In

Computer
Graphics

Introduction to Computer Graphics

John T. Demel and Michael J. Miller
The Ohio State University

PWS ENGINEERING
Boston, Massachusetts

We dedicate this book to our wives,
Margaret Demel and Joan Miller,
who were supportive, and to
our children, Craig and Teresa Demel
and Barbara, Michael, and Julie Miller,
from whom we stole many hours.

PWS PUBLISHERS

Prindle, Weber & Schmidt • ✿ • Duxbury Press • ♠ • PWS Engineering • ⚟
Statler Office Building • 20 Park Plaza • Boston, Massachusetts 02116

Printed in the United States of America
10 9 8 7 6 5 4 3

PWS Publishers is a division of Wadsworth, Inc.

Library of Congress Cataloging in Publication
Data
Demel, John T.
   Introduction to computer graphics.
   1. Computer graphics.   I. Miller, Michael J.
II. Title.
T385.D46 1984   001.64′43   83-25202
ISBN 0-534-03053-X

Sponsoring Editor: Ray Kingman
Production Services Coordinator: Bill Murdock
Production: Del Mar Associates
Manuscript Editor: David Estrada
Interior and Cover Design: Louis Neiheisel
Cover Photo: Courtesy of Evans & Sutherland
Composition: Thompson Type
Printer and Binder: R.R. Donnelley & Sons

/ISBN 0-534-03053-X/

Preface

Introduction to Computer Graphics grew out of our experiences teaching computer graphics programming to freshman engineering students. Our course objectives included creating graphics entities such as lines, polygons, circles, arcs, and special shapes. The data for these entities had to be retrievable so that the figures could be redrawn on the screen or on a hardcopy device and so that portions of the drawings could be selectively erased. Further, the routines for doing the various tasks had to be built into a menu-driven program that was easy to use.

We have found that, while there are a number of texts that might be suitable for graduate students, most presume a level of mathematical and computer-programming sophistication that freshmen have not yet achieved. Our goal in writing this book is to present these topics on a level that can be readily understood by people who do not have extensive math backgrounds while still providing enough depth of coverage to make the material truly instructive and useful. Topics covered include writing a screen dump to a dot matrix printer, outputting to a pen plotter, and using digitizing tablets and joysticks as alternates to the keyboard for data input. We show step by step how to write computer code to accomplish these and many more tasks, such as creating and using data files for storage and retrieval of drawings (both data and image representations) and combining the routines for individual graphics entities into a program that facilitates creating usable drawings as well as charts and graphs. We wrote a drawing package to develop and test the techniques presented in this book, and we used it to create the sample drawings and flow charts.

Introduction to Computer Graphics is intended for use in a classroom setting, but we have tried to present the material in a complete and straightforward manner that should make it easily understood by any reader who wishes to use the book for self-study. All of the example code is presented in both FORTRAN/PLOT10, for large shared-use computers such as DEC VAX 11/750s, and in BASIC, for IBM PCs. In addition, most of the routines are duplicated in Appendix A in Applesoft BASIC for use with the Apple II computers. Appendix B contains Tektronix series 4050 BASIC/PLOT50 versions of the routines of Chapters 4, 5, and 6 for drawing points, lines, polygons, circles, and arcs. With these three versions of BASIC code as examples, the reader should be able to create coded routines for most microcomputers. Sample coded routines and complete, usable programs in BASIC for IBM PC and Apple II computers are available on disk for readers and instructors who desire to obtain them.

Completion of a book of this type requires the combined efforts of many people. We are indebted to the many individuals and organizations who have provided their support and assistance: the students who helped to check the routines and the computer laboratory support staff who helped to bail us out when things went wrong; the hardware and software firms who provided illustrations and loaned equipment and material to be used for testing routines; the editors and layout staff who refined both the material and the way in which it is presented; and the many others who added their support in a number of ways. We also extend our thanks to the reviewers who provided valuable feedback as to what was good and what needed to be added, changed, or deleted: Jon K. Jensen, Marquette University; Robert S. Lang, Northeastern University; Richard Latimer, California State University, Sacramento; Gerald McClain, Oklahoma State University; Peter W. Miller, Purdue University; Donald Riley, University of Minnesota; and Harsh V. Zadoo, Wichita State University. These people all have our undying gratitude. Special thanks is due our families for their understanding and patience when work on the book took precedence over family activities, as well as for their reading of the manuscript and their helpful suggestions.

John T. Demel
Michael J. Miller

Contents

15 Turnkey Drawing and Graphing Programs 349

Introduction to
Computer
Graphics

1

Computer Graphics Purposes and Procedures

This chapter will provide the reader with information about the impact of computer graphics, its application in various fields, and the benefits it brings to these fields. In addition, this chapter will provide details about how the book can be used, what background and materials are needed to best utilize the book, and what will be found in the coming chapters.

The Impact of Computer Graphics

A picture is said to be worth a thousand words. Although this statement is trite, it is true, and computer graphics expresses it in a modern way. Computer graphics seems to be tuned to the way people think; that is, to the way that the brain is designed to work. Engineers and scientists have always capitalized on the value of pictures by expressing the results of their design work and calculations in the form of engineering drawings and charts and graphs. However, it is now possible to create and modify pictures using modern computer graphics systems. These new systems have led to great changes in the methods that are used to produce drawings and, in some cases, the nature of the drawings themselves.

Figure 1-1 shows a typical computer-aided drafting (CAD) system. Such systems are already powerful tools for aiding people in their work, but we are only at the threshold of the changes that will be brought about by computers and computer graphics. While engineers and scientists have used graphics for hundreds of years to record and transmit ideas, and while they have used computers for at least thirty years, it

Figure 1-1. People working at a Bausch & Lomb computer-aided drafting system. (Courtesy Bausch & Lomb)

is only the past five to fifteen years that computer graphics systems have become less expensive and easier to use.

As computer graphics systems become more commonplace, a typical design-to-manufacturing process may occur in the following manner. First, the manufacturing companies will provide the engineer and the designer with computer graphics systems. As their ideas reach the formative stage, the engineers and designers will be able to put the descriptive information (data base) into their own systems. These systems will communicate with larger computers, which will store and distribute the information to the process planning and manufacturing personnel, who, in turn, will take the information, modify it, and make the changes to the data base. These changes will be immediately available to the machines that handle material and that shape or form the product. Thus, it will be possible to go from the design stage to the finished product without having to put the drawing on paper. The machines used in manufacturing will be "intelligent" machines (that is, they will have computers for local control) such as robots, stacker cranes, flexible manufacturing centers, and numerically controlled milling machines and lathes. Two such machines are shown in Figures 1-2 and 1-3. When systems such as these are common, the net savings in total design-to-manufacturing cost will be large, but the greatest savings will be in the reduction in changes to product design necessary to meet regulations or to correct flaws. The net result should be better products and systems and ones that are easier to update.

Engineers have estimated the magnitude of time savings to be on the order of one-half to one-third of the total time to bring a new

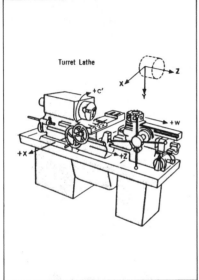

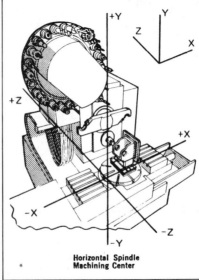

Figure 1-2. An American Tool Eagle 3000 unmanned turning center and a White-Sundstrand Series 20 numerically controlled machining center. (Courtesy White Consolidated Industries)

Figure 1-3. A Cincinnati Millicron robot used for welding.

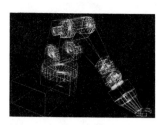

Figure 1-4. Assembly drawing created by Romulus software on the Evans and Sutherland PS300 display system. (Courtesy of Evans & Sutherland)

product from the design stage to manufacture. This time savings will enable the engineers to look at more designs, which should result in an even better, less expensive product.

The "picture" in the design-to-manufacturing example just given has become the representation of the data base used for design and manufacturing. Computer graphics is simply a faster way to draw this picture and to change it.

Applications

Engineers, scientists, businessmen, artists, and educators have all made use of computer graphics to provide more or better information to their coworkers, but each of their fields requires different features in the computer graphics systems that is used. Here we will describe the applications and the particular needs for each of these fields.

Engineering

Engineering activities can be organized into five areas: design, analysis, drawing, manufacturing/construction/processing, and quality control.

In the design phase of an engineering project, engineers are looking at alternatives that may provide the solution for their problem. In general, engineers must examine each alternative in some detail. This examination can involve quick drawings to show relative locations of various parts or sizing of various parts. (Figure 1-4 shows a typical parts assembly.) These drawings can then be put into the computer data base so that the analysis phase can take place.

For example, design of a road construction project in a certain area will depend on the terrain where the road will be located. The terrain information will be put into the computer's data base (the collection of numbers and letters that are recorded by the surveyors). The engineers' calculated numbers that make up the designs proposed for the road will be added to the data base to form the alternatives. Then the cost and benefit analyses will take place to choose the alternative that appears to maximize function and minimize cost. Figure 1-5 shows the contour plot (A), the proposed road center line (B) and the proposed road width (C). Note that the road profile in Figure 1-5C shows how the road would appear if the viewer's line of sight were coincident with the centerline of the road.

In a road construction project the amount of earth to be removed from some areas (cut) and the earth to be added to other areas (fill) must balance, or additional fill must be purchased and moved. Figures 1-5D and 1-5E show a road constructed at two different elevations. Note that the road constructed at an elevation of 20 feet has a better balance of cut and fill than the one at an elevation of 30 feet. In general, roads are built to minimize steep grades. This constraint can be in direct conflict with minimizing the amount of earth to be moved.

The computer, with its computer graphics display, can provide

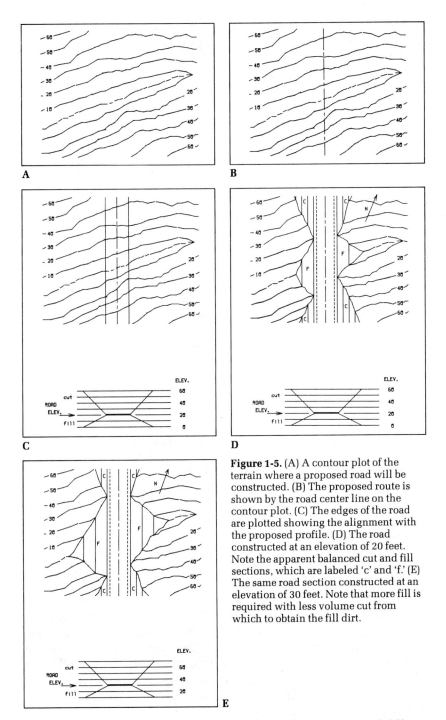

Figure 1-5. (A) A contour plot of the terrain where a proposed road will be constructed. (B) The proposed route is shown by the road center line on the contour plot. (C) The edges of the road are plotted showing the alignment with the proposed profile. (D) The road constructed at an elevation of 20 feet. Note the apparent balanced cut and fill sections, which are labeled 'c' and 'f.' (E) The same road section constructed at an elevation of 30 feet. Note that more fill is required with less volume cut from which to obtain the fill dirt.

engineers with graphic information about the amounts of fill required at any particular slope for each of the various areas. The engineers can look at many alternatives and determine which provides the best combination of function and economy.

When the decision has been made about the location of the roadway, the engineers have the responsibility to produce the drawings for construction. The data base (surveyors' information) can provide the coordinates for drawing the terrain features. The terrain can be displayed on the graphics terminal but must be modified so that construction personnel can get the needed dimensions. It takes an experienced draftsperson to be able to make decisions about the symbols and lines used to portray the desired design. When the design drawing on the graphics terminal screen is ready, the plotter provides rapid inking of the lines and the symbols. The greatest time-savings occur in the transfer of the drawing process from pencil layout in the old-style drawings to electronic layout in the new method. If the drawings need to be revised because, say, the land to be used for the chosen route cannot be obtained, this revision is easily done with computer graphics.

During construction of the highway, the information about the changes to the land and the amount of fuel and manpower used can be added to the computer data base to provide a running record of the progress of the project. Drawings of the as-built (finished) highway can be created by changing the original drawings on the basis of information collected in the field, showing actual locations of the highway, culverts, power lines, gas lines, and any other elements that may have affected the construction.

Quality control in the construction project is determined by the accuracy with which the plans are followed. Slopes vary depending on the type of soil that is available for fill material and the methods used to pack the earth during the preparation phase. This information will have been stored as part of the data base, and the inspectors can turn in their findings about soil type and compaction to be checked by the designers as the construction progresses.

Science

Scientists use computer graphics in a variety of ways. The application described here will be the study of the structure of chemical substances. Scientists who do chemical crystal-structure determination are called crystallographers.

Crystallographers use x-rays to determine the location of atoms in molecular structures. Determining the locations of the atoms in chemical structures provides information about the bonds that hold the atoms in the molecule together. This information shows the scientist why certain alloys are brittle (fracture easily) and why others are ductile (easy to form). Knowledge about relative sizes of atoms and bond strengths between atoms allows creation of better materials.

Crystallographers use a beam of x-rays to strike a crystal of the unknown material. The information about the way the x-ray beam is reflected by the electron clouds surrounding the nuclei provides clues to the crystal structure. Crystallographers then study sub-

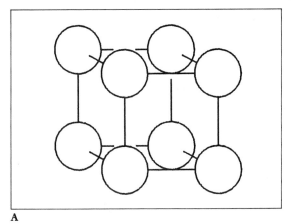

A

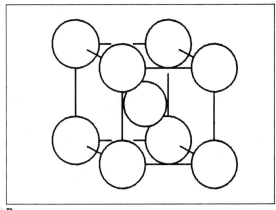

B

Figure 1-6. (A) A unit cell of a simple cubic structure. (B) A unit cell of a body-centered cubic structure.

stances with similar structures—substances that have some of the same groupings of atoms—and propose locations in space for atoms that make up the unknown molecule. On the basis of their experience with crystal structures, the crystallographers give each atom X, Y, and Z coordinates relative to some origin. Figure 1-6A shows a simple cubic structure with one atom at each corner of the unit cell. Figure 1-6B shows a structure with one atom added in the center of the unit cell.

A comparison is made between information from the proposed structure and the actual structure. If the sets of information agree, then the structure is solved. If they do not, then new atom positions must be proposed. Computer graphics allows scientists to see their model for the structure on the display. They can rotate the proposed structure and see whether the angles between certain atoms or sets of atoms match known structures. If the angles displayed do not match the known bond angles, the scientists can manipulate the image on the screen and let the computer provide the information from the scattered x-rays. This modeled data can then be compared to the original data, and the iterative process started again. Figure 1-7 shows atoms arranged in rings of five and six. Figure 1-8A shows a structure with groups of five and six atoms while Figure 1-8B shows the structure with just the recognizable groups displayed and the rest of the structure removed. This process has allowed many structures to be determined in the amount of time that just one could be determined using traditional methods. It has also allowed more complicated structure determinations to be completed. This knowledge of atomic structures allows scientists to understand the behavior of structures under heat or pressure and to predict behavior of similar structures.

Business

Business personnel have used graphs and charts for years to show the progress of a particular activity over a period of time. They also use graphics to display relative distributions for costs or sales of

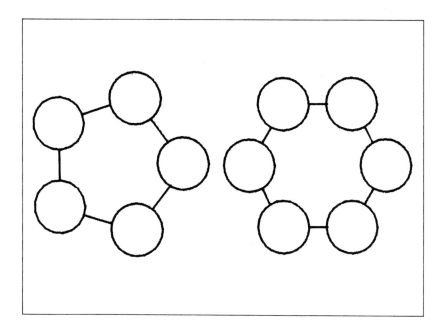

Figure 1-7. Five- and six-sided rings of atoms.

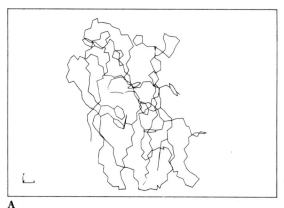

A

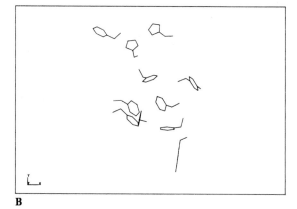

B

Figure 1-8. (A) A protein structure partially composed of the pentagonal and hexagonal groups of atoms shown in Figure 1-7. (B) The same structure with all but the pentagonal and hexagonal groups removed. (Courtesy of Lauric Rellick, Ohio State University)

goods and services (see Figure 1-9). Normally these graphics are included in reports sent to management and serve as aids to making decisions about buying and selling or expanding production. Before computer graphics was used, the pertinent data had to be extracted from reams of information, hand drawn, and then colored in, to emphasize the proper items. Now it is possible to access the information and then use the computer graphics display to draw the picture in either color or black and white (monochrome). It is also possible to integrate text with graphics so that reports can be prepared, proofread, corrected, and published in a relatively short period of time.

In reviewing data, managers look for trends that can govern their decisions. When considering yearly or longer periods of historical

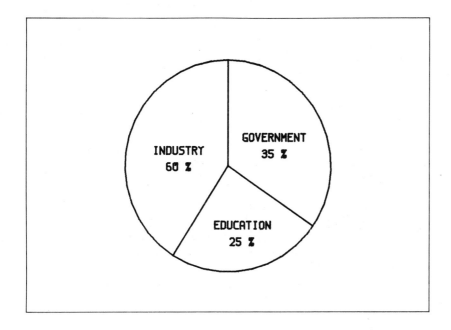

Figure 1-9. Business graph showing percentage of sales apportioned to each type of customer.

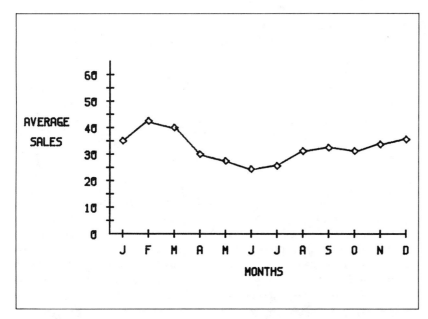

Figure 1-10. A graph showing average sales for each month over a five-year period.

performance, it is easier for them to see the upward or downward trend of a particular quantity if it is graphed, as in Figure 1-10, showing average monthly sales for a five-year period. It can be very difficult for managers to see these trends if they are just looking at pages of numbers.

Another use of computers in the business world is the modeling of a particular activity by writing a program that simulates the action of

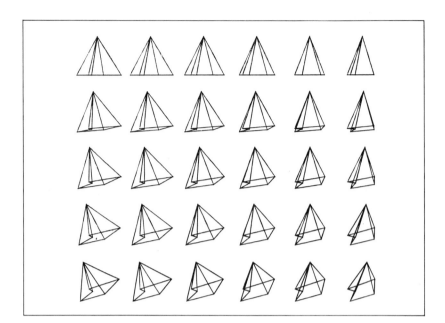

Figure 1-11. Example of a three-dimensional shape rotated about two axes to produce a modified repetitive structure.

the marketplace. A model can be the mathematical equations that govern the motion of a mechanism or the actions and reactions in the marketplace where a product is sold. "Simulation" means that most or all of the information known about the product and the product's buyers that can be reduced to mathematical equations has been included in the model. The output from such a program can be numerical or it can be graphical in nature, and it can also be interactive, allowing the user to input proposed changes to determine their probable effect on the marketplace.

Art

The artist has always been able to choose the media that suit his talents. Computer graphics is another available medium that allows another degree of freedom of expression. Computer graphics can be used for illustration, for creating images of real items and surreal objects, for repetitive patterns with minor changes, for animation of cartoon characters, and for dynamic or changing displays. Figure 1-11 shows an example of a repetitive pattern.

One type of illustration consists of converting engineering drawings of technical hardware to pictorial drawings that can be easily understood by the hardware service personnel and by the user. If three-dimensional information about the object is available in the computer data base created by the engineers and designers, there is no need to create a pictorial from the engineering drawings through laborious measurement and layout. Almost all computer graphics systems can take the information from the data base and create a pictorial. The illustrator can then draw enough information from the pictorial to create an illustration that emphasizes the important details.

Animation is a tedious activity that requires an extremely large number of separate drawings or pictures. Each picture is changed only slightly from the previous one. Using computer graphics, it is possible to define a figure as consisting of several elements or pieces and then to move the pieces to simulate the motion of a body part. An arm, for example, can be divided into relatively rigid parts, with motion occurring at the shoulder, elbow, and wrist. Prior to the use of computer graphics the images of the arm would be drawn by hand. They would be arranged in front of the camera, and each slightly different image would be photographed individually for two or three frames to create the illusion of motion. Now, as the computer creates the images, they are stored on a disk and can then be retrieved from the disk and displayed on the computer graphics system. This procedure saves much of the manual labor and gives the artist much more time for creativity.

Mobiles and films have allowed artists to create dynamic images, but the artists could not change these images without disassembling the mobiles or remaking the films. Computer graphics allows artists to change the images as they are being displayed.

Education

The greatest benefit that the computer and computer graphics provide in the educational environment is that the students always have a response for their input if the computer system is designed properly. Correct answers get approval and incorrect ones direct the students to go back, review the information, and try again. The addition of graphics to the question-and-answer mode allows the students to visualize items being discussed and increases the range of topics that can be presented.

A computer presentation can be just as impersonal as a television presentation if the software is poorly designed. Good interaction between the system and the student is the key to successful educational systems. Each individual has his or her own learning rate. If the computer can aid the teacher in presenting information to the student when he or she is ready, both student and teacher can make more efficient use of their time.

There is no doubt that the advent of color displays has made computer graphics much more attractive to both educators and students. Objects appear more real and the accompanying shading and texturing allow three-dimensional visualization to be part of the learning process. The option for dynamic motion is also a big benefit to certain topics. For example, the motion of a bouncing ball is far easier to describe if there are balls bouncing on the terminal screen for the student to observe.

Now that audio input as well as output is available to the programmer of educational systems, the range of interaction has been increased. For small children who cannot read, the voice of the system can provide access to another sense, hearing. In addition, some systems are able to accept the spoken word as input. This capability will further open up computer use to children and those with learning or communications disabilities. Through a variety of electronic hardware devices it is now possible for a student to provide input by simply pointing to an object on a touch-sensitive display. Sound and touch add exciting alternatives to the traditional input method of typing an answer on the keyboard.

New graphics systems provide pictures of real objects or actions for the user to point to or select. These pictures are called icons. An example of an icon would be a picture of a trash can to indicate the action of throwing something away or deleting it. Another example would be a file cabinet to represent the computer's storage. Each of the icons allows the user to think in real terms about the electronic information and actions. This means that very little instruction is needed for successful use of a system.

If good teachers' ideas can be captured by computer graphics systems, the teachers will be freed to spend more creative time with each individual in the class.

Benefits

The benefits of the various applications of computer graphics are tied into productivity, creativity, and speed. There is no doubt that computer graphics systems cost a significant amount of money. However, the benefits that can be reaped will be worth the expense if people can be relieved from the drudgery of repetitive tasks and can become more creative and, therefore, more productive. In addition, because computers and computer graphics systems can provide the means to examine efficiently many alternatives and choose the best one, they will reduce the number and size of costly, time-consuming mistakes.

The use of color and three-dimensional modeling will allow people to see how proposed new products will fit into their environment both functionally and aesthetically. The pictures created by computer graphics will allow people to consider proposed changes before making decisions.

Using This Book

Introduction to Computer Graphics is primarily for freshman and sophomore engineering and technology students. The examples used will be from the various fields of engineering and technology. This book can also be used as a tutorial by practicing engineers who need to know something about the basic operations of computer graphics systems. However, the material is not limited to engineers and technologists. Science and education students and teachers will be able to make use of the information and the exercises.

This book can be used by individuals for self-study, helping them become familiar with computer graphics and enabling them to see applications for systems that will improve their productivity. It is important for these individuals to have a system available for testing their knowledge. Although the book starts by defining terminology and the basic computer graphics operations, it leads to programs that allow the creation of graphical images that can be stored, retrieved, and modified by the user. Many examples are provided for the readers to type into their systems to test their understanding and to let them see the results of their learning efforts.

Background and Materials

In order to use this book effectively you must be able to write computer programs in a high-level programming language. There are three approaches to meeting this requirement. You may have taken a course prior to using this text; you may be taking a course in parallel with the course that uses this book; or you must be willing to learn the language for your computer through self-study as you read this book. We have deliberately staged the presentation of material so that the last two options are viable.

Programming Language

Three languages are presented in this book and two are used for the examples. FORTRAN, BASIC, and Pascal statements will all be presented in Chapter 3, but only FORTRAN and BASIC will be used in the examples in subsequent chapters. More engineering programs have been written in FORTRAN than in any other language, and the second most popular language for engineering programs is BASIC. This is not to say that either of them is the ideal language for graphics, but they are so widely available that almost any system will have them. Pascal appears to be a good language for many applications and overcomes some of the limitations of both FORTRAN and BASIC. In addition to the languages, a set of graphics statements will be used for each language. These graphics statements will be presented in the chapters as needed. Appendixes provide equivalent versions of the programs contained in the chapters for the Tektronix 4050 series desktop computer graphics systems and for the Apple II microcomputer.

You should have a textbook or reference book in the language that you will be using to solve the exercises. It can be a textbook that makes a general presentation of the language and its capabilities, or it can present the specific version of the language that is used by your computer graphics system.

This book will make use of FORTRAN 77, which is an American National Standards Institute version of FORTRAN agreed upon by experts in the language in 1977. The version of BASIC is one provided by IBM for personal computers and was written by Microsoft Corporation. Microsoft BASIC has become a defacto standard because it is available for and used with many systems. The programming statements for both languages that will be needed for this book, as well as information on the equivalent Pascal statements, are presented in Chapter 3.

Mathematics
The math required to solve the exercises in this book includes algebra and trigonometry. A knowledge of matrices will help you understand some of the exercises. This is normally the beginning level of mathematics required at most technical and engineering schools today. If you are at all rusty at algebra and trigonometry, it would be advisable to have a mathematics book handy to use as a reference.

Systems
In order for the learning process to have the proper reinforcement, you must have a computer system at your disposal. It is assumed that you will have an interactive system, one that can "talk" to you while it is running and respond to your commands.

This also means that you should have manuals for the system that tell you how to communicate with it. As a minimum you should have a user's manual, a manual for the operating system, and a manual for the language being used.

The systems that will be used to provide the examples for this book are (1) the IBM personal computer, using the IBM disk operating system (DOS) and BASIC with graphics statements, and (2) the DEC VAX computer, using the VMS operating system and FORTRAN 77 with the Tektronix PLOT10 graphics statements. The references to BASIC will be for IBM's version of Microsoft BASIC, which will enable most Apple computer owners to use the book as well. And, as we have noted, the appendixes will provide the examples written for Tektronix 4050 series computers and Apple II microcomputers.

Some currently available books that provide more information on computer graphics are those written by Newman and Sproull, Giloi, Foley and Van Dam, and Chasen (see Bibliography).

What You Are Going to Learn
This book will provide you with additions to your vocabulary that will allow you to progress through the chapters of the book and communicate with people using computer graphics. It also provides a review of programming languages, which will prepare you for the computer graphics exercises, including programming, that will follow.

Vocabulary
The vocabulary can be broken into two parts: terms that deal with the physical devices—hardware—that are part of a computer graphics system and terms that deal with the programs or code—

software—that allow that hardware to serve the user. Chapter 2 is devoted to an explanation of these terms and contains pictures and diagrams to help you visualize the items for your new vocabulary.

Programming Language Review

Chapter 3 covers all of the programming language statements (with the exception of graphics statements) that will be used in this book, and it provides a brief explanation of statements and what they do. These statements are presented and explained in the parallel mode so that you can see the sister statements in the two languages that you are not using. Graphics statements are presented beginning in Chapter 4.

Computer Graphics Exercises

The first graphics tasks presented in this text deal with methods for putting points and lines on the screen. These methods are the foundation for all other graphics tasks because complicated figures are composed of lines and points.

Once you are confident that you can put lines and points on the screen, you can progress to the other tasks, which include: (1) drawing two-dimensional geometric figures such as polygons, circles, arcs, and axes for graphs, and producing other graph items (such as labeling); and (2) interacting with the computer through selection devices that can be used to "point" to items on the screen. Chapters 4, 5, 6, and 7 will cover these topics. These chapters provide enough knowledge to create an engineering drawing or a technical graph. They discuss methods for scaling figures and for looking at only a particular section of a drawing (clipping).

Chapters 8, 9, and 10 cover the modification of the graphic image through removal and replacement of lines and features on a drawing. These techniques involve the storage and retrieval of information. Other topics covered in these chapters include additional methods for scaling, clipping, and repositioning figures (translation).

Chapter 11 deals with the interfacing of peripherals with computer graphics systems. Among topics covered is the use of graphics input and output devices.

Chapter 12 presents methods for working in three dimensions through the use of wire-frame models (three-dimensional images created by using lines to show the intersection of surfaces). Two-dimensional drawings are the type that technical people have traditionally used to document their ideas and designs. These have included orthographic drawings, which provide two-dimensional shapes for dimensioning, and pictorial drawings, which help convey the shape and function of a particular object. Three-dimensional representation has generally required various types of physical models, but now the computer allows the user to think and work more easily in three dimensions. This approach is very powerful and allows engineers to deal with the normal three-dimensional world rather than be confined to the two-dimensional world of paper.

In Chapter 12 you will create a three-dimensional data base for wire-frame drawings using two different schemes. One approach is concerned with connecting the vertices of the object with lines, while the other deals with the faces of the object. The faces are planar and each face is drawn separately. Chapter 12 presents methods for deriving orthographic and pictorial drawings from both schemes and the pictorials include oblique and isometric drawings. You will not be expected to create routines to remove hidden lines other than through the removal of lines by visual selection.

Chapter 13 covers the rotation of an object about the X and Y axes, the creation of a perspective, and the removal of hidden lines from a convex polyhedron. The approach used for hidden-line configurations allows for a simple shading algorithm. Hidden-line elimination and shading are presented for only one of the methods of describing an object.

The final chapters, 14 and 15, provide the opportunity for you to write an interactive drafting package that will tie many of the concepts together and demonstrate the power of computer graphics systems. This is not intended to be a commercial package but rather a device to show the complexity required by a good interactive software package and to help you develop a sense of what you should expect from software packages and graphics systems when you need to purchase one. It should also allow you to develop a method for attacking large programming projects yourself or for supervising ones that are created by your subordinates.

Programming Techniques

Writing programs to control the computer's actions requires a logical approach and, as in any engineering problem, the steps must be well documented. The key concepts here are *top-down approach*, *modular construction*, and *good documentation*.

TOP-DOWN APPROACH "Top down" means that the programmer must consider the whole task that is to be accomplished and define all of the tasks that the program must perform. These tasks must be broken down into subtasks, and those portions of the program that direct the action of other portions must be written first. Then the individual subtasks that will be linked together by these portions must be written. This is equivalent to hiring the company's top management first, then the second-line managers, and on down until the level of the worker has been reached. The workers in this case are the portions of the program that draw lines or put points on the screen.

MODULAR CONSTRUCTION The subtasks are termed *routines* in this text, and all programming is done with routines that can be linked together. A routine is seldom more than a page of program statements, including the explanation of the routine function. Routines are called by a variety of names, but the words "subroutine" and "function" are used in both BASIC and FORTRAN to describe them.

DOCUMENTATION One of the most important factors in any program you will write is the quality of the documentation. Good documentation answers the questions who, when, what, why, and how. If these questions are not answered by the documentation of the program, it should be rewritten or not purchased.

The documentation should include (1) the name of the author or authors, (2) when the program was written and the date and version number of the latest revision, (3) explanations for each module (what the module does and how it performs each task), (4) lists of variable names and identification of their use, and (5) lists of the input to and output from every routine or module.

This text provides examples of proper documentation in Appendix C for FORTRAN so that you can pattern program documentation after the example. The example is included in the appendix. Some of the documentation may seem excessive to the novice, but it will prove to be invaluable. For example, you will need to have a variable list with the main program that includes the name of every variable used in the entire program, including all modules. This list prevents the programmer from using a name twice, which can lead to problems that are difficult to trace.

Interactivity

Interactive programs allow the user to provide input and receive output (feedback) as the program executes. *Batch* programs do not allow interaction.

One form of interactivity can be questions printed on the screen that require answers from the user. The user types the answers in from the keyboard, and the computer uses the input information to formulate the program output. The answers can be given by simply choosing numbers or they may require the input of names, labels, or other data.

Part of the input can also be graphical in nature, as when the user traces a drawing with an electronic pointer or uses the pointer to choose an item displayed on the screen. Both keyboards and graphical input devices are shown in the next chapter.

Presentation of Material

This book first establishes a vocabulary of terms that are used in industry to describe the software and hardware used for computer graphics. Once necessary language statements, commands, and terms and concepts have been presented, the book progresses from simple lines and shapes to combinations of lines and shapes in both two and three dimensions. The progression is gradual, with the reintroduction of necessary programming statements in order to make you comfortable with the required tasks. As each graphics task or subtask is introduced, the need for that item in the area of computer graphics is explained, including the place the item is used.

The modules written in the early chapters can be assembled to form a drawing package. The last portion of the book describes how that package can be assembled to allow your interactive computer graphics system to create simple engineering drawings.

This is a book for beginners in the world of computer graphics. As with any technical field, a new vocabulary is required to understand the information that is presented. This may be the first text you use that will require some degree of structure and form in your programming. When you finish the text and the exercises, you will have ventured only a small distance into the world of computer graphics and CAD/CAM (computer-aided drafting/computer-aided manufacturing). A good foundation is necessary to begin this important venture because so many technical activities now depend on the computer and its output.

We believe that there is still a place for many of the traditional methods for producing graphics and that, while computer graphics can play a major role in some areas, it cannot outperform traditional methods in others. The decrease in cost and subsequent increase in capability of computer graphics systems may affect additional areas, but it will take time and considerable software development before the majority of technical graphics production can be taken over by such systems.

Exercises

1. Select your reference texts for programming language, graphics, and mathematics. Write the titles and names of authors on a sheet of paper. Determine whether there are reference manuals for your system and, if so, obtain them.

2. Define the terms *software* and *hardware*.

3. Define the terms *orthographic*, *oblique*, *isometric*, and *axonometric* as applied to graphic projections.

4. Find five or six magazines or journals that describe computer graphics applications in your field.

5. Define the terms *top down* and *modular*.

6. Read the documentation examples that are printed in Appendix C and list the essential elements that are included in the headers (opening COMMENT or REMARK statements) for the main programs and for the subroutines.

2
Computer Graphics Systems- Components and Interaction

Computer graphics systems are composed of three elements. The first element is the *hardware*—the physical devices that can be seen occupying space. The second element is the *software*—the computer programs that allow the system to be used effectively for computer graphics applications. The last and most important element is the *operator*— the user of the hardware and software. This chapter will give you a working vocabulary and a little insight into the elements of a system. While the chapter will provide a recognition level of information for the potential user of computer graphics systems, it should not be considered a source of detailed information.

System Hardware Components

The hardware components in a system fall into three categories: *computers, display* and *output devices,* and *input devices*. The computer is the "heart" of the system and can be one of three types: mainframe computer, minicomputer, or microcomputer. In addition, many of the input and output devices contain microprocessors (small special-purpose computers) programmed for specific tasks. The computer includes the processor, memory, and storage for programs and files. Figures 2-1 and 2-2 show complete computer graphics systems used for drafting. Figure 2-3 shows a typical minicomputer, and Figure 2-4 shows a typical microcomputer.

The display and output devices, reasonably familiar to most people, include plotters that produce pictures or drawings for people to use in their work and TV-like screens that show an electronic version of a picture. Printers are also required as a

Figure 2-1. Bausch & Lomb Producer electronic drafting system. (Courtesy of Bausch & Lomb)

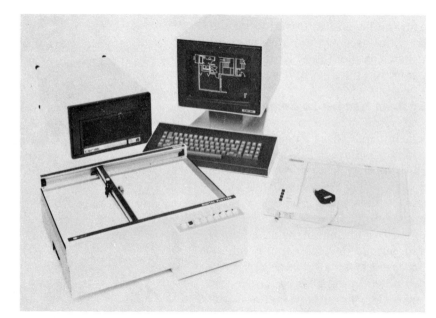

Figure 2-2. T & W Systems T-Square drafting system with computer (upper left), terminal (upper middle), plotter (lower left), and digitizer (right). (Courtesy of T & W Systems)

Figure 2-3. Digital Equipment Corporation (DEC) VAX 11/750 minicomputer.

Figure 2-4. IBM Personal Computer (microcomputer).

Figure 2-5. Houston Instrument DMP 40 plotter. (Courtesy of Houston Instrument)

Figure 2-6. ID Systems ID 100 color graphics terminal. (Courtesy of ID Systems)

part of most systems. See Figures 2-5 and 2-6 for typical graphics output devices.

Input devices include joysticks and light pens for positioning cursors on the displays. These devices can be thought of as electronic pencils. Figure 2-7 shows the IBM 3277 GA workstation, which uses a terminal for alphanumeric (word) display and a screen for graphics display. The joystick is used with the graphic display and the light pen is used with the alphanumeric display. Digitizers are devices used for coordinate input, which might include tracing drawings that were prepared prior to the purchase of a computer graphics system. Digitizers can also be used to display a *menu*—a table of command options available to the user—and thus allow easy, "user-friendly" selection of system functions. Figure 2-8 shows a large digitizer being used to enter coordinate information for a drawing. Note the menu on the lower portion of the digitizer.

Figure 2-7. IBM 3277 GA dual-screen graphics workstation, including an alphanumeric terminal and a graphics display. The light pen is to the right of the alphanumeric keyboard and the joystick can be seen in the lower right-hand corner of the photograph.

Figure 2-8. Houston Instrument digitizer, used for entering existing drawings. This device can also be used for menu input (note menu on lower portion of digitizer). (Courtesy of Bausch & Lomb)

We will now take a closer look at each of the hardware components of a computer graphics system.

Computers

A computer is classified by its capacity for work, which includes such factors as the number of people who can use the computer simultaneously, the speed with which the computer can perform difficult mathematical operations, the computer's memory size, and the size of the unit of information or "word" that the computer uses for basic operations. The computer's price tag will be proportional to its capacity for work.

A *digital* computer is an electronic device that operates by recognizing switches that are turned on or off. The switches are binary digits, or *bits*. Collections of bits are called *bytes* and *words*. Bytes consist of 8 bits and words can be 8, 16, 24, 32, 36, 48, 60, or 64 bits in length.

MAINFRAME COMPUTERS Large or *mainframe* computers normally use word lengths of 32 bits or more. Such large computers can accommodate many users and can handle programs that do many arithmetic operations. General Motors' Fisher Body Division uses two mainframe computers to support more than a hundred designers using computer graphics. These computers can also be linked together, or networked, to become a large central-computer resource.

MINICOMPUTERS Prior to 1979, minicomputers traditionally had 16-bit word lengths and were limited to a relatively small number of users—say, one to fifteen. Newer minicomputers have 32-bit word lengths and can support many more users, which has made the dividing line between mainframe computers and minicomputers very vague. There is still a considerable difference in processor speed, however. For instance, if an arithmetic operation or calculation takes 1 hour on a large computer it will probably take from 10 to 100 hours on a minicomputer.

The minicomputer probably did more to spawn the proliferation of computer graphics systems than any other device, with the possible exception of the storage-tube graphics terminal. The attributes of low price, simplicity of operation, and ability to be assembled in different ways for different applications were all important to the men and women looking for the increases in productivity that could be obtained through CAD/CAM and computer graphics.

MICROCOMPUTERS Microcomputers have all of the same elements that are found in the larger systems, but they are also small and low-priced, attributes that made the minicomputers so popular. The price difference has been another order of magnitude smaller than minicomputers. In 1978, the common microcomputer word size was 8 bits, although the 16-bit microprocessor was available, but there are now 16-bit and 32-bit microcomputers and the lines that separate the three traditional classifications are again very vague. The only real distinction in all of the different classifications of computer is processor speed and the addressable memory. Speed translates to the number of possible users and to the number of calculations per unit of time.

MICROPROCESSORS The *microprocessor* is literally a computer on a piece of silicon, which may be only a quarter of an inch square. Figure 2-9 shows an Intel 8088 microprocessor installed on the printed circuit board that forms the heart of the IBM microcomputer. In order for a microprocessor to be a useful tool it must have addi-

Figure 2-9. Intel 8088 microprocessor, shown installed on the main circuit board of the IBM Personal Computer. Note the empty socket for the Intel 8087 math processor to the right of the 8088 chip.

tional components, such as memory and interface devices. If enough memory and interfaces are provided, a microprocessor can become a microcomputer, but with small amounts of memory the microprocessor can perform only limited tasks, such as controlling the pen on a plotter. By performing such a task, however, the microprocessor removes a load from the main computer, freeing it for other tasks. Such controllers add only a small increment in price and allow the system to serve the user instead of making the user wait while a particular task, such as plotting, is being done. The microprocessor can be used to enhance all of the hardware devices in a system.

MEMORY As we have noted, memory is required by a computer to hold the programs that make it useful. The more memory that a computer has available, the more tasks it can perform. Memory is measured in bytes. In general, thousands of bytes are required for any computer to perform its tasks and *kilobyte* has become a more common unit than byte. Now that computers have been developed that can use millions of bytes of memory, the *megabyte,* or *M byte,* has also become common. Memory has become much less expensive due to technological developments and to high production volumes, which distribute the development costs over many units. Memory is now so inexpensive that microcomputers can have 1 million bytes and minicomputers can make use of 16 million bytes of memory. A minicomputer can support additional users if additional memory is added (assuming that the minicomputer has the processor speed and disk space to support the additional users). Figure 2-10 shows a 256-kilobyte memory board for an IBM Personal Computer.

Figure 2-10. An AlphaByte 256-kilobyte memory board for the IBM Personal Computer.

Figure 2-11. DEC TU-77 tape drive with tape reel in place above controls.

Storage Devices

Magnetic tape and *magnetic disks* are the storage devices most commonly used to keep information on file in computer systems. The magnetic tape is a strip of plastic coated with magnetic metal oxide, which can have its magnetic character changed by the application of electric fields. It will remain in a modified state until another field strong enough to change it is applied. Tape allows for the storage of large amounts of information in a relatively small space, and a reel of tape is inexpensive. Tape drives, however, are not inexpensive. In addition, getting information from a tape is a slow process because access (moving and reading the tape) is sequential. This means that all of the information from the beginning of the tape must be read before a piece of information (file) at the end can be read. Tapes are generally used for long-term storage of information or for periodic short-term storage of user files in case of system failure. Figure 2-11 shows a tape drive with a reel of tape installed.

Figure 2-12. DEC RL-02 disk drive and disk pack.

The disk, the other common storage device, is similar to a phonograph record and a disk drive is similar to a phonograph. The disk is made of a material such as plastic and it has a magnetic coating just as the tape does. The advantage of disk over tape is that the disk read head (similar to a phonograph tone arm) can be positioned anywhere on the disk, thus allowing random access to stored information. Information can be stored easily on unused portions of the disk and can be deleted or read rapidly. In most systems some sort of disk drive is a necessity, whereas a tape drive can be an important option to improve system usability but is not required for the user to do his minute by minute tasks.

The cost of disk drives per megabyte of information stored is decreasing because rapid developments are being made in density of storage and in quality control during manufacture. Figure 2-12 shows a disk drive and a disk pack that stores 10 megabytes of information on a removable disk.

Figure 2-13. Tandon 5.25-inch floppy disk drive, which can be used in the IBM microcomputer.

Figure 2-14. Scotch 5.25-inch floppy disk. Note slot that allows the read head to contact the diskette.

There are two different disk types: hard and flexible. The *hard disks* can have multiple platters and multiple read heads and can be fixed or removable, but if they are fixed they must be used in conjunction with some other type of storage device, such as tape or removable disk. The hard disk is the fastest device for randomly reading or writing stored information other than adding massive amounts of memory to the computer.

Flexible disks are called *floppy disks* and are removable. Floppy disk drives and floppy disks, or *diskettes*, have been used on systems of all sizes but have found most favor on minicomputer and microcomputer systems because of the relatively low cost. The technology has been developed that allows storage on both sides of a floppy disk and at a high enough density that no other mass storage is needed. There are 8-inch, 5.25-inch, and 3.5-inch diameter diskettes and drives. The cost of the actual diskettes is in the range of a few dollars each. The diskettes are subject to bending damage if the cardboard cover is creased in such a way that the disk cannot move. The diskette surface is uncovered at the points where the disk head reads the information. This means that fingerprints and dust can get to the surface and damage the oxide coating. Figure 2-13 shows a floppy disk drive and Figure 2-14 shows the floppy disk.

Output Devices

Early computers used typewriter like devices for communicating with the users. These devices were slow and noisy but were much better than punched tape. While variations of these early devices are still in use today, most modern systems employ the efficient and quiet cathode ray tube, or CRT, for computer output. These terminals come in a variety of configurations but the mechanism is basically the same in each. A beam of electrons leaves a "gun" and strikes a layer of phosphors on a flat or slightly rounded surface. Wherever

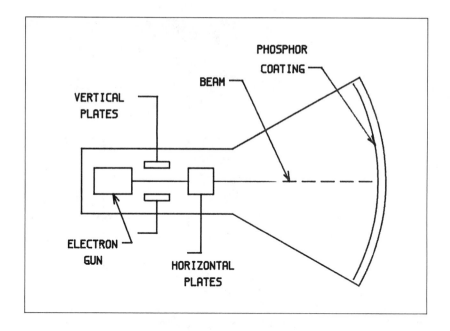

Figure 2-15. A schematic representation of a CRT.

Figure 2-16. DEC VT 100 alphanumeric terminal.

the beam hits the surface the phosphors glow. Electromagnets control the direction of the beam and circuitry controls the power of the electromagnets. Figure 2-15 shows a schematic drawing of a CRT.

There are two types of terminals: those for displaying alphanumeric characters and those for displaying pictures or graphics. In general, alphanumeric terminals, like the one shown in Figure 2-16, are less expensive than graphics terminals. Graphics terminals

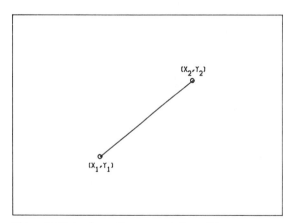

Figure 2-17. A schematic representation of the movement of the electron beam on the screen of a vector CRT.

Figure 2-18. Tektronix 4010 storage terminal for both alphanumeric and graphic display.

are classified by the mechanism for displaying the picture. There are storage terminals, vector refresh terminals, and raster refresh terminals. Terminals are also classified according to whether they are high-resolution or low-resolution and whether they can display more than one color or intensity.

STORAGE TERMINALS The *storage terminal* is a vector terminal. This means that the electron beam moves from any point on the screen to any other point on the screen. Figure 2-17 shows a schematic representation of the movement of the beam on the screen of a vector CRT. The phosphors used stay glowing for a given period of time in such a CRT because of a special capacitive storage grid located behind the screen. Thus the beam can continue to draw more vectors and add to the patterns on the screen without having the pattern or picture already on the screen disappear. These CRTs are relatively expensive but have a very high resolution and provide an excellent picture. However, the user cannot erase lines that have already been drawn except by marking the line to be erased, then erasing the entire screen, and then commanding the computer to redraw the picture minus the marked line.

Tektronix, the company that manufactures the storage tube, has developed a modification that allows a beam of lower intensity to excite the phosphor to an intermediate state that glows with lesser brightness and that will not continue to glow for very long unless the beam hits it again. The beam must retrace its path rapidly to allow this intermediate picture to be drawn. If the user is satisfied with the picture or pattern, the power of the beam can be increased and the picture is thus "stored" on the screen. The limitation is that the number of lines that can be drawn in the intermediate mode is far less than can be drawn in the storage mode. Figure 2-18 shows a combination graphics and alphanumeric storage terminal.

Figure 2-19. Evans & Sutherland PS 300 vector refresh graphics terminal.

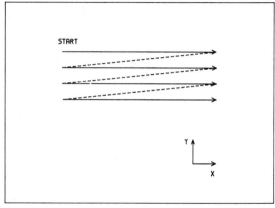

Figure 2-20. A schematic representation of the motion of the beam on a raster scan CRT.

VECTOR REFRESH TERMINALS The operation of the vector refresh CRT is similar to the intermediate mode of the storage CRT. The beam can be directed to the desired locations on the screen to create any patterns, but the phosphor will not glow for very long, so the beam must keep retracing its path to keep the picture on the screen. Storing the path that the beam follows requires memory either in the computer supporting the terminal or in the terminal itself. Any changes in the path are calculated by the computer and sent to the terminal. The advantage of the vector refresh terminal is that the pictures created on the screen can be moved simply by drawing the lines in a new position. When the phosphors in the "old" position cease to glow the picture appears to have moved. Thus the vector refresh terminal can provide dynamic, or moving, pictures. These terminals are relatively expensive, but if high-resolution, dynamic displays are needed for a particular application, such as simulating robot arm movement, then vector refresh terminals are highly desirable. Figure 2-19 shows such a vector refresh terminal.

RASTER TERMINALS A *raster terminal* operates by directing the electron beam over a set path of horizontal lines beginning at the upper left corner of the screen and tracing a line across the screen, then moving down one line, or raster, and back to the left-hand side of the screen and starting the next horizontal line. (See Figure 2-20 for a pictorial representation of the raster screen.) The actual pattern on the screen is created by turning the beam on or off at the appropriate spot or *pixel* (picture element).

The raster CRT can make use of television-technology cathode ray tubes, so these terminals are much less expensive than storage and vector refresh terminals. Unfortunately, television technology of the early 1980s does not produce tubes that have very many pixels, so the picture resolution is not very high. There are two types of raster

Figure 2-21. Raster Technologies color raster refresh terminal.

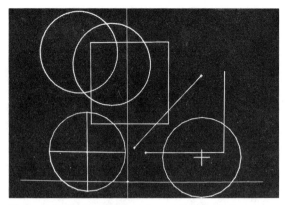

Figure 2-22. Picture displayed on a high-resolution (1024 × 780) Tektronix 4010 terminal.

graphics CRTs in use: relatively low-resolution CRTs, which are designed for displaying television pictures, and higher-resolution CRTs designed for use with digital systems. Figure 2-21 shows a raster refresh graphics terminal.

Resolution provides one basis of comparison for the three CRT terminals described thus far. The vector refresh and storage tubes can have resolutions ranging from 1024 pixels in the horizontal direction by 780 pixels in the vertical direction (1024 × 780) to 4096 × 4096 resolution. Figure 2-22 shows a picture drawn on such a high-resolution storage terminal. The smaller television tubes used by the raster terminals allow 500 pixels in the horizontal direction and have 250 rasters. Figure 2-23 shows a picture drawn on a 640 × 200 resolution raster terminal. Larger, newer CRTs make more vertical lines or rasters available and resolutions can climb to 1280 × 1024, but these tubes are not produced in the same quantities as the smaller television tubes and therefore are much more expensive. As production goes up the cost should come down, although the decrease in cost of the CRT may be offset by the cost of the electronics to display the higher resolution picture.

Monochrome raster terminals have only one gun to create the electron stream, and for most applications the phosphors available are either green, white, or amber. Terminals that provide color have phosphors on the screen that glow with different colors when they are struck by the electron beam, and they also can have three guns: one for red, one for blue, and one for green. These guns are adjustable in intensity in order to produce different color values. In color terminals each of the guns individually produces its own color and the following combinations are possible: Blue and red produce magenta, red and green produce yellow, and blue and green produce cyan. In addition, having all three guns on produces white, while having all three guns off produces black. Thus there are eight colors available. This arrangement also requires memory in the terminal so that the on/off

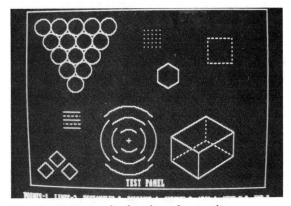

Figure 2-23. Picture displayed on a low-medium resolution (640 × 200) raster terminal.

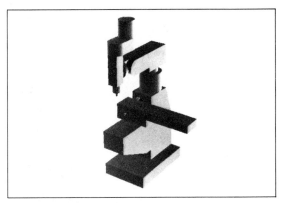

Figure 2-24. Three-dimensional modeling using the University of Rochester's PADL II software. (Courtesy of James Dallam and Lloyd Fields, Ohio State University)

condition of the three guns is available for each pixel on the screen. For a 512 × 250 screen this means that at least 128,000 bytes of information must be stored. Obviously, if more colors are to be used and more resolution is required, more memory will be required. The developments in integrated circuit technology are making memory less expensive each year and thus high-resolution, color raster CRTs will be available at relatively low prices. This will make possible more realistic graphic displays, which can be used to great advantage in geometric modeling (the creation of objects from basic or primitive three-dimensional shapes). Figure 2-24 shows a three-dimensional object created using PADL II, a geometric modeling software package.

PLOTTERS *Plotters* produce the pictures or drawings that the machinist, for instance, will use when making a part for a new product. Plotters are available in a variety of plot sizes and operating mechanisms. They include pen plotters, electrostatic plotters, thermal plotters, and printer plotters. Most plotters now have built-in microprocessors that direct pens to draw standard shapes and characters. The computer can send directions for the location, size, and actual characters to be plotted, and can then move on to another task while the plotter does the drawing.

Some *pen plotters* have been constructed so that the pen does all the moving while the paper stays in one place. The pen can move up, down, left, right, or in combinations, such as up and to the right. Any figures produced must be combinations of these movements; thus curves produced by these plotters are actually a series of short lines. These devices are called *flat-bed plotters* and are now available in sizes from 8.5 × 11 inches to 8 × 20 feet. Flatbed plotters are also available with eight or more pens, making multicolor plots available.

Engineering drawings and other pictures require both thin lines

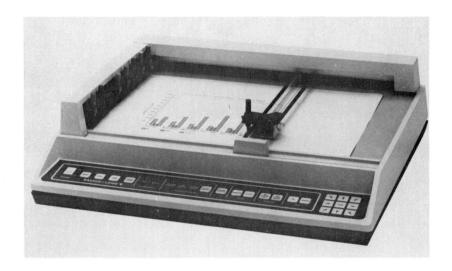

Figure 2-25. Houston Instrument DMP-29 flatbed pen plotter. (Courtesy of Houston Instrument)

and thick lines. Thick lines are achieved by using pens of different line widths or by using a thin-line-width pen to make multiple strokes, each stroke being slightly offset from the previous one. The pens can be felt-tip, ball-point, or liquid-ink. Liquid ink requires pens with very hard tips so that the tips are not worn by movement over paper or mylar. The paper must be held in place with tape, mechanical grippers, or vacuum-hold devices.

Speeds are available in the range of 15 to 30 inches per second. Acceleration of the pen from rest to high speed and change of direction are important parameters. When plotters are designed to move at very high speeds, the plotter mechanism must allow for a linear increase in speed from rest to the maximum speed. The resolution and the repeatability of the plotter mechanism are also important. The pen must be able to move long distances and return to the original starting position with a high degree of precision. Resolutions are in the range of 0.005 inches to 0.002 inches (0.12 mm to .05 mm). Figure 2-25 shows a flatbed plotter.

Drum plotters move the pen left and right and move the paper up and down to achieve the same pictures that the flatbed plotters produce. The big advantage of the drum plotter is that a large roll of paper can be loaded into the plotter, allowing many plots to be produced without having to go through a setup procedure each time. The widths for the rolls range from 8–10 inches to up to 72 inches and the length can be many feet. The mechanisms used to drive drum plotters can be either stepper motors or servo motors. The stepper motor produces a finite step and thus can govern the resolution available in the plotter. Plotters with servo motors can provide greater speed and an infinite range of plotting resolutions. Multiple pens are also available on drum plotters, along with microprocessor control. Figure 2-26 shows a drum plotter.

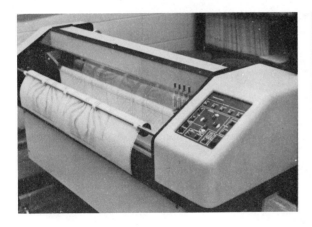

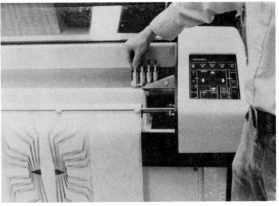

Figure 2-26. Houston Instrument DP-15 drum plotter with multiple pens, used as a plotter for the Bausch & Lomb Producer graphics system.

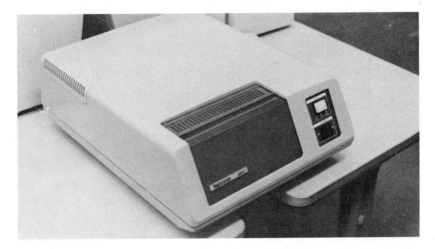

Figure 2-27. Tektronix 4611 electrostatic plotter.

An *electrostatic plotter* is, in effect, a raster device that works like the raster CRTs in some ways. It must get the information from the screen line by line. When it does, it then sends the information to the multiple brushes, which charge the paper that is going past. The charged portion of the paper attracts the toner, which is fixed by heat to produce a permanent picture. Thus the multiple brushes are equivalent to pixels on the screen. When a raster display is being used, the information can be sent to the plotter directly if the resolution matches, or it can be approximated if the screen resolution is higher or lower than the plotter resolution. If the information coming to the plotter is in the form of vectors, either the computer or the plotter controller must change the vector into a series of pixels.

The conversion of vector to raster data can absorb all of the computing power of a small computer, and many electrostatic plotters have a controller (either built-in or external) to serve as an interface. Electrostatic plotters are limited to one color. The resolution can be in the range of 200 × 200 dots to the square inch. An electrostatic plotter is shown in Figure 2-27.

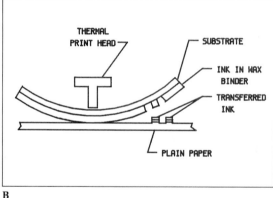

A   B

Figure 2-28. (A) Tektronix thermal hardcopy unit. (B) Schematic of a thermal print process.

Some *thermal plotters* require thermally sensitive paper that has been coated with heat-reactive microcapsules. The picture is transferred from the screen by brushes similar to those in the electrostatic plotter. The brushes provide heat to break the microcapsules, which release a liquid to create the graphic information. The paper tends to be rather expensive on a per-sheet basis and the maintenance costs can be fairly high. Figure 2-28A shows a thermal plotter.

Color thermal display copiers are also available. These copiers use three colors of wax pigment on consecutive sheets on an ink roll. Each picture requires a sheet of plain paper to be subjected to three passes of the ink roll. The cost per copy from these units is less than twenty-five cents. Figure 2-28B shows a schematic of the color thermal display copier.

Printer-plotters operate by using the print head to produce dots on the page that can represent lines. One type of printer capable of this is the *dot matrix printer,* which has print heads with a vertical line of very small, closely spaced wires, each of which can be individually called to strike the ribbon. The picture must be converted to pixels and then adjusted to the printer's resolution to be able to produce the facsimile.

Printer-plotters cannot produce plots with the resolution that electrostatic plotters provide, but for some applications they provide a relatively quick hardcopy of the desired picture. Additionally, using one device for two purposes can save money for certain applications, particularly because the cost per plot is relatively low.

Dot matrix printers can be used to produce color plots by installing a multicolored striped ribbon and a control mechanism to move the colored stripes up and down as needed. Colors are achieved through a combining method, similar to that used in CRTs. Again, resolution is not as good as on a pen plotter but more apparent colors can be available, depending on the controller for the print head and its multistrike and offset capabilities. Figure 2-29 shows a dot matrix

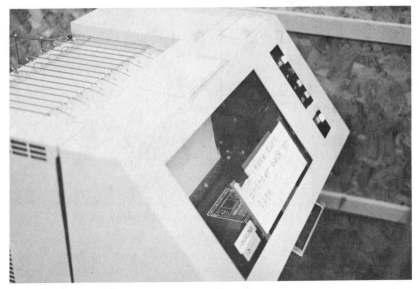

Figure 2-29. Printronix P-600 dot matrix printer-plotter.

printer-plotter. See Figure 2-30 for examples of plots from the various types of plotters we have discussed.

Lasers and *ink jets* are mechanisms now available for doing plotting, including, in the case of ink jets, color drawings. The cost of these devices is somewhat higher than that of the dot matrix printer-plotters and of some pen plotters, but further development and increased production should result in more laser and ink-jet printers in the marketplace.

A final device that can be used for copying, including color copying, is the camera. Special cameras have been produced just for copying from CRT displays. They provide high-quality copy within minutes. It is also possible to get reasonably good copy using a 35mm camera or a Polaroid-type camera.

PRINTERS Two types of alphanumeric printers can be used with computer graphics systems: the dot matrix printer and the formed-character printer. The dot matrix printer is used to keep a written record of system operation and for hardcopies of software changes. The formed-character printer is used for higher-quality output, such as system-instructional manuals.

The print head of a dot matrix printer is composed of a block with a matrix of holes in it that each contain a wire. A typical matrix may be 7 × 9. This means that the characters may be 7 dots wide and 8 dots high with a 1 dot descender (1 dot below the rest of the dots in characters without descenders). A ribbon passes between the print head and the paper and, in response to signals from the computer, various wires are forced out and hit the ribbon against the paper. The printer has a microprocessor built in to help control the print-head

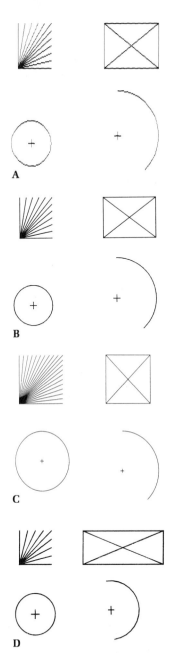

Figure 2-30. Examples of plots from various plotters. (A) NEC 8023A printer-plotter. (B) Houston Instrument HIPLOT pen plotter. (C) Tektronix Xerographic hardcopy unit. (D) Houston Instrument DP-15 drum plotter.

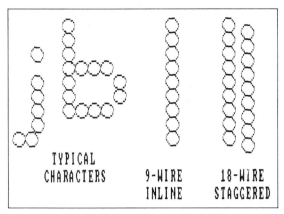

Figure 2-31. Dot matrix characters and print-head wire layouts.

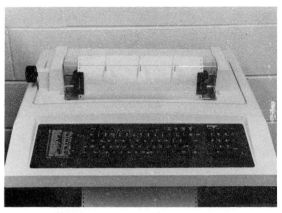

Figure 2-32. DECwriter III dot matrix printer.

Figure 2-33. (A) Print wheel for a daisy wheel printer. (B) Diablo daisy wheel printer.

A

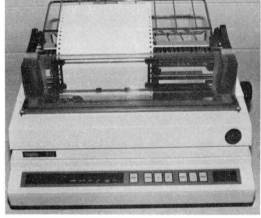

B

movement across the paper and to control the movement of the paper up and down. Figure 2-31 shows a schematic drawing of some letters and wire placement patterns for dot matrix print heads, and Figure 2-32 shows a typical dot matrix printer.

The *formed-character printer,* which can use a daisy-wheel, golf-ball, or band print head, produces letter-quality printing. Figure 2-33 shows a daisy-wheel printer and the print wheel.

Electrostatic and xerographic printers have the capability of combining text with graphics and it is conceivable that the laser and ink-jet printers will also have this capability in the near future.

Input Devices

A computer graphics system that does not allow users to see the display until after the design has been completed cannot be used efficiently for design work. A variety of devices are available to permit users to transmit their thoughts at the proper time to control

Figure 2-34. IBM Personal Computer keyboard.

the picture during its creation. The following paragraphs provide a partial listing of these devices.

The terminal (standard typewriter) *keyboard* can be used effectively to communicate with the computer to alter the display. Many times this may be slower than some of the other methods and devices available, but almost every system does provide a keyboard for either primary or secondary input. The addition of function keys—keys for particular actions (such as arrow keys)—can allow the user to control a screen cursor. This cursor can perform a variety of operations, such as selecting the end points of a vector or choosing an item from a menu. Many times beginners use other input devices, but they may revert to keyboard use for more than 50 percent of their interaction with the system once they are experienced in using the system. In some cases, such as in the Ford Motor Co. graphics systems, there is no keyboard at all. This system uses light-pen input only, and characters and numbers are selected from menus displayed on the screen. Figure 2-34 shows a typical computer terminal keyboard. Note the extra keys on the left and right of the standard typewriter keys.

Digitizer tablets are graphics input devices that allow the user to send the location (coordinates) of a point to the computer. That location may signify the end of a line or may specify a box in a menu that contains a word or a graphic action. Digitizers, which have work areas that can range in size from 11 × 11 inches to 4 × 6 feet, can be used to enter the information about a drawing by "tracing" lines and figures. In general, the drafter touches ends of a line to store the line information and touches the center and one point on the circumference to store a circle. Prior to performing these actions, she must select the item that she is preparing to store so that the computer knows which storage area will be used to keep the information that she has added to the drawing.

Digitizers vary in the precision and repeatability of the informa-

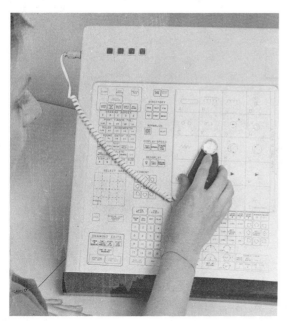

Figure 2-35. Houston Instrument HIPAD digitizer showing details of the menu and cursor. (Courtesy of Bausch & Lomb)

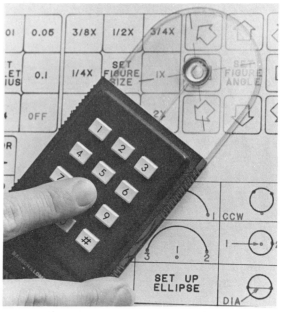

Figure 2-36. Digitizer cursor with multiple buttons for a large Houston Instrument digitizer. (Courtesy of Bausch & Lomb)

tion that they can send to the computer, but most are capable of measuring in increments of between 0.001 and 0.01 inches. There are several ways that the information about X and Y locations can be sent. One way is to use wires sandwiched between two plastic sheets to receive a signal sent from a coil contained in the sending device. The coil will send a signal when a button on the cursor is pressed. The cursor can have the shape of a pen or pointer, or it can be shaped to fit in the hand, with a transparent portion containing a set of cross hairs. Figure 2-35 shows a digitizer board with its menu and handheld cursor, and Figure 2-36 shows a close-up of another type of handheld cursor.

The cursor cross hairs allow the user to accurately position the cursor over the desired point on a drawing. A handheld cursor can also be used to control the cursor on the CRT screen so that every movement of the hand cursor provides a corresponding movement of the screen cursor. When the digitizer is set up in this manner it is said to be in *stream mode*. This means that a stream of coordinates is being sent at regular time intervals. Sound can also be used to input graphic information, but this is not common. The sound or *sonic digitizer* uses two or three strip microphones that are placed at 90 degrees to each other. These microphones pick up sound and transmit it to the computer.

Digitizers and the type and characteristics of signals that they send to the computer will be discussed in Chapter 11.

Thumbwheels are analog devices. Analog in this case means that a

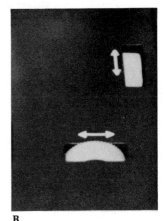

A   B

Figure 2-37. (A) Tektronix 4010 keyboard. (B) Thumbwheels for controlling the cross-hair graphics cursor on the Tektronix 4010 CRT.

A   B

Figure 2-38. (A) Lear-Siegler ADM-3A+ alphanumeric CRT with a Digital Engineering RG-512 Retrographics printed-circuit board and graphics cursor-control keypad installed. (B) Digital Engineering keypad for controlling the cursor on a Lear-Siegler terminal with graphics conversion.

physical movement of the wheel is translated into an electrical signal that positions the cursor on the screen. Thumbwheels, which have been used on the Tektronix graphics terminal shown in Figure 2-37, control a screen cursor that is composed of two lines at right angles, one vertical and the other horizontal, in cross-hair fashion. The movement of a wheel positions the cursor along the horizontal or vertical line and can also position the cursor relative to a grid displayed on the edge of the screen.

Pushbuttons, or *function keys,* can be used to replace thumbwheels for controlling the screen's graphics cursor. Four buttons can replace two thumbwheels, one pair of buttons being for up-down motion and the other for left-right motion. The design can also allow for adjacent buttons to provide motion at a 45-degree angle. A set of buttons can be an addition to a terminal and housed in a separate box, as shown in Figure 2-38, or it can be additional keys on a

Figure 2-39. DEC VT 100 terminal keyboard with cursor-control (arrow) keys used for controlling the graphics cursor when an ID Systems graphics board is installed.

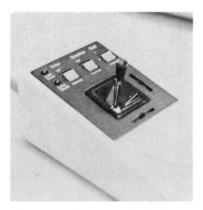

Figure 2-40. Joystick used with the graphics display on the IBM 3277 GA dual-screen workstation (shown in Figure 2-7).

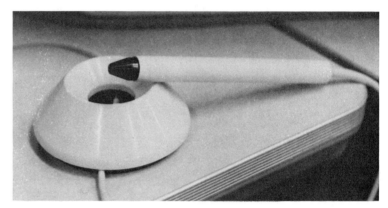

Figure 2-41. Light-pen attachment for use with the alphanumeric display in the IBM 3277 GA dual-screen workstation (shown in Figure 2-7).

"standard" keyboard, as shown in Figure 2-39. In some systems, the buttons are lit when the cursor-control function is active, which helps the user to be efficient when operating the system. Some systems also allow the user to write programs to specify cursor-control (or other) functions for particular keys. This contributes to system flexibility. Unlike thumbwheels, which are analog devices, pushbuttons are digital devices that send one character at a time.

A *joystick* is shown in Figure 2-40. Joysticks are analog devices that can be used to move the screen cursor in any direction rather than in specified directions as the pushbuttons do. Some systems depend on joysticks as their only graphics input device, while others use them in conjunction with other input devices.

A *light pen* is a pencil-shaped device with a cord attached to one end and a light sensor at the other end (see Figure 2-41). A light pen can be used on vector and raster refresh terminals to point to objects displayed on the screen. When the light pen points to an object and the electron beam sweeps by that position, the pen picks up the signal and sends it to either the computer or the microprocessor that controls the display. The signal interrupts the computer and the computer asks the CRT for the screen location of the light pen. This coordinate information is then available to be used by the system. In general, the pen must be pointed at relatively large objects. One dot on the screen is difficult for the pen to detect.

Less common input devices include the human voice and light-sensitive scanning devices. If certain words in an individual's vocabulary are tested and characterized, that individual can then operate particular systems using only his or her voice to indicate a desired action. A trained individual can look at a signal pattern recorded on paper or displayed on the terminal and translate what he or she sees in cryptic, or coded, sets of words, which can be understood and stored by the computer.

Scanning devices pick up the difference between light and dark areas. Through a variety of means, the differences are detected and stored in a computer system and can be decoded into objects recognizable by the computer and by the system operator. A typical scanning device is the type of television camera used on space vehicles. The information recorded by such a camera is coded and sent back to earth, where it is decoded and displayed as recognizable pictures.

Interfaces

The term *interface* is used to signify the physical device connecting two computer system components. The hardware can consist of printed circuit boards, electronic chips, and wires. An interface is like the outlet that allows you to connect a light to a power source. In the case of the interface, however, one additional item must be considered. The system must have enough intelligence to recognize the information being exchanged so that communication occurs. The intelligence is obtained through the system software or programs resident in each device.

There are two types of interfaces: serial and parallel. A *serial interface* is one that sends one bit at a time between the connected devices. Characters are made up of a combination of 8 high and low voltages (bits) that move along the wires one after the other. These 8 bits (1 character) can be sent at a variety of speeds, varying from approximately 15 cps (characters per second) to 2400 cps or higher, or from an industry standard of 110 to more than 19,200 bits per second. A serial interface can require as few as three wires to connect two devices, and in general, they are less expensive than parallel interfaces if the signals are to be carried more than 100 feet.

A *parallel interface* sends the 8 bits that make up one character

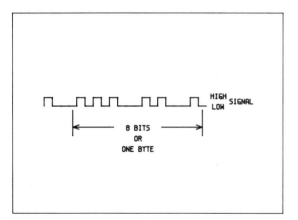 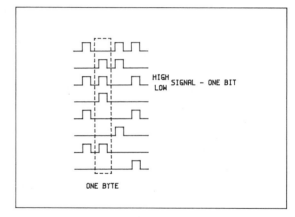

Figure 2-42. Pictorial representation of serial and parallel interfaces.

over eight parallel wires (one bit per wire) rather than over one wire. Thus the bits for the character all arrive at the destination at the same time and are then decoded. Figure 2-42 shows a pictorial representation of serial and parallel interfaces.

System Software Components

Computer graphics systems require instructions or programs to tell them what to do. This *system software* has several components, including: (1) operating software, which controls the computer and manages the hardware devices; (2) editors, which allow programs to be written by the user; and (3) programming languages, which are English-like instructions to the machine that it then decodes into words it can understand. Editors are used to prepare programs for specific applications using the programming language.

Operating System Software

In simplified form the computer has a processing unit, a memory unit, a tape or disk storage unit, communications (interfaces) among these units, and interfaces for users. *Operating system software* is written by specialists in computer programming so that these components interact efficiently. In machines with sufficient capacity, system software can allow several users to be active at any one time, sharing the machine's resources. Microcomputers generally allow only one user at a time, so their operating software can be much simpler.

The users must be able to utilize the computer's operating system to gain access to the memory, disk space, and computing power. A *command language* is available for this purpose. The user's manual for your system will give you these commands and define their function. In some systems the commands are one-, two-, or three-letter shorthand representations of the word that forms the command. In other systems the command word must be entered in full. For example, COPY is a command used to copy the contents of a portion of a disk to another portion of the disk. This command can be entered as COP or CP on some systems.

The operating system must assign memory locations to be sure that memory space being utilized is not already being used to store items entered earlier. In addition, the operating system must keep track of where numbers and words are stored so that it can find them when the user wants them. If the memory is full, then information must be stored on the tape or disk. Some systems do this automatically, while others tell you that the memory is full and let you decide what information must be put on the tape or disk. The disk storage is limited, and each stored item must have a labeled space so that it can be found when needed. The items stored on the disk are known as *files*.

Sophisticated operating systems on very fast computers appear to allow the user to get immediate response on each request. Slower computers may make the user wait to get the answers to the problems that he or she wants solved. Some of the slower systems give messages that the computer is busy, while others simply do not respond to input until the calculations are finished.

If there are multiple users on the system, the operating system must have the capability to manage its resources so as to serve each user on either an equitable or on a biased basis if the system operators choose. The operating system must know how many users are assigned to the system and what the required communications rates are for each user. The user terminals are generally serial interfaces whereas the printer could well be a parallel interface.

Editors

Editors are text-processing programs written to allow the user to write his or her programs easily. Editors take care of naming the programs so that they can be stored on the disk in files and called when needed. Editor programs have their own set of commands for doing different operations. For example, if you wish to change a plus sign to a minus sign some systems will require you to find the statement where the plus sign occurs. Once you have found the line you type C/+/−/, meaning "change the first plus sign in this statement to a minus, but don't go past the first one and don't look in any other lines." This type of editor is called a *line editor* because the user enters the program line by line and must find all errors by line.

Full-screen editors allow the user to enter the program line by line but then to move the cursor to any the line visible on the terminal or CRT and change, add, or delete any item that is incorrect. Full-screen editors may take longer to learn and generally require more system capacity but the payback is in the speed with which program creation and editing are performed.

Programming Languages

Programming languages have been created so that humans can talk to computers. These languages can be divided into three basic categories:

1. *High-level languages*, which are collections of words that people understand and which must be translated into words that the computer understands. In general, each word means a series of operations that the computer must perform.

2. *Assembler languages*, which are very cryptic in terms of the words used and much more specific in terms of machine operations. They specify one operation of the computer using a two- or three-letter code.

3. *Machine code*, which is the series of binary digits or bits (high or low voltages represented as 1's and 0's) that the computer can use directly.

HIGH-LEVEL LANGUAGES The common languages used by engineers and scientists include FORTRAN, BASIC, Pascal, PL/I, APL, C, and ADA. Some of these, BASIC for example, are interpreted. This means that each time a line of code is executed it must be changed from the high-level language into machine code that the computer can execute. Others, like FORTRAN, are compiled. For these languages there is a program called a *compiler* that reads all of the statements and converts the entire program to machine code before any statements are executed. Compiled code generally runs faster on a system because the compiler organizes the tasks in the order that makes best use of the computer's resources.

Each of the high-level languages has certain advantages. FORTRAN is most commonly used by engineers because it is good for scientific calculations that require manipulating numbers. BASIC is easy to learn and is good for manipulating words as well as numbers, but programs written in interpretive BASIC run rather slowly in comparison to compiled languages. For this reason there are now BASIC compilers. Pascal was written to overcome some of the shortcomings of both BASIC and FORTRAN and has been written to be used on both large and small computers. These three languages are used more by engineers than are any of the others. PL/I, APL, and the others form a very small portion of the total code in use in industry today. ADA may become popular because the government is supporting the development of this language. The American National Standards Institute (ANSI) has attempted to develop standards for each of the commonly used languages so that software will be more transportable among computer systems.

ASSEMBLER LANGUAGES Assembler code is more efficient than high-level languages but it requires the user to know the computer's internal operations. The user must specify that a number is to be stored in a certain memory location, for example, rather than specifying the value for that number and then letting the system decide where to store it. The "words" used by the programmer are cryptic two- or three-letter codes. One statement in BASIC is often equivalent to several statements in assembler. Each computer or microprocessor has its own assembler code. Some have a very small number of instructions while others have many.

MACHINE CODES Machine code is the code that the computer understands. It is indecipherable to most programmers, and printing the file on a terminal can cause the terminal to quit working. The digital computer only understands combinations of 1's and 0's or high and low voltages. For most programmers to work at the level of the machine code would not only be difficult but would be inefficient as well.

Libraries

The computer is able to store commonly used programs or pieces of programs. A series of pieces of programs that can be added to any other program is called a *library*. A library of programs can be focused on a particular application, such as statistics or computer graphics. If the piece of program performs a complex task (one consisting of several actions), such as drawing a rectangle, it is called a *subroutine*. If the piece of program performs only one action, such as calculating the value of the sine of an angle, it is called a *function*.

In a computer graphics system there is frequently a library of subroutines and a library of functions. PLOT10 was written by Tektronix to support their graphics terminals and is a library of functions and subroutines that is used for scaling, rotating, and drawing objects. The drawing routines that PLOT10 provides produce lines of various types, such as solid lines, dashed lines, and center lines. This book draws on two libraries: PLOT10, written in FORTRAN for the Digital Equipment Corporation minicomputer paired with a Tektronix compatible terminal, and IBM's graphics functions, written in BASIC.

Libraries can also be written by the system programmer by developing subroutines for graphical actions needed to create pictures. These libraries contain the most commonly needed routines. A graphing software package such as SAS/GRAPH needs routines to draw axes, label axes, fill areas with patterns, draw lines to connect data points, and create titles for graphs. Each of these routines would be part of the library.

Functions are required for most programs to operate efficiently. Examples of functions would be the calculation of sines, cosines, tangents and square roots. Matrix operations can also be functions.

Applications Software

When programmers have a computer system, they have at their disposal the operating system, the language, and the libraries, but in

Figure 2-43. Manuals for documentation of the BASIC language, for the disk operating system (DOS) for an IBM microcomputer, and for WordStar, a word-processing software package from MicroPro International Corporation.

most cases these alone are insufficient for solving the problems at hand. The users must also obtain or create software or programs that answer their particular needs. These programs are called *applications software*.

In the process of creating applications software users must invest considerable time and money. At this point, before beginning a sizable programming project, they must consider cost, time, documentation, the database, and many other factors. If software that will solve the immediate problem is available on the open market, it is generally cheaper to buy this software rather than to create it. Each case must be considered individually, particularly if any proprietary information or process is involved. Figure 2-43 shows the manuals for the BASIC language and the disk operating system (DOS) for an IBM microcomputer. The figure also shows the manual for WordStar, a word processing software package (one form of applications software).

A program can be written to solve any problem imaginable, but the time needed to finish the project is generally longer than the creator might imagine. Several companies have created their own graphics programs, but they have had large resources at their disposal and could ask computer manufacturers to create hardware to suit their needs. On a software project it is almost impossible to gain back time that has been lost. If a project gets behind schedule, even adding extra people seldom gains back any measurable amount of time.

Documentation of what a program does and how it is to be used is critical for the user/purchaser. Just as important for the user is the degree of *internal documentation* that is available for maintenance and upgrading of software packages. The internal documentation is the explanation that is included with listings of the source code. The *external documentation* includes the manuals for daily use and for training users.

This text will give examples of internal documentation that should provide guides for those students who intend to create their own code. Good documentation for software is so critical that students might be wise to sacrifice learning more techniques in favor of properly documenting the ones that they have already learned.

Utilities are programs or segments of programs that are created for solving a particular problem, such as copying a disk file or a whole disk onto another disk. Utilities may be part of the operating system or they may be incorporated as part of the user programs. Most of the utilities that you will deal with in this book will be part of the DEC or IBM operating system.

Database is a term used to represent the information that is stored in files on the computer. When a picture is created, many types of information must be stored and retrieved. This book will deal primarily with storing the information used to create graphical images drawn with line segments.

Programs are assigned *version* numbers to indicate to users which chronological model of a software package they are employing on their system. There are often multiple versions because most packages are initially designed and created to do a certain number of tasks. When it becomes apparent that additional tasks must be performed using a particular software package, the authors add new modules and the modified package is given a new version number. For example, the first version of a software package may be labeled 1.0 and any minor changes are taken care of by calling the new versions 1.1, 1.2, 1.3, and so on. A version embodying a major change is generally given a higher number, such as 2.0.

In almost every known case a language or a program will be dependent on the hardware of the system. Thus FORTRAN on an IBM mainframe computer will be very similar to the FORTRAN used on a minicomputer or a microcomputer, but it will seldom be identical.

This chapter has introduced some of the terms you will be encountering with regard to the computer hardware and software used in computer graphics. We anticipate that you will find yourself learning much more about the operation of computer graphics systems as you complete the reading and programming exercises provided in the following chapters. At this point you should have a mental picture of the computer and the peripherals needed for a computer graphics system, and you should have an idea of the software necessary to make the system operate. This picture will have a minimum amount of detail now, but by the end of the book your mental image should be considerably more accurate and detailed. You should expect to follow up your study of this book with a great deal of additional study of computer science if you wish to be a successful creator of system or applications software.

Exercises

1. Determine whether the system that you are to use to complete the programming exercises in this book is a mainframe computer, a minicomputer, or a microcomputer and whether the processor is classified as an 8-bit, a 16-bit, a 32-bit, or some other word length processor.

2. Read the user's manuals to determine which language you will be using and, if possible, whether it conforms to one of the ANSI standards.

3. Determine which graphics package you will be using and the number of different graphics commands or functions that are available to you.

4. By reading the user's manuals and beginning to work on the system, determine whether there are help files available.

5. List all of the graphics peripherals that are available to you. Assuming that you have a graphics terminal, indicate the resolution of the terminal as part of your list. Determine whether the digitizer and plotter have equivalent resolutions and list them as well.

Language Review and Programming Techniques

A sound working knowledge of the programming language you will use is critical to effective computer programming, and graphics programming is no exception. Graphics programs use the same program statements that are used by any other program as well as unique graphics language statements. We assume that, if you are using this textbook, you have completed an introductory course in FORTRAN, Advanced BASIC, or Pascal, or have had equivalent experience. Therefore, the intent of this chapter is to review language elements rather than to provide first-time instruction in any of these languages. If you have a strong programming background, you may wish to skim this chapter. If you feel you need more in-depth instruction, you may wish to refer to the programming texts listed in the appendixes. Graphics language elements, which are not normally covered in conventional programming courses, will be covered in detail in the following chapters.

Language Elements

This chapter will discuss the language features most used in graphics programming. Each feature will be presented in conjunction with a general discussion of its use and limitations, then each feature's availability and form will be discussed for each of the three languages.

Working with Values

The values—constants or variables—and other information used by a computer program must be stored in the computer's memory in a form that it can use. Values are stored in one of several ways. Fixed numerical values are stored as *constants*; fixed non-numeric information is stored as *literals*, which are usually enclosed in quotation marks (such as the date "July 11, 1982"). Variables are treated in various ways depending on their type. Variable types with which we will be concerned are integer, real, character (or string), and logical (boolean).

INTEGER VARIABLES Integers—numbers without decimal points—are, in general, treated much differently from numbers with decimal points. Integers are stored as whole numbers with no provision for storing anything but the digits and the sign of the number (+ or −). Since the numbers are stored in binary form, the size of number that can be stored is 2^{n-1}, where n is the number of bits (generally 16 or 32) that the system uses to store the number and its sign. If 16 bits are used, for instance, the number can range in size from -2^{15} to 2^{15-1}, or −32768 to +32767. An integer stored using 32 bits can range from −2147483648 to +2147483647.

Arithmetic operations on real numbers generally produce the same answer on the computer that one would get using a pencil and paper. Operations with integers, on the other hand, generally produce a result that is truncated or rounded according to one of the following conventions:

1. Rounded to the nearest integer.
2. Rounded toward zero (truncated).
3. Rounded to next smaller integer (−1.2 would become −2 using this convention).

Integers normally take less storage space than real numbers (those with decimal points) because they do not have to store location information for the decimal point.

- FORTRAN: Any variable name beginning with the letter I through the letter N is recognized by default as an integer unless declared otherwise in a type statement.
- BASIC: Integers are those variables whose name ends with %.
- PASCAL: Integers are those variables that have been declared as integer in a type statement such as the following:

```
VAR vname:INTEGER;
```

REAL VARIABLES *Real numbers* are used when it is necessary to keep track of decimal portions of the numbers or when the number is very large. Scientific notation allows the computer to handle very large numbers as reals. The number is stored as a decimal value along with its sign and an exponent. The sign takes one binary digit, the exponent uses seven, and the number is stored in the remaining 24 bits of a 32-bit storage location. While a number of any practical size can be handled, only seven significant digits will be retained (that is the capacity of the 24 bits), so extremely large numbers or those with a large number of digits to the right of the decimal point are approximated.

- FORTRAN: Real variables are those whose names begin with any letter except I through N (by default) or those that have been declared to be real as follows:

```
REAL number
```

The default typing can be modified with an IMPLICIT REAL statement such as

```
IMPLICIT REAL n
```

This statement declares that any variable whose name begins with the letter n will be real instead of integer. All other default typing will remain in effect.
- BASIC: Real variables are those whose names do not end with % or $. Thus, MYVALUE is real while MYVALUE% is integer and MYVALUE$ is character or string. Some BASICs that are written for computers with limited memory allow only a single character or a character followed by a single digit, such as B or B1, for real variables and do not recognize integers at all.
- PASCAL: All variables must be declared. Real variables are declared using

```
VAR
    myvalue:REAL
```

Once declared, the variable is global (the same throughout the program) and its type cannot be changed. There are ways of redeclaring a variable as local within a procedure (subroutine) and changing its type for the purposes of that one procedure, but this technique is not recommended and will not be covered here.

CHARACTER VARIABLES *Character variables* are used to store letters, words, numbers that are not going to be used in computation (such as dates), and any other non-numeric data. Some language implementations can handle only one character per variable element. Others can handle more than one character per element and thus are known as *string* variables.

- FORTRAN: Some versions recognize BYTE, which is equivalent to LOGICAL*1 and will hold one alphanumeric character per element. FORTRAN will allow the use of real or integer variables for character information as long as the read and write formats are for character information. Real variables will generally handle 8 characters per element and integer variables will handle 2 or 4, depending on whether the computer is a 16-bit or 32-bit-word machine. It is important to check the machine and the FORTRAN version being used.

- BASIC: BASIC will handle strings of up to 255 characters in length. Some BASIC versions require that strings longer than a particular value (such as 18 characters) be explicitly dimensioned or they default to that length. Most versions, however, will accept any string length from zero to the maximum and do not require a dimension statement.

- PASCAL: Original versions of Pascal recognized only character variables (string of length 1), but many versions have extensions that recognize longer strings. As with other variables in Pascal, all character and string variables have to be declared as either character or string (two different things to Pascal). An example of a character declaration would be

```
VAR
    myword: CHAR;
```

LOGICAL VARIABLES *Logical*, or *Boolean*, variable types come into play when the variable is to be used in decision making. The logical variable can take on only one of two values (TRUE or FALSE). In some implementations of BASIC the value FALSE is represented by a zero (0) and TRUE is represented by a negative one (−1). It may be possible to use these values in numeric computations, but in FOR-TRAN or Pascal this will not be the case.

- FORTRAN: FORTRAN generally requires that logical variables be declared as such. A typical type declaration would be

```
LOGICAL  MYTEST
```

In this case, the two permissible values, ".TRUE." and ".FALSE." each have a length of four (occupy four bytes of memory). Some implementations use LOGICAL*1, in which case the values are ".T." and ".F.", which are of length 1.

- BASIC: BASIC does not have a separate variable type for logical variables, but string variables can be assigned the value TRUE or FALSE and the variable can be used in a test. For example

```
200   A$="TRUE"
210   IF A$ THEN  GOTO 600
```

In this example, the program will always branch to line 600 because A$ is always TRUE. However the code

```
100 IF X<=30 THEN A$="TRUE":ELSE A$="FALSE"
110 IF A$="TRUE" THEN GOTO 600
```

will cause a conditional branch to line 600 depending on the value of X. Use of logical tests to control conditional branching is a very powerful tool. Statements may be designed to test multiple conditions by joining individual tests together through the use of AND, OR, and NOT.

- PASCAL: All logical variables must be declared as BOOLEAN before they can be used. Boolean variables may take on only one of two values, TRUE or FALSE, and they may be used only in logical operations.

Equations

Equations are always evaluated according to the generally well-defined rules of mathematics. The order of execution is as follows:

1. Function calls are evaluated.
2. Arithmetic operations are performed.
3. Relational operations are performed.
4. Logical operations are performed.

Since we are concerned here with mathematical operations, the operators with which we need to deal and their order of execution are:

1. Expressions within parentheses. Nested parenthesis are evaluated from the inside out (innermost set first).
2. Exponentiation, which is done starting at the right-hand side of the equation and working to the left.
3. Multiplication and division. These have equal priority and are performed as they are encountered, working from left to right.
4. Addition and subtraction. These have equal priority and are performed from left to right in the order encountered.

Functions

Functions can be of two types. The first are so-called *built-in* or *library functions*. They are part of the system software for the language being used and have only to be called when needed. Library functions are generally available to provide the following:

- Trigonometric functions
- Logarithmic and exponential functions
- Absolute value and transfer of sign
- Rounding and truncation
- Modular arithmetic
- Type conversion
- Base conversion

The second type of function is the *user-defined* function. This type is written by you, the applications programmer, to fit your specific needs, and can be whatever is needed. For instance, some language versions offer SIN and COS functions, but no TAN. You could write your own TAN function as being the SIN divided by the COS.

Subroutines

Subroutines are special routines, either within or external to user programs, that may be called from any point in the program. Subroutines perform a specific set of operations and then return control to the calling segment at the first executable statement following the call. Their operation is quite different in the three languages being reviewed here.

- FORTRAN: Subroutines are separate program segments with their own variable names. They begin with the reserved word SUBROUTINE and the name of the subroutine, and they end with the reserved word RETURN. Any type declaration statements or dimension statements that would be required for a main program segment are required for the subroutine, since it must stand on its own. Variables passed from the main program to the subroutine may have a different name in the different program segments since they are, in effect, separate programs. Variables are passed by use of a COMMON statement or by use of an argument list in the subroutine call and a corresponding parameter list in the subroutine. They can also be passed by a combination of the two.

  Since all variables are local, that is, they have meaning only within their own program segment, values are passed between segments in the order in which the names appear in the statement or list. Thus, the value of the first variable in the argument list of the calling statement will be assigned to the first parameter in the subroutine list. The second argument will be assigned to the second parameter, and so on. If the argument list contains an array, every element of the array will be passed before the next named variable is passed. Likewise, if the parameter list contains an array, the array, when encountered, will be filled before any values are assigned to the next variable. For this reason it is critical that variables be listed in corresponding order in both lists and that arrays be properly and consistently dimensioned.

  When a subroutine call is made, any values required by the subroutine must be passed to it. Results are returned to the calling routine by assigning the values of the variables in the parameter list back to the argument list in the same order as they were passed to the subroutine.

  The second way of passing values is through the COMMON statement. COMMON statements have variable lists that must agree in type and number of elements in each program segment in which they are used. Values are passed between segments according to the variable's position in the list rather than the variable's name. As with argument and parameter lists, the variable names do not have to be the same. It is their position in the list that determines their value. If a value is passed between two program segments by a COMMON statement, it must not be passed in a parameter list. If a value is in a parameter list, it must not be passed in a COMMON statement. Program segments may have a variable named in a COMMON statement and may use the same variable in argument lists for subroutine calls so long as the called subroutine does not contain that COMMON statement. There are many options available in the use of COMMON statements and blocks. We recommend that a FORTRAN text be consulted for further discussion of this area.

- BASIC: Subroutine use is rather informal in BASIC. The subroutines are an integral part of the main program and all variables are global (they mean the same thing throughout the program). Variables may not be redefined or redimensioned in the subroutines. However, their values may be changed at will. A subroutine is called by use of the command GOSUB followed by the starting line number of the subroutine. Upon encountering a RETURN, control will be returned to the statement following the GOSUB. It is not necessary to enter the subroutine at any specific point but, from the point of entry, the subroutine must be logically and syntactically correct. If a subroutine is encountered in normal execution of a program (no GOSUB is in effect) the program will attempt to execute the statements and will produce an error when the RETURN is encountered. For this reason most programs either put subroutines after the program END statement or else use transfer statements to bypass the subroutines.

- PASCAL: Pascal has very specific rules regarding subroutines. These subroutines are called *procedures*. All procedures must precede the main body of the program. Each procedure begins with the word PROCEDURE followed by the name of the procedure. Variables used in the main program are global and thus do not need to be called out as parameters in the procedure call. However, parameter lists may be used to pass variables by location (address) or by value to local variables that are defined within the procedure. When variables are passed by location, changes made to their values in the procedure will change the values of the variables in the calling segment. When variables are passed by value, changes made in the procedure will not cause changes in the variables in the calling segment. Procedures are called by simply naming the procedure. The procedure ends with an END statement and control is then returned to the calling segment at the next statement following the call.

Data Storage and Retrieval

Data storage and retrieval capability is a prime requirement of any computer program and it is particularly important to graphics programs. Chapter 2 noted that in order to delete a graphic entity from a storage tube terminal, the entity had to be marked, the screen erased, and the display redrawn minus the marked entity. Redrawing the display would not be possible without reentering all of the data, unless the data were stored in the system.

There are many different techniques for storing data, the choice of which depends on the interrelationship of the data elements (structure of the data). Some data consist of values that are all independent of one another. These data are often stored as independent data items (primitives). However, data are often grouped into a set of related items that have a fixed relationship to each other. Data of this type are best stored in a data structure that retains the integrity of the set.

Arrays

A type of data structure that is particularly well suited for storing computer graphics data is called an *array*. An array is a set of data that is stored with a single variable name and uses subscripts to refer to the various data elements in the set. Arrays allow all related data to be handled as a single unit. This makes accounting for all of the elements much easier. The elements of the set may be integers or real values or characters. They must, however be of the same type for the entire set. It is not permissible to mix data types within one array. An exception to this rule is found in Pascal, which supports *record* structures. Records are composed of several fields each of which is declared as to type. A Pascal array of records is permitted.

Arrays may contain the equivalent of a single line of data. For instance, the days of the week could be stored in a seven-element array named DAY. The first day would be DAY(1), the second day DAY(2), and so on. This is known as a singly subscripted array. Another example of a singly subscripted array would be all of the homework grades for one student in one class, let us call it GRADE(I), where I is the subscript and can take on any positive integer value within the range for which the array was dimensioned. A singly subscripted array could be used to store all the data needed to draw one graphic entity on the screen. For instance, the X-Y coordinates of a point could be stored in an array with two elements. Similarly, the end points of a line could be stored in an array of four elements, two for the starting point and two more for the ending point.

Double-subscripted arrays can store the equivalent of many lines of data. All the days of the month could be stored in a 42-element double-subscripted array. The array would have seven columns and six rows, as shown in the example on page 57. If the first subscript represents the row and the second subscript represents the column, then the third day of the second week would be DAY(2,3).

Another example of a double-subscripted array would be homework grades for all of the students in a single class. A value for the fifth homework grade for the twelfth student in the class might then be stored in GRADE(12,5). A double-subscripted array could store

JANUARY 1983							
WEEK	S	M	T	W	T	F	S
1							1
2	2	3	4	5	6	7	8
3	9	10	11	12	13	14	15
4	16	17	18	19	20	21	22
5	23	24	25	26	27	28	29
6	30	31					

the data for a number of graphics entities. The first subscript would refer to the elements of an entity and the second subscript would define which particular entity the data are for. Of course, the arrays have to be dimensioned for two subscripts before they can be used.

Triple-subscripted arrays can be thought of as being several pages of double-subscripted array data. Going back to our calendar example, the third subscript could be the month. Thus the third day of the second week of the seventh month would be DAY(2,3,7). In the student grade example, the third subscript could record the section of the course. GRADE(12,5,2) would then be the second homework-paper grade for student number 12 in the second section of the course. A triple-subscripted array might be used to store graphics that are grouped by type: Points would be one type, lines another, and circles and arcs a third. The third subscript, then, would denote the group. In this example, data for all circles and arcs could be retrieved by calling up all array elements whose third subscript was 3.

Arrays of more than three dimensions are somewhat more difficult to visualize. Most people are able to visualize one-, two-, or three-dimensional space and can relate an array to that space, but additional dimensions are hard to represent physically. Returning to our earlier examples, a fourth subscript (dimension) might represent the year in the calendar example or the courses offered in the student example. Thus DAY(2,3,7,83) would be the second week, the third day, the seventh month, in the year 1983. Similarly, GRADE (12,5,2,141) would be the grade for the fifth homework paper of student number 12 in section 2 of course 141. The graphics array could use the fourth subscript to denote the drawing or picture to which the array belonged, thus allowing storage of data for several different drawings in one array. For our purposes it will not be necessary to go beyond two dimensions in most cases.

- FORTRAN: All arrays must be declared and dimensioned before being used. They must be dimensioned in every program segment in which they are used, since all variables are local. The rules for variable types, including default typing, apply to array variables. If the FORTRAN version being used does not recognize character strings (that is, if it is necessary to use BYTE or LOGICAL*1 or a real or integer variable name), then it will be necessary to use arrays for character strings.

- BASIC: All arrays must be dimensioned. Some versions of BASIC provide for dimensioning the length of the string as well as the number of elements (one string of whatever length is thought of as being one element). Other versions handle the string length and only require dimensioning for the number of elements. For example, a drawing title could be stored in an array variable named TITLE if it were dimensioned to provide one element for each line of the title. Thus, if the title contained three lines, the array would need three elements and would be dimensioned as follows:

```
DIMENSION  TITLE(3)
```

Then the lines of characters forming the title could be stored and retrieved by use of a loop to write to or read from the array.

- PASCAL: All arrays must be declared as arrays and must be declared as to type. This must be done as part of the declaration of all data types at the start of the program. A typical declaration statement would look like

```
VAR
     ivalue : ARRAY [1..9] OF INTEGER;
     xvalue : ARRAY [-5..5] OF REAL;
     aword : PACKED ARRAY [1..20] OF CHAR;
```

where the name to the left of the colon is the name assigned to the variable and the values within the brackets specify the number of elements. Note that the character array is described as PACKED. Packed arrays are used for character variables because they allow the storage of two characters per computer word instead of the one per word in a standard array. Also note that the arrays shown are one-dimensional. A two-dimensional (double-subscripted) array might be declared as follows:

```
VAR
     xyvalue : ARRAY [1..10,1..20] OF REAL;
```

where the two ranges 1..10 and 1..20 define the ranges of the two subscripts.

Files

It is difficult to conceive of any computer program of any practical use that does not use files. Although some files are kept on magnetic tape, most files are on magnetic disk mass-storage devices. Some files for large computers are kept in the form of punch (Hollerith) cards. Were it not for these mass-storage devices, most programs either would not be able to fit into computers without massive main memories or would use up so much of the available memory as to make it difficult for the machine to accommodate any other users.

Disk files are used for a variety of storage and retrieval functions. First, the computer's operating system is generally stored on disk. This includes such items as the compiler or interpreter for the language being used and a library of functions and subroutines. Second, your program is generally stored on disk in a source-code file and, in the case of FORTRAN or Pascal, in an object-code file and a complete linked executable-task file. If your program is to generate or use much data, it should use one or more data files to provide input data to the program and to store intermediate and final results. Another use of files is to store instructions and prompts that will be displayed for the operator while the program is running.

Some programs are so large that even with maximum use of these types of files, the entire program will still not fit into the available computer memory. In this case it will be necessary to divide the program into segments and chain from one to another (in the case of BASIC) or to overlay (replace) program segments from time to time while the program is running (in the case of FORTRAN or PASCAL). Some sophisticated computers use the disk space as extensions of main memory (virtual machines), thus making it seem to the user that the machine has essentially unlimited main memory space.

There are several types of files, each with its own function. While the types available on any system and their type names will vary, the following are typical.

- FORTRAN: Source-code files (the ones you use for your program) may be identified with the extension .FTN or .FOR, depending on the computer system being used. When the program is compiled, an object file (.OBJ) is produced, which contains the machine language version of your program. A listing file (.LST) is also produced. This file has a complete listing of your source code along with line numbers, error messages for compile-time errors, and other diagnostics. When the program is linked with the system library, the runnable program that results (if all goes well) is stored in a task-image file (.TSK or .EXE). Files of data to be used for input or output of the program are type .DAT or, in the case of text files, type .TXT. Text files are used for instructions, help files, and other textual material.

  Sequential-access files only allow access to records (groups or sets of related values and/or non-numeric information) in the file in a sequential manner—the first access for retrieving information is to the first record in the file, the second access is to the second record, and so on. Each access to store information (write it to the file) adds the information onto the end of the file. Some systems allow files to be opened only for input or for output (specify which), while others allow both input and output. If a file is open for input only and you desire to write to it, you must close the file and reopen it for output prior to writing the record.

Random-access files—often called direct-access files or record-access files—allow access to any record in the file by simply specifying the number of the record to be accessed. Again, the file may be opened for input (read) only, for output (write) only, or for both. The ability to specify input only or output only protects an input file from an unintentional attempt to write over an existing record and protects a program from mistakenly reading from a file that was not intended for input.

- BASIC: BASIC does not use object, listing, and task files (unless it is compiled BASIC). The source-code file may have the file type (.BAS). Data files typed as (.DAT) are common, as are text files described as (.TXT). In some cases backup copies of files will be produced by a system and will have the file type (.BAK).
- PASCAL: File types used in Pascal conform pretty much to the arrangement for FORTRAN files but will vary from system to system. IBM Pascal for the IBM PC, for example, uses .PAS for the source-code file, .OBJ for the object-code file, .LST for the source-listing file, .CRF for a cross-reference file, and .EXE for the executable-task image file.

Program Structure

Unless a program specifies otherwise, statements are executed in order from the beginning of the program to the end, at which point the program terminates. There are three techniques that are often used to modify the order in which program statements are executed. The first, which we have already discussed, is to group some statements into subroutines that may be called as often as desired from any point in the program. The second technique is a method of repeatedly executing a group of statements by a procedure called *looping*. The third technique is to use a *branching* (GOTO) statement.

Loops

Loops are often called DO loops or FOR loops. There are several different ways of controlling loops, but each depends on the outcome of a logical (boolean) test to determine whether to repeat the group of statements in the loop. In some loops the test is performed at the beginning (top) and it is possible that the statements in the loop will not be executed at all. In other arrangements the test is made after the loop has executed (at the bottom). In this case, the statements in the loop are always executed at least once.

- FORTRAN: Standard FORTRAN provides for only one type of loop. It is called a DO loop and is written as follows

```
          DO 50  I=1,10,2
             statement
                 *
             statement
       50    CONTINUE
```

In this example, DO 50 states that the range of the loop, that is, the statements to be repeated, ends at statement 50. The letter K is the name of the counter, the numeral 1 is the initial value of the counter, the numeral 10 is the final (test) value that, if exceeded, causes the test to be FALSE and the loop to quit repeating, and the numeral 2 indicates the amount by which the counter is to be incremented each time the statement is repeated. The counter, the initial value, the test value, and the increment must all be positive integers.

Another type of DO loop that is available in structured versions of FORTRAN is the WHILE DO, or DO WHILE, loop. This loop, which makes the test at the top, executes the statements in the loop if and only if the test condition is found to be TRUE. There is no set initial value or incrementing arrangement, as there is in the standard DO loop. The test may never be TRUE, in which case the statements in the loop will never execute. At the other extreme, the test may always be TRUE, in which case the loop will keep repeating forever. This is a very powerful construct, since it allows much more flexibility in loop control than does the standard DO loop.

- BASIC: The standard loop in BASIC is the FOR-NEXT loop. The operation of the FOR-NEXT loop is similar to that of the DO loop in standard FORTRAN—that is, the loop is repeated a fixed number of times based on the counter value, a test value, and an increment. However, the FOR-NEXT loop is more flexible than its FORTRAN counterpart in that the counter, initial value, test value, and increment can all be positive or negative real numbers. Some versions of BASIC also support a WHILE DO type of loop. A typical loop would look like the following:

```
          WHILE avg <> 5
             statement
                 *
                 *
                 *
             statement
          WEND
```

In this loop, as in the FORTRAN WHILE DO, the test is made before the loop executes. If the test is TRUE, the statements in the loop between WHILE and WEND are executed. If the test is FALSE, control transfers to the statement following WEND.

- PASCAL: Pascal also supports a loop of the FOR-NEXT variety. This loop consists of a statement that looks like one of the following:

```
FOR counter := starting value TO test value DO
    statement;
```

or:

```
FOR counter := start val DOWNTO test val DO
    statement;
```

or:

```
FOR counter := start val TO test val DO
    BEGIN
        statement;
            *
            *
            *
        statement;
    END;
```

In the first example there is only one statement to be executed each time. In the second example, there is also only one statement, but the loop is decremented rather than incremented. In the third example, the loop is incremented as in the first one, but instead of one statement, there is a block or group of statements to be executed. Notice that the loop has no end statement as such. Instead, the range of the loop is defined as only one statement or block of statements. The start value and test value are typically integer, and the amount of the increment or decrement is 1.

Pascal also supports WHILE DO, which works as it does in FORTRAN or BASIC except that there is no END WHILE or WEND statement. As with the FOR-TO-DO type loop, the range of the loop is one statement or block of statements. A typical WHILE statement would look like the following:

```
WHILE variable >= test val DO
    statement;
```

A third type of loop supported by Pascal is often called REPEAT-UNTIL. Its form is

```
REPEAT
    statement;
        *
        *
        *
    statement;
UNTIL variable < test val;
```

Note that this loop has an end statement (UNTIL) and that the test is performed at the bottom of the loop rather than the top. Thus, the loop will always execute at least once.

Branching: Transfer of Control

A common way in which the order of execution of a program is controlled is through the use of branching statements. The most familiar of these is GOTO, a statement that directs an unconditional transfer of control to the point in the program specified after the word GOTO. For example

```
30   GOTO 50
```

in BASIC would cause an unconditional transfer to line number 50.

```
GOTO 50
```

in FORTRAN would cause an unconditional branch to statement number 50 (not necessarily the same as line number 50). Either of these statements can be converted into a conditional branching statement by preceding GOTO with an IF statement:

```
IF condition is true THEN GOTO 50
```

in which case a test is made on the specified condition to determine whether the transfer to statement 50 (or line 50) is to be made. Of course, the statement must have a line number if it is in BASIC. Should the condition be FALSE, the program simply executes the next statement. Another variation of this conditional branch is to add an ELSE statement:

```
IF condition is true THEN GOTO 50 ELSE GOTO 20
```

Now either a TRUE or FALSE result will cause a branch, but to different points in the program. A third variation is to not branch at all but to perform one set of statements if the condition is TRUE, another set if the condition is FALSE, and, in either case, to continue execution of the program with the next statement following the IF-THEN-ELSE group.

Still another type of branching statement will transfer control to one of a list of program locations based on the value of a test integer that is in the range of +1 to the last transfer location on the list. One such statement looks like

```
GOTO (10,20,30,40,50), number
```

In this case, if the value of the variable "number" is 1, the program branches to statement 10, if the value is 2, the branch is to statement 20, and so on. Since there are only five destination statements listed, any number other than 1,2,3,4, or 5 will not cause a branch—instead, control will pass to the very next statement. A structured variation of this is called DO CASE (or simply CASE). It might look like

```
DO CASE number
    CASE
            statement
                *
                *
                *
            statement
    CASE
            statement
    CASE

    CASE
            statement
                *
                *
            statement
END CASE
```

If the number is 1, the statements following the first CASE are executed, if the number is 2, the statements following the second CASE are executed, and so on. Note that no statements follow the third CASE in this example. This is to demonstrate that one or more values may transfer control to an empty case group. If this happens, nothing is executed as a result of DO CASE. Likewise, if the number is less than 1 or greater than 4 (outside the range of CASEs) nothing will be executed—control simply passes to the statement following END CASE.

- FORTRAN: All versions support GOTO, IF-GOTO, and computed GOTO. The typical statement for each of these three would look like

```
GOTO 50
IF (A .NE. B) GOTO 50
GOTO (50,60,70), I
```

In each of these statements, numbers are statement numbers, not line numbers. Structured FORTRAN also supports IF-THEN-ELSE. An IF-THEN-ELSE construct would look like

```
IF (A .NE. B) THEN DO
    statement
        *
        *
    statement
ELSE DO
    statement
        *
        *
        *
    statement
END IF
```

In this example, if A is not equal to B then the first group of statements is executed. If A is equal to B then the second group of statements is executed. In either case, control then passes to the next statement following END IF.

FORTRAN also supports DO CASE constructs. The DO CASE example given earlier is in FORTRAN.

- BASIC: GOTO and IF-GOTO are available in all versions of BASIC, as is a computed GOTO. Typical statements would be

```
100 GOTO 350
120 IF A <> B  GOTO 350
150 ON C GOTO 400,500,600
```

The first number of each statement is its line number (all BASIC statements must have line numbers), and the other numbers are the line numbers to which the transfer is to be made. Some BASICs use a slightly different syntax for the computed GOTO that looks like

```
150 GOTO (400,500,600) ON C
```

Advanced BASIC supports IF-THEN-ELSE. The entire construct is contained on one line (that is, one line number). The action to be taken can be either a transfer or an execution of one or more BASIC statements. The ELSE group can contain another IF-THEN, or it can contain one or more BASIC statements (including GOTO, if desired), or it can be eliminated. Typical statements are

```
30 IF A<>B THEN C=500:D=3.78:ELSE C=-20:D=45
60 IF A<>B GOTO 100:ELSE GOTO 200
80 IF A<>B THEN C=1000:GOTO 600
```

In statement 30, if A does not equal B the value 500 is assigned to C and 3.78 is assigned to D. However, if A does equal B, the values assigned are −20 and 45. In either case, control then passes to the next program statement. Statement 60 executes one of two branches, depending on whether A equals B. Statement 80 assigns 1000 to C and then branches to line 600 if A is not equal to B. Since there is no ELSE statement, there is no action (control simply passes to the next statement) if the test is FALSE—that is, if A equals B.

- PASCAL: Pascal provides an IF-THEN-ELSE construct and also a DO CASE. A typical example of the former is

```
IF a<>b THEN
             statement
        ELSE
             statement;
```

while an example of the latter is

```
CASE  myvalu  OF
      value1 : statement;
      value2 : statement;
      value3 : statement;
      END;
```

In this example, myvalu is some variable that is compared to value1, value2, and value3. If myvalu is found to match one of the three values, the appropriate statement is executed. When the matching statement has been executed (or no match is found), control passes to the next statement after END. The variable being tested can be integer, character, or boolean.

Pascal does support GOTO, but such use is discouraged in this highly structured language.

Logical Operations

The basis for conditional transfer of control and looping operations is a logical decision. When a conditional transfer statement is executed, the action taken depends on whether some predefined condition is TRUE. Every time a loop is executed, the "truth value" of some test determines whether to repeat the loop. The arithmetic used to make these tests is called *boolean algebra* and the result of the arithmetic operations is a *logical* or *boolean* value. *Logical* or *boolean* constants or variables can take on only one of two different values, TRUE or FALSE. The values are represented within the system by binary numeric digits, just as are all other letters, numbers, punctuation marks, and other symbols the computer uses, but the values, however they are represented, mean, literally, TRUE or FALSE.

Logical operations—those that determine the truth value of a test—employ a variety of logical operators and relational operators to permit the programmer to represent almost any conceivable condition or set of conditions to be tested. These logical and relational operators may be used singly for simple tests or in combination to test more complex relationships. The available logical operators and their meanings are as follows:

LANGUAGE	OPERATOR	MEANING
FORTRAN	.NOT.	not
	.AND.	and
	.OR.	or
BASIC	NOT	not
	AND	and
	OR	or
Pascal	not	not
	and	and
	or	or

Relational operators available are

LANGUAGE	OPERATOR	MEANING
FORTRAN	.LT.	less than
	.GT.	greater than
	.EQ.	equal to
	.NE.	not equal to
	.LE.	less than or equal to
	.GE.	greater than or equal to

BASIC	<	less than
	>	greater than
	=	equal to
	<>	not equal to
	<= or =<	less than or equal to
	>= or =>	greater than or equal to
Pascal	<	less than
	>	greater than
	=	equal to
	<>	not equal to
	<=	less than or equal to
	>=	greater than or equal to

Logical operators AND and OR are used to permit the making of complex comparisons. NOT is used to negate the truth value of an expression. Examples of use of the various logical and relational operators (in BASIC) are

```
50 IF A>B AND C<=D THEN GOTO 200
60 IF A>B OR C<=D THEN GOTO 300
70 IF A>B AND C<=D OR E<>F THEN GOTO 400
80 IF NOT E>=G THEN GOTO 500
```

In statement 50, the value of A is compared to that of B. If A is greater, then that part of the test is TRUE. Next, C is compared to D. If C is less than or equal to D, then that part of the test is TRUE. Finally, AND says that if both tests are TRUE, then the entire test is TRUE, and the THEN statement will execute (the program will branch to line 200). Statement 60 compares A to B and C to D, just as 50 did, but the OR operator says that if either of the two conditions is TRUE, or if both are TRUE, the entire test is TRUE and a branch will be executed. Thus, the test in 60 may be TRUE even though the test in 50 was FALSE. Statement 70 uses the same test as statement 50 and then adds "OR E<>F." This statement will test TRUE if statement 50 tests TRUE, and it will also test TRUE if E does not equal F (regardless of the truth value of A>B and of C<=D). Finally, statement 80 looks at the relational value of E>=G and then says that the test is TRUE if and only if E>=G is NOT TRUE. Statement 80 reverses the normal truth value of the relational operation.

Now that we have examined some statements using logical and relational operators, it is time to discuss the priority order in which they are considered. Relational operators have equal priority with each other and higher priority than the logical operators. Among the logical operators, the highest priority is given to NOT, followed by AND and then OR. For example, in the statement

```
90 IF NOT E>=G AND A<B OR C<>E THEN GOTO 1000
```

the truth values of E>=G, A<B, and C<>E are determined, then the truth value of NOT E>=G is determined. Next, NOT E>=G is

ANDed with A<B—that is, the known truth value of NOT E>=G is tested in combination with the known truth value of A<B to see if the combination NOT E>=G AND A<B is TRUE. Finally, the result of this test is ORed with the known truth value of C<>E to obtain the truth of the entire statement. The order of evaluation can be changed by enclosing portions of the expression in parentheses, since, just as with other arithmetic operations, the operations within parentheses are performed first. When parentheses are nested, the operations in the innermost set will be evaluated first, followed by the next innermost set, and so on.

Inputting and Outputting Data

Computer programs, in order to function, need data on which to operate. The data may be included in the program in data statements or may be generated by the program through use of a number generator or a function, but most often data are input to the program during execution. Inputs may come from many sources. Computers that are controlling processes or events often obtain data from sensors and measuring devices, which can include volt or ampere meters, thermometers, clocks, cameras, and a wide variety of other devices. However, for our purposes most data input will come from one of four sources. The most common is the keyboard, followed by disk files, direct cursor controls such as joysticks and light pens, and digitizing tablets.

Input from disk is generally performed by the system without operator intervention. A statement in the program directs a read from the disk file and the system responds. Input from the keyboard, joysticks, or digitizing tablets, however, is accomplished by the operator and is generally in response to a prompt from the program (such as a flashing cursor, a printed message, or a "beep"), but may be initiated by the operator when he or she perceives a need to direct progress of the program (this is particularly evident in computer games). Of course, such a program must be prepared to accept input, or the operator's efforts will be wasted. Techniques by which the program can be made to scan the input devices on a continuing basis will be presented as needed in the following chapters.

Output from the computer program can, like input, go to a wide variety of devices, such as machine and process-control units, to name just two. For our purposes, most output will be directed to one of four devices. The most common is the display screen (which can also be thought of as an input device), followed by the printer, the plotter, and of course, the disk files.

Program output, like input, can be performed by the program as needed or can be done only when requested by the operator. Some output requires two steps. For instance, many systems require that printer or plotter output first be stored in a disk file. The actual printout or plot is then performed by the system accessing that file and sending the data, record by record, to the appropriate output device. This approach is common when more than one user shares a printer or plotter.

Disk read-and-write operations are often different on different systems. You should study the manuals for the system you are using in order to become familiar with the system's requirements. Of particular importance are procedures for creating, naming, opening, and closing files, both sequential-access files and random- (sometimes called record- or direct-) access files.

Rules for Writing

Many programmers who have been writing short, uncomplicated programs tend to develop very bad programming habits. It is easy to sit down at a computer keyboard and write a short program without much prior thought. If the program does not run, it is usually a simple matter to analyze it right on the screen, make some changes, and try again. However, this approach does not work for large programs.

Some large CAD/CAM programs will occupy 200 megabytes of disk storage or more. Only a very small portion of these huge programs will be in memory at any one time. Routines will be overlaid (replaced) in the computer as needed to perform the required operations. These overlays may take place hundreds or even thousands of times during the running of the program. In such situations, control of the program's progress and maintenance and transfer of data from one program segment to another becomes a task of major proportions. This task is complicated by the fact that many different programmers will be responsible for different portions of the package, and their program segments must all work with each other and with the main control segment.

While the programs you will be writing will not approach this size or complexity (at least for some time), it is important to develop good programming habits early. It is not unusual for a college freshman to write a computer graphics program containing 2000 to 3000 lines of code, 40 to 50 subroutines, and a complex menu-driven control system. Many of the subroutines may be contained in libraries or invokable modules and thus may not be readily available for study during the debugging process.

The First Rule: Structure

When you write a paper you first organize your thoughts, grouping related points or ideas, and then, to make it easier for the reader to follow and understand, you divide the paper into sections (or chapters) and the sections into paragraphs. The same technique should be used in writing computer programs. Early programmers tended to write in a way that was very esoteric and obscure, but they soon found that their programs became obsolete very quickly, since no one could modify them to keep them current and usable with new computers. It became apparent that programs needed organization (structure) if they were to be maintained by anyone but their author.

Programs contain three types of structure: (1) order of execution or flow of control, (2) decisions and selection, and (3) looping. Early languages were often impediments to writing programs with good structure. Consequently, all new programming languages are designed for structured programming (they are called structured languages). Structured versions of the older languages are also being developed.

CONSTRUCTS The primary features of structured languages are the *constructs* they offer. Constructs provide for the orderly creation of good program structures. Most structured versions of modern languages contain IF-THEN-ELSE and WHILE DO constructs. Some support DO CASE and DO UNTIL. Some FORTRAN versions support AT END DO and WHILE EXECUTE. Pascal has a WITH statement that simplifies working with records. Pascal also makes extensive use of BEGIN-END to define groups of code that form compound statements as well as to begin and end each program segment.

Prior to the availability of decision and selection constructs, such as IF-THEN-ELSE and DO CASE, all decisions required a conditional branch to another part of the program (GOTO). As a result, control often jumped back and forth from one part of the program to another and the sequence of execution was nearly impossible to follow. Constructs provide for execution of the appropriate code at the point of decision, thus alleviating this problem.

Constructs that aid in building recursion or looping structures are WHILE DO and DO UNTIL (called REPEAT UNTIL in Pascal). Their main advantage over the older FOR-NEXT loop controls is their provision for executing the loop an indefinite number of times. The FOR-NEXT loop executed a predetermined fixed number of times (and always at least once), but the WHILE DO and DO UNTIL constructs execute as many times as is necessary (as long as a specified condition exists or until a specified condition exists). In the case of WHILE DO, the loop may not execute at all, since the test is made at the top—before the loop executes.

MODULARITY *Modularity* is a most important part of the design structure of any program. A modular program is one in which each distinct task is written as a separate module, usually in the form of a subroutine. Pascal programmers often recommend that *all* of the operations be written as procedures (subroutines) and that the main program segment consist of nothing but calls to the appropriate procedures. This approach is equally effective using FORTRAN or BASIC.

Both FORTRAN and Pascal require that their subroutines be separated from the main body of the program. Pascal requires that all procedures within the program be placed before the main segment. FORTRAN permits them to be either before or after the main segment, or even in separate files, as long as they are compiled and linked to the main segment in the executable-task image file. BASIC permits subroutines to be embedded in the body of the main program; however if a RETURN is encountered when no GOSUB is active, an execution error occurs. It is good programming style to place all BASIC subroutines after the END statement so that the flow of control in the main segment is easier to follow.

The Second Rule: Stepped Approach

You should always develop a stepped approach to any programming problem—that is, you should follow a logical and consistent set of steps to get from initial formulation of the problem to final solution.

DEFINE THE PROBLEM The first step is to define the problem completely. It is easy to say, "Oh, I know what is needed," but do you really? Inadequate definition of the problem can cause many headaches and much lost time later on. On the other hand, a good definition of the problem can be half of the solution. There is no universal approach to problem definition; different people tend to define problems in terms that make sense to them. There are, however, two elements that must be present in a good problem definition, regardless of how it is formulated. These two elements are (1) a complete statement of the given information and (2) a complete statement of what is required for the final solution. Proper attention to these two elements will ensure that you have a thorough knowledge of the task that lies ahead of you. Formal statements of the "given" and of the "required" should be set down on paper to be referred to from time to time during the programming exercise.

PRELIMINARY IDEAS When the problem has been completely defined, it is time to begin developing a solution. The first thing to do is to develop some preliminary ideas. It is important at this point to avoid being too critical of the ideas that come to mind. The main thing is to get your mind working. All the ideas you can think of should be written down. You will find during this process that one idea will give rise to another. This is a sort of one-person brainstorming session.

REFINEMENT The next step is to review and refine the ideas that you have generated. This is the point at which unworkable ideas are discarded, as they have already served their purpose in the creative process. The initial list of ideas should be pared down to five or fewer.

TESTING Now, with a list of your best ideas in hand, it is time to try them on the system. Different systems behave in different ways, so you must design for the particular system you are using.

ANALYSIS AND FURTHER REFINEMENT When the concepts have been tested, any unexpected or unwanted results can be studied and further refinements made to fine tune the program. Then the concepts should be retested to determine whether the changes worked.

When the concepts are worked out, it is time to design the program itself. First you should outline the overall structure of the program so that you can decide what is to go where. Your first outline should not contain too much detail. Attempting to deal with a lot of detail will obscure the overall structure of the program. When the major building blocks are in place, take them one by one and develop them in greater detail. The logic of a computer program is best outlined with an algorithm—that is, a logical list of ordered steps that will lead to the desired solution. Many programmers prefer to write this algorithm in the form of a flow chart. Flow charts are easy to analyze, easy to change, and easy to use as a basis for coding (writing) the program. Appendix C contains a list of flow chart symbols, example flow charts, and example code.

Execution of Concepts (Writing)

If you have done well with the previous steps, writing the program statements should be a simple matter of writing the appropriate code to execute the logic of each of the flow chart boxes. If your program is very large or has a number of subroutines, you should write the code for the main part of the program first, inserting references to the as yet unwritten subroutines. The subroutine calls can be to "dummy" subroutines that simply return the user to the main program. In this way, the overall communication paths of the program can be checked out before all of the subroutines are completed.

TESTING EACH MODULE As each subroutine is written, it should be checked for proper interfacing with the main program and correct performance of its assigned task. If it does not work correctly, you have only the one subroutine to debug. This is a much easier approach than trying to test the entire program at one time.

TESTING THE COMPLETED PROGRAM By the time you have written and tested the main program segment and then written and tested each subroutine separately, most of the bugs should be worked out. Testing the completed program may seem to be a mere formality. However, problems can crop up in the most carefully written and tested programs—in fact, they nearly always do. Therefore, you should test the completed program as thoroughly as possible before you declare it finished.

Documentation

You might think that when your computer program has been written and tested it is a finished piece of work. Experienced professional programmers, however, often find that they spend more time modifying previously written programs than writing new ones. Even if the program to be modified is one they personally wrote, it can be very difficult after a period of months or years to remember all of the carefully thought-out detail that went into the logic of the code. Approaches that made sense at the time can seem utterly baffling when the programmer goes back to correct or modify an old program. Worse, people change jobs frequently and it is not at all unusual to have to work on a program someone else wrote. Good *documentation* is indispensible in these situations. But what is documentation? How is it done?

The main program segment documentation should contain (1) a thorough but concise overview description of the entire program—its purpose, design, and important features; (2) a list of all subroutines and user-written functions that are called from the main segment, along with their location if not in the same file; (3) input/output specifications—that is, what input devices (name, type, and important requirements) and files (name, location, type, and access method) are used; (4) a list of all global variable (and constant) names and all local variables used in the segment along with their types (and dimensions if they are array variables); and (5) any other important information relating to the program's design or operation.

Subprogram documentation should contain (1) a description of what the subprogram is and what it does along with a description of its important features, (2) a list of the program segments that call the subprogram and any program segments the subprogram calls, (3) input/output specifications, (4) a variable list, and (5) any other important details.

Program Description

A well-written program will usually contain a number of subprograms in addition to the main program segment. As we have indicated, each segment should be completely described, including information about what it does and how it relates (interfaces) with other program segments. Program descriptions may be included in the source code as comments or may be written in a programmer's or user's manual, or both. It is common practice to include an abundance of documentation in the source code of FORTRAN or other compiled languages. In interpretive languages such as BASIC, however, such comments both take up space and, in the case of comments imbedded in the code, slow down execution. Therefore, thorough documentation for a program written in BASIC is best done in a separate manual.

Interaction with Other Segments

Each segment should contain a complete listing of the other program segments with which it interfaces, whether subroutines called by the segment or routines that call the segment. Such listings are extremely helpful in debugging a faulty program. It is not unusual to have a mismatch of parameter lists or to have the value of a variable changed in an unexpected place. A thorough search of all interfacing routines is often necessary to find the source of such problems.

Listing of Input/Output Devices and Files Used
While listing input/output (I/O) devices and files used may seem redundant, since this information is contained in the program statements themselves, such a list is a good reference when trying to get the program to run on another system with a different hardware configuration. For example, a new plotter or CRT may be available, and the software to communicate with it may have to be altered.

Variable List
While most programmers attempt to choose good mnemonic names (names that sound like the variable they represent), there is no substitute for a good listing with adequate description. Some versions of BASIC do not permit use of mnemonic names, so a variable list is the only way to keep track of the names.

Intraline Documentation
So far all of the documentation we have discussed is either written at the beginning of the source code or is contained in a separate documentation manual. Comment statements throughout the program are another very important type of documentation. Good comments are a great help when debugging a program and are invaluable when making modifications at a later date.

A good working knowledge of the elements of computer programming is essential to the study of computer graphics. Particularly important are the concepts of modular programming and the effective use of subroutines. The reader is encouraged to consult other good programming texts for more detailed programming instruction and language review.

Input/output statements vary from system to system. The material in the following chapters has been developed on two systems: (1) an IBM PC with disk operating system and advanced BASIC and (2) a Digital Equipment Corporation minicomputer with FORTRAN IV-plus and Tektronix PLOT10 graphics subroutines. The techniques are readily adaptable to other systems. They have been tested in part on Apple II, Apple III, Tektronix 4051/52, and Northstar computers. Coded examples of several routines have been included in the Appendixes for the Apple II and Tektronix computers. You should consult the operating manuals for your system to determine the specific techniques for file handling and other I/O tasks.

Exercises

1. List the arithmetic operators for your system for addition, multiplication, subtraction, division, and exponentiation.

2. How many bytes do each of the following require on your system: (a) integers? (b) Real numbers? (c) Characters?

3. How many characters may be used for names of (a) variables? (b) Subroutines or procedures? (c) Functions?

4. How many types of looping statements are available on your system? Name them.

5. How many types of branching statements are available on your system? Name them.

6. What are the logical operators for your system?

7. What library (built-in) functions are available on your system?

8. Is there a library of graphics routines on your system? If so, list the functions and statements that are available.

Creating
Points and
Lines on
the Screen

We have all seen words, pictures, and even computer-generated graphics on our television sets. Most of us have also seen the television-like display screens, called monitors or CRTs, that are used with computers to display words and pictures. Figure 4-1 shows a popular CRT. There is very little difference between these monitors and a television set. In fact, low-cost personal computers often use televisions in place of monitors. Only an inexpensive adapter is required to make televisions serve as monitors. However, monitors specifically intended for use with computers do produce a higher-quality picture.

Every letter, number, picture, or other image displayed on the computer display screen is made up of individual points. These points, when assembled properly, produce lines. In this chapter we will learn how to create points and lines on the screen so as to create drawings.

The graphics screen consists of a grid of picture elements or pixels, often called dots or points. The typical screen contains between 100,000 and 1,000,000 pixels. Each pixel, when energized, creates one visible point or picture element on the screen. Graphics pictures can be created by selecting and energizing the pixels that form the desired pattern.

Suppose we wish to energize a certain pixel. To do so we must tell the system which one we have selected. How can we do that? Referring to Figure 4-2 we see that the grid can be thought of as being composed of many rows of dots. Suppose

Figure 4-1. A popular CRT.

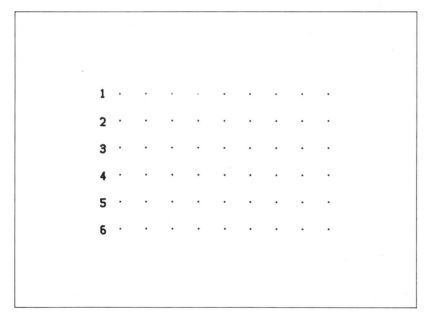

Figure 4-2.

we number the rows as shown in the figure. Now we can identify the row that contains the desired dot. This certainly helps but we still haven't identified which dot in the row is the correct one. We can see, however, that the grid can also be thought of as consisting of several columns of dots. Suppose we number both the rows and the columns as shown in Figure 4-3. We can now specify the precise location of the dot by its row number and its column number, since there can be only one dot that is located at the intersection of that

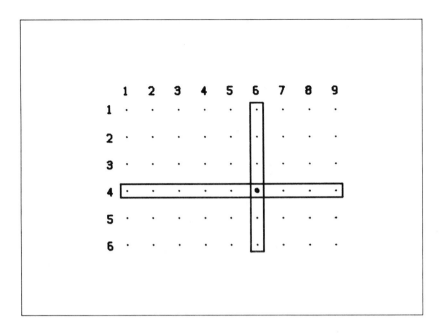

Figure 4-3.

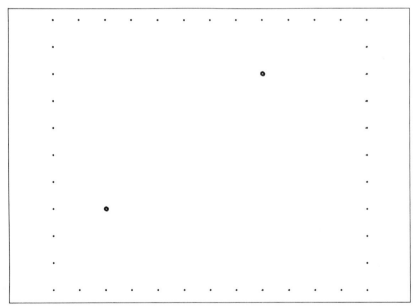

Figure 4-4.

row and that column. We can completely describe the location of any dot or point on the entire screen by specifying the row and the column in which it is contained. If we think of the graphics display as a coordinate system, with the X coordinate being the column number and the Y coordinate being the row number, we see that we can identify any point on the screen by identifying its location in terms of its X and Y coordinates. Figure 4-4 shows a typical raster display with two pixels (points) lighted.

Table 4-1.

Point No.	X Value	Y Value
1	1	1
2	2	6
3	3	4
4	4	1
5	5	5
6	6	3
7	7	3
8	8	4
9	9	2

It should now be apparent that we can create a picture, an alphabetic or numeric character—or whatever we desire—by plotting, one by one, all of the points that would be needed to complete the image. In fact, some low-resolution personal computers use this method to create crude graphics. Higher-resolution systems (those with a large number of pixels) would require locating such a large number of points to create an image that the user would grow tired before completing it. Fortunately, graphics languages allow us to draw lines in a much easier fashion.

Plotting Points

Suppose we want to create a plot of the points in Table 4-1. We will first plot them on a standard sheet of coordinate or graph paper. To do so, we must construct a coordinate system consisting of an X axis, a Y axis, and a scale for each axis. Since all of the points have positive coordinates, they will all be located in the first quadrant. Therefore, we could draw the X axis at the bottom of the paper and the Y axis along the left side. After choosing a scale that will allow all of the points to be contained on the paper and still provide a large enough display to be read and interpreted easily, we simply need to plot in the points. Figure 4-5 shows the completed chart based on Table 4-1, using two graduations per unit. Note that only a few of the grid intersections are shown.

We will now plot the points on a graphics display. Referring again to Figure 4-2, we see that each pixel in the grid of the display is analogous to an intersection on a grid of graph paper. With this in mind it is a simple matter to represent the coordinate system of the paper on the screen. The X and Y axes can be established along the bottom and left edges of the screen just as was done on the paper. We decided on a scale of two graduations per unit for the scale on the paper. Since the graphics screen contains many times more pixels than the paper does graduations, a scale of two pixels per unit would create an extremely small chart. In order to select an appropriate scale it would be helpful to know the number of pixels (the resolution) available on the system being used. Assuming that the res-

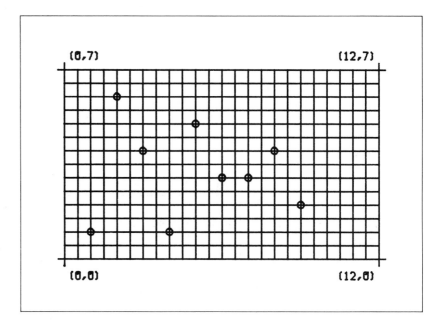

(0,7)   (12,7)

(0,0)   (12,0)

Figure 4-5.

olution is 1000 × 800—that is, 1000 pixels horizontally by 800 vertically—the largest possible X scale would be about 166 pixels per unit (1000/6) and the largest possible Y scale would be about 133 pixels per unit (800/6). Neither of these scales, however, would be easy to use. It is easier to work with scales of 2:1, 4:1, 5:1, or multiples of 10:1.

If we desire to keep the same shape graph on the screen as on the paper, it is important to use the same ratio between the horizontal and vertical scales. A scale ratio of 1:1 was used for the X and Y scales on the paper. We will use a scale of 80 pixels per unit horizontally and vertically on the screen. With this scale, we will have space for a title block, if desired, and we can move the origin to provide room on the screen to draw and label the X and Y axes. Of course, a larger or smaller scale could be used if desired. Using a scale of 80 pixels per unit and drawing axes at X = 2 (160 pixels from the left edge) and Y = 2 (160 pixels from the bottom) it is now possible to calculate the row and column number of the appropriate pixel for each point. Remember that (0,0) is at (160,160) on the screen. Table 4-2 lists the points, their coordinates, and the row and column numbers of the corresponding pixels. The column number represents the X coordinate and the row number represents the Y coordinate. Figure 4-6 is a representation of the finished plot on the computer screen.

Preparing the System to Draw
Computer systems with graphics capability are designed to operate in either text mode or graphics mode, but not in both at the same

Table 4-2.

Point No.	X Value	Y Value	X Pixel	Y Pixel
1	1	1	240	240
2	2	6	320	640
3	3	4	400	480
4	4	1	480	240
5	5	5	560	560
6	6	3	640	400
7	7	3	720	400
8	8	4	800	480
9	9	2	880	320

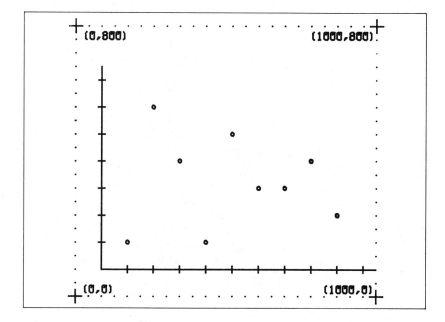

Figure 4-6.

time. When computer systems are in text mode, they will print characters on the screen but will not draw lines. When they are in graphics mode, they will draw lines but will not print characters unless special provision is made for them to do so. The characters that can be printed while in the graphics mode are often a different size or shape than those printed in character mode. Character output will be discussed in more detail in Chapter 7.

The statements required to put a system in graphics mode will vary from system to system but these statements usually must accomplish the following: (1) put the system in graphics mode; (2) specify the graphics language to be used; (3) describe the workspace size—that is, the resolution of the screen; (4) define the background (screen) and foreground (pen) colors to be used if the system has color or grayscale capability; and, on some systems, (5) define the portion of the screen to be used (the entire screen may be a default setting). Some of these tasks may be performed automatically on your system. For normal black-and-white drawing, a screen color of BLACK (or NONE) and a pen color of WHITE are generally best. Statements required for some representative systems include the following:

LANGUAGE/SYSTEM	STATEMENT
FORTRAN/PLOT10	CALL INITT (960)
	CALL TERM (1,1024)
BASIC/Apple II	HGR2
	COLOR= 3
BASIC/Apple III	OPEN#1,".GRAFIX"
	INVOKE".D1/BGRAF.INV"
	PERFORM INITGRAFIX
	PERFORM GRAFIXMODE
	(%1,%1)
	PERFORM GRAFIXON
	PERFORM PENCOLOR(%15)
	PERFORM FILLCOLOR(%0)
	PERFORM FILLPORT
BASIC/IBM PC (High resolution)	SCREEN 2
BASIC/IBM PC (Med resolution)	SCREEN 1
	COLOR 0,1
BASIC/Tektronix 4051/52	PAGE
	INIT
Pascal/Apple II TURTLE-GRAPHICS and UCSD TURTLEGRAPHICS	uses TURTLEGRAPHICS;
	INITTURTLE;
	VIEWPORT (0,279,0,191);
	FILLSCREEN (NONE);
	PENCOLOR (WHITE);

At first these statements might seem overwhelming, but they are nearly always the same for every graphics program on any given system, except that the parameter lists may be different. Consequently they can be copied from program to program.

Selecting the Points

The pixels, or points on the screen, are energized (lighted) by means of an electronic beam inside the CRT tube. Before a specific point can be energized, the beam must be moved into the proper position. Of course, this must be done without leaving a trace on the screen and can be accomplished with a graphics statement of the form

MOVE ABSOLUTE (X,Y)

where X and Y are integers that represent the coordinates of the destination point. The exact syntax of the statement will vary for different graphics languages. It is not possible to include here every available variation of the MOVE ABSOLUTE statement but the following are representative:

LANGUAGE/SYSTEM	STATEMENT
FORTRAN/PLOT10	CALL MOVABS (IX,IY)
BASIC/TRS-80 Level 3	RESET (X,Y)
BASIC/Apple II	HCOLOR= 0:HPLOT X,Y
BASIC/Apple III	PERFORM MOVETO (%X,%Y)
BASIC/IBM PC	PRESET (X,Y)
BASIC/Tektronix 4051/52	MOVE X,Y
Pascal/Apple II	PENCOLOR (NONE);
TURTLEGRAPHICS and	MOVETO (X,Y);
UCSD TURTLEGRAPHICS	

We will now write a program in FORTRAN with PLOT10 to move the graphics beam to each point in Table 4.1. We will assume that the screen has a resolution of 1000 × 800 pixels, though an actual screen resolution might be 1024 × 780. First, we will write an *algorithm*, in the form of a set of instructions, that will accomplish the task. Second, we will convert these instructions into a flow chart. Finally, we will code the logic of the flow chart in FORTRAN.

Algorithm:

1. Start up (initialize) the system.
   a. Initialize the graphics routine.
   b. Define the terminal to be used.
2. Enter the coordinates of a data point.
3. Move the beam to the location specified by the coordinates.
4. Check whether there are more points.
5. If there are more points, repeat steps 2 and 3, otherwise go to the next step.
6. End program.

Flow chart:

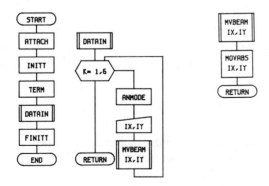

FORTRAN code:

```
C ** DRAWING PROGRAM **
        CALL INITT (960)
        CALL TERM (1,1024)
        CALL DATAIN
        CALL FINITT (0,0)
        END


C ** INPUT COORDINATES OF SIX POINTS **
C ** COORDINATES TO BE ENTERED FROM KEYBOARD **
        SUBROUTINE DATAIN
        DO 50   K=1,6
C ** MOVE BEAM TO PROMPT LOCATION
        CALL MOVABS(1,840-80*K)
        CALL ANMODE
        WRITE (5,*) 'ENTER COORDINATES OF POINT (X,Y)'
        READ (5,*) IX,IY
        CALL MVBEAM (IX,IY)
  50    CONTINUE
C ** DUMMY READ STATEMENT TO CREATE PAUSE **
        CALL ANMODE
        READ (5,25) IDUMMY
  25    FORMAT(A1)
        RETURN
        END


C ** MOVE GRAPHICS BEAM TO SELECTED POINT **
        SUBROUTINE MVBEAM (IX,IY)
        CALL MOVABS (IX,IY)
        RETURN
        END
```

The same program coded in BASIC for a personal computer (IBM PC) but using the same algorithm and flow chart would be as follows (note the use of INKEY$ to create a pause in the program when the plotting is finished):

```
10      REM ** DRAWING PROGRAM **
30      SCREEN 2
70      GOSUB 1000
80      SCREEN 0
90      END


1000    REM ** SUBROUTINE TO INPUT COORDINATES **
1010    REM ** OF SIX POINTS **
1020    REM ** COORDINATES ENTERED FROM KEYBOARD **
1040    FOR K=1 TO 6
1050      INPUT "ENTER COORDINATES OF POINT (X,Y)";X,Y
1110      GOSUB 1200
1120      NEXT K
1130    PAUS$=INKEY$:IF PAUS$="" THEN GOTO 1130:'PAUSE
1190    RETURN


1200    REM ** SUBROUTINE TO MOVE BEAM TO POINTS **
1230    PRESET (X,Y)
1390    RETURN
```

The program for this example has also been coded in BASIC for the Apple II (see Appendix A) and for the Tektronix 4051/52 (see Appendix B).

Creating a Plot

The MOVE ABSOLUTE statement will move the graphics beam to any designated location on the screen. However, this statement does not energize any pixels, so no display is created.

In order to create a visible plot of the selected points, it is necessary to combine the MOVE ABSOLUTE statement with one that says "create a visible point at (X,Y)." Most graphics languages contain a statement of the type

```
POINT ABSOLUTE (X,Y)
```

that accomplishes this task. As with the MOVE statement, the exact syntax will vary from language to language. Examples of the POINT ABSOLUTE statement include:

LANGUAGE/SYSTEM	STATEMENT
FORTRAN/PLOT10	CALL PNTABS (IX,IY)
BASIC/TRS-80 Level 3	SET (X,Y)
BASIC/Apple II	HCOLOR= 3:HPLOT X,Y
BASIC/Apple III	PERFORM DOTAT (%X,%Y)
BASIC/IBM PC	PSET (X,Y)
BASIC/Tektronix 4051/52	None (use DRAW to create a short line)
Pascal/Apple II TURTLEGRAPHICS and UCSD TURTLEGRAPHICS	PENCOLOR (NONE); MOVETO (X,Y) PENCOLOR (WHITE); MOVE (1)

The concept of TURTLEGRAPHICS needs some explanation at this point. TURTLEGRAPHICS got its name from an experiment with a robot at the Massachusetts Institute of Technology. The robot, which was called a turtle, was programmed to move around on the floor. In order that its movements could be studied, the robot was equipped with a marking instrument that left a line on the floor marking its path. The resulting drawing was called turtlegraphics. TURTLEGRAPHICS uses this same concept of a "turtle" moving about on the screen, dragging a pen with it and producing lines on the display. The user can control the operation by specifying the pen color the turtle is to use. A pen color of NONE will result in a move without leaving a trace. In the POINT ABSOLUTE example, the turtle moved to the desired location using pen color NONE and then made a one-pixel move using pen color WHITE, thus producing a very short line (or point) at the desired location.

When the statement (or group of statements) representing

```
POINT ABSOLUTE (X,Y)
```

is executed, the following events take place:

1. The graphics beam is moved to the point whose coordinates are (X,Y).
2. A visible dot or point is created on the screen at (X,Y).
3. The beam remains at (X,Y) until another graphics statement is executed.

The algorithm and code developed to move the graphics beam around the screen can be used, with minor modification, to plot the points as well as to move the beam:

1. Start up (initialize) the system.
   a. Initialize the graphics routine.
   b. Define the terminal to be used.
2. Enter the coordinates of a data point.
3. Move the beam to the location specified by the coordinates and plot a point.
4. Check whether there are more points.
5. If there are more points, repeat steps 2 and 3, otherwise go to the next step.
6. End program.

Flow chart:

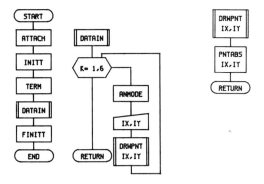

FORTRAN code:

```
C ** DRAWING PROGRAM **
      CALL INITT (960)
      CALL TERM (1,1024)
      CALL DATAIN
      CALL FINITT (0,0)
      END


C ** INPUT COORDINATES OF SIX POINTS FOR PLOTTING **
C ** COORDINATES ENTERED FROM KEYBOARD **
      SUBROUTINE DATAIN
      DO 50  K=1,6
C ** MOVE BEAM TO PROMPT LOCATION
      CALL MOVABS(1,840-80*K)
      CALL ANMODE
      WRITE (5,*) 'ENTER COORDINATES OF POINT (X,Y)'
```

```
            READ (5,*) IX,IY
            CALL DRWPNT (IX,IY)
      50    CONTINUE
C ** DUMMY READ STATEMENT TO CREATE PAUSE **
            CALL ANMODE
            READ (5,25) IDUMMY
      25    FORMAT(A1)
            RETURN
            END


C ** MOVE GRAPHICS BEAM AND PLOT SELECTED POINT **
            SUBROUTINE DRWPNT (IX,IY)
            CALL PNTABS (IX,IY)
            RETURN
            END
```

The same program coded in BASIC for a personal computer (IBM PC) but using the same algorithm and flow chart would be as follows:

```
10      REM ** DRAWING PROGRAM **
30      SCREEN 2
70      GOSUB 1000
80      SCREEN 0
90      END


1000    REM ** SUBROUTINE TO INPUT COORDINATES **
1010    REM ** OF SIX POINTS FOR PLOTTING **
1020    REM ** COORDINATES ENTERED FROM KEYBOARD **
1040    FOR K=1 TO 6
1050      INPUT"ENTER COORDINATES OF POINT (X,Y)";X,Y
1110      GOSUB 1200
1120      NEXT K
1130    PAUS$=INKEY$:IF PAUS$="" THEN GOTO 1130:'PAUSE
1190    RETURN


1200    REM ** SUBROUTINE TO MOVE BEAM AND PLOT POINTS **
1230    PSET (X,Y),1
1390    RETURN
```

The program for this example has also been coded in BASIC for the Apple II (see Appendix A) and for the Tektronix 4051/52 (see Appendix B).

Drawing a Line

Suppose that the points that were plotted in Figure 4-6 are to be connected by straight lines to create a chart. The first and second points are to be connected, then the second and third, the third and fourth, the fourth and fifth, and, finally, the fifth and sixth. A drafter would be likely to accomplish the task as follows:

1. Move the pencil to point 1.
2. Draw a straight line to point 2 (probably with the aid of a straightedge).
3. Reposition the straightedge (if used).
4. Move the pencil to point 2.

5. Draw a straight line to point 3.

6. Repeat steps 3, 4, and 5 for the remaining points.

A graphics system will use a MOVE ABSOLUTE statement to accomplish the equivalent of step 1 or step 4. The statement to accomplish step 2 or step 5 is

```
DRAW ABSOLUTE (X,Y)
```

which tells the system, "Draw a visible line from the present beam position to the location specified by the coordinates (X,Y)." This is accomplished by moving the beam "hot" and energizing all pixels in the path of the move. Examples of this statement are:

LANGUAGE/SYSTEM	STATEMENT
FORTRAN/PLOT10	CALL DRWABS (IX,IY)
BASIC/TRS-80 Level 3	None—plot point by point using SET (X,Y)
BASIC/Apple II	HPLOT TO X,Y
BASIC/Apple III	PERFORM LINETO (%X,%Y)
BASIC/IBM PC	LINE −(X,Y)
BASIC/Tektronix 4051/52	DRAW X,Y
Pascal/Apple II and UCSD TURTLEGRAPHICS	PENCOLOR (WHITE); MOVETO (X,Y);

Note that the draw statement HPLOT TO X,Y for BASIC/Apple II will draw the line in the color of the last point plotted. Therefore, any color statement preceding it will have no effect. If the last HPLOT X,Y statement was a move, it will be necessary either to plot the beginning point of the line before using this statement or to use

```
HPLOT X1,Y1 TO X2,Y2
```

where X1,Y1 is the beginning point of the line and X2,Y2 is the ending point of the line. This statement combines HPLOT X1,Y1 and HPLOT TO X2,Y2.

By referring to Figure 4-7 you can see that, except in the case of a horizontal or vertical line, very few of the pixels will be located directly in the path of the move. Your system will use an algorithm to determine which pixels to energize to obtain a line that is as straight and as uniform as possible. Each of the lines connecting corresponding points can be drawn by repeated use of the appropriate form of the graphics statements

```
MOVE ABSOLUTE (X1,Y1)
DRAW ABSOLUTE (X2,Y2)
```

where (X1, Y1) represents the coordinates of the beginning point of the line and (X2, Y2) represents the coordinates of the ending point

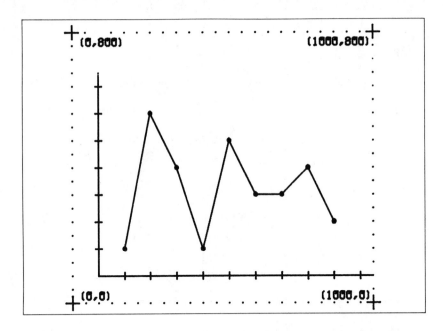

Figure 4-7.

of the line. The procedure to move the beam will now be modified to draw a line from point to point as the beam moves about the screen. Note that, as before, only minor changes need to be made to the algorithm used in our first example:

1. Start up (initialize) the system.
   a. Initialize the graphics routine.
   b. Define the terminal to be used.
2. Enter the coordinates of the first data point.
3. Move the beam to the location specified by the coordinates.
4. Enter the coordinates of the second point.
5. Draw a line from the first point to the second point.
6. Check whether there are more points.
7. If there are more points, repeat steps 4 and 5, otherwise go to the next step.
8. End program.

Flow chart: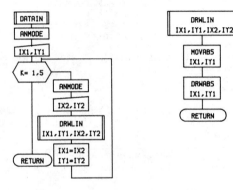

FORTRAN code:

```
C ** DRAWING PROGRAM **
      CALL INITT (960)
      CALL TERM (1,1024)
      CALL DATAIN
      CALL FINITT (0,0)
      END


C ** INPUT COORDINATES OF SIX POINTS FOR DRAWING **
C ** COORDINATES WILL BE ENTERED FROM KEYBOARD **
      SUBROUTINE DATAIN
      CALL MOVABS(1,760)
      CALL ANMODE
      WRITE (5,*) 'ENTER COORDINATES OF FIRST POINT (X,Y)'
      READ (5,*) IX1,IY1
      DO 50  K=1,5
        CALL MOVABS(1,760-80*K)
        CALL ANMODE
        WRITE (5,*) 'ENTER COORDINATES OF NEXT POINT (X,Y)'
        READ (5,*) IX2,IY2
        CALL DRWLIN (IX1,IY1,IX2,IY2)
        IX1=IX2
        IY1=IY2
 50     CONTINUE
C ** DUMMY READ STATEMENT TO CREATE PAUSE **
      CALL ANMODE
      READ (5,25) IDUMMY
 25   FORMAT(A1)
      RETURN
      END


C ** DRAW LINE BETWEEN POINTS **
      SUBROUTINE DRWLIN (IX1,IY1,IX2,IY2)
      CALL MOVABS (IX1,IY1)
      CALL DRWABS (IX2,IY2)
      RETURN
      END
```

The same program coded in BASIC for a personal computer (IBM PC) but using the same algorithm and flow chart would be as follows:

```
10      REM ** DRAWING PROGRAM **
30      SCREEN 2
70      GOSUB 2000
80      SCREEN 0
90      END


2000    REM ** SUBROUTINE TO INPUT COORDINATES **
2010    REM ** OF SIX POINTS FOR LINE DRAWING **
2020    REM ** COORDINATES ENTERED FROM KEYBOARD **
2030    INPUT"ENTER COORDINATES OF FIRST POINT (X,Y)";X1,Y1
2040    FOR K=1 TO 5
2050      INPUT"ENTER COORDINATES OF NEXT POINT (X,Y)";X2,Y2
2110      GOSUB 2200
2115      X1=X2
2116      Y1=Y2
2120      NEXT K
2130    PAUS$=INKEY$:IF PAUS$="" THEN GOTO 2130:'PAUSE
2190    RETURN


2200    REM ** SUBROUTINE TO DRAW LINE BETWEEN POINTS **
2230    LINE (X1,Y1)-(X2,Y2),1
2390    RETURN
```

The program for this example has also been coded in BASIC for the Apple II (see Appendix A) and for the Tektronix 4051/52 (see Appendix B).

Note that it is not necessary that the lines be connected for these programs to work, since the beam is always moved to the starting point before beginning to draw. The BASIC statement

```
LINE (X1,Y1)-(X2,Y2),1
```

combines the functions of the generic statements

```
MOVE ABSOLUTE (X1,Y1)
DRAW ABSOLUTE (X2,Y2)
```

Since the lines are connected in this case, it would be possible to eliminate all MOVE statements except the first. This would be analogous to leaving out step 4 of the pencil-and-paper procedure used by the drafter. The simplified procedure is as follows:

1. Start up (initialize) the system.
   a. Initialize the graphics routine.
   b. Define the terminal to be used.
2. Enter the coordinates of the first data point.
3. Move the beam to the location specified by the coordinates.
4. Enter the coordinates of the second point.
5. Draw a line from the first point to the second point.
6. Check whether there are more points.
7. If there are more points, repeat steps 4 and 5, otherwise go to the next step.
8. End program.

Flow chart:

FORTRAN code:

```
C ** DRAWING PROGRAM **
      CALL INITT (960)
      CALL TERM (1,1024)
      CALL DATAIN
      CALL FINITT (0,0)
      END
```

```
C ** INPUT COORDINATES OF SIX POINTS FOR DRAWING **
C ** COORDINATES WILL BE ENTERED FROM KEYBOARD **
      SUBROUTINE DATAIN
      CALL MOVABS(1,760)
      CALL ANMODE
      WRITE (5,*) 'ENTER COORDINATES OF FIRST POINT (X,Y)'
      READ (5,*) IX1,IY1
      CALL MOVABS (IX1,IY1)
      DO 50  K=1,5
        CALL ANMODE
        WRITE (5,*) 'ENTER COORDINATES OF NEXT POINT (X,Y)'
        READ (5,*) IX2,IY2
        CALL DRWABS (IX2,IY2)
   50   CONTINUE
C ** DUMMY READ STATEMENT TO CREATE PAUSE **
      CALL ANMODE
      READ (5,25) IDUMMY
   25 FORMAT(A1)
      RETURN
      END
```

The same program coded in BASIC for a personal computer (IBM PC) but using the same algorithm and flow chart would be as follows:

```
10      REM ** DRAWING PROGRAM **
30      SCREEN 2
70      GOSUB 2000
80      SCREEN 0
90      END

2000    REM ** SUBROUTINE TO INPUT COORDINATES **
2010    REM ** OF SIX POINTS FOR LINE DRAWING **
2020    REM ** DATA ENTERED FROM KEYBOARD **
2030    INPUT"ENTER COORDINATES OF FIRST POINT (X,Y)";X1,Y1
2035    PRESET (X1,Y1)
2040    FOR K=1 TO 5
2050      INPUT"ENTER COORDINATES OF NEXT POINT (X,Y) ";X2,Y2
2110      LINE -(X2,Y2),1
2120      NEXT K
2130    PAUS$=INKEY$:IF PAUS$="" THEN GOTO 2130:'PAUSE
2190    RETURN
```

The program for this example has also been coded in BASIC for the Apple II (see Appendix A) and for the Tektronix 4051/52 (see Appendix B).

Moving and Drawing in Relative Coordinates

Sometimes it is desirable to be able to specify the distance to be moved or the length of the line to be drawn rather than the coordinates involved. Suppose you wished to draw a number of identical figures separated by a uniform fixed distance. You could accomplish this task by using MOVE ABSOLUTE and DRAW ABSOLUTE statements but it would be necessary to determine and specify the coordinates of each point involved. However, if you could describe the first figure in terms of moves and draws of certain distances and directions, the statements used to draw the figure could be repeated to draw a second identical figure. The only requirement would be that the beam be moved to the starting point of the new figure before beginning to draw. In fact, the same set of statements could be repeated any number of times to produce several identical figures. Additionally, the starting point of each successive figure could be specified in terms of distance and direction from the ending point of the previous figure, thus permitting reuse of the statement for the move between figures. Moves and draws specified in this way are executed using statements of the type

```
MOVE RELATIVE (dX,dY)
POINT RELATIVE (dX,dY)
DRAW RELATIVE (dX,dY)
```

where (dX, dY) refers not to the coordinates of the destination point but rather to the X and Y components of the distance between the starting and ending points.

Appropriate statements to accomplish these tasks would include the following:

LANGUAGE/SYSTEM	STATEMENT
FORTRAN/PLOT10	CALL MOVREL (IdX,IdY)
	CALL PNTREL (IdX,IdY)
	CALL DRWREL (IdX,IdY)
BASIC/TRS-80 Level 3	None available
BASIC/Apple II	None available
BASIC/Apple III	PERFORM MOVEREL (%dX,%dY)
	PERFORM DOTREL (%dX,%dY)
	PERFORM LINEREL (%dX,%dY)
BASIC/IBM PC	PRESET STEP (dX,dY)
	PSET STEP (dX,dY)
	LINE STEP −(dX,dY)
BASIC/Tektronix 4051/52	RMOVE dX,dY
	RDRAW dX,dY
Pascal/Apple II and UCSD TURTLEGRAPHICS	
MOVE command sequence	PENCOLOR (NONE);
	MOVE (distance);
POINT command sequence	PENCOLOR (NONE);
	MOVE (distance);
	PENCOLOR (WHITE);
	MOVE (1);
DRAW command sequence	PENCOLOR (WHITE);
	MOVE (distance);

In order to use RELATIVE statements it is necessary to know the distance and the direction in which the graphics beam must travel to execute each command. Referring to Figure 4-8 we see that the distance and direction necessary to get from point 1 to point 2 can be stated in terms of the X component and the Y component of that

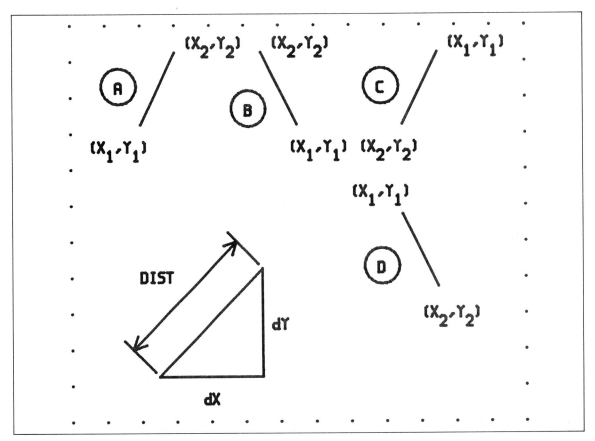

Figure 4-8.

distance. These components are referred to as dX and dY. Four different lines are shown in Figure 4-8. In each case the line length or distance traveled is identical. However, the directions are different. In 4-8A both dX and dY are positive. As a result, the line is drawn upward and to the right. Such a line is said to be in the first quadrant.

Here again, an explanation of the TURTLEGRAPHICS commands is in order. Since the turtle's only action is to move about dragging a pen, the POINT RELATIVE command must be accomplished through a sequence of commands that first moves the turtle to the desired location with pen color of NONE and then moves it a very short distance with pen color WHITE. The RELATIVE operations in TURTLEGRAPHICS are all accomplished by first orienting the turtle in the desired direction and then moving it the desired distance. Consequently, a calculation of direction should be made and the turtle turned before the MOVE (distance); command is executed. Calculations for distance and direction are easily made using the dX and dY values as the legs of a right triangle and calculating the

Table 4-3.

Point No.	X Value	Y Value	dX	dY	dX Pixel	dY Pixel
1	1	1	1	1	240	240
2	2	6	1	5,	80	400
3	3	4	1	−2	80	−160
4	4	1	1	−3	80	−240
5	5	5	1	4	80	320
6	6	3	1	−2	80	−160
7	7	3	1	0	80	0
8	8	4	1	1	80	80
9	9	2	1	−2	80	−160

hypotenuse to obtain the distance, then using a trigonometric formula to obtain the direction.

The line in 4-8B has a positive dY but a negative dX. Consequently, it is drawn upward and to the left, or in the second quadrant. Figure 4-8C shows a line with a negative dX and negative dY, which is drawn downward and to the left, or in the third quadrant. Finally, the line in 4-8D has a positive dX and a negative dY. It is drawn downward and to the right, or in the fourth quadrant. You can see that a dX of zero will result in a vertical line and a dY of zero will produce a horizontal line. If both dX and dY are zero the beam will not move at all.

Plotting the Points

We will now plot the points from Table 4-2 to the screen using our initial screen layout, only this time our graphics statements will use RELATIVE Coordinates. Before we can do any plotting, however, it will be necessary to determine the dX and dY to use for each point. Therefore let us modify Table 4-2 to show those values. To do this we will add a column labeled dX and one labeled dY (see Table 4-3), and we will calculate the values to enter for each point by taking each coordinate of the current point in turn and subtracting the corresponding coordinate for the previous point. For example, dX for point 5 is 5−4, or 1, and dY for point 5 is 5−1, or 4. We run into trouble when we apply this method to point 1 because there is no previous point. The coordinates we subtract in this case are the coordinates of the actual beam location at the time the plotting exercise is started. In many actual cases, this position is known or can be determined by interrogating the system. If this is not possible, the beam's starting position can be fixed by first moving the beam to a known location, such as (0,0). These coordinates can then be used in the calculation of X and Y for point 1. Alternatively, the move to point 1 can be accomplished with MOVE ABSOLUTE or POINT ABSOLUTE using the absolute coordinates of point 1. In the following code, the beam is moved to the initial position (0,0) and then all plotting is done using RELATIVE coordinates.

Flow chart:

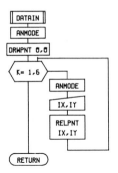

FORTRAN code:

```
C ** DRAWING PROGRAM **
        CALL INITT (960)
        CALL TERM (1,1024)
        CALL DATAIN
        CALL FINITT (0,0)
        END

C ** INPUT COORDINATES OF SIX POINTS FOR PLOTTING **
C ** COORDINATES ENTERED FROM KEYBOARD **
        SUBROUTINE DATAIN
        CALL MVBEAM (0,0)
        DO 50  K=1,6
          CALL ANMODE
          WRITE (5,*) 'ENTER DISTANCE TO POINT (X,Y)'
          READ (5,*) IX,IY
          CALL PNTREL (IX,IY)
        50      CONTINUE
C ** DUMMY READ STATEMENT TO CREATE PAUSE **
        CALL ANMODE
        READ (5,25) IDUMMY
     25 FORMAT(A1)
        RETURN
        END
```

The same program coded in BASIC for a personal computer (IBM PC) but using the same flow chart would be as follows:

```
10      REM ** DRAWING PROGRAM **
30      SCREEN 2
70      GOSUB 1000
80      SCREEN 0
90      END

1000    REM ** SUBROUTINE TO INPUT COORDINATES **
1010    REM ** OF SIX POINTS FOR PLOTTING **
1020    REM ** COORDINATES ENTERED FROM KEYBOARD **
1030    PRESET (0,0):GOSUB 1200
1040    FOR K=1 TO 6
1050      INPUT"ENTER DISTANCE TO POINT (X,Y)";X,Y
1110      PSET STEP (X,Y),1
1120      NEXT K
1130    PAUS$=INKEY$:IF PAUS$="" THEN GOTO 1130:'PAUSE
1190    RETURN
```

The program for this example has also been coded in BASIC for the Apple II (see Appendix A) and for the Tektronix 4051/52 (see Appendix B).

All of the graphics statements discussed up to this point have required that the user specify the exact pixel to which the MOVE, POINT, or DRAW statement will move the graphics beam. As a result, it has been necessary to convert the X and Y values given for each point in Table 4-3 to the corresponding column and row numbers of the pixel on the screen and then to use these column and row numbers as the X and Y values of the MOVE ABSOLUTE (X,Y), POINT ABSOLUTE (X,Y), or DRAW ABSOLUTE (X,Y) statements. Similarly, it has been necessary to convert each dX and dY value in Table 4-3 to an equivalent number of pixels and then to specify the distance and directions—in terms of numbers of pixels—as the dX and dY of the MOVE RELATIVE (dX,dY), POINT RELATIVE (dX,dY), and DRAW RELATIVE (dX,dY) statements. These statements are said to be in screen coordinates, since the actual column and row numbers of the screen are used.

It would be much more convenient if the selected scale could be entered into the system. The system could then accept the original coordinates of each point and, using the scale, make the necessary conversion to determine the row number and column number of the proper pixel. Some graphics languages provide this capability. The arrangement varies somewhat from language to language, but the typical arrangement is for the user to define the minimum and maximum X and Y values that the screen is to display. The system then assigns the minimum X value to the first—or left-most—column of pixels, assigns the maximum X value to the last—or right-most—column of pixels and, using standard scaling techniques, establishes a column number for every value between these extremes. Similarly, the minimum Y value is assigned to the bottom (sometimes the top) row of pixels, the maximum Y to the top (or bottom) row of pixels, and row numbers are calculated for Y values between the extremes.

We are now able to create the two graphic elements that are the basis of all drawings: points and lines. The next two chapters will present techniques for creating rectangles and polygons through repeated drawing of points and lines under program control, thus freeing the user from having to enter each line individually.

Exercises

1. Determine the resolution of your screen in terms of the number of pixels horizontally and vertically.

2. Does your graphics language or set of graphics commands map (correspond) 1:1 with the number of dots? If so, you are ready to begin the rest of the exercises. If not, you must determine this ratio before proceeding.

3. Write out the graphics commands for your system to match each of the following generic commands and put the list in a reserved section of your notebook: MOVE ABSOLUTE (X,Y), MOVE RELATIVE (X,Y), DRAW ABSOLUTE (X,Y), DRAW RELATIVE (X,Y), POINT ABSOLUTE (X,Y), POINT RELATIVE (X,Y).

4. Plot the following sets of points on your system by writing the graphics commands using either ABSOLUTE coordinates or RELATIVE coordinates, as specified by your instructor:

    a. (200,50)
    b. (225,60)
    c. (250,75)
    d. (0,0)
    e. (25,10)
    f. (319,191)
    g. (319,0)
    h. (0,191)

5. Plot enough points between the ABSOLUTE coordinates given below to create a line. Use either ABSOLUTE coordinates or RELATIVE coordinates, as specified by your instructor:

    a. (100,100) (200,50)
    b. (100,50) (200,100)
    c. (200,100) (100,100)
    d. (100,100) (100,50)
    e. (100,50) (200,50)
    f. (200,50) (200,100)

Rectangles and Other Polygons

All drawing in computer graphics is done with some combination of the three commands MOVE, POINT, and DRAW, which were discussed in Chapter 4. Some graphics languages offer other commands, such as CIRCLE, to draw shapes. These commands access a built-in routine or procedure that uses the appropriate sequence of MOVE, POINT, and DRAW commands to accomplish the task, thus relieving programmers from having to write their own routines. Most graphics languages, however, do not provide routines to draw shapes. In this chapter and in Chapter 6 we will learn how to write our own routines to draw these shapes.

Any figure, no matter how complex, can be represented by a number of appropriately placed points. In fact, this is precisely how a picture is produced on the graphics display. However, it would be extremely tedious to produce any but the most elementary figure by specifying each point or pixel individually. As we saw in Chapter 4, the DRAW command allows us to specify with one statement all of the points to be used to create any straight line, thus greatly simplifying the task of completing a drawing. Although the DRAW command is a powerful tool, examination of a drawing of medium complexity will show that its creation on a graphics display will require hundreds or even thousands of lines. Many of the lines are used to create basic shapes, such as rectangles, hexagons, and other polygons. Frequently these are regular shapes—square or rectangular window and door openings in a building or hexagonal bolt heads on an assembly drawing.

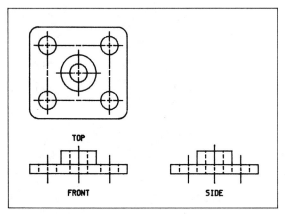

Figure 5-1.

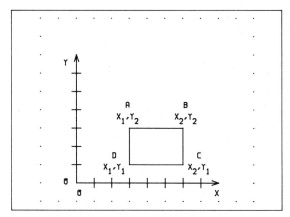

Figure 5-2.

The drawing in Figure 5-1 is quite simple, yet it contains several hundred separate lines. The circles are each composed of between 30 and 60 separate lines and the quarter-circle arcs are each created with one-fourth that number. While it is entirely possible to create these shapes one line at a time, or even one point at a time, such a procedure would require the system user to specify the coordinates of each point needed to complete the drawing—a very time-consuming process. However, many of these frequently used shapes are regular polygons (have equal sides and equal angles and can be inscribed in a circle) or are rectangles in standard position—that is, their sides are parallel to the X and Y axes. Shapes of this type can be completely described by writing a formula specifying the coordinates of two points and, in the case of a regular polygon, the radius and location of the circle in which it can be inscribed.

Rectangles

In Figure 5-2 we see a rectangle whose sides are parallel to the axes. Notice that the X coordinate for the lower left corner of the figure is the same as for the upper left corner and that the X coordinate for the lower right corner is the same as for the upper right corner. Similarly, the Y coordinates for the upper left and upper right corners are the same, as are the Y coordinates for the lower left and lower right corners. There are only two distinct X values and two distinct Y values. Thus, we can completely describe a rectangle in standard position with two X coordinates and two Y coordinates. Further study shows that if we select the pair of coordinates for any corner and the pair of coordinates for the diagonally opposite corner, we will have both required X values and both required Y values. Points A (X_1, Y_2) and C (X_2, Y_1) in Figure 5-2 are typical and illustrate the procedure.

Suppose the rectangle is drawn as in Figure 5-3. What additional information is required to describe it? In the example shown in Figure 5-2 we knew that the rectangle was parallel to the X and Y

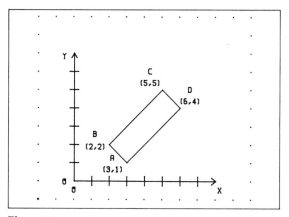

Figure 5-3.

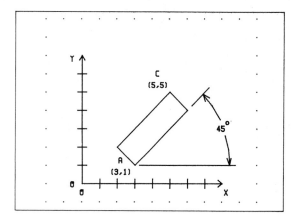

Figure 5-4.

axes. That information was a necessary part of our description of the rectangle. If, in the example of Figure 5-3, we specify the angle made by one side with the X axis or the Y axis along with the coordinates of opposite corners (see Figure 5-4), we have completely described the rectangle, but the calculations required to obtain the rest of the coordinates are somewhat more involved than in the first example. We do not know the length of any side, but the length of the diagonal AC can be calculated as

$$\text{Diagonal} = \sqrt{(5-3)^2 + (5-1)^2}$$
$$= \sqrt{2^2 + 4^2}$$
$$= 4.47$$

The angle this diagonal makes with the X axis is

$$\phi = \arctan\left(\frac{5-1}{5-3}\right)$$
$$= 63.4°$$

The angle made by the diagonal with side AD is then calculated as

$$\theta = 63.4 - 45$$
$$= 18.4°$$

Next, the length of the side AD is calculated as

$$AD = \text{Diagonal} \times \cos(\phi - \theta)$$
$$= 4.24$$

and the length of side AB is

$$AB = \text{Diagonal} \times \sin(\phi - \theta)$$
$$= 1.41$$

Finally, the coordinates of corner D are calculated as

$$X_D = 3 + 4.24 \cos(45)$$
$$= 6$$
$$Y_D = 1 + 4.24 \sin(45)$$
$$= 4$$

and the coordinates of corner B are

$$X_B = 3 + 1.41 \cos(45 + 90)$$
$$= 2$$
$$Y_B = 1 + 1.41 \sin(45 + 90)$$
$$= 2$$

In what other ways could we describe the rectangle of Figure 5-3? Suppose we know the angle formed by one side and an axis, and the lengths of two adjacent sides, as shown in Figure 5-5. We can then calculate the coordinates as follows:

$$X_D = 3 + 4.24 \cos(45)$$
$$= 6$$
$$Y_D = 1 + 4.24 \sin(45)$$
$$= 4$$
$$X_B = 3 + 1.41 \cos(45 + 90)$$
$$= 2$$
$$Y_B = 1 + 1.41 \sin(45 + 90)$$
$$= 2$$
$$X_C = 2 + 4.24 \cos(45)$$
$$= 5$$
$$Y_C = 2 + 4.24 \sin(45)$$
$$= 5$$

This set of calculations is much easier than the previous set, since the lengths of the sides do not have to be determined.

Suppose we do not know the rectangle's orientation. It can still be described by specifying the coordinates of any three corners, as shown in Figure 5-6. Referring to the previous calculations, we can see that obtaining the coordinates of the fourth corner is relatively simple. In practice, however, it is difficult to accurately locate the three required corners with a light pen or other direct input device unless the rectangle is in standard position. Consequently this method is not often used.

It is now clear that three separate values or, in the case of coordinates, pairs of values are required to describe a rectangle: location, size, and orientation. Data options include coordinates, lengths of the sides, and angles formed by the sides and the axes. There are several possible combinations of data that will be sufficient to form a rectangle, but, from a programming standpoint, it is not practical to

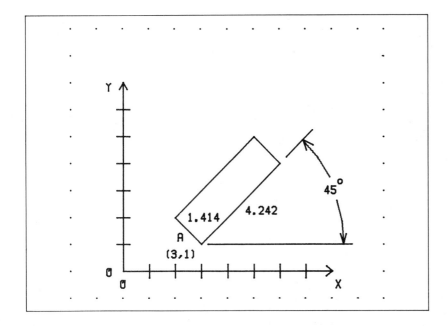

Figure 5-5.

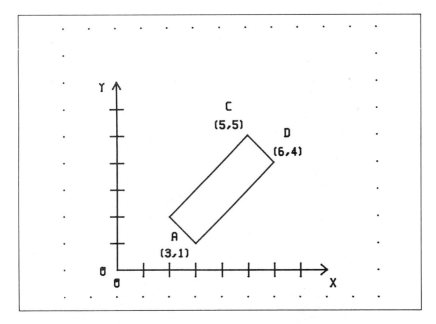

Figure 5-6.

write routines to provide for every possibility. The program would be too large and unwieldy. Therefore, most drafting programs limit themselves to two or three of the most useful options.

The most useful form of rectangle is the rectangle in standard position. It can be used for drawing object outlines, borders, title blocks, and many other details. This form is so useful that most drawing packages contain special input routines that allow you to create rectangles by entering the coordinates of any two diagonally opposite corners. A procedure for this technique is presented in the following flow chart and accompanying FORTRAN code.

Flow chart:

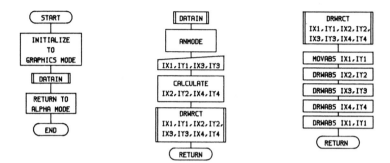

FORTRAN code:

```
C ** DRAWING PROGRAM **
      CALL INITT (960)
      CALL TERM (1,1024)
      CALL DATAIN
      CALL FINITT (0,0)
      END


C ** ENTER COORDINATES FOR RECTANGLE **
C ** COORDINATES TO BE ENTERED FROM KEYBOARD **
      SUBROUTINE DATAIN
      CALL MOVABS(1,760)
      CALL ANMODE
      WRITE (5,*) 'ENTER FIRST CORNER (X1,Y1)'
      READ (5,*) IX1,IY1
      WRITE (5,*) 'ENTER THIRD CORNER (X3,Y3)'
      READ (5,*) IX3,IY3
      IX2=IX1
      IY2=IY3
      IX4=IX3
      IY4=IY1
      CALL DRWRCT (IX1,IY1,IX2,IY2,IX3,IY3,IX4,IY4)
C ** DUMMY READ STATEMENT TO CREATE PAUSE **
      CALL ANMODE
      READ (5,25) IDUMMY
   25 FORMAT(A1)
      RETURN
      END


C ** DRAW RECTANGLE **
      SUBROUTINE DRWRCT(IX1,IY1,IX2,IY2,IX3,IY3,IX4,IY4)
      CALL MOVABS(IX1,IY1)
      CALL DRWABS(IX2,IY2)
      CALL DRWABS(IX3,IY3)
      CALL DRWABS(IX4,IY4)
      CALL DRWABS(IX1,IY1)
      RETURN
      END
```

Some comments are in order regarding this code. First, two subroutines are presented, one to input the data and another to do the drawing. Throughout this book we will strive to have all tasks performed by subroutines. Each subroutine will have a simple, straightforward task. When we are finished, we will have a set of subroutines that can be assembled into a sophisticated program, yet each subroutine will be very simple and easy to understand. In fact, some of the subroutines will be used in several different parts of the program, which will reduce duplication of code and keep the program manageable. Second, we have used the same start-up routine that was used in Chapter 4. This routine will not be presented again since it is always the same. In fact, it occurs only once in any one program even though there may be a great number of subroutines. In our examples, the main program accesses the data-input routine, but when there are many subroutines, the main program should access a menu subroutine, which then controls access to the various task subroutines.

The following code implements the data-input and rectangle-drawing subroutines in BASIC for the IBM PC. Note statement 3130. This statement causes the program to keep looping back to the same line number until any key is pressed on the keyboard, thus creating a pause in the program.

```
10 REM ** DRAWING PROGRAM **
30 SCREEN 2
70 GOSUB 3000
80 SCREEN 0
90 END


3000   REM ** SUBROUTINE TO INPUT COORDINATES **
3010   REM ** OF RECTANGLE **
3020   REM ** COORDINATES ENTERED FROM  KEYBOARD **
3050   INPUT"ENTER FIRST CORNER (X1,Y1)"; X1,Y1
3070   INPUT"ENTER THIRD CORNER (X3,Y3)"; X3,Y3
3080   X2=X1:Y2=Y3:X4=X3:Y4=Y1
3110   GOSUB 3200
3130   PAUS$=INKEY$:IF PAUS$="" THEN GOTO 3130
3190   RETURN


3200   REM ** SUBROUTINE TO DRAW RECTANGLE **
3220   PRESET (X1,Y1)
3230   LINE -(X2,Y2),1
3240   LINE -(X3,Y3),1
3250   LINE -(X4,Y4),1
3260   LINE -(X1,Y1),1
3390   RETURN
```

The program for this example has also been coded in BASIC for the Apple II (see Appendix A) and for the Tektronix 4051/52 (see Appendix B).

Rectangles in nonstandard positions—that is, not parallel to the X and Y axes—are not often used. When needed, they may be put in by eye with the aid of a grid or put in by a package that has the capability of drawing lines at specified angles or perpendicular to other specified lines. Some packages allow the user to draw the rectangle in standard position and then rotate it to the desired position.

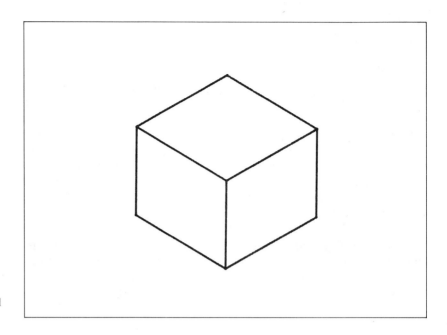

Figure 5-7. A cube formed using parallelograms.

Parallelograms

A geometric figure that is often found in drawings is the parallelogram. It is somewhat like a rectangle in that opposite sides are parallel and of equal length. However, the angles between adjacent sides are not necessarily 90 degrees. One common use of parallelograms is to create two-dimensional representations of three-dimensional objects. The isometric drawing of a box in Figure 5-7 is composed of three parallelograms, each representing one of the rectangular sides of the box.

How can we describe a parallelogram? A common way, shown in Figure 5-8, is to specify the coordinates of any three of the four vertices. Another approach is to specify the lengths of two adjacent sides, the angle between them, and the angle one of them makes with a specified axis (see Figure 5-9). There are several other possibilities.

We will use the common method of describing a parallelogram—that is, we will specify the coordinates of three corners or vertices and have the system determine the coordinates of the fourth. We will enter the coordinates of three vertices, starting with any one of the four and proceeding in a clockwise (or counterclockwise) direction around the parallelogram. Does it matter whether we go clockwise or counterclockwise? Study of Figure 5-8 will show that, regardless of which coordinate is taken as the starting point, the coordinates (X_4, Y_4) can be calculated as

$$X_4 = X_3 - (X_2 - X_1)$$
$$Y_4 = Y_3 - (Y_2 - Y_1)$$

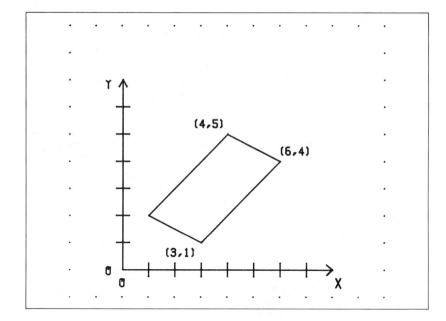

Figure 5-8.

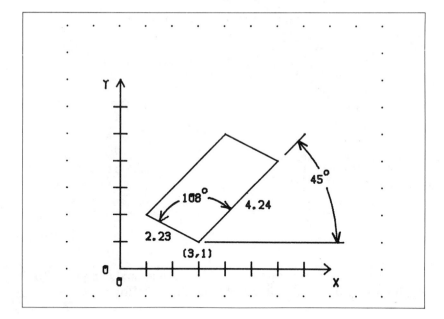

Figure 5-9.

The following flow chart and FORTRAN code can be used for drawing parallelograms. Notice the similarity of the code to that for drawing the rectangle. If the coordinates of all four corners of the figure were calculated in the input routine, could the same drawing routine be used for both rectangles and parallelograms? Try it.

Flow chart:

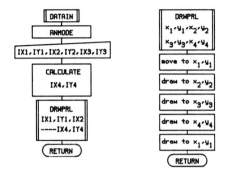

FORTRAN code:

```
C ** ENTER COORDINATES FOR PARALLELOGRAM **
C ** COORDINATES TO BE ENTERED FROM KEYBOARD **
      SUBROUTINE DATAIN
      CALL MOVABS(1,760)
      CALL ANMODE
      WRITE (5,*) 'ENTER FIRST CORNER (X1,Y1)'
      READ (5,*) IX1,IY1
      WRITE (5,*) 'ENTER SECOND CORNER (X2,Y2)'
      READ (5,*) IX2,IY2
      WRITE (5,*) 'ENTER THIRD CORNER (X3,Y3)'
      READ (5,*) IX3,IY3
      IX4=IX3-(IX2-IX1)
      IY4=IY3-(IY2-IY1)
      CALL DRWPRL (IX1,IY1,IX2,IY2,IX3,IY3,IX4,IY4)
C ** DUMMY READ STATEMENT TO CREATE PAUSE **
      CALL ANMODE
      READ (5,25) IDUMMY
  25  FORMAT(A1)
      RETURN
      END


C ** DRAW RECTANGLE OR PARALLELOGRAM **
      SUBROUTINE DRWPRL(IX1,IY1,IX2,IY2,IX3,IY3,IX4,IY4)
      CALL MOVABS(IX1,IY1)
      CALL DRWABS(IX2,IY2)
      CALL DRWABS(IX3,IY3)
      CALL DRWABS(IX4,IY4)
      CALL DRWABS(IX1,IY1)
      RETURN
      END
```

The same program coded in BASIC for a personal computer (IBM PC) but using the same flow chart would be as follows:

```
10 REM ** DRAWING PROGRAM **
30 SCREEN 2
70 GOSUB 3800
80 SCREEN 0
90 END


3800   REM ** SUBROUTINE TO INPUT COORDINATES **
3810   REM ** OF PARALLELOGRAM **
3820   REM ** COORDINATES ENTERED FROM  KEYBOARD **
3850   INPUT"ENTER FIRST  CORNER (X1,Y1)"; X1,Y1
3860   INPUT"ENTER SECOND CORNER (X2,Y2)"; X2,Y2
```

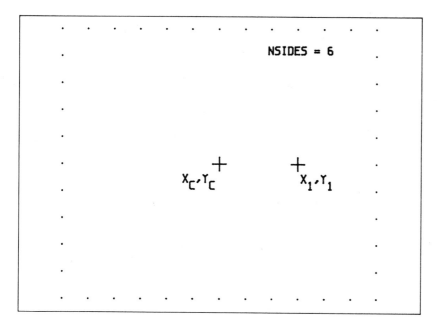

Figure 5-10.

```
3870   INPUT"ENTER THIRD  CORNER (X3,Y3)"; X3,Y3
3880   X4=X3-(X2-X1):Y4=Y3-(Y2-Y1)
3910   GOSUB 3200
3930   PAUS$=INKEY$:IF PAUS$="" THEN GOTO 3930
3990   RETURN


3200   REM ** SUBROUTINE TO DRAW RECTANGLE **
3210   REM ** OR PARALLELOGRAM **
3220   PRESET (X1,Y1)
3230   LINE -(X2,Y2),1
3240   LINE -(X3,Y3),1
3250   LINE -(X4,Y4),1
3260   LINE -(X1,Y1),1
3390   RETURN
```

The program for this example has also been coded in BASIC for the Apple II (see Appendix A) and for the Tektronix 4051/52 (see Appendix B).

Regular Polygons

Regular polygons—that is, polygons that have equal sides and equal angles and can be inscribed in a circle—are often found in drawings. Equilateral triangles, squares, and hexagons are three common regular polygons.

An effective way to define a polygon is to specify the coordinates of the center of the circumscribed circle and one vertex of the polygon along with the number of sides (see Figure 5-10). This common method makes drawing concentric polygons of various sizes or number of sides very easy. Also, it is often more convenient to locate polygons in this way, as in the case of bolt heads, for example, which are either squares or hexagons and which must be concentric with the body of the bolt.

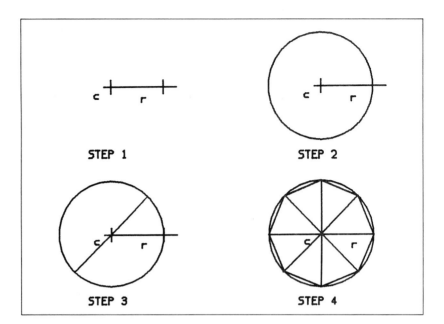

Figure 5-11.

Drafters working with instruments on paper have a number of techniques available to them for constructing polygons. One approach that will always work is to draw the circumscribed circle, locate one vertex, and mark off the other vertex locations with a protractor by drawing lines at the proper incremental angles, as shown in Figure 5-11. The vertices are then connected by straight lines and the circle, having served its purpose, is erased.

The technique we will use for drawing the polygon on the computer is similar to the manual method: The center of the circumscribed circle is located and then a starting vertex is located. The radius of the circle is calculated, as is the incremental angle of rotation between sides. The figure is then drawn by calculating the coordinates of each successive vertex. The coordinate of a vertex is the respective coordinate of the center plus the product of the radius times the sine (or cosine, as appropriate) of the incremental angle. Thus, if the starting vertex is at 0 radians relative to the center point (dY = 0—see Figure 5-12), then the first vertex to be calculated will be at

$$X = X_C + radius \times \cos(2 \times \pi/n)$$
$$Y = Y_C + radius \times \sin(2 \times \pi/n)$$

Generalizing these formulas, the kth vertex will be at

$$X = X_C + radius \times \cos(2k \times \pi/n + start)$$
$$Y = Y_C + radius \times \sin(2k \times \pi/n + start)$$

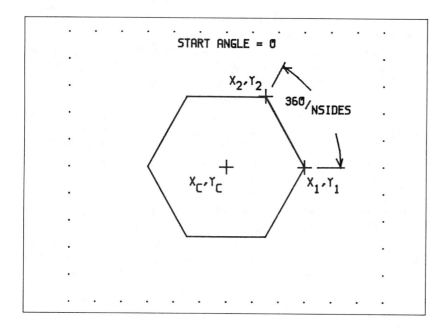

Figure 5-12.

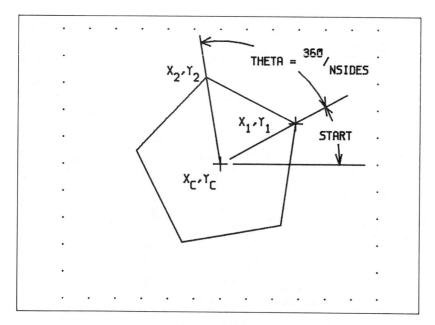

Figure 5-13.

where *k* is the *k*th vertex, *n* is the number of sides, and *start* is the angle formed by a line from the center (X_C, Y_C) to the starting vertex, as shown in Figure 5-13. Note that when $k = n$, the angle is equal to the starting angle, $X = X_{start}$, $Y = Y_{start}$, and the polygon is closed. Due to rounding errors in calculations, the closure may not be perfect.

For this reason, many packages eliminate the calculation for the last vertex and simply draw to the starting point X_{start}, Y_{start}.

The following flow chart describes one method of drawing an n-sided polygon on a computer. The procedure is then coded in FORTRAN and in BASIC. Note that a FACTOR of 2.5 has been used to scale the X values in the BASIC code (written for the IBM PC). A factor is required to obtain a correctly proportioned polygon if the screen has a different number of pixels per inch in the X direction than in the Y. The value 2.5 is correct for a system with a 640 × 200 screen resolution but may vary for other systems. Try various factors to see what value is best for your system.

A new subroutine has been added to the data input and drawing subroutines used up to this point. The purpose of this new subroutine is to calculate the angle made by an imaginary line drawn from the center of the figure (or circumscribed circle) to the coordinates of the starting point. Why is this angle needed? (Note also that the FORTRAN code takes advantage of the function ATAN2—not available in BASIC—to simplify the calculation of this angle.)

Flow chart:

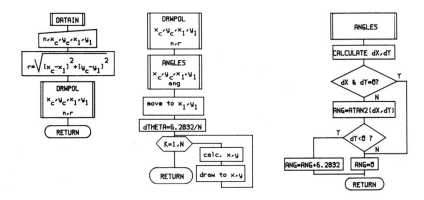

FORTRAN code:

```
C ** ENTER COORDINATES FOR POLYGON **
C ** COORDINATES TO BE ENTERED FROM KEYBOARD **
      SUBROUTINE DATAIN
      CALL MOVABS(1,760)
      CALL ANMODE
      WRITE (5,*) 'ENTER NUMBER OF SIDES'
      READ (5,*) N
      WRITE (5,*) 'ENTER CENTER (XC,YC)'
      READ (5,*) IXC,IYC
      WRITE (5,*) 'ENTER STARTING POINT (X1,Y1)'
      READ (5,*) IX1,IY1
      RADIUS=((IX1-IXC)**2+(IY1-IYC)**2)**.5
      CALL DRWPOL (IXC,IYC,IX1,IY1,N,RADIUS)
C ** DUMMY READ STATEMENT TO CREATE PAUSE **
      CALL ANMODE
      READ (5,25) IDUMMY
25    FORMAT(A1)
      RETURN
      END
```

```
C ** DRAW POLYGON **
      SUBROUTINE DRWPOL(IXC,IYC,IX1,IY1,N,RADIUS)
C ** CALCULATE STARTING ANGLE **
      CALL ANGLES (IXC,IYC,IX1,IY1,ANG)
      CALL MOVABS (IX1,IY1)
      DTHETA=6.2832/N
      DO 50 K=1,N
        IX=COS(ANG+K*DTHETA)*RADIUS+IXC
        IY=SIN(ANG+K*DTHETA)*RADIUS+IYC
        CALL DRWABS (IX,IY)
  50    CONTINUE
      RETURN
      END


C ** CALCULATE STARTING ANGLE **
      SUBROUTINE ANGLES (IXC,IYC,IX1,IY1,ANG)
      X=IX1-IXC
      Y=IY1-IYC
C ** ERROR TRAP **
      IF (X .EQ. 0. .AND. Y .EQ. 0.) GOTO 10
C ** CALCULATION **
      ANG=ATAN2(Y,X)
      IF (Y .LT. 0.) ANG=ANG+6.2832
      GOTO 999
  10  ANG=0
 999  RETURN
      END
```

BASIC code:

```
10    REM ** DRAWING PROGRAM **
30    SCREEN 2
40    FACTOR=2.5
70    GOSUB 4000
80    SCREEN 0
90    END


4000  REM ** SUBROUTINE TO INPUT COORDINATES **
4010  REM ** OF POLYGON **
4020  REM ** COORDINATES ENTERED FROM KEYBOARD **
4040  INPUT "ENTER NUMBER OF SIDES";N
4050  INPUT "ENTER CENTER (XC,YC)";XC,YC
4060  INPUT "ENTER STARTING POINT (X1,Y1)";X1,Y1
4080  RADIUS=SQR(((X1-XC)/FACTOR)^2+(Y1-YC)^2)
4110  GOSUB 4200
4130  PAUS$=INKEY$:IF PAUS$="" THEN GOTO 4130
4190  RETURN


4200  REM ** SUBROUTINE TO DRAW POLYGON **
4210  REM ** CALCULATE STARTING ANGLE **
4230  GOSUB 5100
4260  PRESET (X1,Y1)
4270  DTHETA=6.2832/N
4280  FOR  K=1 TO N
4290    X=COS(START+K*DTHETA)*RADIUS*FACTOR+XC
4300    Y=SIN(START+K*DTHETA)*RADIUS+YC
4320    LINE -(X,Y)
4340    NEXT K
4390  RETURN


5100  REM ** SUBROUTINE TO CALCULATE START ANGLE **
5150  IF X1-XC=0 THEN IF Y1>YC THEN START=1.5708
      :GOTO 5190 ELSE START=4.7124:GOTO 5190
5160  START=ATN((Y1-YC)/((X1-XC)/FACTOR))
5170  IF X1-XC<0 THEN START=START+3.1416
5190  RETURN
```

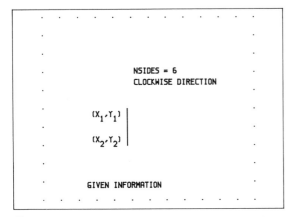

Figure 5-14.

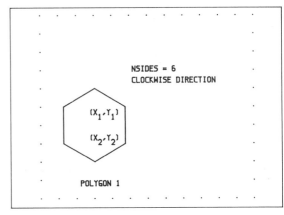

Figure 5-15.

The program for this example has also been coded in BASIC for the Apple II (see Appendix A) and for the Tektronix 4051/52 (see Appendix B).

Another way regular polygons can be completely defined is by specifying two adjacent corner points (vertices) and the number of sides plus the direction of rotation to be used to complete the figure. The radius of the circumscribed circle is readily calculated as

$$radius = \frac{\text{side length}}{2 \sin(\pi/n)}$$

where π is 3.1416 radians and n is the number of sides.

Figure 5-14 describes a six-sided polygon. Clockwise rotation is specified. The radius can be calculated without specifying the direction of rotation, but when this is done there can be two different polygons sharing the common side. The specification of clockwise rotation eliminates one of the two, leaving just one polygon that can meet all of the requirements. The polygon will be drawn by starting at (X_1,Y_1) and proceeding in a clockwise direction around the perimeter. Each successive side will be drawn at an angle of $2 \times \pi/n$ radians or 360/n degrees to the previous side (where n is the number of sides). Figure 5-15 shows the completed polygon.

In practice, many drafting systems draw counterclockwise. The specification of clockwise drawing appears to be limited to those systems that locate the origin in the upper left corner of the screen, as does the IBM PC. If you wish to draw counterclockwise, you can accomplish this on the PC by using a negative increment for the angle of turn. Thus, a hexagon would be drawn by rotating from 0 to −6.2832 radians using an increment of −1.0472 radians.

Irregular Polygons

Since their shapes do not follow any set pattern, irregular polygons must be completely defined—that is, either all vertices must be

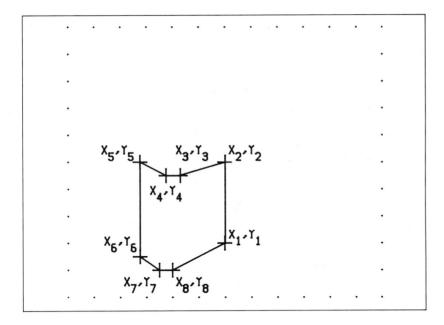

Figure 5-16.

Table 5-1.

Point No.	X	Y	Angle (degrees)	Distance (units)
1	8	2.5		
2			0	2.50
3			127	5.00
4			180	2.75
5			150	1.73
6			270	2.50
7			217	5.00
8			37	4.75

known, or at least one vertex plus a combination of side lengths and angles must be known in order to determine the coordinates of the other vertices. Surveyors drawing descriptions of land parcels generally find these parcels to be irregular polygons. Figure 5-16 is an example of an irregular polygon.

If you wish to draw an irregular polygon using DRAW ABSOLUTE commands, then you must determine the coordinates of each vertex from the available information regarding the lengths of the sides and the angles they make with the axes. Table 5-1 lists location data for eight points. The X and Y coordinates are listed for the first point (point 1). Location of the second point is described relative to the first by an angle (measured counterclockwise from the positive X axis) and a direction, and location of each successive point is similarly described. Figure 5-17 was drawn by calculating the coordinates of each point and then using the line-drawing routine from Chapter 4 to draw each of the lines. Table 5-2 lists the X and Y

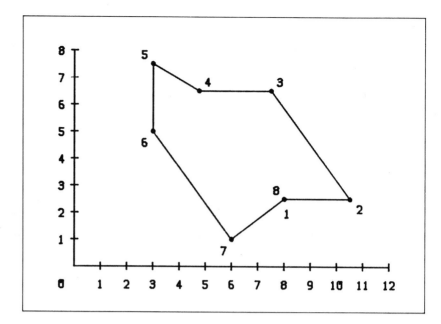

Figure 5-17.

Table 5-2.

Point No.	X	Y	Angle (degrees)	Distance (units)
1	8.00	2.50		
2	10.50	2.50	0	2.50
3	7.50	6.50	127	5.00
4	4.75	6.50	180	2.75
5	4.75	7.50	150	1.73
6	3.02	5.00	270	2.50
7	6.03	1.01	217	5.00
8	8.00	2.50	37	4.75

coordinates that were calculated in order to produce Figure 5-17. The calculation procedure used was to start with point 2 and perform the following operations:

1. Multiply the cosine of the angle between the current point and the previous point by the distance between them to get the X coordinate of the distance; then add the X coordinate of the location of the previous point to get the X coordinate of the location of the current point.

2. Multiply the sine of the angle between the current point and the previous point by the distance between them to get the Y coordinate of the distance; then add the Y coordinate of the location of the previous point to get the Y coordinate of the location of the current point.

If you wish to draw irregular polygons using DRAW RELATIVE commands, the distances and directions will be used and the actual

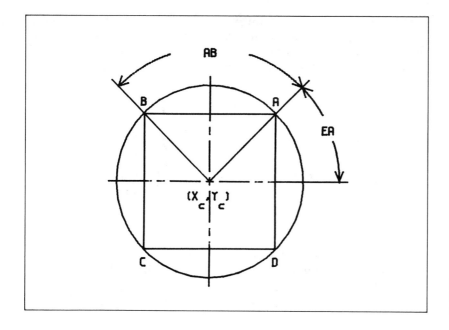

Figure 5-18. Square inscribed in a circle with a radius of 5 units.

coordinates of the vertices will not need to be calculated. The distance and direction data will still be used to calculate the X and Y coordinates of the distance between points unless the system being used can work directly with distance and direction data.

A frequent problem when drawing with DRAW RELATIVE commands is the failure of the last line drawn to connect to the starting point. This happens due to (1) the rounding that takes place in calculating lengths and angles and (2) the fact that the resolution of the display creates additional rounding with resulting inaccuracies. A common solution to this problem is to use an "auto close after n − 1 sides" procedure—that is, to draw the last line using a DRAW ABSOLUTE command with the coordinates of the starting point, or, at least, to use the coordinates of the starting point to calculate the distance and direction for the last DRAW RELATIVE command. Using the coordinates with DRAW ABSOLUTE is, of course, more accurate.

Figure 5-18 shows a square inscribed in a circle of radius 5 units. The center of the square is at (X_c, Y_c). Our task is to draw this square on the screen using RELATIVE drawing commands.

We can see that the location of any vertex (X_n, Y_n) can be described as

$$X_n = X_{n-1} + dX_n$$
$$Y_n = Y_{n-1} + dY_n$$

where dX_n and dY_n are the X and Y components, respectively, of the distance from the previous vertex X_{n-1}, Y_{n-1} to the current vertex.

The location of the first point is calculated relative to some known point, such as the center of the square. In Figure 5-18, point A (X_1,Y_1) is located 5 units from (X_c,Y_c) at an angle of 3.1416/4 radians (45 degrees). If the center of the square is at (300,100), then

$$dX_1 = 5 \cos\left(\frac{3.1416}{4}\right)$$
$$dY_1 = 5 \sin\left(\frac{3.1416}{4}\right)$$

If the beam is located at the center of the square (300,100), then it can be moved to the first vertex using a command of the form

```
DRAW RELATIVE (dX(1),dY(1))
```

Based on our knowledge of regular polygons, we can calculate the angle of the line from point A (X_1,Y_1) to point B as

$$\angle AB = \angle EA + \frac{1}{2} \times \frac{3.1416 - 6.2832}{n}$$
$$= 3.1416 + \frac{1}{2} \times \frac{3.1416 - 6.2832}{4}$$
$$= 3.9270$$

and the length of the side as

$$\text{side length} = 2 \times radius \times \sin\left(\frac{6.2832}{4}\right)$$

We also know that the direction to BC can be calculated as

$$\angle BC = \angle AB + \frac{6.2832}{n}$$

and each successive direction can be obtained by adding 6.2832/n to the previous one.

Comparison of this procedure to our existing code for drawing a regular polygon discloses great similarities. The angle from the center to point 1 is the same as the starting angle we used previously, the incremental angle 6.2832/n is $d\theta$, and the calculations for X and Y make use of the calculations for dX and dY. Obviously, only minor changes are needed to convert our original code to RELATIVE drawing code. This task will be left to you.

Keeping Track of Progress and Making Choices

During the process of running a drafting program, it is generally necessary to keep track of the progress of the operations being executed and, at points in the process where there are alternate ways of proceeding, to make choices as to which of the available options to use. The program needs some type of ongoing record of what has been done, what choices have already been made, and the status of each of the various procedures that make up the program. This process of "keeping score" is accomplished through the use of *flags* and *pointers*.

Flags

Flags can best be described as markers that have two possible states: Either they exist (are set) or they do not exist (are not set). Flags are not physical devices but it is easier to understand their function if they are thought of in that way. The flag itself is simply a variable to which the appropriate condition value is assigned. Since flags have only two states, they provide a binary "yes/no" type of message and are only useful for keeping track of the status of on/off, true/false, or other two-state conditions.

A boolean (logical) variable type is particularly appropriate for use as a flag, but an integer variable can be used with the two states being, say, 0 and 1. In this case, the condition "off" or "false" could be represented by 0 and "on" or "true" could be represented by 1. An example of the use of a flag would be to signify whether a drawing feature is to be deleted. A commonly used method of correcting a drawing is to flag the items to be deleted, then erase the display and, using stored data, redraw everything except the flagged items. Other uses for flags will be presented as they are needed in the following chapters.

Pointers

Pointers are similar in many respects to flags, but they can take on many values and thus can represent a variety of different conditions, states, or positions. Consequently, they are used to keep track of location or position. For instance, a pointer could be used in a data list to identify the next value to be used. Use of the RESET command in a program written in BASIC will move the pointer back to the first value in the list. Of course, like a flag, a pointer is not a physical device but, rather, a variable to which a value is assigned. This value records or "points at" the appropriate position in the data list. Pointers, like flags, are very important in computer graphics and will be used in many ways throughout the following chapters.

We have now developed subroutines to easily create some of the most-used drafting figures: rectangles and other polygons. Chapter 6 will cover creation of circles and arcs, along with techniques for drawing curves of various shapes. These various entities, along with lettering of titles and labels (to be covered in Chapter 7), form the basis of interactive drafting programs.

Exercises

1. Write a subroutine on your system to draw rectangles oriented parallel to the X and Y axes. Test your routine by using it to draw a border and title block.

2. Write a data-entry subroutine for rectangles that uses the length of two sides, the coordinates of one vertex (corner), and the angle one side makes with the abscissa as the input data. The subroutine should calculate the required coordinates for the rectangle-drawing subroutine.

3. Write a subroutine on your system to draw regular polygons. Plot polygons with sides from $n = 3$ to $n = 9$ using your system and turn in the plot to demonstrate the output for your instructor.

4. Write a subroutine to enter information for a regular polygon starting at any vertex and a subroutine to draw the specified polygon.

5. Rewrite either the rectangle subroutine or the polygon subroutine given in this chapter to plot in the opposite rotational direction (clockwise or counterclockwise).

6. Write a rectangle subroutine using RELATIVE moves and draws.

7. Write a polygon subroutine using RELATIVE moves and draws.

8. Use your polygon subroutine to draw a polygon with the center as the screen's center and the first vertex as the screen's extreme right edge. How much of your polygon is displayed? What happened in areas where the routine tried to draw beyond the edge of the screen? (This problem will be discussed in later chapters.)

9. Plot polygons of 5 through 80 sides using increments of 5 or 10 sides. Which ones produce a reasonable representation of a circle on your system?

We learned in Chapter 4 how to use the three basic graphics commands—MOVE, POINT, and DRAW—to create points, lines, and simple shapes on the graphics screen. Chapter 5 introduced techniques for efficient drawing of more sophisticated shapes. However, both of these chapters were devoted to graphics that contain only straight lines. In this chapter we will extend our drawing capabilities to include figures with curved edges or sides.

In actuality, it is very difficult to produce a truly curved line with computer graphics. The two drawing commands we have available—DRAW ABSOLUTE and DRAW RELATIVE—are capable of producing only straight lines. The POINT ABSOLUTE and POINT RELATIVE commands would allow us to create a curve one point at a time, but, as we explained in Chapter 4, the number of points required on a high-resolution screen, or even on a medium-resolution screen, would make the job very time consuming. Fortunately, it is not generally necessary to create a true curved line. A line composed of a large number of short line segments will appear to be curved; consequently we can create a suitable approximation to a curve by drawing it as a series of short straight lines.

The question that comes immediately to mind is, "How many lines are required to approximate a curve?" The answer is, "That depends." In other words, there is no single answer. Enough lines are required to make the drawing look like a curve, but not so many that additional lines do not make a significant improvement in the curve's appear-

6
Circles, Arcs, and Curves

ance. Factors that enter into this decision are (1) the resolution of the screen, (2) the degree (amount) of curvature, (3) the level of quality desired by the user, and (4) the time required to draw a large number of lines.

A low-resolution screen will not produce an accurate circle even if it is plotted point by point. On such a screen a "circle" with 8 sides may appear as good as one with 200 sides. A high-resolution screen, on the other hand, will produce better-looking circles if the circles are composed of a large number of very short lines.

Experimentation shows that, to produce good-looking circles of practical size, the number of line segments needed for a circle increases as the radius increases. The number of lines needed for a circle of, say, 20 units radius will not be twice the number needed for a circle of 10 units radius, however, since the degree of curvature per unit distance in the larger circle is less than that of the smaller one. Also, the line length can be increased somewhat, thus reducing the number of lines. Very complex formulas can be developed to calculate the number of lines needed to produce a circle, but a simple one that works well on a typical microcomputer screen (vertical resolution of about 200) is

$$n = 12 + 0.4 \times r$$

where r is the radius in pixels in the Y direction and n is the number of lines (polygon sides) required. The minimum (12) and the constant multiplier (0.4) can be adjusted to produce acceptable results on other screens.

Circles

Circles are special forms of curves. Their rate of curvature is constant and they are closed (begin and end at the same point), so they are easily drawn by hand using a compass. They are also relatively easy to draw with computer graphics. We learned in Chapter 5 to draw regular polygons with any desired number of sides. If we think of a circle as a polygon with an arbitrarily large number of sides we see that we can use the polygon routine to draw circles. The data-input routine should, of course, be modified to incorporate the calculation for number of sides so that the user does not have to worry about that detail. The modified data input routine would appear as follows.

Flow chart:

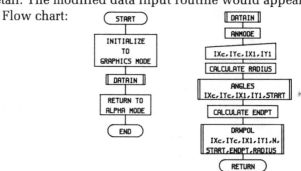

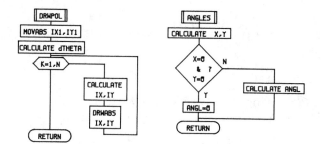

FORTRAN code:

```
C ** DRAWING PROGRAM **
      CALL INITT (960)
      CALL TERM (1,1024)
      CALL DATAIN
      CALL FINITT (0,0)
      END


C ** INPUT COORDINATES OF CENTER AND **
C ** STARTING POINT OF CIRCLE **
C ** COORDINATES TO BE INPUT FROM KEYBOARD **
      SUBROUTINE DATAIN
      CALL MOVABS(1,760)
      CALL ANMODE
      WRITE (5,*) 'ENTER CENTER (XC,YC)'
      READ (5,*) IXC,IYC
      WRITE (5,*) 'ENTER STARTING POINT (X1,Y1)'
      READ (5,*) IX1,IY1
      RADIUS = ((IX1-IXC)**2+(IY1-IYC)**2)**.5
      CALL ANGLES (IXC,IYC,IX1,IY1,START)
      ENDPT=START+6.2832
      N=12+0.4*RADIUS
      CALL DRWPOL (IXC,IYC,IX1,IY1,N,
     1START,ENDPT,RADIUS)
C ** DUMMY READ STATEMENT TO CREATE PAUSE **
      CALL ANMODE
      READ (5,25) IDUMMY
   25 FORMAT(A1)
      RETURN
      END


C ** DRAW POLYGON OR CIRCLE **
      SUBROUTINE DRWPOL (IXC,IYC,IX1,IY1,N,
     1START,ENDPT,RADIUS)
      CALL MOVABS(IX1,IY1)
      DTHETA=(ENDPT-START)/N
      DO 50 K=1,N
        IX=COS(START+K*DTHETA)*RADIUS+IXC
        IY=SIN(START+K*DTHETA)*RADIUS+IYC
        CALL DRWABS (IX,IY)
   50   CONTINUE
      RETURN
      END


C ** CALCULATE ANGLE **
      SUBROUTINE ANGLES (IXC,IYC,IX1,IY1,ANGL)
      X=IX1-IXC
      Y=IY1-IYC
C ** ERROR TRAP **
      IF (X .EQ. 0. .AND. Y .EQ. 0.) GOTO 10
```

```
C ** CALCULATION **
      ANGL=ATAN2 (Y,X)
      IF (Y .LT. 0.) ANGL=ANGL+6.2832
      GOTO 999
  10  ANGL=0
 999  RETURN
      END
```

The following BASIC code was written for the IBM PC. Note the use of INKEY$ to create a pause when the figure is completed.

```
10 REM **** DRAWING PROGRAM ****
30 SCREEN 2:FACTOR=2.5
70 GOSUB 4000
75 IF INKEY$="" THEN GOTO 75
80 SCREEN 0
90 END


4000 REM ** SUBROUTINE TO INPUT COORDINATES **
4010 REM ** FOR ARC **
4020 REM ** COORDINATES ENTERED FROM KEYBOARD **
4050 INPUT "ENTER CENTER        (XC,YC)";XC,YC
4060 INPUT "ENTER STARTING POINT (X1,Y1)";X1,Y1
4070 INPUT "ENTER ENDING POINT   (X2,Y2)";X2,Y2
4080 RADIUS=SQR(((X1-XC)/FACTOR)^2+(Y1-YC)^2)
4090 XX=X1:YY=Y1:GOSUB 5100
4100 START=ANGL
4110 XX=X2:YY=Y2:GOSUB 5100
4120 ENDPT=ANGL:IF ENDPT-START<=0 THEN
     ENDPT=ENDPT+6.2832
4140 N=INT((20+.4*RADIUS)*(ENDPT-START)/6.2832)
4150 GOSUB 4200
4160 PAUS$=INKEY$:IF PAUS$="" THEN GOTO 4160
4190 RETURN


4200 REM ** SUBROUTINE TO DRAW POLYGON **
4210 REM ** CIRCLE OR ARC **
4240 X1=COS(START)*RADIUS*FACTOR+XC
4250 Y1=SIN(START)*RADIUS+YC
4260 PRESET (X1,Y1)
4270 DTHETA=(ENDPT-START)/N
4280 FOR K=1 TO N
4290   X=COS(START+K*DTHETA)*RADIUS*FACTOR+XC
4300   Y=SIN(START+K*DTHETA)*RADIUS+YC
4320   LINE -(X,Y)
4340   NEXT K
4390 RETURN


5100 REM ** SUBROUTINE TO CALCULATE ANGLE **
5150 IF XX-XC=0 THEN IF YY>YC THEN ANGL=1.5708
     :GOTO 5190 ELSE ANGL=4.7124:GOTO 5190
5160 ANGL=ATN((YY-YC)/((XX-XC)/FACTOR))
5170 IF XX-XC<0 THEN ANGL=ANGL+3.1416
5190 RETURN
```

The program for this example has also been coded in BASIC for the Apple II (see Appendix A) and for the Tektronix 4051/52 (see Appendix B).

The most common method of drawing a circle by hand is to determine the center, select a starting point, and rotate the compass around the center point. Location of a circle by its center and a starting point is also one of the most common methods used in computer graphics. Another method that is sometimes used when it is necessary to "fit" a portion of the circle to some other feature of the drawing is to input three points on the circumference. Since three points define a circle, it is possible to calculate the equation of the circle and, from that, its center and radius. However, because of the difficulty, in most cases, of locating a circle using three points, and because of the extra calculations required to obtain the data to draw the circle, this method is not used except when absolutely necessary. We will cover this method in more detail when discussing arcs later in this chapter.

When we think of a circle, we generally visualize a round figure created by a solid curved line. Many circles are drawn using dashed or dotted lines. As an aid in locating concentric features, it is often desirable to mark the center of the circle by placing a dot or a small cross at the center point or even to draw center lines through the center point in the X and Y direction. The ability to draw circles with different line styles, to automatically draw a cross in the center of the circle, or to draw automatic center lines is very important in computer-aided drawing. These options are provided in computer-aided-drafting packages and their activation is controlled through a system of flags (discussed in Chapter 5). Provision of some of these options and their control will be covered in later chapters.

Arcs

Arcs are portions of circles. They are drawn manually in exactly the same way as circles except that the compass is not turned through a full 360 degrees. One method we used to draw circles was to locate the center of the circle and an arbitrarily selected starting point. We then drew the circle by dividing 360 degrees (2π radians) by the number of sides or line segments to be used. The result of that calculation was used as the incremental angle in our polygon routine. Had we originally selected some lesser angle—say 90 degrees ($\pi/2$ radians)—we would have ended up with an arc instead of a complete circle (try it). Our polygon drawing routine that became a circle-drawing routine is now an arc-drawing routine.

Of course, we need a way to determine the number of degrees our arc should contain and a data input routine to implement it. One way to do this is to select an ending point for the arc in addition to its starting point and center of curvature. Then the angle between the line from the center to the starting point and the line from the center to the ending point can be calculated and used in the polygon routine. As Figure 6-1 shows, it is not necessary that the ending point be accurately located on the curve itself. What is important is that the line from the center through the selected point also go through the desired end point of the arc. This procedure makes locating and drawing an arc much easier when working with a light pen or graphics cursor.

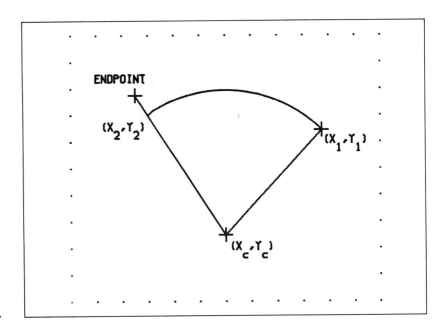

Figure 6-1.

The following flow chart and codes can be used to generate arcs:

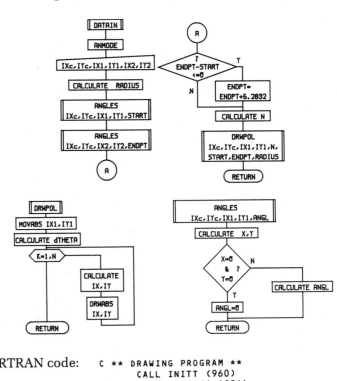

FORTRAN code:

```
C ** DRAWING PROGRAM **
   CALL INITT (960)
   CALL TERM (1,1024)
   CALL DATAIN
   CALL FINITT (0,0)
   END
```

```
C ** INPUT COORDINATES OF CENTER, STARTING POINT, AND **
C ** ENDING POINT OF ARC **
C ** COORDINATES TO BE INPUT FROM KEYBOARD **
      SUBROUTINE DATAIN
      CALL MOVABS(1,760)
      CALL ANMODE
      WRITE (5,*) 'ENTER CENTER (XC,YC)'
      READ (5,*) IXC,IYC
      WRITE (5,*) 'ENTER STARTING POINT (X1,Y1)'
      READ (5,*) IX1,IY1
      WRITE (5,*) 'ENTER ENDING POINT (X2,Y2)'
      READ (5,*) IX2,IY2
      RADIUS = ((IX1-IXC)**2+(IY1-IYC)**2)**.5
      CALL ANGLES (IXC,IYC,IX1,IY1,START)
      CALL ANGLES (IXC,IYC,IX2,IY2,ENDPT)
      IF ((ENDPT-START) .LE. 0.) ENDPT=ENDPT+6.2832
      N=(20+0.4*RADIUS)*(ENDPT-START)/6.2832
      CALL DRWPOL (IXC,IYC,IX1,IY1,N,
     1START,ENDPT,RADIUS)
C ** DUMMY READ STATEMENT TO CREATE PAUSE **
      CALL ANMODE
      READ (5,25) IDUMMY
   25 FORMAT(A1)
      RETURN
      END


C ** DRAW POLYGON, CIRCLE OR ARC **
      SUBROUTINE DRWPOL (IXC,IYC,IX1,IY1,N,
     1START,ENDPT,RADIUS)
      CALL MOVABS(IX1,IY1)
      DTHETA=(ENDPT-START)/N
      DO 50 K=1,N
        IX=COS(START+K*DTHETA)*RADIUS+IXC
        IY=SIN(START+K*DTHETA)*RADIUS+IYC
        CALL DRWABS (IX,IY)
   50   CONTINUE
      RETURN
      END


C ** CALCULATE ANGLE **
      SUBROUTINE ANGLES (IXC,IYC,IX1,IY1,ANGL)
      X=IX1-IXC
      Y=IY1-IYC
C ** ERROR TRAP **
      IF (X .EQ. 0. .AND. Y .EQ. 0.) GOTO 10
C ** CALCULATION **
      ANGL=ATAN2 (Y,X)
      IF (Y .LT. 0.) ANGL=ANGL+6.2832
      GOTO 999
   10 ANGL=0
  999 RETURN
      END
```

BASIC code (IBM PC version):

```
10 REM **** DRAWING PROGRAM ****
30 SCREEN 2:FACTOR=2.5
70 GOSUB 4000
80 SCREEN 0
90 END


4000 REM ** SUBROUTINE TO INPUT COORDINATES OF **
4010 REM ** CENTER AND STARTING POINT OF CIRCLE **
4020 REM ** COORDINATES ENTERED FROM KEYBOARD **
4050 INPUT "ENTER CENTER      (XC,YC)";XC,YC
4060 INPUT "ENTER STARTING POINT (X1,Y1)";X1,Y1
```

```
4080 RADIUS=SQR(((X1-XC)/FACTOR)^2+(Y1-YC)^2)
4090 XX=X1:YY=Y1:GOSUB 5100
4100 START=ANGL
4120 ENDPT=START+6.2832
4140 N=INT(12+.4*RADIUS)
4150 GOSUB 4200
4160 PAUS$=INKEY$:IF PAUS$="" THEN GOTO 4160
4190 RETURN


4200 REM ** SUBROUTINE TO DRAW POLYGON OR CIRCLE **
4210 REM
4240 X1=COS(START)*RADIUS*FACTOR+XC
4250 Y1=SIN(START)*RADIUS+YC
4260 PRESET (X1,Y1)
4270 FOR K=1 TO N
4280   DTHETA=(ENDPT-START)/N
4290   X=COS(START+K*DTHETA)*RADIUS*FACTOR+XC
4300   Y=SIN(START+K*DTHETA)*RADIUS+YC
4320   LINE -(X,Y)
4340   NEXT K
4390 RETURN


5100 REM ** SUBROUTINE TO CALCULATE ANGLE **
5150 IF XX-XC=0 THEN IF YY>YC THEN ANGL=1.5708
     :GOTO 5190 ELSE ANGL=4.7124:GOTO 5190
5160 ANGL=ATN((YY-YC)/((XX-XC)/FACTOR))
5170 IF XX-XC<0 THEN ANGL=ANGL+3.1416
5190 RETURN
```

The program for this example has also been coded in BASIC for the Apple II (see Appendix A) and for the Tektronix 4051/52 (see Appendix B).

A second data-input technique that was discussed for drawing a circle was to select three points on the circumference. We can use this technique to draw an arc as well as a full circle. The three points can represent the two end points and an intermediate point on the arc. This method is generally more difficult to use than the center-and-two-end-points method, but it is sometimes the only acceptable method (such as when the arc must fit a specific set of points and its center is not determined).

Figure 6-2 shows the construction necessary to locate the center and determine the radius of an arc that is defined by three points. The technique used here is to draw a chord through two of the points on the arc and then to construct the perpendicular bisector of the chord. This bisector will pass through the center of curvature of the arc. Another chord is then drawn through another pair of points and its perpendicular bisector constructed. The intersection of these two bisectors is the center of curvature of the arc. Of course, the construction will not actually be done on the computer. Instead, the equations of the perpendicular bisectors will be derived and solved for the common point.

Referring again to Figure 6-2, we see that the end points of one chord (ab) are (X_1,Y_1) and (X_2,Y_2). The slope of the chord is then

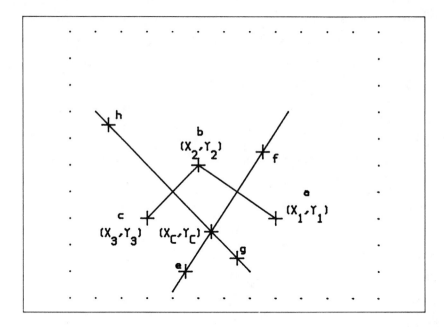

Figure 6-2.

$$M_{ab} = \frac{Y_2 - Y_1}{X_2 - X_1}$$

and the midpoint is at

$$X = \frac{X_1 + X_2}{2}$$

$$Y = \frac{Y_1 + Y_2}{2}$$

The perpendicular bisector (ef) of the chord passes through this point and has a slope of $-(1/M)$. These values can be used in the equation of a line as follows

$$Y = \left(\frac{1}{M_{ab}}\right)X + B_{ef}$$

to obtain the value of the intercept B.

The bisector (gh) of the second chord (bc) is similarly determined and the two equations are solved as simultaneous equations using the intersection of the two bisectors as the common point:

$$Y_i = -\left(\frac{1}{M_{ab}}\right)X_i + B_{ef}$$

$$Y_i = -\left(\frac{1}{M_{bc}}\right)X_i + B_{gh}$$

$$X_i = \frac{B_{gh} - B_{ef}}{\frac{1}{M_{bc}} - \frac{1}{M_{ab}}}$$

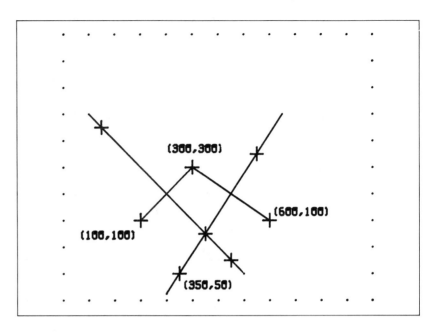

Figure 6-3.

The value of X_i can now be inserted in the equation of either of the bisectors to solve for Y_i. Figure 6-3 presents the solution using numbers for the coordinates involved.

Several potential problem areas must be addressed if this method is to be used effectively. First, the method cannot be used if the three points are in a straight line. In such a case, the perpendicular bisectors will be parallel (will not intersect) and, of course, the "arc" will have infinite radius. The program should test for this condition and take appropriate action if it is found. Appropriate action might be (1) to draw a straight line through the three points or (2) to signal the user that the condition exists and await further instructions.

A second potential problem is that one of the chords might be horizontal ($Y_1 = Y_2$ or $Y_2 = Y_3$). In this case, the perpendicular bisector would be vertical, which means it would have infinite slope and would not have an intercept on the Y axis. If this condition exists, the X coordinate of the vertical line can be inserted into the equation of the other bisector to solve for the Y coordinate of the intersection (Y_i). A test should be made for this condition if the straight-line test fails. If both tests fail, then the intersection of the bisectors can be calculated as described.

The third problem condition occurs when working with a display that has a nonsquare pixel pattern, as most microcomputers do. In this case, a circle will not appear to be round. We have compensated for this condition in our polygon, circle, and arc code by fixing two points, the center point and the starting point, and then "adjusting" the coordinates of all other points to obtain a true circle or circular arc on the screen. The adjusting (multiplying) factor 2.5, applied to the X coordinates, has been used in the example code. When dealing

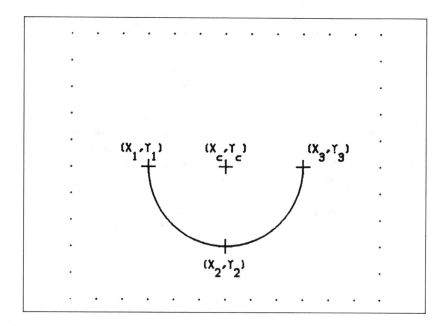

Figure 6-4A.

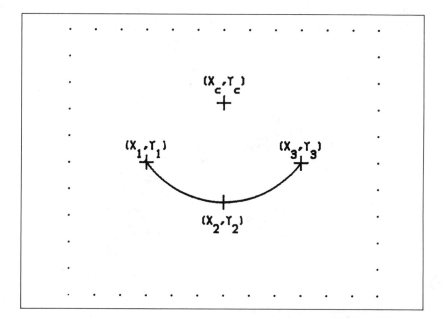

Figure 6-4B.

with a three-point input, however, it is necessary that the arc go through all three points. If the coordinates of the points are chosen without regard to screen distortion, the arc will not appear circular on the screen. If, on the other hand, the coordinates are chosen to give a circular arc on the screen, they cannot be used in the calculations.

Referring to Figure 6-4A, we see that the coordinates (200,100),

(300,60), (400,100), when plotted on our nonsquare screen, will define a semicircular arc of π radians. Using these coordinates directly in our equations, we find that the arc is calculated as shown in Figure 6-4B. To overcome this distortion problem it is necessary to *map* the coordinates to a square coordinate system, perform the calculations, and map the results back. *Mapping* is a term applied to the transfer of values from one system to another. In our case, all X coordinates will be divided by 2.5 to obtain (80,100), (120,60), (160,100). Calculations using these coordinates determine the center to be at X = 120, Y = 100. Mapping the points back we find the three points to again be (200,100), (300,60), (400,100) and the center to be (300,100).

The center-and-two-points arc-drawing routine will need only minor modifications to become the three-point routine. It will still use the center coordinates (X_c,Y_c) and the beginning and ending coordinates (X_1,Y_1) and (X_3,Y_3) supplied by the data-input routine.

Note that in the following flow chart, the points are first tested to determine that there are three separate points (otherwise they cannot define an arc). Next, tests are made for vertical bisectors and then for parallel bisectors. Only if all three tests fail is the intersection of the bisectors calculated in the normal manner. The FORTRAN code for this routine assumes a square pixel pattern on the display, while the BASIC code assumes a nonsquare pattern with an X-Y spacing ratio of 2.5 to 1.

Flow chart:

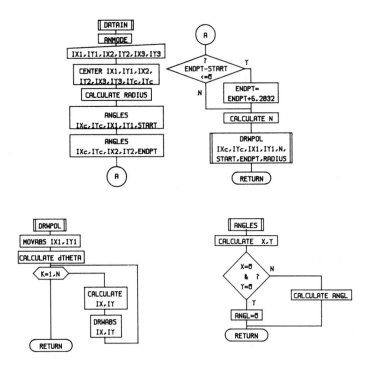

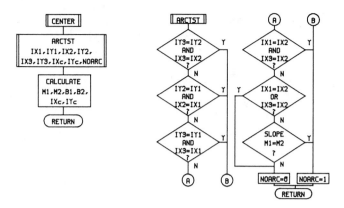

FORTRAN code:

```
C ** DRAWING PROGRAM **
      CALL ATTACH
      CALL INITT (960)
      CALL TERM (1,1024)
      CALL DATAIN
      CALL FINITT (0,0)
      END


C ** INPUT COORDINATES OF THREE POINT ARC **
C ** COORDINATES TO BE INPUT FROM KEYBOARD **
      SUBROUTINE DATAIN
    5 CALL MOVABS(1,760)
      CALL ANMODE
      WRITE (5,*) 'ENTER STARTING POINT (X1,Y1)'
      READ (5,*) IX1,IY1
      WRITE (5,*) 'ENTER NEXT POINT (X2,Y2)'
      READ (5,*) IX2,IY2
      WRITE (5,*) 'ENTER ENDING POINT (X3,Y3)'
      READ (5,*) IX3,IY3
      CALL CENTER (IX1,IY1,IX2,IY2,
     $IX3,IY3,IXC,IYC,NOARC)
      IF (NOARC .NE. 4) GOTO 10
      CALL BELL
      CALL ERASE
      GOTO 5
   10 RADIUS = ((IX1-IXC)**2+(IY1-IYC)**2)**.5
      CALL ANGLES (IXC,IYC,IX1,IY1,START)
      CALL ANGLES (IXC,IYC,IX3,IY3,ENDPT)
      IF (ENDPT-START .LE. 0.) ENDPT=ENDPT+6.2832
      N=(20+0.4*RADIUS)*(ENDPT-START)/6.2832
      CALL DRWPOL (IXC,IYC,IX1,IY1,N,
     $START,ENDPT,RADIUS)
C ** DUMMY READ STATEMENT TO CREATE PAUSE **
      CALL ANMODE
      READ (5,25) IDUMMY
   25 FORMAT(A1)
      RETURN
      END


C ** DRAW POLYGON, CIRCLE OR ARC **
      SUBROUTINE DRWPOL (IXC,IYC,IX1,IY1,N,
     $START,ENDPT,RADIUS)
      CALL MOVABS(IX1,IY1)
      DTHETA=(ENDPT-START)/N
      DO 50 K=1,N
        IX=COS(START+K*DTHETA)*RADIUS+IXC
        IY=SIN(START+K*DTHETA)*RADIUS+IYC
        CALL DRWABS (IX,IY)
```

```
       50      CONTINUE
               RETURN
               END


C  ** CALCULATE ANGLE **
               SUBROUTINE ANGLES (IXC,IYC,IX1,IY1,ANGL)
               X=IX1-IXC
               Y=IY1-IYC
C  ** ERROR TRAP **
               IF (X .EQ. 0. .AND. Y .EQ. 0.) GOTO 10
C  ** CALCULATION **
               ANGL=ATAN2 (Y,X)
               IF (Y .LT. 0.) ANGL=ANGL+6.2832
               GOTO 999
       10      ANGL=0
      999      RETURN
               END


C  ** CALCULATE CENTER OF 3 POINT ARC **
               SUBROUTINE CENTER (IX1,IY1,IX2,IY2,
              1IX3,IY3,IXC,IYC,NOARC)
               REAL M1,M2
               CALL ARCTST (IX1,IY1,IX2,IY2,IX3,IY3,
              2IXC,IYC,NOARC)
               GOTO (10,20,30,999),NOARC
       10      IF (IX2-IX1 .EQ. 0) THEN
                 M1=0
               ELSE
                 M1=-(1.0/(FLOAT(IY2-IY1)/FLOAT(IX2-IX1)))
               ENDIF
               IF (IX3-IX2 .EQ. 0) THEN
                 M2=0
               ELSE
                 M2=-(1.0/(FLOAT(IY3-IY2)/FLOAT(IX3-IX2)))
               ENDIF
               B1=(IY1+IY2)/2.0 - M1*((IX1+IX2)/2.0)
               B2=(IY2+IY3)/2.0 - M2*((IX2+IX3)/2.0)
               IXC=(B2-B1)/(M1-M2)
               IYC=M1*IXC + B1
               GOTO 999
       20      IF (IX3-IX2 .EQ. 0) THEN
                 M2=0
               ELSE
                 M2=-(1.0/(FLOAT(IY3-IY2)/FLOAT(IX3-IX2)))
               ENDIF
               B2=(IY2+IY3)/2.0 - M2*((IX2+IX3)/2.0)
               IXC=(IX1+IX2)/2.0
               IYC=M2*IXC+B2
               GOTO 999
       30      IF (IX2-IX1 .EQ. 0) THEN
                 M1=0
               ELSE
                 M1=-(1.0/(FLOAT(IY2-IY1)/FLOAT(IX2-IX1)))
               ENDIF
               B1=(IY1+IY2)/2.0 - M1*((IX1+IX2)/2.0)
               IXC=(IX2+IX3)/2.0
               IYC=M1*IXC+B1
      999      RETURN
               END


C  ** DETERMINE WHETHER POINTS CAN DEFINE AN ARC **
               SUBROUTINE ARCTST (IX1,IY1,IX2,IY2,IX3,IY3,
              1IXC,IYC,NOARC)
               NOARC=1
C  ** CHECK FOR THREE DIFFERENT POINTS **
               IF((IY3-IY2.EQ.0.AND.IX3-IX2.EQ.0).OR.
              1(IY2-IY1.EQ.0.AND.IX2-IX1.EQ.0).OR.
              1(IY3-IY1.EQ.0.AND.IX3-IX1.EQ.0)) THEN
```

```
            NOARC=4
            GOTO 999
         ENDIF
C ** NEXT, CHECK FOR TWO VERTICAL LINES **
         IF (IY3-IY2.EQ.0.AND.IY2-IY1.EQ.0) THEN
            NOARC=4
            GOTO 999
         ENDIF
C ** CHECK FOR ONE VERTICAL LINE **
         IF (IY2-IY1.EQ.0) NOARC=2
         IF (IY3-IY2.EQ.0) NOARC=3
         IF (NOARC .EQ. 2 .OR. NOARC .EQ. 3) GOTO 999
C ** CHECK FOR PARALLEL LINES **
         IF (FLOAT(IY3-IY2)/FLOAT(IX3-IX2).EQ.FLOAT(IY2-IY1)
        1/FLOAT(IX2-IX1)) NOARC=4
     999 RETURN
         END
```

BASIC code (IBM PC version):

```
10 REM **** DRAWING PROGRAM ****
30 SCREEN 2:FACTOR=2.5
70 GOSUB 4000
80 SCREEN 0
90 END


4000 REM ** SUBROUTINE TO INPUT COORDINATES **
4010 REM ** OF THREE-POINT ARC **
4020 REM ** COORDINATES ENTERED FROM KEYBOARD **
4050 INPUT "ENTER STARTING POINT (X1,Y1)";X1,Y1
4060 INPUT "ENTER NEXT POINT    (X2,Y2)";X2,Y2
4070 INPUT "ENTER ENDING POINT  (X3,Y3)";X3,Y3
4072 X1=X1/FACTOR:X2=X2/FACTOR:X3=X3/FACTOR:
     GOSUB 6000
4073 X1=X1*FACTOR:X2=X2*FACTOR:X3=X3*FACTOR:
     XC=XC*FACTOR
4074 IF ARCTYP=4 THEN BEEP:GOTO 4050
4080 RADIUS=SQR(((X1-XC)/FACTOR)^2+(Y1-YC)^2)
4090 XX=X1:YY=Y1:GOSUB 5100
4100 START=ANGL
4110 XX=X3:YY=Y3:GOSUB 5100
4120 ENDPT=ANGL:IF ENDPT-START<=0 THEN
     ENDPT=ENDPT+6.2832
4140 N=INT((20+.4*RADIUS)*(ENDPT-START)/6.2832)
4150 GOSUB 4200
4160 PAUS$=INKEY$:IF PAUS$="" THEN GOTO 4160
4190 RETURN


4200 REM ** SUBROUTINE TO DRAW POLYGON OR CIRCLE **
4210 REM
4240 X1=COS(START)*RADIUS*FACTOR+XC
4250 Y1=SIN(START)*RADIUS+YC
4260 PRESET (X1,Y1)
4270 DTHETA=(ENDPT-START)/N
4280 FOR K=1 TO N
4290   X=COS(START+K*DTHETA)*RADIUS*FACTOR+XC
4300   Y=SIN(START+K*DTHETA)*RADIUS+YC
4320   LINE -(X,Y)
4340   NEXT K
4350 LINE -(X3,Y3)
4390 RETURN


5100 REM ** SUBROUTINE TO CALCULATE ANGLE **
5150 IF XX-XC=0 THEN IF YY>YC THEN ANGL=1.5708
     :GOTO 5190 ELSE ANGL=4.7124:GOTO 5190
5160 ANGL=ATN((YY-YC)/((XX-XC)/FACTOR))
5170 IF XX-XC<0 THEN ANGL=ANGL+3.1416
5190 RETURN
```

```
6000 REM ** SUBROUTINE TO CALCULATE CENTER **
6010 REM ** OF 3-POINT ARC **
6020 GOSUB 6400
6030 ON ARCTYP GOTO 6040,6110,6160,6390
6040 IF X2-X1=0 THEN M1=0 ELSE M1=-(1/((Y2-Y1)/(X2-X1)))
6050 IF X3-X2=0 THEN M2=0 ELSE M2=-(1/((Y3-Y2)/(X3-X2)))
6060 B1=(Y1+Y2)/2 - M1*((X1+X2)/2)
6070 B2=(Y2+Y3)/2 - M2*((X2+X3)/2)
6080 XC=(B2-B1)/(M1-M2)
6090 YC=M1*XC+B1
6100 GOTO 6390
6110 IF X3-X2=0 THEN M2=0 ELSE M2=-(1/((Y3-Y2)/(X3-X2)))
6120 B2=(Y2+Y3)/2 - M2*((X2+X3)/2)
6130 XC=(X1+X2)/2
6135 YC=M2*XC+B2
6150 GOTO 6390
6160 IF X2-X1=0 THEN M1=0 ELSE M1=-(1/((Y2-Y1)/(X2-X1)))
6170 B1=(Y1+Y2)/2 - M1*((X1+X2)/2)
6180 XC=(X2+X3)/2
6190 YC=M1*XC+B1
6390 RETURN

6400 REM ** SUBROUTINE TO DETERMINE WHETHER **
6410 REM ** POINTS CAN DEFINE AN ARC **
6420 ARCTYP=1
6430 REM ** CHECK FOR THREE DIFFERENT POINTS **
6440 IF (Y3-Y2=0 AND X3-X2=0) OR (Y2-Y1=0 AND X2-X1=0)
     OR (Y3-Y1=0 AND X3-X1=0) THEN ARCTYP=4:GOTO 6550
     ELSE GOTO 6460
6450 REM ** NEXT, CHECK FOR TWO VERTICAL LINES **
6460 IF Y3-Y2=0 AND Y2-Y1=0 THEN ARCTYP=4:GOTO 6550 ELSE GOTO 6480
6470 REM ** CHECK FOR ONE VERTICAL LINE **
6480 IF Y2-Y1=0 THEN ARCTYP=2
6490 IF Y3-Y2=0 THEN ARCTYP=3
6500 IF ARCTYP =2 OR ARCTYP=3 THEN GOTO 6550
6510 REM ** CHECK FOR PARALLEL LINES **
6520 IF X3-X2=0 AND X2-X1=0 THEN ARCTYP=4:GOTO 6550
6530 IF X3-X2=0 OR X2-X1=0 THEN GOTO 6550
6540 IF (Y3-Y2)/(X3-X2)=((Y2-Y1)/(X2-X1)) THEN ARCTYP=4
6550 RETURN
```

The program for this example has also been coded in BASIC for the Apple II (see Appendix A) and for the Tektronix 4051/52 (see Appendix B).

Both of these methods for drawing an arc have a weakness: Each defines two semicircles or arcs, one to be drawn and the other not. The problem is to make sure our routine draws the correct one. This problem is resolved by specifying the points in a set order. The center, if used, is specified first. If the curve is to be drawn in a counterclockwise direction around the center—as in Figure 6-1—the beginning, intermediate (if used), and ending point must be specified in counterclockwise order. If, however, the curve will be drawn in a clockwise direction, the order of input must be reversed.

A further problem that will sometimes be encountered when drawing an arc is that the trigonometric functions used to determine beginning and ending angles will sometimes return an ending angle that is less than the beginning angle. Figure 6-5 shows a case where the beginning angle is in the first quadrant and is thus positive. The ending angle, however, is in the fourth quadrant and is returned as a negative value. The system must test for this problem and, if it is found, the values of the angles must be adjusted.

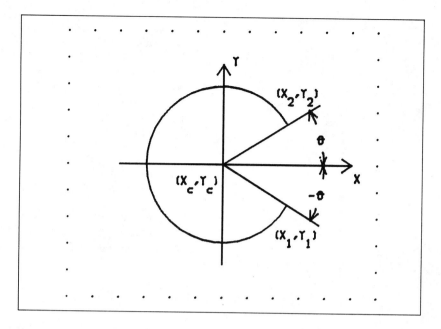

Figure 6-5.

Another Drawing Routine

All of our regular polygons, circles, and arcs have been drawn with the same routine, based on calculating the ending point of each successive line segment using the sine and cosine functions. While this method is very effective, the need to calculate the sine and cosine for each of the many line segments in a circle makes the drawing process relatively slow. We will now examine another approach that depends on calculating the sine and cosine of only the incremental angle $d\theta$. The sine and cosine calculations need to be performed only once to draw the figure.

The equation of a circle with its center at (X_c, Y_c) is

$$(X - X_c)^2 + (Y - Y_c)^2 = r^2$$

where X and Y are the coordinates of any point on the circle, X_c and Y_c are the coordinates of the center, and r is the radius.

From trigonometry we know:

$$\frac{X_n - X_c}{r} = \cos\theta \qquad \frac{X_{n+1} - X_c}{r} = \cos(\theta + d\theta)$$

$$\frac{Y_n - Y_c}{r} = \sin\theta \qquad \frac{Y_{n+1} - Y_c}{r} = \sin(\theta + d\theta)$$

But:

$$\cos(\theta + d\theta) = \cos\theta \times \cos d\theta - \sin\theta \times \sin d\theta$$

and:

$$\sin(\theta + d\theta) = \cos\theta \times \sin d\theta + \sin\theta \times \cos d\theta$$

So by substituting and simplifying we have:

$$X_{n+1} = X_c + (X_n - X_c)\cos d\theta - (Y_n - Y_c)\sin d\theta$$

and:

$$Y_{n+1} = Y_c + (X_n - X_c)\sin d\theta + (Y_n - Y_c)\cos d\theta$$

where (X_{n+1}, Y_{n+1}) is the coordinate of the line end to which we are drawing and (X_n, Y_n) is the coordinate of the starting point of the line (the end of the previous line). Substituting these equations into our FORTRAN drawing code we have:

```
C ** DRAW CIRCLE **
      SUBROUTINE DRWPOL (IXC,IYC,IX1,IY1,N,
     1START,ENDPT,RADIUS)
      CALL MOVABS(IX1,IY1)
      DTHETA=(ENDPT-START)/N
      COSDTH=COS(DTHETA)
      SINDTH=SIN(DTHETA)
      IXN=IX1
      IYN=IY1
      DO 50 K=1,N
        IX=IXC+(IXN-IXC)*COSDTH-(IYN-IYC)*SINDTH
        IY=IYC+(IXN-IXC)*SINDTH+(IYN-IYC)*COSDTH
        CALL DRWABS (IX,IY)
        IXN=IX
        IYN=IY
   50   CONTINUE
C ** DUMMY READ STATEMENT TO CREATE PAUSE **
      CALL ANMODE
      READ (5,25) IDUMMY
   25 FORMAT(A1)
      RETURN
      END
```

Since the grid system of the display used for the BASIC version of our code is not square, it is necessary to remap the coordinates to a square system before performing the calculations. This is accomplished in statement 4265 of the following code. The calculated values are mapped back to the system's grid in statement 4310 for drawing purposes. However, the system continues to perform calculations in the square grid system.

BASIC code (IBM PC version):

```
4200 REM ** SUBROUTINE TO DRAW POLYGON OR CIRCLE **
4210 REM
4240 X1=COS(START)*RADIUS*FACTOR+XC
4250 Y1=SIN(START)*RADIUS+YC
4260 PRESET (X1,Y1)
4265 XN=(X1-XC)/FACTOR+XC:YN=Y1
4270 DTHETA=(ENDPT-START)/N
4272 COSDTH=COS(DTHETA)
4274 SINDTH=SIN(DTHETA)
```

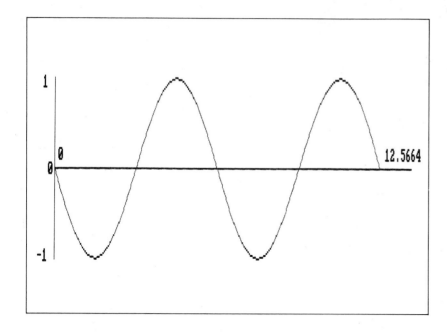

Figure 6-6A.

```
4280 FOR K=1 TO N
4290   X=XC+(XN-XC)*COSDTH-(YN-YC)*SINDTH
4300   Y=YC+(XN-XC)*SINDTH+(YN-YC)*COSDTH
4310   XD=(X-XC)*FACTOR+XC:YD=Y
4320   LINE -(XD,YD)
4330   XN=X:YN=Y
4340   NEXT K
4360 PAUS$=INKEY$:IF PAUS$="" THEN GOTO 4360
4390 RETURN
```

The program for this example has also been coded in BASIC for the Apple II (see Appendix A) and for the Tektronix 4051/52 (see Appendix B).

Curves

Circles and circular arcs are only two of the many types of curves that are encountered in graphics. Some of the other types that will be encountered behave according to a known formula and some do not. Those in which the relationship of the X coordinate and Y coordinate of each point can be reduced to a formula include ellipses and elliptical arcs, parabolas, hyperbolas, trigonometric relationships (such as the familiar sine wave), and logarithmic relationships (such as $Y = X^3$).

Figure 6-6A shows the plot of two cycles of the sine wave $Y = \sin(X)$. The curve was generated by evaluating the formula for values of X ranging from 0 degrees to 720 degrees (0 to 4π radians) at X intervals of 0.2616 ($\pi/12$ radians). Since the sine of any angle varies between $+1$ and -1, the value of $\sin(X)$ will never be greater than 1 nor less than -1 and the curve will always be continuous (no sharp changes of direction).

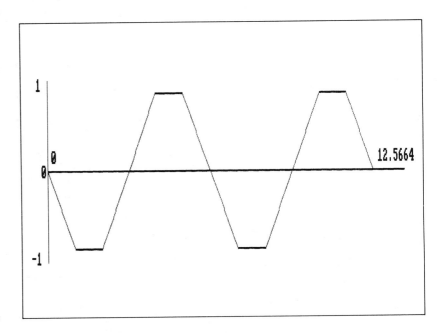

Figure 6-6B.

In order that the plot be large enough to see on our graphics screen (resolution 1024 × 780) and to be able to display the negative half of the Y values, we mapped the curve to the screen using an X scale of 40 pixels per unit, a Y scale of 50 pixels per unit, and an origin located at screen coordinates (50,99). If we drew this curve on our graphics screen by evaluating the formula at X intervals of 1.0464 ($\pi/3$) radians we would get a very poor representation of the actual curve (see Figure 6-6B). At the other extreme, we could evaluate the formula for X at intervals of 0.001 radians and plot all of the points. The resulting curve would be very accurate but its production would be extremely slow. Unless we are using exceptionally high-resolution equipment, the accuracy of the data could still be compromised by the system. Our chosen interval size is a compromise that produces a realistic curve in a reasonable length of time.

Let us now look at the code that was used to create the plot. Remember that the parameters used were (1) an X scale, (2) a Y scale, (3) a new origin, (4) minimum and maximum values of the independent variable x for which the equation was to be evaluated (thus defining the *range*), and (5) the interval at which x was to be evaluated. These parameters are defined as constants in our code but could be defined as variables to be entered by the user or to be calculated by the system to fit the curve to the data.

In the following FORTRAN code, the screen resolution is assumed to be 1024 × 780. The X scale is set at 64, the Y scale at 195, and the origin at (80,390) to get the same picture size and placement as on the 640 × 200 screen:

```
C ** DRAW SINE WAVE **
C ** A SUBROUTINE ACCESSED FROM A MAIN PROGRAM **
      SUBROUTINE DRWSIN
      CALL MOVABS (80,195)
      CALL DRWABS (80,585)
      CALL MOVABS (80,390)
      CALL DRWABS (960,390)
      CALL MOVABS (80,390)
      X=0
      DO 50 K=1,48
        X=X+0.2617
        Y=SIN (X)
        IY=195*Y+390
        IX=64*X+80
        CALL DRWABS (IX,IY)
  50    CONTINUE
C ** DUMMY READ STATEMENT TO CREATE PAUSE **
      CALL ANMODE
      READ (5,25) IDUMMY
  25  FORMAT(A1)
      RETURN
      END
```

In the following BASIC code (IBM PC version), values have been adjusted to maintain proper scale in the drawing. In addition, the value of Y is changed to $-Y$ to invert the image because our screen had the origin in the upper-left corner:

```
11000 REM ** SINEWAVE DRAWING SUBROUTINE **
11010 REM ** ACCESSED FROM A MAIN PROGRAM **
11020 REM ** SYSTEM ALREADY IN GRAPHICS MODE **
11030 LINE (50,49)-(50,199)
11040 LINE (50,99)-(600,99)
11050 PRESET (50,99)
11060 FOR X=0 TO 12.5664 STEP .2617
11070     Y=SIN (X)
11080     YD= -50*Y + 99
11090     XD=  40*X + 50
11100     LINE -(XD,YD),1
11110     NEXT X
11120 PAUS$=INKEY$:IF PAUS$="" THEN GOTO 11120
11130 RETURN
```

The program for this example has also been coded in BASIC for the Apple II (see Appendix A) and for the Tektronix 4051/52 (see Appendix B).

Many other curves, such as a line of constant elevation on a surveyor's map, do not follow any set pattern and so must be produced by entering data into the system one point at a time. Often the data are recorded in the field by taking measurements. Since it is impractical to record every data point—for instance, every point in the area a surveyor is mapping—data are often recorded at selected intervals and the values between these intervals are assumed to follow some fixed pattern. Sometimes, for convenience, data points are connected by straight lines. Table 6-1 shows a set of data that depicts the outline of an irregular area. The data are plotted in Figure 6-7A on an X-Y coordinate system.

Table 6-1.

Point No.	X_i	Y_i
1	300	350
2	400	550
3	800	350
4	650	150
5	450	50
6	200	150
7	50	350
8	200	400

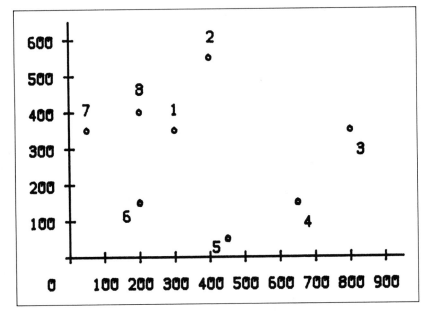

Figure 6-7A.

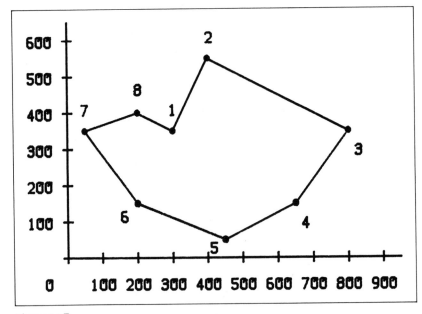

Figure 6-7B.

In Figure 6-7B the points have been connected by straight lines. While the resulting plot may be a reasonable representation of the relationship of the X and Y values over the range of the plot, the surface of the earth is not generally discontinuous (does not change direction abruptly) at each plotted point, nor is the surface contour between points really a straight line. The quality of the plot could be

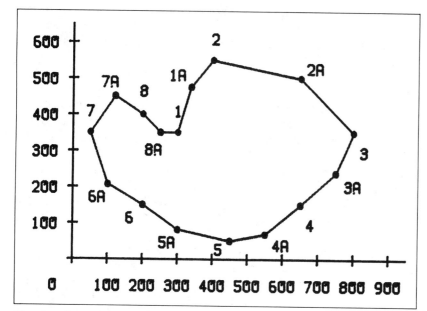

Figure 6-7 C.

Table 6-2.

Point No.	X_i	Y_i
1	300	350
1A	340	475
2	400	550
2A	650	500
3	800	350
3A	750	240
4	650	150
4A	550	70
5	450	50
5A	350	80
6	200	150
6A	100	200
7	50	350
7A	125	450
8	200	400
8A	250	350

improved by plotting in more data points if they are available. Figure 6-7C shows the plot of Figure 6-7B with additional data points (see Table 6-2). More points may not be available, in which case the curve might be improved by developing a more reasonable projection of what happens between known points.

Curve Smoothing
The data that are gathered by making measurements in the field are often distorted by inaccuracies of measurement caused either by human error or by the limitations of the measuring equipment being used. We know that the data should conform to a particular pattern—a straight line relationship, a trigonometric or logarithmic relationship, or simply a continuous curve (with no sharp breaks) over the range of the data. A number of techniques have been developed for creating "smoother," more realistic curves to match these patterns. One of the most used techniques is called the moving average. This technique will be discussed in Chapter 7 as part of the presentation on charts and graphs.

Fitting Curves to Data
Sometimes there is an expected relationship between the X and Y values of a set of data. The expected relationship may be linear, for instance, or it may be logarithmic. Or the data may be expected to conform to a certain pattern, such as the binomial distribution or the Poisson distribution used in statistical analysis. In these cases we often assume that the data really do conform to that pattern and that any nonconformities are due to errors in measurement. It is common

practice to draw the expected curve form through the data in such a way as to create the fewest and smallest deviations between the plotted data and the hypothetical curve. This is known as *curve fitting*.

A common curve-fitting technique, when the data are expected to be linear, is known as the *method of least squares*. This is an arithmetic technique in which a straight line is superimposed on the data in a location such that the square of all the deviations of the actual points from the line is the minimum possible value. Once the equation of the optimum line is determined, it is easy to solve it for a point at the lower limit of the data and another at the upper limit of the data and then draw a line between the two points. Of course, the two points do not have to be at the data limits, but this will result in a more accurately drawn line.

We are now able to create points, lines, rectangles, regular polygons, circles, and circular arcs on the display screen. In addition, we are able to create curves and irregular polygons through repeated use of the line-drawing routine. In Chapter 7 we will use these capabilities to create graphs and charts and will add lettering of titles and labels. Chapter 7 will also introduce the subjects of data storage and retrieval, modification of the drawing, and scaling. These topics will be developed further in Chapters 8, 9, and 10, respectively.

Up to this point all data entry has been from the keyboard. Interactive drafting programs, however, need a means of working directly on the screen to make menu selections, enter data, and create graphics entities. Such drafting programs typically use digitizing tablets, light pens, or graphics cross hairs controlled by joysticks, thumbwheels, or keypads to perform these functions. Programming the system to use these devices will be covered in Chapter 11.

Exercises

1. Write a subroutine to draw circles on your system. Determine the adjustment factor that must be applied to the X-coordinate values to obtain a true circle on your display screen.

2. Write a subroutine on your system to calculate the starting angle for a circle. Modify this routine to work for any angle to be determined from two points.

3. Modify the circle subroutine to draw circular arcs on your system. Does your subroutine draw the correct portion of the circle?

4. Write a main program on your system that calls a data-input subroutine, an angle-calculation subroutine, and the circle-drawing subroutine.

5. Modify the routines of exercise 4 to work for arcs.

6. Write a subroutine to draw the curves for

$$Y = X^2$$
$$Y = X^3$$
$$Y = X^2 - 5X$$

Use the limits $X = -8$ to $X = +8$.

7. Modify the subroutines of Exercise 6 to permit the user to enter the desired minimum and maximum X values from the keyboard.

8. Write a main program that will call the subroutines (developed in Exercises 6 and 7) that will allow you to input data, to draw circles to indicate data points, and to plot the curve.

9. Write the circle subroutine using the incremental angle, $d\theta$, method.

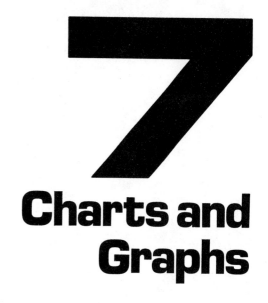

Charts and Graphs

Charts and graphs are among the most useful tools available to the professional in any discipline. They show at a glance information that might otherwise require hours of study to obtain. They are easy to read and easy to understand. Pictures transcend language barriers, technical terminology, and deficiencies in basic reading skills. That is why so many signs in buildings and on our streets and highways use pictures to present their messages.

One weakness of charts and graphs is that they are not precise—it is not always easy or even possible to read a data point to a high degree of accuracy. This shortcoming can often be remedied by printing important values on the chart. The main purpose of charts and graphs, however, is to show relationships and trends, and they do this very well. Precise values can always be obtained by studying the supporting data.

Another shortcoming of charts is that the data are not readily usable in calculations. They must first be read and quantified. Any errors in reading or interpreting the data will affect the subsequent calculations. For this reason, the supporting data should be used whenever possible for calculations.

Uses of Charts and Graphs

A serious attempt to list all of the uses of charts and graphs would probably fill several volumes. They are used in games of all types, from football to computer games. Business executives, physicians, educators, engineers, and scientists are but a few of the professionals who use them regularly in their occupations.

Business executives use charts to present a wide variety of information in easily understood form: to show sales, market share, profit margins, sources and uses of funds, and trends in all of these areas. The business executive looking at a sales chart can tell immediately whether sales are improving and whether they are following the expected trend for the period.

Physicians use charts to follow a patient's progress. Charts are used to keep track of a patient's temperature, blood pressure, weight, and, in the hospital, such vital signs as pulse and respiration.

Educators use charts to present many types of information, and students involved in laboratory experiments often find that their reports require a chart of some kind.

Engineers and scientists find charts invaluable for analyzing manufacturing processes, for studying performance characteristics, and for a variety of other analytical procedures.

Types of Charts and Graphs

There are many types of charts. Indeed, it seems that every use has its own chart form. Most types, however, are variations on one of four basic types: the pie chart, the line or curve chart, the bar or column chart, and the map. Surface charts, often thought of as a fifth chart type, are really variations of line or bar charts.

Pie charts are generally used to show the relative impact each element of an entity has on the whole. The chart is drawn in the form of a circle, or pie, which is then subdivided into segments, or slices, to represent the individual elements. Figure 7-1 is a pie chart representation of a budget. The size of each slice of the pie is proportional to the percentage of the budget dollar that is allocated to the item represented by that slice.

Line charts, also called curve charts, are used to show the relationship between two variables. A line chart has a horizontal axis, called the abscissa, and a vertical axis, called the ordinate. Each value plotted has to have two coordinates, one for each axis. Line charts are particularly useful for plotting data in relationship to time. For example, the flight of a rocket might be recorded by using the abscissa to represent time from lift-off. The ordinate could record the acceleration, speed, distance traveled, or other data. Sometimes it is desirable to plot more than one curve on a chart, in which case it may be necessary to establish multiple scales on the ordinate. Figure 7-2 shows a plot of the data in Table 7-1 for a rocket flight.

Bar charts, like line charts, show the relationship between two variables. Some writers distinguish between charts with horizontal bars and those with vertical bars, calling the latter column charts. Both types will be called bar charts in this chapter. Figure 7-3 shows a bar chart with horizontal bars and Figure 7-4 shows a bar chart with vertical bars.

Whereas line charts connect all data points with straight lines or

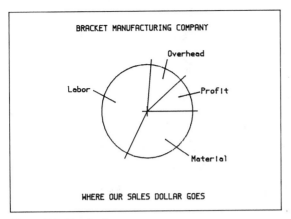

Figure 7-1. Pie chart.

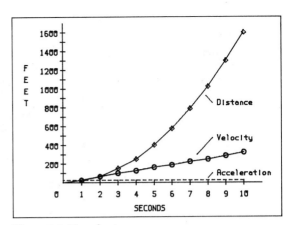

Figure 7-2. Line chart.

Table 7-1. Rocket Flight Data

Time (seconds)	Acceleration (ft/sec/sec)	Velocity (ft/sec)	Distance (feet)
0	32	0	0
1	32	32	16
2	32	64	64
3	32	96	144
4	32	128	256
5	32	160	400
6	32	192	576
7	32	224	784
8	32	256	1024
9	32	288	1296
10	32	320	1600

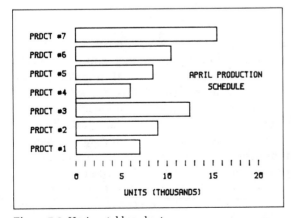

Figure 7-3. Horizontal bar chart.

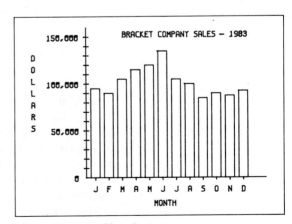

Figure 7-4. Vertical bar chart.

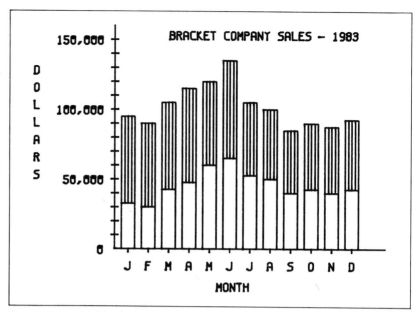

Figure 7-5. Stacked bar chart.

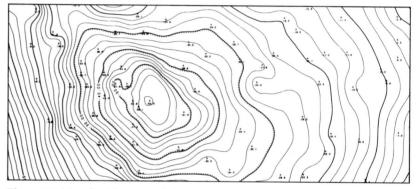

Figure 7-6. Map chart (contour plot).

with a continuous curve, bar charts have separate bars for each X-Y coordinate pair. As a result, line charts convey continuous data while bar charts are better used to present discontinuous or discrete data. Plots of the rocket flight presented in Figure 7-2 would not be appropriate with bar charts. Representative uses for bar charts in industry include production schedules and sales comparisons. Dual or stacked bar charts are sometimes used to present data in a manner similar to that used in pie charts: Each bar can be made to represent the equivalent of the whole pie and can be subdivided to show the relative weights of the parts that make up the whole (see Figure 7-5).

Maps, as their name implies, are used to convey data with geographic significance. Figure 7-6 shows a contour plot, a common

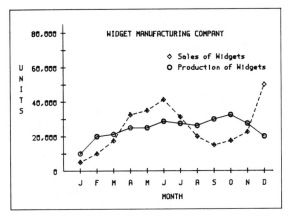

Figure 7-7. Line chart with two lines.

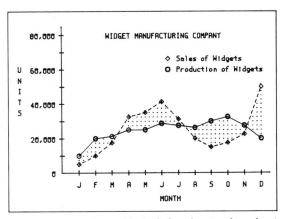

Figure 7-8. Line chart with shaded surface (surface chart).

type of map. Weather forecasters make extensive use of map charts to show temperatures, rainfall, and other meteorological information. Businesses often use map charts to show geographic areas in which they have sales offices, the geographic makeup of their total sales, or similar information. You should be aware of the uses of map charts, even though we will not cover them in as much detail as the other types of charts.

Surface charts are particularly useful for conveying a feeling of volume. As we mentioned, surface charts are adaptations of bar or line charts. Figure 7-7 shows a line chart with two lines, one representing production of widgets and the other representing sales of widgets. The difference between the quantities represented by these two lines is an increase or decrease in inventory of widgets in the warehouse. During periods when sales exceed production, inventory decreases. When production exceeds sales, inventory increases. Figure 7-8 shows this same chart with the space between the two lines shaded to represent a surface. Note that the shading makes it much easier to see the effect on inventory as production and sales fluctuate.

Subtasks in a Chart-Drawing Routine

The process of drawing a chart can be divided into a number of subtasks, each of which can be accomplished relatively independently of the others. Approaching the task in this way will permit each subtask to be written as a separate routine and tested independently of the other subtask routines.

Creation of charts and graphs typically begins with information (data) that is to be presented in graphic form. The type of chart to be used is chosen on the basis of the nature of the data and the manner and purpose of the presentation. The data will then be restructured as necessary to suit the type of chart, chart labels and titles will be chosen, the chart form will be drawn and labeled, and, finally, the data will be plotted. If the finished chart is not acceptable, it will need to be modified through editing techniques.

Choosing a Chart Type

As we have mentioned, each type of chart is best suited to presenting a particular type of information. When choosing a chart type, make sure that the nature of the data you wish to present is consistent with the nature of the chart you choose.

Pie charts are used to represent the parts that make up an entire quantity. For example, a pie chart could be used to show the division of total car sales into compact, intermediate, full-size, and limousine categories. Another use for a pie chart would be to show the proportional distribution of our tax dollar among various government agencies.

Bar charts are useful when comparing numbers, such as sales of different automobile manufacturers for a particular car size, the yield strengths of various alloys, or the clock speed of different microprocessors.

Line charts could be used to present such information as the load-equation curves for metal tensile specimens or to represent a chemical reaction coming to equilibrium. Each of these uses would require continuous lines, or smooth curves. Broken-line charts could show monthly sales of microcomputers, where one month's sales are not mathematically related to the previous month's sales.

Surface charts are used to represent the difference between two or more quantities. A surface chart comparing sales and inventories could provide valuable information about added manufacturing costs when inventories are high.

Entering the Data

Once you have chosen a chart type, the next task in a computer-based chart-drawing routine is to enter the data. The entire process of drawing the chart is dependent upon the data. Most chart data entries will have two parts, the first part being the independent variable. In the case of X-Y type charts, such as line or vertical bar charts, the independent variable is the X-axis locational information. In the case of a pie chart, this first part of the data will be the identification of the particular element, or slice of the pie. For either type chart, the independent variable may be either string data or numeric data.

The second part of the data is the value of the element being charted. In the case of the line or vertical bar chart, it is the Y-axis value. In the case of the pie chart, it is the information for calculating the size of the slice. In all cases this information is usually numeric. Both parts of each entry should be retained as a pair for each data element.

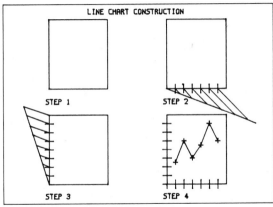

Figure 7-9. Line-chart construction.

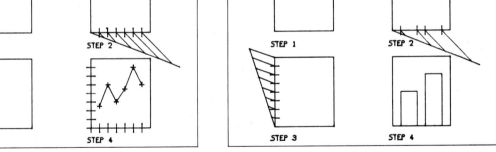

Figure 7-10. Bar-chart construction.

Entering Labels and Titles

Every chart, to be understandable, must have labels and titles. Line and bar charts generally have labels for the X axis and the Y axis. In addition, the data points may be labled finally. Of course, the chart needs a title.

In pie charts, labels are used to identify each slice of the pie and value labels are provided to show the size of the slice. Pie charts often have two chart titles (see Figure 7-1), one to tell who or what organization the chart is for and they other to tell what information is being presented.

When entering labels and titles, you need some means of controlling what labels and titles you wish to use. Computer charting routines are inherently less flexible in this regard than manual methods. The amount of variation provided may range all the way from none (you must use the number and types of labels and titles the system is programmed to accept) to very flexible systems (you can enter whatever you want and position each item precisely by use of a cross-hair graphics cursor or light pen). Of course, the complexity of the program will increase with the amount of flexibility provided.

Drawing the Chart

When all of the data have been entered, it is time to draw the chart. If the drawing were being done manually, your first step would be to draw the form on which the chart is to be created. If it is to be a line or bar chart, the first thing you need is a set of axes. If it is to be a pie chart, you might draw a circle to represent the pie. Figures 7-9, 7-10, and 7-11 show how the line, bar, and pie charts might be drawn.

Your next step might be to develop a scale. In the case of a line or bar chart, you must develop scales for both the X axis and the Y axis. The X-axis scale is usually the easiest to develop, since you normally take the space available and divide it by the number of elements to

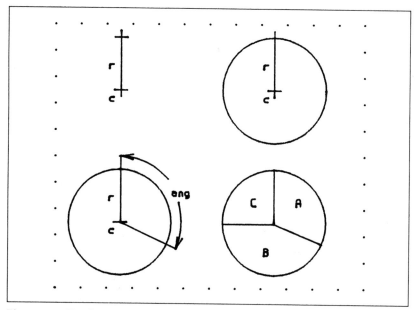

Figure 7-11. Pie-chart construction.

be plotted to get the space to be allotted to each element. The Y-axis scale is somewhat more difficult. Generally, you should choose a scale that will just accommodate the largest data values, and you should set the minimum value at zero, unless there are negative values to be accounted for or unless there is good reason to set the minimum at some other value. The *range*—the difference between the minimum and the maximum values—must be subdivided into a convenient number of parts. Unless the data values are very small, you should make each increment a whole number and present the values in a manner that will make it easy for the reader to extract information from the chart. When the scale has been developed, mark each increment with a short line perpendicular to the axis and print its value next to the mark. Do this for both axes.

With the axes marked, you are now ready to plot the data. To do so, select one element of the data pair and find its coordinate on the appropriate axis. Then go perpendicular to that axis until you are opposite the point on the second axis that represents the second data element. Finally, mark the spot. Repeat this procedure for each data pair.

When all of the points have been plotted, you are ready to complete the plot by connecting the points (line chart) or drawing the bars (bar chart). The last step is to add the labels and titles. Note that axis labels have already been completed.

Pie charts are scaled somewhat differently from line and bar charts. The scale is determined by taking the total angular measure of the pie (2π radians if the pie is to be drawn as a full circle) and dividing by the total of all the data elements to get the number of data units per unit of angular measure. Consequently, the scale cannot be calculated until all of the data have been entered. Each segment of the pie can then be laid out and lines drawn to define the segments. Labels and titles are added after the pie is completed.

Drawing the chart on the computer is not much different from doing it manually. Normally an algorithm is built into the program to determine the appropriate scales to use. You are generally given the option of selecting your own scales and increments or of letting the computer make the selection. The computer also typically decides where to place the labels and titles but is subject to being overruled by the users during editing.

Editing the Data

Editing is an important capability in any charting routine. You may often need to correct values or the spelling of string data, to change the arrangement or order of the data, or to delete some data pairs and add others. In addition, editing capability allows time-series charts to be added to each time period without having to reenter the existing data.

As with data entry, there are a number of ways data-correction capability can be built into the program. One procedure is to have the program display each entry in sequence and ask the user whether it is to be modified. This is relatively easy to program and is satisfactory from the user's standpoint if there are few data. However, if the chart has a great deal of data it will be very time consuming to review every entry in order to make one or two changes. In situations where there are many data and where each pair is identifiable, a more satisfactory editing routine is to permit the user to enter the data pair to be changed along with the change to be made. The system then replaces the old values with the new ones or, if the data pair is to be eliminated, removes it and, if necessary, closes up the space that is created.

Rearrangement of the data is often desirable in order to improve the chart's appearance, readability, or accuracy. Pie charts with many segments are often improved by intermixing the small and large segments so that very small segments are not located next to each other. Line or bar charts may have had their data entered in the wrong order. If rearrangement is to involve moving a large percentage of the data pairs, it may be easier to simply start at the beginning and reenter all of the data in the correct order. However, if only one or two data pairs are to be moved, an editing routine can be very valuable.

The key to rearranging data is to be able to identify the data pairs. There are a number of ways to do so. One is to assign a sequence number to each data pair as it is entered. The first pair is number 1, the next is number 2, and so on. Then, if a data pair is to be moved, the user can enter the number of that pair and the number of the pair either preceding or following the location to which it is to be moved.

Table 7-2. Chart Data

Number of Data Pair	First Element	Second Element
1	12	192
2	16	83
3	21	67
4	4	133
5	27	86
6	18	54
7	9	76
8	15	91
9	23	156
10	7	121

Table 7-3. Chart Data with Pointers

Number of Data Pair	First Element	Second Element	Pointer (next pair)
1	12	192	2
2	16	83	3
3	21	67	4
4	4	133	5
5	27	86	6
6	18	54	7
7	9	76	8
8	15	91	9
9	23	156	10
10	7	121	0

Of course, the numbers assigned to the data pairs will have to be reassigned to accommodate the move.

Suppose that the data in Table 7-2 are to be reorganized so that data pair number 7 will follow data pair number 3. To do this manually, you would change the number of data pair 7 to 4 and then change number 4 to number 5, 5 to 6, and 6 to 7. The procedure is similar on the computer, but since the computer does not have the same mental processes you do, it is necessary to follow a slightly different procedure to keep from losing data. Suppose that you establish a pair of temporary storage locations and store the data for pair number 7. Now you can move the data from number 6 to number 7, then from 5 to 6, and from 4 to 5. All that remains at this point is to transfer the original pair number 7 from temporary storage to location number 4.

Another technique that can be used is to assign each data pair an additional value whose function is to act as a pointer to record which pair follows it. Referring to Table 7-3, we see that you can now change the order so that number 7 follows number 3 by simply changing the pointer value of number 3 from 4 to 7 and changing the

Table 7-4. Chart Data with Data-Point Labels

Number of Data Pair	First Element	Second Element	Pointer (next pair)	Label
1	12	192	2	TG
2	16	83	3	BK
3	21	67	4	RS
4	4	133	5	DG
5	27	86	6	MM
6	18	54	7	QC
7	9	76	8	ND
8	15	91	9	SK
9	23	156	10	FW
10	7	121	0	BL

pointer value of number 7 from 8 to 4. The advantage of this technique over the previous one becomes more obvious as the number of points on the list of data grows: You can "move" a data pair by changing two pointers even if the list is hundreds of values long. Note that the pointer for pair number 10 is 0. This means that number 10 is the last pair.

Adding data to the list is a fairly simple procedure if the data are to go at the end of the list. Suppose, however, that you want to add a data pair to the list in Table 7-2 right after pair number 1. Again you are faced with moving each item in the list down one number to make room. If, however, you are using the list in Table 7-3, you can simply change the pointer on pair number 1 to 11, the location of the new data pair, and set the pointer on the new data pair to 2. Procedures for storing and retrieving data will be covered later in this chapter and again in greater detail in Chapter 8.

Editing the Labels and Titles

Sometimes the labels and titles come out just right the first time. More often, however, you will want to make changes to improve the appearance of the chart or to add detail or correct errors. The procedures for correcting labels and titles are similar to those for editing data. A straightforward approach is for the computer to display the labels and titles in sequence and ask the user to approve them or else change them. If the labels correspond to data points, any change in the order of the data pairs will change the order of the corresponding labels. A useful technique for keeping track of the data-point labels is to store them with their corresponding data pair. Table 7-4 shows the data of Table 7-3 with the addition of data-point labels.

Storing the Data

If you were going to create a chart just one time, never change it, and never use the data again, there would be no reason to store the data. However, in nearly all cases, you will want to make changes to improve the chart, and you may also want to re-create the chart on a pen plotter or a printer plotter. Therefore, you will need to store the data as they are entered so that they can be reused. There are two places that the data can be stored: in main memory or on a disk or tape. Temporary storage in main memory is probably the most convenient method and provides the fastest access. There are, however, some disadvantages to use of main memory for data storage. First, such storage takes up valuable working space. There might not be enough memory to store all the data that are needed. Second, main-memory storage is volatile—when the program terminates, the data are lost. The alternative is to store data permanently on magnetic disk or magnetic tape. Punch cards and punched paper tape are other means of storing data but are not used with interactive systems. In fact, magnetic tape is rarely used, except for long-term mass storage, because access is too slow. Magnetic disk, either hard disk or floppy, is the best storage medium for all but small amounts of data and is the only suitable permanent working storage for interactive systems.

Retrieving the Data

Once the information has been stored, retrieval is a matter of accessing the disk file or main memory locations and reading what has been stored. The key to successful data storage and retrieval is the organization of the data. If the data are well organized in accord with their natural structure, they will be easy to store and retrieve. Chapter 8 will present storage structures and the mechanics of using them in greater detail.

Adjusting the Chart Form

Adjustment of the chart form is a function of the editing process. In this process you are generally given the option of moving axes, changing diameter and/or location of the pie, changing the scale, and reworking the labels and titles.

Another very important adjustment that you might wish to make to the chart is in the plotted data. Often it is desirable to *smooth* the data to eliminate irregularities that detract from the information to be derived from the chart. For instance, the data in a line chart may be so inconsistent that the trend of the line is difficult to follow. Figure 7-12 shows such a chart. Figure 7-13 shows the same chart except that the line has been smoothed by a moving average calculation.

Many times measured data are compared to a theoretical distribution. In such cases the theoretical curve that best fits the data is calculated and is drawn on the chart instead of trying to draw a curve to connect the actual data. This is known as *curve fitting*.

Sometimes it is desirable to adjust the location or size of the chart. The scale may need to be altered to make the chart better fit the space, or the pie may need to be moved to make more room for text

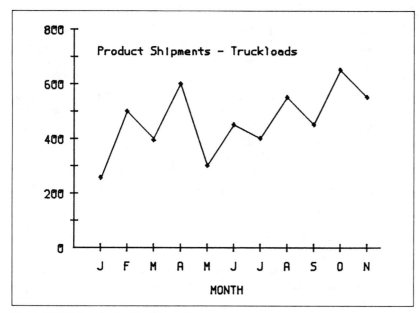

Figure 7-12. Line chart with data scatter.

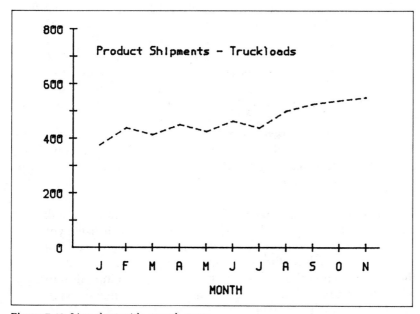

Figure 7-13. Line chart with smooth curve.

above, below, or beside it. The size of the pie may also need to be changed, or the axes on a line or bar chart to be moved. All of these changes are part of the editing procedures that should be built into the program. As with most procedures, these are not difficult to accomplish if the routines that create the features are modular and use variables for their parameters.

Data-Entry Techniques

When you sit down at the terminal, you will typically load a program and type RUN. You then expect to be given instructions, prompts, and maybe a menu of choices from which to select the desired task. Without these, you would be at a loss as to how to proceed. Your data-entry program should contain instructions and prompts of the type you would expect from someone else's program. You should be prompted for each item of data needed by the system.

Suppose a mistake is made in entering the data. What then? One possible outcome is that the program terminates with an error message and you have to start over again. A much better solution is for the program to contain an error-recovery routine that allows you to correct the error and then continue. Since the data being entered will be of various types, it may be necessary to have more than one error-recovery routine. Each such routine should provide you with a message describing the error and a list of the available recovery alternatives. The appropriate alternatives will vary depending on the nature of the program. A set that is often seen is: (1) REENTER, (2) IGNORE, (3) ABORT.

Occasionally, incorrect data will be entered that will not result in an error message. For instance, a character string may have a misspelled word or a number may have incorrect digits. In these cases, you will wish to correct the entry but the system will not offer you the chance. A user-initiated error-correction routine will solve this problem. Such routines are often called "undo" or "oops" routines. To initiate them, you press a key or key sequence that the system is programmed to recognize and act upon by branching to a recovery routine.

At the end of the data-entry process the system must branch to the next task or return to the menu. Recognition by the system of the end-of-data condition is generally programmed to occur in one of the following three ways:

1. The computer may request that you enter the number of data pairs before entering any data. When this technique is used, you can simply use the entered number as the number of repetitions of a loop. This method has the advantage of simplicity. A disadvantage is that you may enter the wrong number and then run into difficulty when the system will not accept all of the data or when the system insists on having more data than there are.

2. You may be asked, after each data pair is entered, whether there are more data. This approach is much more flexible since it permits you to enter as much data as you desire and to stop at any time. The primary disadvantage of this method is that it is slow and cumbersome. You have to respond to a YES/NO question for every data pair. This method also requires that you constantly read the screen to keep track of the prompts.

3. You may use a code to inform the system when all of the data have been entered. The code can be entered as one part of the data pair, but it must be something that would never be a part of a legitimate data entry. Many data pairs have string information as one part and numerical information as the other part. Entering a unique character string such as DONE would signal the system that all of the data have been entered. In the case of data where both parts of the pair are numeric, a value or pair of values that would not occur in legitimate data could be used as the code. Of course, the system must be programmed to test the data entries and recognize the agreed-upon code.

The following code (given in FORTRAN and BASIC) is an example of a routine to enter data. Which of the three methods we discussed does this code use to recognize the end of the data? Can you modify it to use one of the other methods?

FORTRAN code:

```
C ** ENTER DATA FOR PIE CHART **
        SUBROUTINE PIEDTA (VALUE,ELNAME,TOTAL,ENTRES)
        DIMENSION VALUE(25)
        CHARACTER*1 ELNAME(25,25),NAMWRK(25)
        TOTAL=0
        ENTRES=0
        CALL ANMODE
        WRITE (6,10) 'ENTER DATA FOR PIE CHART'
 10     FORMAT (' ',A50)
 20     FORMAT (25A1)
        DO 50 K=1,25
          CALL ANMODE
          WRITE (6,10) 'ENTER VALUE FOR ELEMENT (0 IF DONE)'
          READ (5,*) VALUE(K)
          IF (VALUE(K) .EQ. 0.) GOTO 999
          WRITE (6,10) 'ENTER NAME OF ELEMENT (MAX 25 CHARACTERS)'
          READ (5,20) NAMWRK
          DO 25 J=1,25
            ELNAME(K,J)=NAMWRK(J)
 25         CONTINUE
          TOTAL=TOTAL+VALUE(K)
          ENTRES=ENTRES+1
          CALL VMODE
          CALL ERASE
 50       CONTINUE
 999    RETURN
        END
```

BASIC code:

```
1200 REM *** SUBROUTINE TO ENTER DATA FOR PIE CHART ***
1205 REM *** DIMENSIONED FOR 25 ENTRIES MAXIMUM ***
1210 CLS:ENTRIES=0:TOTAL=0:K=0
1220 PRINT"ENTER DATA FOR PIE CHART":PRINT
1230 FOR K=1 TO 25
1240   INPUT "ENTER VALUE FOR ELEMENT (0 IF DONE) >";VALUE(K)
1250   IF VALUE(K)=0 THEN GOTO 1290
1260   INPUT "ENTER NAME OF ELEMENT >";NAM$(K)
1270   TOTAL=TOTAL+VALUE(K):ENTRIES=ENTRIES+1
1280   NEXT K
1290 RETURN
```

Some charts will require that more than one set of data be entered. For instance, a line chart for the flight of a rocket may have one line for acceleration, one for velocity, and one for distance, all as a function of time from launch. These data must be entered in sets. Most likely, the acceleration data would be one set, the velocity data another set, and the distance data a third set. Or, if the data are being entered as they are being generated, acceleration, velocity, and distance might be entered as a set for each time frame being plotted. In the first case, you might enter the number of sets to be plotted before starting data entry. In the latter case, since the number of sets might not be known before hand, you will need some means of signalling the system to exit data entry.

Label and Title Entry

Entry techniques for labels and titles are similar to those for data in that you are prompted for each entry. One difference, however, is that there are normally a set number of entries to make. Line and bar charts, for example, usually have a title for the abscissa, a title for the ordinate, and a chart title. You are always prompted for three entries. The following code (in FORTRAN and BASIC) is an example of a routine to enter chart names for a pie chart.

FORTRAN code:

```
C ** ENTER CHART NAMES FOR PIE CHART **
        SUBROUTINE CHRTNM (CHART)
        CHARACTER*1 CHART(2,50),CHRTWK(50)
        CALL ANMODE
        WRITE (6,*) 'ENTER NAME FOR   TOP  OF CHART'
        READ (5,10) CHRTWK
10      FORMAT (50A1)
          DO 25 J=1,50
            CHART(1,J)=CHRTWK(J)
25        CONTINUE
        WRITE (6,*) 'ENTER NAME FOR BOTTOM OF CHART'
        READ (5,10) CHRTWK
          DO 35 J=1,50
            CHART(2,J)=CHRTWK(J)
35        CONTINUE
        RETURN
        END
```

BASIC code:

```
1300 REM *** SUBROUTINE TO ENTER CHART NAMES FOR PIE CHART ***
1310 REM
1320 INPUT "ENTER NAME FOR   TOP  OF CHART >";CHART$(1)
1330 INPUT "ENTER NAME FOR BOTTOM OF CHART >";CHART$(2)
1340 RETURN
```

Drawing a Pie Chart

Let us now draw a pie chart. Table 7-5 shows the cost elements that make up the total manufacturing cost of widgets. Since the whole is the sum of its parts, this information is readily represented by a pie chart.

To construct the pie we first need to draw a circle. The circle

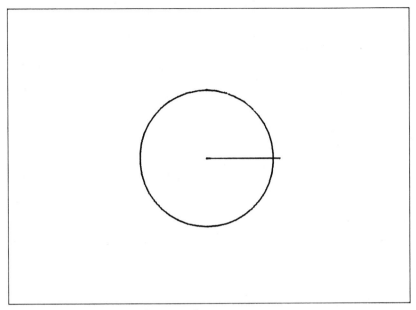

Figure 7-14. (A) Pie chart with starting line.

Table 7.5. Cost Elements for Widgets

Description	Cost	Percentage of Total
Raw material	2.28	20
Purchased parts	1.14	10
Packaging material	.57	5
Direct labor	4.56	40
Indirect cost	2.85	25
Total	11.40	100

routine of Chapter 6 can be employed to accomplish this task. Figure 7-14A shows the circle with one line drawn. This line is the beginning line from which the first cost element (slice) will be marked off.

Our next task is to establish a scale for the data. Adding up all of the cost elements, we find that the total cost is $11.40. Dividing this total by 6.28, the approximate number of radians in a circle, we find that one radian represents $1.82, or that $1.00 can be represented by about 0.55 radians. Multiplying our data in Table 7-5 by 0.55 radians/dollar, we get a new column (see Table 7-6) giving the angular measure of each slice of the pie. We can now calculate the coordinates of each line required to divide the pie into slices. To do this we will first draw a horizontal line from the pie's center to the rightmost edge, as shown in Figure 7-14A. Since the first slice is to be 1.26 radians in size, the end point of the next line will have the coordinates $X_1 = X_c + r \times \cos(1.26)$ and $Y_1 = Y_c + r \times \sin(1.26)$, where X_c and Y_c are the X and Y coordinates of the center and r is the radius of the circle. We can now draw the line from (X_c, Y_c) to (X_1, Y_1).

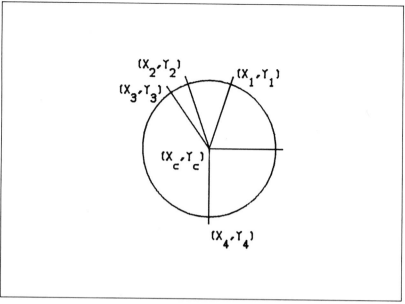

Figure 7-14. (B) Pie chart with all subdivisions made.

Table 7.6. Cost Elements for Widgets with Angular Measure of Slices

Description	Cost	Percentage of Total	Radians
Raw material	2.28	20	1.26
Purchased parts	1.14	10	.63
Packaging material	.57	5	.31
Direct labor	4.56	40	2.51
Indirect cost	2.85	25	1.57
Total	11.40	100	6.28

Our second line is calculated by adding the angular measure of the second slice (.63 radians) to that of the first slice, giving 1.89 radians, and using this value to calculate the end point of our second line, (X_c,Y_c) to (X_2,Y_2). When the coordinates of each line have been calculated, we can draw the line on the chart. The following routine (given in FORTRAN and BASIC) will draw in all of the lines, as shown in Figure 7-14B.

FORTRAN code:

```
C ** SUBDIVIDE PIE **
C ** USES DATA FROM ENTRY ROUTINE **
      SUBROUTINE SUBDIV (VALUE,RADIUS,IXC,IYC,ENTRES,TOTAL)
      DIMENSION VALUE(25),ANGL(25)
      INTEGER RADIUS
      CALL MOVABS (IXC,IYC)
      CALL DRWABS (IXC+RADIUS,IYC)
      PIESUM=0
      DO 50 K=1,ENTRES
        ANGL(K)=((PIESUM+VALUE(K))/TOTAL)*6.2832
        IX=COS(ANGL(K))*RADIUS+IXC
        IY=SIN(ANGL(K))*RADIUS+IYC
```

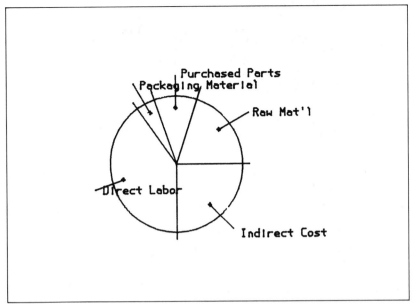

Figure 7-14. (C) Pie chart with sections labeled incorrectly.

```
        CALL MOVABS(IXC,IYC)
        CALL DRWABS(IX,IY)
        PIESUM=PIESUM+VALUE(K)
50      CONTINUE
      RETURN
      END
```

BASIC code:

```
100 REM *** SUBROUTINE TO SUBDIVIDE PIE ***
110 REM *** USES DATA FROM ENTRY ROUTINE ***
120 LINE (XC,YC) - (XC+RADIUS*FACTOR,YC)
130 PIESUM=0
140 FOR K=1 TO ENTRIES
150    ANGL(K)=((PIESUM+VALUE(K))/TOTAL)*6.2832
160    X=COS(ANGL(K))*RADIUS*FACTOR+XC
170    Y=SIN(ANGL(K))*RADIUS+YC
180    LINE (XC,YC) - (X,Y)
185    PIESUM=PIESUM+VALUE(K)
190    NEXT K
200 RETURN
```

Labeling the sections of the pie can be done in a variety of ways. One is to draw a line from the midpoint of each slice radially outward beyond the edge of the pie and then to enter the label. Figure 7-14C shows the pie with sections labeled in this manner. The following FORTRAN and BASIC codes are an example of a labeling routine.

FORTRAN code:

```
C ** LABEL SECTIONS OF PIE **
        SUBROUTINE LABLPI (ENTRES,ELNAME,VALUE,RADIUS,IXC,IYC,TOTAL)
        DIMENSION ANGL(25),VALUE(25)
        CHARACTER*1 ELNAME(25,25)
        INTEGER RADIUS
```

```
                PIESUM=0
                DO 50 K=1,ENTRES
                  ANGL (K)=((PIESUM+VALUE(K)/2)/TOTAL)*6.2832
                  IXS=COS(ANGL(K))*.75*RADIUS+IXC
                  IX=COS(ANGL(K))*1.1*RADIUS+IXC
                  IYS=SIN(ANGL(K))*.75*RADIUS+IYC
                  IY=SIN(ANGL(K))*1.1*RADIUS+IYC
                  CALL MOVABS(IXS,IYS)
                  CALL DRWABS(IX,IY)
                  PIESUM=PIESUM+VALUE(K)
C ** CALL ROUTINE TO WRITE LABEL
                  CALL PRNLBL (ELNAME,K,IX,IY)
      50          CONTINUE
                RETURN
                END

C ** PRINT SECTION LABELS FOR PIE **
                SUBROUTINE PRNLBL (ELNAME,K,IX,IY)
                CHARACTER*1 ELNAME(25,25)
                CALL MOVABS (IX,IY)
                CALL ANMODE
                WRITE (5,10) (ELNAME(K,J),J=1,25)
      10        FORMAT('+',25A1)
                RETURN
                END
```

BASIC code:

```
210 REM *** LABEL SECTIONS OF PIE
215 PIESUM=0
220 FOR K=1 TO ENTRIES
230 ANGL(K)=((PIESUM + VALUE(K)/2)/TOTAL)*6.2832
240    XS=COS(ANGL(K))*.75*RADIUS*FACTOR+XC
250    X=COS(ANGL(K))*1.1*RADIUS*FACTOR+XC
260    YS=SIN(ANGL(K))*.75*RADIUS+YC
270    Y=SIN(ANGL(K))*1.1*RADIUS+YC
280    LINE (XS,YS) - (X,Y)
282    REM ** PRINT LABEL NAME
283    GOSUB 5500
284 GOSUB 810
285    PIESUM=PIESUM+VALUE(K)
290    NEXT K
300 RETURN

5500 REM ** SUBROUTINE TO PRINT LABELS FOR PIE SECTIONS **
5510 REM
5520 COLM=(X\8)+3
5530 RO=(Y\8)+1
5535 GOSUB 5620
5540 LOCATE RO,COLM
5550 PRINT NAM$(K)
5560 RETURN
```

Note that the chart resulting from these code examples will have some labels written toward the pie from the line end and some away from the pie. This has been corrected in Figure 7-14D, which uses the algorithm of the following coded example to decide where to start the label. This subroutine would be called from the label-printing subroutine prior to locating the beam at the print start position.

FORTRAN code:

```
C ** CALCULATE STARTING POINT OF PIE LABEL **
                SUBROUTINE STRT (ANGL,K,IX,IY,ELNAME)
                DIMENSION ANGL(25)
                CHARACTER*1 ELNAME(25,25)
                IF (ANGL(K) .LT. 1.58 .OR. ANGL(K) .GT.4.7) GOTO 999
```

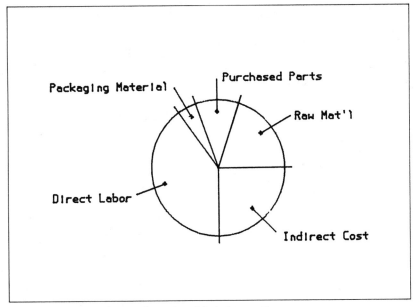

Figure 7-14. (D) Pie chart with sections labeled correctly.

```
        LNGTH=0
        DO 50 J=1,25
          IF (ELNAME(K,J) .NE. ' ') LNGTH=J
  50      CONTINUE
        IX=IX - ((1024/80)*LNGTH+1)
 999    RETURN
        END
```

BASIC code:

```
5600 REM *** SUBROUTINE TO CHANGE LOCATION OF PRINT START
5610 REM
5620 IF ANGL(K)<1.58 OR ANGL(K)>4.7 THEN GOTO 5640
5630 COLM=COLM - (LEN(NAM$(K))+3)
5640 RETURN
```

Chart titles are another feature that can take many forms. One approach is to permit the user to enter a one-line title above the pie and another one-line title below the pie. Either of the titles can be eliminated simply by entering a null string—that is, one without any characters. The program should center the string on the display by counting the number of characters it contains, subtracting that number from the number of characters the screen can display on one line, and indenting the string by half of the remaining character positions. Thus, a 20-character title string on a 40-character display would start in position 11. Figure 7-14E shows the title centered above the completed pie chart. The following example (given in FORTRAN and BASIC) presents the code to create pie-chart labels.

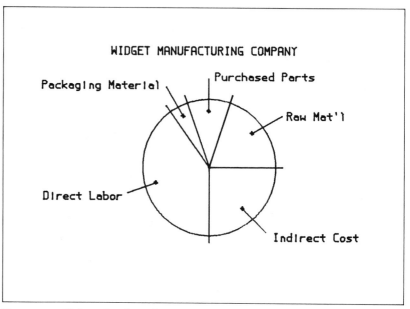

Figure 7-14. (E) Completed pie chart.

FORTRAN code:

```
C ** PRINT PIE CHART TITLES **
        SUBROUTINE CTITLE (CHART)
        CHARACTER*1 CHART(2,50)
        LNGTH=0
        DO 30 J=1,50
          IF (CHART(1,J) .NE. ' ') LNGTH=J
 30       CONTINUE
        IX=513 - ((1024/160)*LNGTH+1)
        CALL MOVABS (IX,760)
        CALL ANMODE
        WRITE (5,40) (CHART (1,J),J=1,LNGTH)
 40     FORMAT('+',50A1)
        LNGTH=0
        DO 60 J=1,50
          IF (CHART(2,J) .NE. ' ') LNGTH=J
 60       CONTINUE
        IX=513 - ((1024/160)*LNGTH+1)
        CALL MOVABS (IX,20)
        CALL ANMODE
        WRITE (5,40) (CHART (2,J),J=1,LNGTH)
        RETURN
        END
```

BASIC code:

```
310 REM *** SUBROUTINE TO PRINT PIE CHART TITLES ***
320 REM
330 XSPOT=INT(41-.5*LEN(CHART$(1)))
340 LOCATE 2,XSPOT
350 PRINT CHART$(1)
360 XSPOT=INT(41-.5*LEN(CHART$(2)))
370 LOCATE 24,XSPOT
380 PRINT CHART$(2);
390 RETURN
```

Drawing a Line Chart

The first step in drawing a line chart is to draw and label the axes. This is a simple matter of drawing two lines, one horizontal and one vertical, from a common point, the origin. Figures 7-15A, B, C and D show the steps in drawing a line chart.

The exact location of the axes is a matter of personal preference. The only requirements are that there be enough room to label and mark scales on the axes, that there be enough room for the chart, and that the areas be in balance for a pleasing appearance. In our example, the chart will be drawn on a system with a resolution of 1024 by 780 for the FORTRAN version and 640 by 200 for the BASIC version. For the FORTRAN version we will arbitrarily choose the point (250,250) as the origin, thus placing the X axis at Y = 250 and the Y axis at X = 250. For the BASIC version the origin will be at (150,70), placing the X axis at Y = 70 and the Y axis at X = 150. Note that the routines draw the axes to the edge of the screen. In many cases it may be desirable to stop short of the edge for aesthetic reasons.

FORTRAN code:

```
C ** DRAW AXES FOR LINE CHART **
        SUBROUTINE DRWAXS (XORGIN,YORGIN)
        INTEGER XORGIN,YORGIN
        XORGIN=250
        YORGIN=250
        CALL MOVABS (XORGIN,YORGIN)
        CALL DRWREL (1024-XORGIN,0)
        CALL MOVABS (XORGIN,YORGIN)
        CALL DRWREL (0,780-YORGIN)
        RETURN
        END
```

Note that the following BASIC code is written for a system with the origin in the upper-left corner of the screen, which is why the Y values are written as they are.

BASIC code:

```
400 REM *** SUBROUTINE TO DRAW AXES FOR LINE CHART ***
410 REM
420 XORGIN=150:YORGIN=199-70
430 PRESET (XORGIN,YORGIN)
440 LINE -STEP (639-XORGIN,0)
450 PRESET (XORGIN,YORGIN)
460 LINE -STEP (0,0-YORGIN)
470 RETURN
```

Labeling the abscissa is a relatively easy task. We will use the same code we used to place titles on the pie chart. Our only modifications will be to change the height at which the characters will be output and to move the starting point so that the label will be slightly to the right of center for better appearance. The required modifications will be left to you.

Labeling the ordinate is a somewhat different matter. We will print the label with the characters in standard position but appearing beneath one another in a vertical line. This requires that the label be output one character at a time and that the cursor be repositioned for

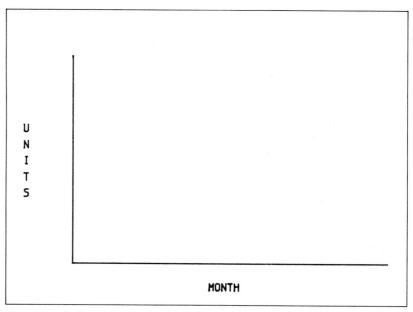

Figure 7-15. (A) Line chart with axes shown and labeled.

each character. The location of the first character will be determined by calculating the number of characters that can be output in the space between the top of the screen and the abscissa and then centering the label in that space. Thus, if the space is adequate for 16 characters and our label has 12, we will leave two blank spaces above the label and two below. This task is handled somewhat differently in the FORTRAN version of the code than in BASIC, since each character in the FORTRAN code is a separate array variable. Figure 7-15A shows the chart at this point, with the abscissa and ordinate drawn in and labeled.

FORTRAN code:

```
C ** LABEL THE ORDINATE **
      SUBROUTINE LBLORD (LABL,XORGIN,YORGIN)
      INTEGER XORGIN,YORGIN
      CHARACTER*1 LABL(50)
      LNGTH=0
      DO 30 J=1,25
        IF (LABL(J) .NE. ' ') LNGTH=J
30      CONTINUE
      CENTER=(780-YORGIN)/2 +YORGIN
      START=CENTER+16*LNGTH
      DO 50 K=1,LNGTH
        IY=START-33*(K-1)
        CALL MOVABS (20,IY)
        CALL ANMODE
        WRITE (5,40) LABL(K)
40      FORMAT ('+',A1)
50      CONTINUE
      RETURN
      END
```

BASIC code:

```
500 REM *** SUBROUTINE TO LABEL THE ORDINATE ***
510 REM
520 CENTER=INT((YORGIN-0)/2/8)
530 START=CENTER-INT(.5*LEN(LABL$))
535 FOR K=1 TO LEN(LABL$)
540    LOCATE START+K,2
550    PRINT MID$(LABL$,K,1)
560    NEXT K
570 RETURN
```

Table 7-7. Widget Production for 1983

Month	Units Produced
January	500
February	575
March	600
April	675
May	725
June	800
July	775
August	800
September	750
October	700
November	625
December	550

Scaling and marking the axes require that the data be entered so that we know what our data range is. For the following example the data of Table 7-7 are to be plotted. These data consist of twelve data pairs and we will plot them evenly spaced along the abscissa. The amount of space available in the FORTRAN version is 1024 − 250, or 774, screen units. In the BASIC version it is 639 — 150, or 489, screen units. To avoid having the last data point at the extreme edge of the screen, 13 spaces are used. The number of screen units available are divided by 13 and the result is truncated to an integer.

FORTRAN code:

```
C ** CALCULATE X INTERVAL **
      SUBROUTINE XINTVL (XORGIN,XINT)
      INTEGER XORGIN,XINT
      XINT=INT((1024-XORGIN)/13)
      RETURN
      END
```

BASIC code:

```
600 REM *** SUBROUTINE TO CALCULATE X INTERVAL ***
610 XINT=FIX(639-XORGIN)/13
620 RETURN
```

We are now ready to mark the abscissa. The tick marks are made by moving to a point XINT units to the right of the ordinate and drawing a short vertical line across the abscissa, moving XINT units to the right again and drawing another short vertical line, and repeating this procedure until all of the tick marks are drawn. This is easily done with a loop as shown in the following example.

FORTRAN code:

```
C ** PLACE TICK MARKS ON ABSCISSA **
      SUBROUTINE TIKMRK (XORGIN,YORGIN,XINT)
      INTEGER XORGIN,YORGIN,XINT
      CALL MOVABS (XORGIN,YORGIN-5)
      DO 50 K=1,12
         CALL MOVREL (XINT,10)
         CALL DRWREL (0,-10)
50       CONTINUE
      RETURN
      END
```

BASIC code:

```
630 REM *** SUBROUTINE TO PLACE TICK MARKS ON ABSCISSA
640 PRESET (XORGIN,YORGIN+2)
650 FOR K=1 TO 12
660    PSET STEP (XINT,-4)
670    LINE -STEP (0,4)
680    NEXT K
685 GOTO 800
690 RETURN
```

Marking the values is done using a similar procedure, only this time the loop must provide for outputting characters and must adjust the starting points so that the characters are centered as nearly as possible on the tick marks. The locations and character outputting routines can be similar to those used to print chart titles and axis labels. This task will be left to you.

Scaling the ordinate is somewhat more complicated. We want the chart to be scaled so that the largest value is nearly at the top, and we also want all graduations to be easy to read and interpret. Since our largest data value is 800 and there are no negative values, we will use 800 as the chart top and 0 as the value at the abscissa. We will use eight increments of 100 units each. Dividing the available vertical plotting space (530 units for the FORTRAN version, 130 for BASIC) by 8, we get 66.25 screen units (FORTRAN version) or 16.25 screen units (BASIC version) per 100 data units. We do not want the data to go off the screen, but we also need some space at the top for a title. [The following example reserves some space for this purpose by placing the top of the chart at 740 (FORTRAN) or 10 (BASIC).]

FORTRAN code:

```
C ** CONVERT DATA "Y" VALUES TO SCREEN "Y" VALUES **
      SUBROUTINE YSCALE (YDATA,YORGIN,YSCREN)
      INTEGER YORGIN,YSCREN
      YSCREN=YORGIN+YDATA*(740-YORGIN)/800
      RETURN
      END
```

BASIC code:

```
700 REM *** SUBROUTINE TO CONVERT DATA "Y" VALUES ***
710 REM ***     TO SCREEN COORDINATE "Y" VALUES    ***
720 YSCREN=YORGIN+(10-YORGIN)/200*YDATA
730 RETURN
```

Drawing the tick marks on the ordinate is done in the same way as for the abscissa except that the lines are drawn horizontally and the cursor is moved vertically between marks. Do you see how the code used for putting tick marks on the abscissa can be modified to mark the ordinate? Can you make the code general enough to be used for both axes by using variable names for all movements and then passing the correct parameters to mark either axis? (The above code can be used to calculate the absolute Y coordinate for each of the tick marks, or it can be used to calculate the Y coordinate of the first tick mark. Then the relative move for each tick mark can be calculated as the distance from YORGIN to the first tick mark.)

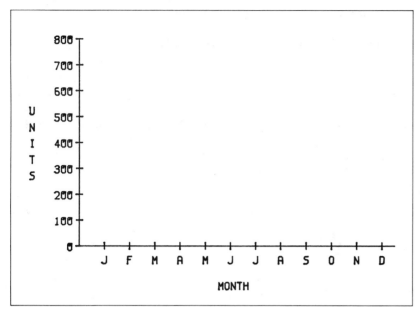

Figure 7-15. (B) Line chart with axes scaled and marked.

Marking the values by each tick mark on the ordinate can be done with a routine similar to the title- and label-printing routines we have already used. In this case, though, the starting point must be the correct number of character spaces to the left of the tick mark for the number of digits to be printed, and the digits must be centered as nearly as possible vertically on the tick mark.

Positioning characters on the screen can be very precise with systems using PLOT10 or any graphics language that permits moving the cursor to any position and outputting a character at that position in graphics mode. The LOCATE command we have been using in our BASIC examples for the IBM PC does not provide as much flexibility in positioning. This problem may be overcome by creating a special character set and plotting the characters instead of printing them. A procedure for placing characters by use of the MICROSOFT BASIC GET and PUT statements will be covered in Chapter 11. Figure 7-15B shows the line chart with axes scaled and marked.

What happens when the data contain no small numbers? Is it necessary to start the ordinate scale at zero? The answer, of course, is no. The chart should be scaled just as we have done. The *data range* is the difference between the maximum and minimum data values. In our example the data range was 800 units. (800 − 0). The subroutines should, of course, be generalized to accept a user-input or program-input data range by replacing the value 800 with a variable. Can you create a chart with data that contain negative values?

Now that the chart has been drawn it is time to enter the data points and connect them. Note that the screen X and Y coordinates are obtained by accessing subroutines (not shown) similar to the one we have already used to convert the data values to screen coordinates.

In many cases, particularly where more than one line is to be drawn on the chart, the data points should be identified by drawing a symbol over them. In our example, we will draw a small cross on each data point. Note that this is done with a separate routine called from the point-plotting routine. Several different symbol routines can be used with the same point-plotting routine.

FORTRAN code:

```
C ** SUBROUTINE TO PLOT POINTS ON CHART **
        SUBROUTINE PLTDTA (VALUE,ELNAME,ENTRES,XORGIN,YORGIN,XINT)
        INTEGER XORGIN,YORGIN,XSCREN,YSCREN,XINT
        DIMENSION VALUE(25)
        CHARACTER*1 ELNAME (25,25)
        DO 50 K=1,ENTRES
          CALL XSCALE (XSCREN,XORGIN,XINT,K)
          CALL YSCALE (VALUE(K),YORGIN,YSCREN)
          CALL PNTABS (XSCREN,YSCREN)
          CALL CROSS
50      CONTINUE
        RETURN
        END

C ** DRAW A SMALL CROSS AT BEAM POSITION **
        SUBROUTINE CROSS
        CALL MOVREL (-5,0)
        CALL DRWREL (10,0)
        CALL MOVREL (-5,5)
        CALL DRWREL (0,-10)
        CALL MOVREL (0,5)
        RETURN
        END
```

BASIC code:

```
800 REM *** SUBROUTINE TO PLOT POINTS ON CHART ***
810 FOR K=1 TO ENTRIES
820    XDATA=ELNAME(K):GOSUB 750:REM XSCALE SUBROUTINE
830    YDATA=VALUE(K):GOSUB 700:REM YSCALE SUBROUTINE
840    PSET (XSCREN,YSCREN)
850    GOSUB 900
860    NEXT K
865 GOTO 970
870 RETURN

900 REM *** SUBROUTINE TO DRAW A CROSS AT BEAM POS ***
910 PRESET STEP (-5,0)
920 LINE -STEP (10,0)
930 PRESET STEP (-5,2)
940 LINE -STEP (0,-4)
950 PRESET STEP (0,2)
960 RETURN
```

Once the points have been plotted, we are ready to connect them. This could have been done as part of the point-plotting routine by drawing a line to the next point to be plotted. Alternatively, the line-drawing routine of Chapter 4 can be used. This task will be left to you. Figure 7-15C shows the chart with points plotted and connected with solid lines.

Finally, we can reuse the code developed for outputting titles on

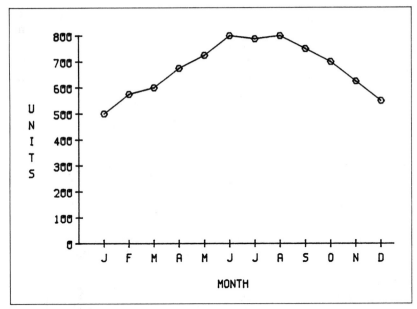

Figure 7-15. (C) Line chart with data points entered and connected.

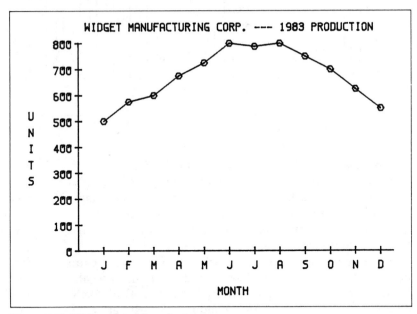

Figure 7-15. (D) Completed line chart.

the pie chart to put a title on our line chart. Figure 7-15D shows the completed chart.

Drawing a Bar Chart

Bar charts are drawn in a manner similar to that of line charts. The axes are drawn, scaled, and labeled in the same manner and the chart

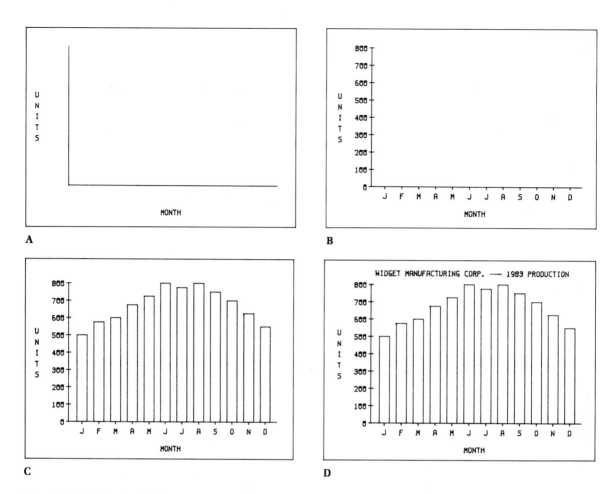

Figure 7-16. (A) Bar chart with axes shown and labeled. (B) Bar chart with axes scaled and marked. (C) Bar chart with bars drawn. (D) Completed bar chart.

title is created in the same manner. One difference is that the distance from the axis to the first data point is generally reduced so that the space between the ordinate and the first bar is equal to the space between the bars. This means that the axis from which the bars are drawn is scaled somewhat differently. Figure 7-16 shows the steps for drawing the bar chart.

Suppose we wish to construct a vertical bar chart using the same data we used for our line chart. In that example, we calculated that the data points would be 59 units apart for the FORTRAN version or 40 units apart for the BASIC version. If the bars are made about 60 percent of this width (35 or 24 units, depending on the version), then the space between the bars will be 24 or 16 units. The edge of the first bar, however, will be half a bar width further than this from the Y axis. To change this to the standard spacing of 19 or 13 units, we will need to move all data points about one-half bar width to the left. The spacing can be adjusted to give the best appearance. Since our routines use relative moves from a starting point, we need only

Table 7-8. Data for Chart of Production Defects

Number of Data Pair	First Element (date data taken)	Second Element (number of defects)
1	6/1	4
2	6/6	3
3	6/9	4
4	6/12	3
5	6/16	4
6	6/18	5
7	6/21	6
8	6/23	6
9	6/26	7
10	6/28	6

change the location of the first data point to accomplish the required adjustment.

The bars may be drawn in outline form or may be drawn solid. To draw them in outline form we must draw a rectangle whose lower edge is centered on the X axis data point location, with corners one-half bar width to the left and one-half bar width to the right of the data point location. The rectangle's upper edge will be directly above the lower edge at the height of the data point. Thus if the first data point is at X = 141, Y = 55 (screen coordinates) and the bar width is 24 units, our rectangle corners will be at (129,199 − 70), (153,199 − 70), (153,55), and (129,55). The bar can be drawn using the rectangle routine given in Chapter 5. If the bars are to be solid, they can be drawn in outline form and then filled in, or they can be created and filled by drawing a series of adjacent parallel lines, using a looping routine to increment X from 129 to 153 and drawing from Y = 55 to Y = 199 − 70.

Editing Techniques

Suppose that the data, labels, and titles of Table 7-8 have been made into the line chart of Figure 7-17A and that we now wish to change some of the items. How do we go about the editing process?

Let us first modify the data that were entered. We want to change the number of defects in the fourth data pair, eliminate the third data pair, insert a new data pair after the first one, and add a new data pair after the last one. Our corrected data are shown in Table 7-9.

Our original data-entry procedure stored the data in two corresponding one-dimensional arrays, one for the abscissa value and one for the ordinate value. The abscissa value array (a string array) was called ELNAME or NAM$, and the ordinate value array was called VALUE. For any entry number i, NAM$($i$) contains the abscissa identifier (the date of the reading), and VALUE(i) contains the ordinate value (number of defects found). To change the values of the

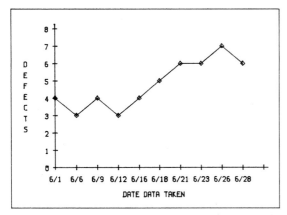

Figure 7-17. (A) Line chart before editing.

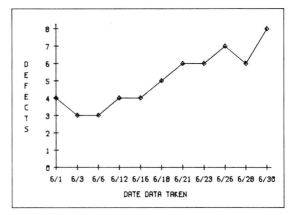

Figure 7-17. (B) Line chart after editing.

Table 7-9. Data for Revised Chart of Production Defects

Number of Data Pair	First Element (date data taken)	Second Element (number of defects)
1	6/1	4
2	6/3	3
3	6/6	3
4	6/12	4
5	6/16	4
6	6/18	5
7	6/21	6
8	6/23	6
9	6/26	7
10	6/28	6
11	6/30	8

fourth data pair we need only replace NAM$(4) with the new string and replace the value of VALUE(4) with its new value. Actually, in this case NAM$(4) will be the same as it was.

How do we eliminate the third data pair? When we remove those data, pair number 4 becomes number 3, pair number 5 becomes number 4, and so on. The following example (coded in FORTRAN and in BASIC) is a routine for moving each pair of data to eliminate data pair number 3. Note that when we are finished we have one less data pair than we had when we started.

FORTRAN code:

```
C ** DELETE A DATA PAIR **
        SUBROUTINE ELIM (ENTRES,ELNAME,VALUE,L)
        DIMENSION VALUE (25)
        CHARACTER*1 ELNAME (25,25)
        DO 50 K=1,ENTRES-L
          KK=K+L
          DO 40 J=1,25
            ELNAME(KK-1,J)=ELNAME(KK,J)
40        CONTINUE
          VALUE(KK-1)=VALUE(KK)
```

```
  50       CONTINUE
          ENTRES=ENTRES-1
          RETURN
          END
```

BASIC code:

```
3000 REM ** SUBROUTINE TO DELETE A DATA PAIR **
3010 FOR K=I+1 TO ENTRIES
3020    NAM$(K-1)=NAM$(K)
3030    VALUE(K-1)=VALUE(K)
3040    NEXT K
3050 ENTRIES=ENTRIES-1
3060 RETURN
```

At this point, we still need to insert a new data pair after the first. This means that pair number 2 will become number 3 and each successive pair will be moved one number forward. This time we cannot just move 2 to 3, 3 to 4, and on to the end, since we will be destroying data. The solution is to move the last pair, number 9, to number 10 and then, working backward, successively move 8 to 9, 7 to 8, and so on until 2 is moved to 3. We now have two identical data pairs, number 2 and number 3, which means we can now store the values for the new pair number 2, thus completing the necessary replacements. The following example (coded in FORTRAN and in BASIC) is a routine for creating space for the new entry. Note that our arrays have now grown one element longer.

FORTRAN code:

```
C ** INSERT A DATA PAIR **
          SUBROUTINE INSRT (ENTRES,ELNAME,VALUE,L)
          DIMENSION VALUE (25)
          CHARACTER*1 ELNAME (25,25)
          DO 50 K=1,ENTRES-L
            KK=ENTRES+1-K
            DO 40 J=1,25
              ELNAME(KK+1,J)=ELNAME(KK,J)
  40          CONTINUE
            VALUE(KK+1)=VALUE(KK)
  50        CONTINUE
          ENTRES=ENTRES+1
          RETURN
          END
```

BASIC code:

```
3200 REM ** SUBROUTINE TO INSERT A DATA PAIR **
3210 FOR K=ENTRIES TO I STEP -1
3220    NAM$(K+1)=NAM$(K)
3230    VALUE(K+1)=VALUE(K)
3240    NEXT K
3242 NAM$(I)=NUNAM$
3244 VALUE(I)=NUVALU
3250 ENTRIES=ENTRIES+1
3260 RETURN
```

Our final task is to add a new data pair at the end of the group. This is the easiest task of all. Since we have eleven data pairs, we simply store the new values in NAM$(11) and VALUE(11). This task will be left to you. The modified chart is shown in Figure 7-17B.

Editing labels and titles is a task that can take many forms. If the labels have been entered as numeric data it is usually easiest to simply enter new values to replace the old ones. String data can also be edited by entering a new string to replace the old. Another string-editing technique that is often more desirable, particularly in the case of long strings or of relatively minor changes, is to replace one substring with another.

Replacing one numeric value or entire string with another requires that the numeric value or string be identified. There are several ways to do this. One way is to enter the value or string to be replaced and instruct the system to search for a match among the stored information. When a match is found, the system may ask for the replacement information. The new number or string is then stored where the old number was stored.

A second replacement approach is to record the order number in which the label or title information was entered. You can then instruct the system to replace the material by entering the appropriate number. Consider this title:

WIDGET MANUFACTURING COMPANY
SMALL WIDGET DIVISION
PRODUCTION SCHEDULE

Let us say that the program (BASIC version) has T$ as a singly subscripted array to store title lines. The third line of the title would then be stored in T$(3). To replace it, you could then identify it as such. The following coded example is a routine that can be used to accomplish this. (The FORTRAN version uses a double-subscripted array of single characters.) Note that the routine displays the selected title for the user to verify before replacing it.

FORTRAN code:

```
C ** REPLACE A TITLE LINE WITH A NEW ONE **
      SUBROUTINE REPLCE (TITLE,N)
      CHARACTER*1 TITLE (2,50), TTLWRK(50)
      CALL ANMODE
      WRITE (5,10) 'ENTER NUMBER OF TITLE LINE TO REPLACE'
10    FORMAT ('+',A50)
      READ (5,20) N
20    FORMAT (I3)
      WRITE (5,10) 'ENTER NEW TITLE LINE'
      READ (5,30) TTLWRK
30    FORMAT (50A1)
        DO 35 J=1,50
          TITLE(N,J)=TTLWRK(J)
35      CONTINUE
      RETURN
      END
```

BASIC code:

```
3400 REM ** SUBROUTINE TO REPLACE A TITLE LINE **
3410 REM **         WITH A NEW ONE            **
3420 INPUT"ENTER NUMBER OF TITLE LINE TO REPLACE";N
3430 INPUT"ENTER NEW TITLE LINE";T$(N)
3440 RETURN
```

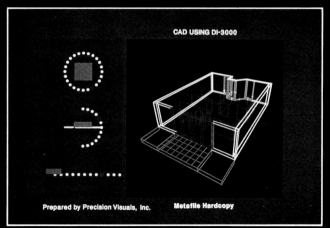

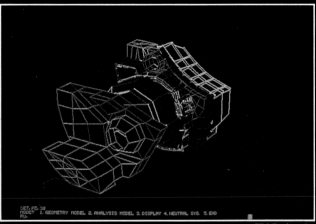

Some of the most exciting and visually striking applications of computer graphics involve the use of color and shading. Computer graphics is, of course, a powerful tool for presenting ideas and information in two and three dimensions, but the use of color and shading provides a fourth dimension, as the illustrations on this and the following pages show. While many of these illustrations display concepts, hardware, and software beyond the scope of this book, the principles we outline in the text provide the foundation for each of the examples, and we have included them here to give the reader an appreciation for the tremendous potential computer graphics holds.

The top figure on this page shows a three-dimensional color display of a simple building. As the user rotates the image, the left portion of the display gives the relative position of the viewer. In the center figure a user is at work at a color computer graphics workstation. The bottom figure shows a portion of a relatively complex machine. Note the use of color to distinguish the various machine parts.

Here are three examples of
how color can enhance
two-dimensional images.
The graphs shown in the
top two figures are much
easier to interpret when
color or shading is used to
highlight critical
information. The bottom
figure, a schematic layout
for process control of a
factory, allows a user to
direct material flow,
activate process machinery,
and modify control
designs.

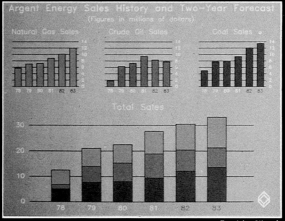

Precision Visuals

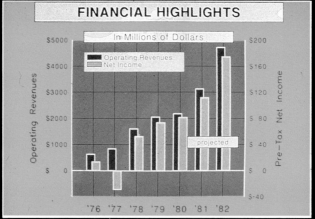

Precision Visuals

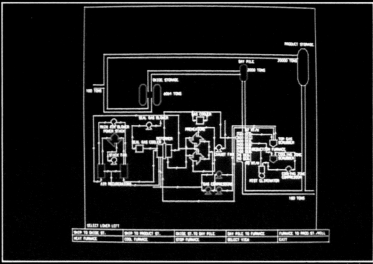

Evans & Sutherland

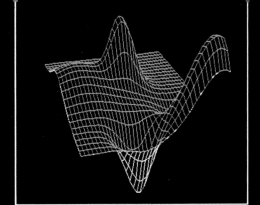

Precision Visuals

These examples are further applications of line meshes used to represent three-dimensional surfaces. The top left figure is of a three-dimensional surface representing a mathematical function. The remaining figures show a portion of a car fender and wire-frame images of an aircraft.

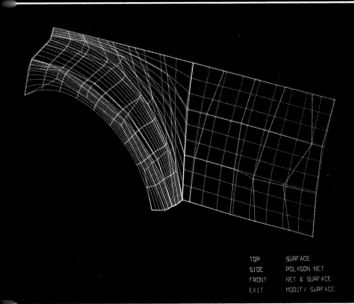

TOP   SURFACE
SIDE   POLYGON NET
FRONT   NET & SURFACE
EXIT   MODIFY SURFACE

Evans & Sutherland

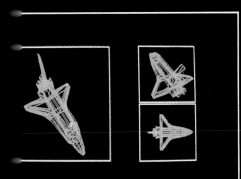

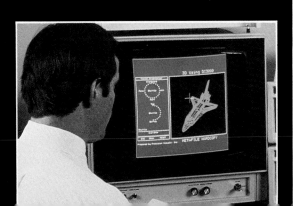

The top four figures shown here illustrate the steps in building a three-dimensional model of a solid object. The bottom two figures show examples of how a system can display the intersection of two solids for modeling.

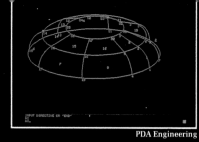 

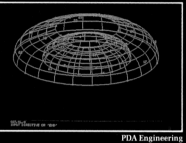 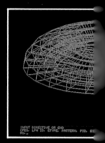

PDA Engineering

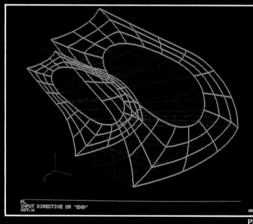

PDA Engineering

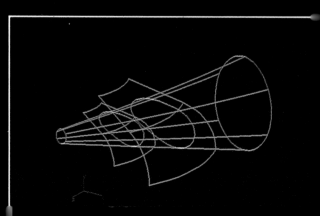

PDA Engineering

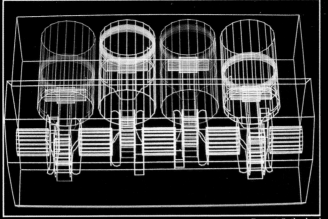

Evans & Sutherland

The top two figures shown here are line drawings, created by a color calligraphic display, that can be animated to show the motion of working parts. The bottom left figure demonstrates how a finite-element program can display stress levels in a machine part. Here the computer graphics display is working as a post-processor for an analysis program that allows the user to pinpoint any areas in the part where the stress levels exceed the material limits. The bottom right figure shows a machine part colored and shaded, resulting in an image that is more realistic than surfaces created with lines only.

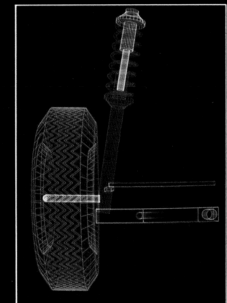

Evans & Sutherland

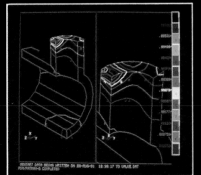

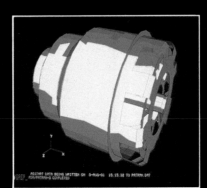

Here are four views of a complex three-dimensional object. The top figure shows the geometric information as lines, while the remaining three show surface areas colored and shaded to provide a better interpretation of the design.

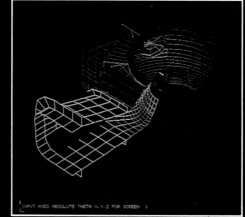

PDA Engineering

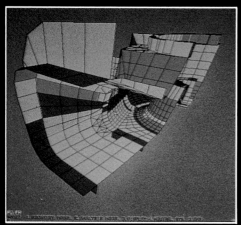

PDA Engineering

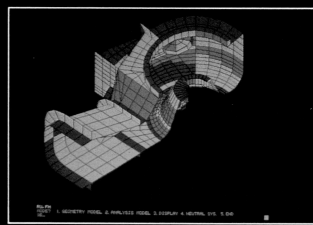

PDA Engineering

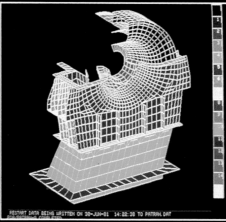

PDA Engineering

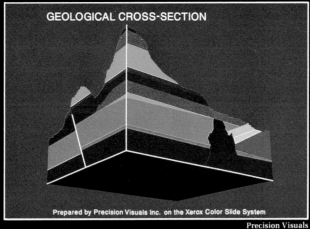

Prepared by Precision Visuals Inc. on the Xerox Color Slide System

Precision Visuals

The top figure here is a geological cross-section that uses color to allow the viewer to distinguish the various strata. The bottom two figures show how an indistinct photograph (on the left) can be enhanced using computer graphics techniques to provide a clearer picture, with sharper, better-defined objects.

Comtal Corporation

Comtal Corporation

These figures combine terrain modeling and geometric modeling of aircraft designs. The systems used to create and display these images can be used to model airports, landing strips, and the interiors and exteriors of aircraft, thus providing realistic flight training for pilots. Such systems are very expensive, but their use allows airlines to save money by eliminating a certain amount of actual flight time.

Evans & Sutherland

Evans & Sutherland

Evans & Sutherland

Evans & Sutherland

Evans & Sutherland

Storing and Retrieving the Data

We have already talked about editing techniques requiring that the data be kept in a form that allows them to be identified, retrieved, and changed. Successful data storage and retrieval requires that a separate data location be maintained for each item of information and that the locations be logically grouped into sets or arrays for ease of manipulation.

When data are to be stored in main memory, enough memory locations must be set aside to store all the data that will be entered and each memory location must have a unique name. Note that each element of an array, by reason of its subscript, has a unique name.

Data that are to be stored on disk or tape are usually logically grouped into records. Each record may contain a data pair, all of the data pairs for one curve, or some other reasonable grouping of information. If arrays are used for data, one record might contain one line of the array. A two- or three-dimensional array could be completely contained in one record, but this would make the record difficult to handle and might also exceed the allowable record length of the disk or tape. Data storage and retrieval using memory (RAM) will be covered in later chapters, as will the techniques for using disk storage and retrieval.

Data Adjustments

There are a number of reasons for wanting to adjust the data. Sometimes the raw data are so irregular that a chart drawn using them will be misleading. It is difficult to see overall trends and patterns when the chart displays confusing inconsistencies.

A frequently used technique for adjusting chart data is *smoothing*. There are a number of ways of smoothing chart data. A very common method and the one we will cover here is called moving average.

Refer back to Figure 7-12, where raw data on product shipments have been charted. Note that the line is very irregular. Figure 7-13 presents the chart using data that have been smoothed using an algorithm that recalculates all of the values as follows: Each data point value is added to the two preceding and two succeeding values and the result divided by 5. Of course, the first value has no preceding values, so it is added to the second and third value and the result divided by 3. The second, next-to-last, and last values are treated similarly. Note that original data values are used in all calculations, not "smoothed" values. Use of the latter could distort the data. Obviously, the curve in Figure 7-13 is much smoother than the one in Figure 7-12. The data could be further smoothed by averaging seven values per data point instead of five. There is no rule of thumb for the amount of smoothing to do; it is a matter of obtaining the best chart for the purpose at hand.

Experimental data are often expected to conform to a predetermined theoretical pattern. For instance, a chart of voltage patterns

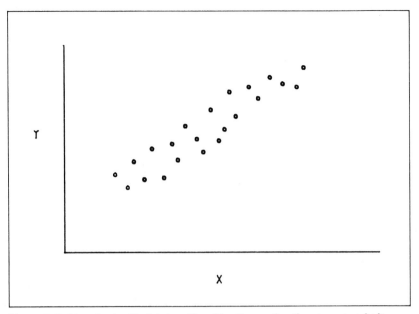

Figure 7-18. Line chart with data in a "band" pattern rather than in a straight line.

with respect to time for alternating current should produce a sine wave. However, experimental data may show variations from that theoretical pattern due to a variety of causes. Similarly, statistical data are generally expected to conform to an expected standard distribution pattern such as the binomial, normal, or Poisson distribution. Finally, many types of data, or their logarithms, are expected to conform to a straight-line distribution. In all of these cases, you may want to determine the parameters of the curve that best fits the data. Figure 7-18 is a list of data that, when plotted, was expected to form a straight-line graph. As you can see from the chart, the data do follow a linear pattern but are spread out in a band rather than a line.

Charts and graphs, unlike most other drawings, are generally created by programs that are written specifically for the type of chart to be drawn. The user typically enters all of the data before the drawing is started. The program contains all of the necessary routines to scale the drawing to fit the input data, lay out the chart, including locations of titles and labels, and create the finished drawing. Editing routines are included to permit the user to alter the data or to change the layout of the chart.

Other routines often found in charting packages permit the user to store the data on a disk and retrieve it at a later time or to create a plot or print-plot of the chart. These techniques, as well as storage of data in memory (RAM) and drawing-modification techniques, will be covered in greater detail in later chapters.

Exercises

1. What are the four basic chart types?

2. List three applications for which a pie chart would be appropriate.

3. What is a surface chart? Describe an application where one might be used.

4. Describe a charting application where (a) a horizontal bar chart would be appropriate; (b) a vertical bar chart would be the proper choice; and (c) a stacked vertical bar chart might be used.

5. What type of chart would you use to present weather information?

6. Name the subtasks in a chart-drawing routine.

7. Define the term "data pair."

8. Give three reasons for editing data that have been entered into the system.

9. What are pointers? How are they used in data sets?

10. Give two reasons for storing the chart data.

11. What is meant by data smoothing? Why might it be desirable to smooth data?

12. What is curve fitting?

13. Describe a technique for automatically centering a string of text on your chart.

14. Write a subroutine to mark values on the axes of a bar or line chart.

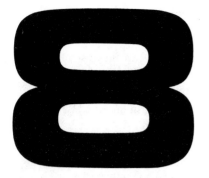

Storing and Retrieving the Data

Pictures and drawings made without provision for storing the data are like drawings made in the sand on the beach. They are soon erased and must be re-created from scratch. The artist who works with sketchpad and crayon or the drafter who works with paper, pencil, and drawing instruments create a lasting image. Their "data storage" device is the paper on which they are working. Computer graphics system users, on the other hand, are working with an electronic medium. Their creations will disappear when they sign off or when the power is shut off. Consequently, if it is necessary to interrupt the drawing task and resume it later, whether on the same system or a different system, the data necessary to re-create the drawing will need to be stored in a permanent file.

Most of the figures and flow charts used in this book were created on an IBM PC using a drawing system created by the authors to illustrate and test the routines and techniques being presented. One way to store this material, of course, is to create a hardcopy, but paper tends to be bulky and difficult to store. A more efficient storage medium is film or magnetic disk or tape. Film storage, however, requires that the drawing be photographed, which may not always be convenient. Magnetic disks or tapes on the other hand, are generally very convenient and, in ordinary situations, they are permanent.

Even if the drafter has a printer or a plotter available on the system and wants only a hardcopy, he or she may need to store the data, because the hardcopy device may work only from a file and not from the image on the display screen. The pen plotter we used to create the drawings used in this book required that the display be redrawn on the plotter, not merely bit-mapped (copying the lighted dots) from the screen.

Data are also stored in order to simplify the task of modifying a drawing. Storage-tube terminals do not permit selective erasure of drawing details. Thus, if a mistake is made, or if a change is desired for any reason, the entire drawing must be erased and redrawn, leaving out the part to be erased. This method is very time consuming and requires that the entire drawing be rechecked for errors. If, however, the data have been stored, the system can recreate the drawing minus the deleted details quickly and accurately.

Some drawing details, such as bolt heads and hole patterns, may be repeated many times on one drawing. How much easier it is to create these if, after the object has been drawn once, the system is able to repeat it in any specified location!

Objectives

The principal reason for storing information is to be able to retrieve it and use it at a later date. If this objective is to be met, the data must be stored in an organized manner. Some data values are totally unrelated to other values, but most often data elements are logically grouped into records or sets. An example of a record might be a student's name, address, ID number, department, and class level. A set of data might be all of that student's homework grades in a particular course. Her exam grades in that course might be another set. Both of these sets could be considered subsets of a larger set containing all of her grades for the course.

All of the data needed to create one graphics entity on the screen could be considered as one set. In Chapter 4 we drew lines using the data (X_1, Y_1) and (X_2, Y_2) as the end points. These four coordinates make up the set of data needed to create one line. The set may be expanded by adding other information, such as the line type (solid, dashed, dotted) to be used. The data for all entities of the same type, for instance all lines, make up a larger set, of which the data for one line are a subset. Carrying this concept further, the data for an entire drawing can be considered as a set, with all of the sets of data for elements of the drawing as subsets of the larger set.

The Nature of Data

All data used by a computer, whether numeric or non-numeric, are composed of "computer words" that are, in turn, made up of one or more bytes. Each byte contains eight bits (binary digits). The bit is the smallest entity of computer information.

We do not usually think of bits and bytes when dealing with data in the computer. However, when allocating file space to store the data, we must know how many bytes each data element contains in order to calculate the file space that will be required. Character information typically requires 1 byte per alphanumeric character.

CHAR.	ASCII DECIMAL	BYTE (8 BITS)
H	072	01001000
E	069	01000101
L	076	01001100
P	080	01010000

Figure 8-1.

Thus, the word HELP would require 4 bytes. Figure 8-1 shows the capital letters used to form the word "HELP," along with their ASCII decimal equivalents and byte, or 8-bit, equivalent representations. Real numbers require 4 bytes per value for single precision (seven-significant-digit accuracy) or 8 bytes for double precision. Integers typically require 2 bytes per value on minicomputers (and 4 bytes for double precision).

Another factor affecting the amount of storage space required for data is the length of one contiguous unit or physical record of storage. Many systems allow variable, or at least user-specified, record lengths. Some, however, do not permit any variation in record length. Most notable in this regard is FORTRAN on large batch-oriented systems, which often uses a fixed 80-byte record. If the data are not organized so that each unit uses up an entire record, much storage space can be wasted.

Data Structures

Data used to draw computer graphics images consist of integer and real numeric values as follows:

- Pairs of values representing coordinates of points, end points of lines, or vertices of figures.
- Single values indicating how the line or figure is to be drawn, including (1) line type (solid, dashed, dotted), (2) draw or erase (add/delete mode), and (3) marking of points (dot, cross, circle).
- Character information for chart labels, headings, title blocks, and the like.

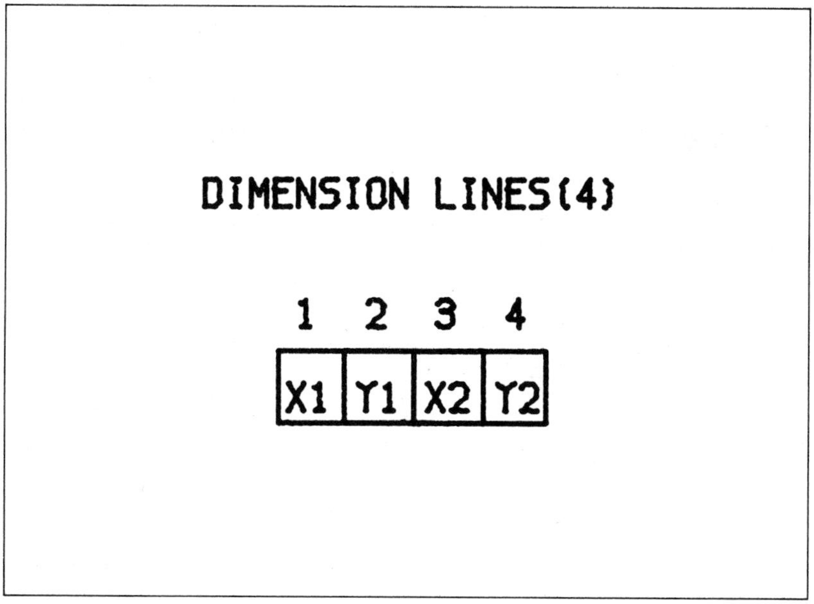

DIMENSION LINES(4)

```
  1   2   3   4
┌───┬───┬───┬───┐
│X1 │Y1 │X2 │Y2 │
└───┴───┴───┴───┘
```

Figure 8-2.

Table 8-1. One-Dimensional Array (Vector)

Array elements	1	2	3	4
Coordinates	X1	Y1	X2	Y2

Data can be represented in many forms. The most practical form is that which most nearly resembles the natural form or structure of the information itself. Since the storage is structured to resemble the natural structure of the data, the storage forms are called *data structures*.

Primitive data elements consist of bits, bytes, words, and registers. The data we use in computer graphics are made up of these primitives in various combinations. The two most commonly used data structures in computer graphics are arrays and lists.

Arrays

Arrays containing data for one graphic entity may be one-dimensional. The four coordinate values representing the two end points of a line can be stored in a one-dimensional array composed of four elements (see Table 8-1 and Figure 8-2). If the set name of the array is LINES, then LINES(1) = X1, LINES(2) = Y1, LINES(3) = X2, and LINES(4) = Y2.

An array used to store several of the same type of entity may be two-dimensional (essentially, a one-dimensional array of one-dimensional arrays). Each of the one-dimensional arrays is thus a subset of the two-dimensional array (see Table 8-2 and Figure 8-3).

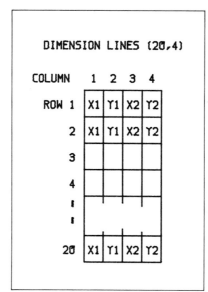

Figure 8-3.

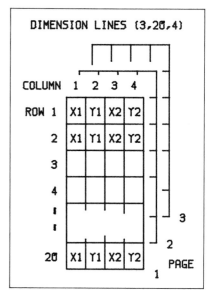

Figure 8-4.

Table 8-2. Two-Dimensional Array

Array Name Is LINES	Columns			
	1	2	3	4
Row 1	X1	Y1	X2	Y2
Row 2	X1	Y1	X2	Y2
Row 3	X1	Y1	X2	Y2
Row 4	X1	Y1	X2	Y2

A three-dimensional array (which can be thought of as a one-dimensional array of two-dimensional arrays) can store the data for a variety of different entities. Each two-dimensional array is now a subset of the three-dimensional array. Another way of thinking of three-dimensional arrays is as several pages of data like Table 8-2, where each page is a two-dimensional array. Figure 8-4 is a symbolic representation of this concept.

The first time a variable is referenced in a computer program, the computer assigns a block of memory to store the variable and records its location in a symbol table. However, when the variable is to be an array having more than one element, the system must be told what the dimensions of the array will be so that enough memory locations can be reserved to store all of the elements. This is done with a DIMENSION statement. The DIMENSION statement (see Figure 8-5A) must appear in the program before the array variable is used. (See Chapter 3 for requirements for DIMENSION statements.) Each time an array is dimensioned, enough memory is assigned to store all of the elements specified. Thus, if the array is dimensioned as

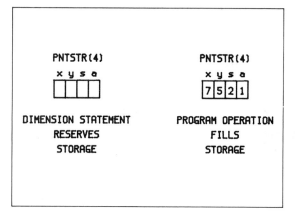

Figure 8-5A.

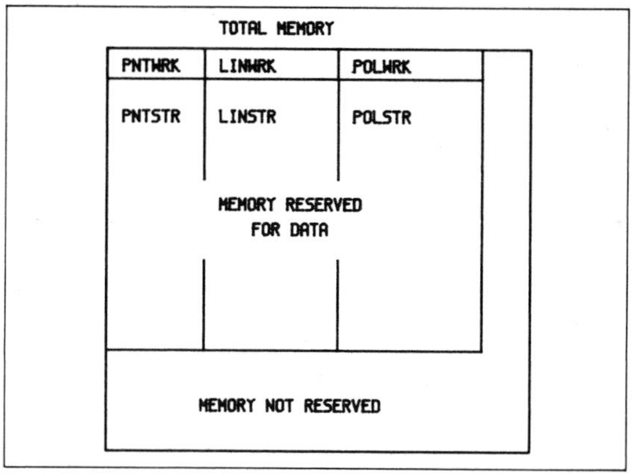

Figure 8-5B.

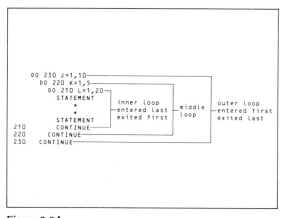

Figure 8-6A.

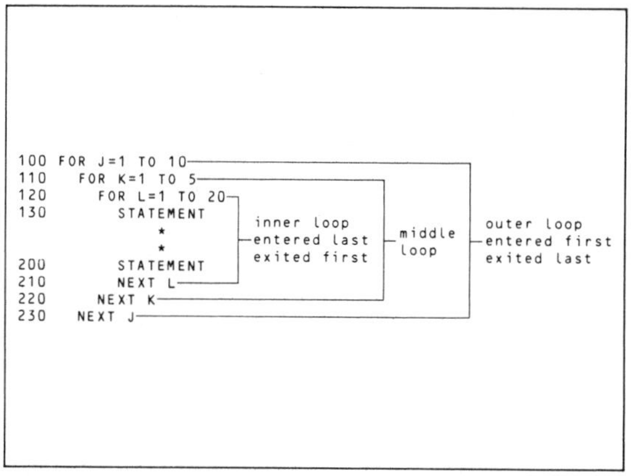

Figure 8-6B.

8×40, the system will allocate 320 memory locations for it. If each element requires 4 bytes, 1320 bytes of space would be reserved for that array. Obviously, large arrays will use up the available memory very quickly, so it is important that arrays not be dimensioned any larger than needed (see Figure 8-5B).

Address calculations for arrays are quite simple. The first subscript (shown in parentheses) of the array always represents the row number and the second subscript is always the column number. The third element in the second row of an array named LINES, for example (see Table 8-2), would be LINES(2,3). This part of the array contains the value of Y1 for line number 2. Many computers store arrays column by column instead of row by row. Consequently, care must be taken to avoid improperly dimensioning and filling an array. Data are typically written into arrays and read from them using statements in nested loops. Figures 8-6A and 8-6B show nested loop code for FORTRAN and BASIC programs respectively. Nesting the statements in the same order for both the WRITE and READ operations will assure that the data is not mixed up in the process. For an

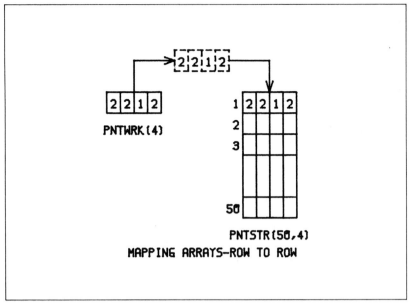

Figure 8-7.

array of more than two dimensions, the third subscript will represent the third dimension (the page) and additional subscripts will represent additional dimensions.

It is often desirable to "map" the data from one array to another array of different dimensions. For instance, a one-dimensional "working" array might be used to manipulate the data needed to draw a point. A two-dimensional array might be used to store the data for all points. Suppose a four-element working array, PNTWRK, is needed for one point. Suppose further that we wish to store the data for 50 points. Then we might define a 4 × 50 array, PNTSTR, and dimension the arrays as

```
DIMENSION   PNTWRK(4),PNTSTR(4,50)
```

Or, alternatively, as

```
DIMENSION   PNTWRK(4),PNTSTR(50,4)
```

Which statement is correct? Are they both correct? If so, which is best? Does it make any difference which one we use?

The array PNTSTR in the first DIMENSION statement contains 4 rows of 50 columns. Thus, there is one row for each element in PNTWRK. The second DIMENSION statement gives PNTSTR 50 rows and 4 columns, or one column for each element in PNTWRK. Consequently, if we use the first dimension statement, we should map to PNTSTR column by column, as represented in Figure 8-7. This is the way the computer will do it if given only the set name.

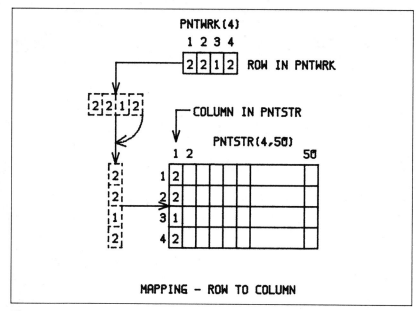

Figure 8-8.

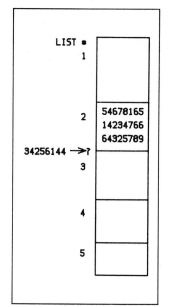

Figure 8-9.

Using the second DIMENSION statement, we need to map row by row, as represented by Figure 8-8. To do this, we simply set up a loop and increment the column subscript while holding the row subscript constant. To do another row, we increment the row subscript and again hold it constant while incrementing the column subscript to fill the row.

Lists

We are all familiar with lists. We have shopping lists, lists of jobs we need to do, lists of our possessions, perhaps even lists of people we like (or do not like). Data structures described as lists are very similar to these. They are simply a collection of individual records. A two-dimensional array could be treated as a list of one-dimensional arrays.

Suppose we have only one long, narrow sheet of paper on which to make a list but that we have several different lists to make and, further, that we will need to add items to each of the lists from time to time. We can reserve a section of the paper for each list if we know how many items to expect to have on each list (see Figure 8-9). What if the amount of space we reserve for a list is too small? Our solution on paper might be to print smaller and try to squeeze more items into the space, but this does not work on a computer. Another solution (the one used on computers) is to simply enter the items in the order that they become known. This procedure produces several lists mixed together. How do we know which items belong to which list? Suppose we number each item. Now suppose that, as part of the information for each item, we include the item number of the previ-

Table 8-3A.

Array Name Is LINES	1	2	3	4	5	6
			Columns			
Row 1		X1	Y1	X2	Y2	
Row 2		X1	Y1	X2	Y2	
Row 3		X1	Y1	X2	Y2	
Row 4		X1	Y1	X2	Y2	
Row 5		X1	Y1	X2	Y2	

Table 8-3B.

Array Name Is LINES	1	2	3	4	5	6
			Columns			
Row 1	0	0	50	50	75	4
Row 2	5	200	120	250	80	0
Row 3	4	100	90	150	60	5
Row 4	1	50	75	100	90	3
Row 5	3	150	60	200	120	2

ous item belonging to that same list and the item number of the next item also belonging to the same list. The first item on any list will, of course, have no previous item, in which case we can enter a null symbol in the space reserved for the previous item. Similarly, the last item will have no succeeding or next item, but, again, a null indicator can be used. In this case, the null indicator will be replaced whenever an item is added to the list. A combined listing of this type (known as a *linked list*) would be difficult to handle on paper but it is surprisingly easy with a computer.

Table 8-3A contains the data of Table 8-2, only this time two more columns have been added, and the data have been shifted one column to the right to make space for a new Column 1. Column 1 will now be used for a pointer to show the row number of the logically previous row of data (record), and Column 6 will be used for a pointer to show the row number of the logically following row of data (record). Note that these are not necessarily the row numbers of the physically preceding or following rows, but of the rows we want to precede and succeed the present row.

In Table 8-3B we have filled in numbers for the coordinates of the lines we wish to represent as well as pointer numbers for the logically previous and following rows. Drawing these lines in the logical sequence shown will plot a line on a line chart (see Figure 8-10). Note that a 0 (zero) in Column 1 means that there is no previous record and a 0 in Column 6 means that there is no following record.

The group of records described in Table 8-3B can be accessed by scanning Column 1 until a 0 is found (in the first physical row), indicating that the first logical record has been found. The next logical record is found by reading the value in Column 6. It is seen to be the fourth physical row. Moving to Row 4, we find a 1 in the first

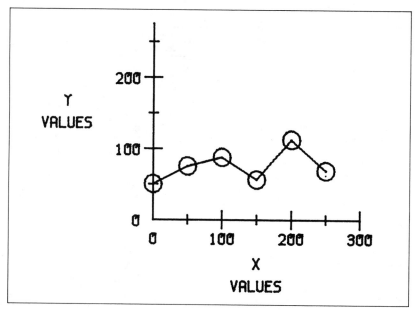

Figure 8-10.

column, indicating that it is preceded by Row 1. Checking Column 6 of Row 4, we find that it is to be followed by Row 3. We can continue on in this manner and check the logical order of all of the rows. Note that we are able to check continuity as well as sequence. If a row of data is missing or has incorrect values in Column 1 or 6, then the "next row" pointer of one row will not match the "previous row" pointer of the logically following row.

A more common use of linked lists is handling ordered data—say, an alphabetical listing of the students in a course. Any new student enrolling in the course must be inserted into the list and any student dropping out must be deleted. The former condition requires that a position be created within the list and the latter condition leaves a hole in the list. If, however, the list is linked, the new student can be added at the end and the pointers to previous item and next item can be changed on the affected records to fit him in. Likewise, the leaving student can be removed by changing the pointers to by-pass him.

Table 8-4A contains the names of several students. The pointers in Columns 1 and 15 arrange the names logically in alphabetical order.

In Table 8-4B a new student, Champion, R. K., has been added. Note that the changed pointers in record number 1 and record number 5 position this new record logically as number 2, even though it is physically in Row 6.

In Table 8-4C, a student, EVERETT, M. T., is to be dropped. Note that her name is still physically present but that the pointers have been changed to exclude her logically. Both pointers for EVERETT

Table 8-4A.

	Columns		
	1	**2 through 14**	**15**
Row 1	5	DOWNS G.S.	3
Row 2	0	BAKER I.R.	5
Row 3	1	EVERETT M.T.	4
Row 4	3	FOREST A.O.	0
Row 5	2	DANE G.T.	1

Table 8-4B.

	Columns		
	1	**2 through 14**	**15**
Row 1	5	DOWNS G.S.	3
Row 2	0	BAKER I.R.	6
Row 3	1	EVERETT M.T.	4
Row 4	3	FOREST A.O.	0
Row 5	6	DANE G.T.	1
Row 6	2	CHAMPION R.K.	5

Table 8-4C.

	Columns		
	1	**2 through 14**	**15**
Row 1	5	DOWNS G.S.	4
Row 2	0	BAKER I.R.	6
Row 3	0	EVERETT M.T.	0
Row 4	1	FOREST A.O.	0
Row 5	6	DANE G.T.	1
Row 6	2	CHAMPION R.K.	5

have been changed to 0, indicating that her record is not logically part of the group.

Stacks, Queues, and Trees

Many other types of data structures exist to serve the needs of particular types of data. Stacks and queues are used extensively within the computer itself. Tree structures are important in programs that are too big to fit in the computer and that must be overlaid (that is, divided into multiple parts that are pulled into memory, one at a time, as needed), as well as for large data bases. For our purposes, however, arrays will be the primary data structures to be used.

STACKS Stacks (see Figure 8-11) get their name from the fact that data can only be added to or removed from the end (top). Their arrangement is similar to that of a stack of paper with information on each sheet. Only the top sheet is accessible. As a result, the last data added to the stack are the first data removed. Computer instructions

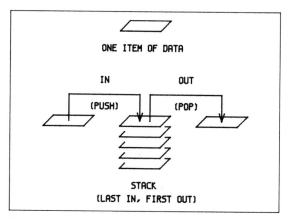

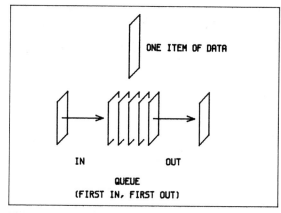

Figure 8-11.   **Figure 8-12.**

using stack structures use PUSH to add instructions to the stack and POP to remove instructions. Stacks may be implemented as arrays or lists, since PUSH operations simply add data to the next available element in the array and POP operations get the data in the last element that was used for PUSH. Stacks are used by the program for storing data, such as the contents of the CPU's registers, before branching to a subroutine. Upon returning from the subroutine, the contents of the registers are retrieved in the reverse order from that in which they were stored. We will not utilize stacks for user data.

QUEUES Queues (see Figure 8-12) are similar to stacks in that data or instructions can only be added to or removed from the end. However, unlike stacks, queues have two ends. Material is added to one end and removed from the other. Thus, the order of accessing the information is "first in, first out," just as it is in a waiting line at a fast-food restaurant. Since a queue is always being added to at one end and taken from at the other, it does not lend itself to implementation as an array. It might, however, be implemented as a linked list, since linked lists can be accessed at any point for addition or removal.

Queues are used for I/O (input/output) operations, such as outputting data to a printer, and for internal operations, such as fetching instructions and data for subsequent computations while the CPU is busy executing the current instructions. The new instructions are put into a queue until the CPU is ready to use them. This speeds up the processing, since the CPU does not have to wait while instructions are being fetched. As we did with stacks, we will leave queues to the operating system for program manipulation and will not utilize them for user data storage.

TREES Trees get their name from the fact that their form resembles that of a tree. They are a very efficient way to design large data bases

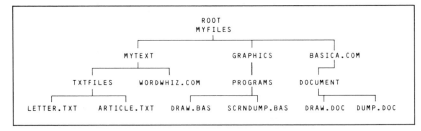

Figure 8-13.

that must be searched frequently. Binary trees, which are a special form of tree, lend themselves to binary search techniques. Linked lists, on the other hand, must be searched linearly. (Search techniques will be discussed later in this chapter.)

Another use for tree structures is to diagram the file-directory structure for systems that may have a large number of files. Many computers, such as the Apple III and the IBM PC running DOS 2.0, use tree structures for their file directories. Figure 8-13 shows a tree structure of a file directory on the IBM PC. The directory consists of a main or root directory that contains the names of files and also the names of other subdirectories that, in turn, contain the names of both files and other lower-level subdirectories. A structure such as this is very valuable when working with a large disk that may have hundreds or even thousands of separate files on it.

Still another use for trees is to diagram the relationship of the many separate routines that make up a large computer program. A tree diagram can be invaluable for describing the structure of the program. Trees will be used for this purpose in Chapter 15.

Use of Arrays to Store Data

We have referred to two types of arrays, "working" and "storage." The *working array* is a singly subscripted array that is sized to hold all of the data needed to create one graphic element. We will now consider what those data are and how to determine the array size needed. Figure 8-14 shows the relationship between a working array and a storage array.

Points Working Array

The minimum information needed to create a point on the screen is the point's location; that is, its X and Y coordinates. A point typically lights one pixel. If our program is to be able to delete, we need to also know whether the pixel is to be turned on or off. In some cases we may want to mark the point with some symbol, such as a small cross, so our information might also include symbol mode (dot, cross, or other symbol). If we are working in color or grayscale we also need to know what color to use. Finally, if we are storing the data in a list structure, we need pointers to previous and successive items in the list. Since we are not working in color or with linked-list

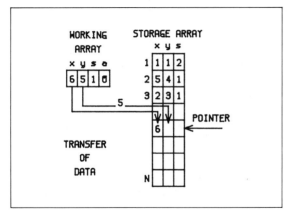

Figure 8-14.

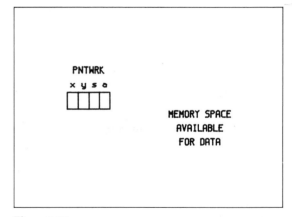

Figure 8-15.

storage structures, we can disregard the color and pointer data. What we have left, then, are four elements: X coordinate, Y coordinate, symbol mode (SYMBOL), and add/delete mode (ADDDEL). As shown in Figure 8-15, we will name this array PNTWRK (for points working array) and will dimension it to contain four elements:

DIMENSION PNTWRK (4)

to be assigned as follows:

Array Name	Element			
	1	**2**	**3**	**4**
PNTWRK	X Coord.	Y Coord.	SYMBOL	ADDDEL

Lines Working Array

Lines require the same information regarding modes, colors, and list pointers as points do. In order to draw a line, however, we need to know the coordinates of both the starting point and the ending point, so we have two pairs of coordinates instead of one. We may also wish to use various line types, such as solid, dotted, dashed, or center line, so we will add LINTYP (line type). Consequently, our working array will have seven elements (disregarding color and list information). We will call this array, shown in Figure 8-16, LINWRK (lines working array) and will dimension it as:

DIMENSION LINWRK (7)

to be assigned as follows:

Array Name	Element						
	1	**2**	**3**	**4**	**5**	**6**	**7**
LINWRK	X1	Y1	X2	Y2	SYMBOL	LINTYP	ADDDEL

Regular Polygon Working Array

One method we have used to draw regular polygons is to specify the center, one vertex as the starting point, and the number of sides

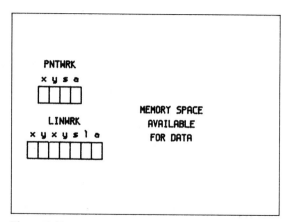

Figure 8-16.

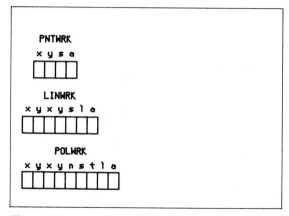

Figure 8-17.

(SIDES). This information requires five elements for storage. In addition, we need to specify add/delete mode. We may also want a choice of line types. A working array (POLWRK) with seven elements will hold all of this information:

```
DIMENSION POLWRK (7)
```

to be assigned as follows:

Array Name	Element						
	1	2	3	4	5	6	7
POLWRK	XC	YC	X1	Y1	SIDES	LINTYP	ADDDEL

An alternate method of defining a polygon is to specify the radius and the angle a line drawn from the center to the starting point makes with an axis. Since we would be eliminating two items of information (coordinates of the starting point) and adding two, we would still need a seven-element array. While this alternate method is very versatile, it has the disadvantage that the actual coordinates of the starting point need to be calculated by the system.

We modified our polygon drawing routine of Chapter 5 to a circle and arc drawing routine in Chapter 6. In order to draw arcs, we needed to know both the beginning and the ending point of the arc. The ending point was specified in terms of the angle of a line from the center through the arc. We then compared that to the angle of a line from the center to the beginning point and calculated the number of degrees in the arc. To make use of our working array for circles and arcs, as well as for polygons, we will need to add an element to store the length of the arc (SWEEP). We will also find it helpful to identify the type (TYPE) of figure being handled; that is, whether it is a polygon, a circle, or an arc. To do this we need to add two more elements (see Figure 8-17) to our working array:

```
DIMENSION POLWRK (9)
```

to be assigned as follows:

Array Name	Element								
	1	2	3	4	5	6	7	8	9
POLWRK	XC	YC	X1	Y1	SIDES	SWEEP	TYPE	LINTYP	ADDDEL

Irregular Polygon Working Array

Since irregular polygons typically do not follow any set pattern (they cannot be reduced to a formula), the coordinates of every vertex must be specified. As a result, irregular polygons are often drawn as a set of individual lines.

Triangles, squares, other rectangles, and parallelograms occur frequently in drawings. While they do not meet our conditions for regular polygons, they are all definable with a maximum of three points. As a result, they are often treated separately from other irregular polygons. An array to store them requires, as a minimum, the coordinates of three points plus the information as to number of sides, linetype, and add/delete mode. With this information, these polygons can be created in a manner similar to the other figures we have discussed.

Storage Arrays

The working arrays we have discussed are each capable of holding all of the data needed to create or delete one entity. In order to create another entity of the same type, we must reuse the same array elements, losing the data for the first entity in the process. Just as we write the data from variables in our programs to files for later retrieval and use, we need some place to write the data from the working array. *Storage arrays* are designed to serve this function. We will dimension a storage array to function with each working array. The storage array will be two-dimensional (double subscripted), and will be dimensioned so that one row (or column) will have the required number of elements to hold all of the data from the working array except for the add/delete flag. The other dimension (row or column) will be sized for the number of entities we expect to store. The add/delete flag will not be stored because we will not retain any data that pertain to deleted details. As we shall see in Chapter 9, this will reduce the amount of memory space required for storage of the data and will also speed up search and retrieval routines.

Figure 8-18 shows the relationship between working and storage arrays for the lines data. Note that the storage array has been named LINSTR (lines storage array):

```
DIMENSION LINWRK (7)
DIMENSION LINSTR (50,6)
```

to be assigned as follows:

Array Name	Element						
	1	2	3	4	5	6	7
LINWRK	X1	Y1	X2	Y2	SYMBOL	LINTYP	ADDDEL

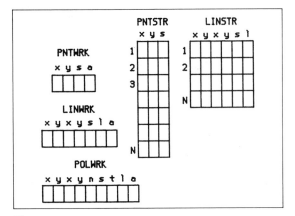

Figure 8-18.

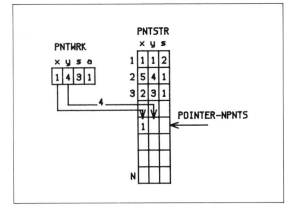

Figure 8-19.

	Array Name	Element					
		1	2	3	4	5	6
Row 1	LINSTR	X1	Y1	X2	Y2	SYMBOL	LINTYP
Row 2		X1	Y1	X2	Y2	SYMBOL	LINTYP
*		X1	Y1	X2	Y2	SYMBOL	LINTYP
*		X1	Y1	X2	Y2	SYMBOL	LINTYP
Row 50		X1	Y1	X2	Y2	SYMBOL	LINTYP

Transferring Data Between Arrays

The method we will use to transfer data from working arrays to storage arrays or from storage arrays to working arrays will be the same for all of the arrays. Figure 8-19 describes the process. We will use a loop to transfer the data, element by element, from one array to the corresponding element of the other array. For example, to transfer data from our points working array, PNTWRK, to the tenth row of our points storage array, PNTSTR, we could use the following code (assuming both arrays are in memory). Note that the add/delete code is not stored.

FORTRAN code:

```
      DIMENSION PNTWRK (4), PNTSTR (50,3)
           *
           *
      DO 50 K=1,3
         PNTSTR(10,K)=PNTWRK(K)
   50    CONTINUE
```

BASIC code:

```
10   DIM PNTWRK (4), PNTSTR (50,3)
          *
          *
100  FOR K=1 TO 3
110     PNTSTR(10,K)=PNTWRK(K)
120     NEXT K
```

To transfer the data for one point from the storage array PNTSTR to the working array PNTWRK with both arrays in memory, we

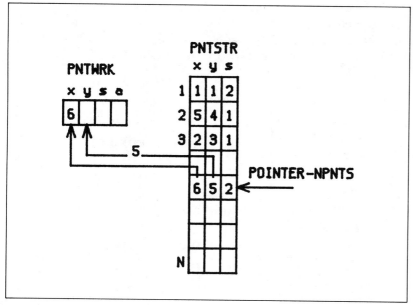

Figure 8-20.

simply reverse the process (see Figure 8-20) and then set the add/delete flag (ADDDEL) to 1 to indicate add mode. For instance, the following code transfers the sixth row.

FORTRAN code:

```
        DO 100 K=1,3
           PNTWRK(K)=PNTSTR(6,K)
100     CONTINUE
        PNTWRK(4)=1
```

BASIC code:

```
200 FOR K=1 TO 3
210    PNTWRK(K)=PNTSTR(6,K)
220    NEXT K
230 PNTWRK(4)=1
```

You may be asking, "How do I know what row of the storage array to use?" If you are adding to the array, you will want to use the next available row. Thus, if the array has the data for nine points stored in its first nine lines and the new point is to be the tenth point stored, you will use line number 10. Knowing what line to use is a matter of setting a pointer to the next available line and updating it each time a set of data is stored.

Searching the storage array to retrieve data is somewhat more complicated but can be readily accomplished. Suppose that the pointer for the storage array PNTSTR indicates that there are data in the array for 15 different points—that is, the first 15 rows contain data. We want to find the date for a point whose X coordinate is 140 and whose Y coordinate is 80. We can read each row of the array in succession and compare the stored coordinates with the ones being sought. For example, using FORTRAN, the data might be found as follows. Note that the code does not retrieve the data, it just locates it and then transfers control to another statement group that will take the appropriate action (retrieve, delete, or whatever):

```
C ** SEARCH POINTS ARRAY FOR DATA
      DO 320 J=1,15
C ** TEST X AND Y VALUES IN ROW J
   310    IF (PNTSTR(J,1) .EQ. PNTWRK(1) .AND.
   #   PNTSTR(J,2) .EQ. PNTWRK(2)) GOTO 390
   320    CONTINUE
C ** POINT NOT FOUND, PROCEED ACCORDINGLY
   340 * STATEMENT *
       * STATEMENT *
C ** POINT FOUND, PROCEED ACCORDINGLY
   390 * STATEMENT *
```

The BASIC version of this procedure could be written in a very similar fashion as follows:

```
280 REM ** SEARCH POINTS ARRAY FOR DATA
290 FOR J=1 TO 15
300 REM ** TEST X AND Y VALUES IN ROW J
310    IF PNTSTR(J,1)=PNTWRK(1) AND
       PNTSTR(J,2)=PNTWRK(2) THEN GOTO 390
320    NEXT J
330 REM ** POINT NOT FOUND. PROCEED ACCORDINGLY
340 * STATEMENT *
350 * STATEMENT *
380 REM ** POINT FOUND. PROCEED ACCORDINGLY
390 * STATEMENT *
```

If coordinates of the point in any row of PNTSTR match the ones we want, we immediately exit the loop. The value of J when we exit tells us which row of the array contains the data we want. If the test in statement 310 (line 310 of the BASIC version) fails—that is, the coordinates do not match—we simply increment J and test the next line. If we test all 15 lines without a match, the program will transfer control to the next statement after the loop (program statement/line 340) and we can take the appropriate action.

A difficulty that arises when we search a storage array is that the coordinates we have may not be quite correct. This is especially true if we are using a light pen or other graphics cursor device to obtain the coordinates. It can be frustrating to have the search fail time after time because the value we are using for one of our coordinates is off one unit. How can we ease this problem? Suppose we decide that we want to accept a point as correct if its X coordinate and Y coordinate are close to the test values, say within five screen units (see Figure 8-21). Can we design our test to allow that margin of error? Looking at our test in statement 310 of the FORTRAN sample code, suppose we changed it to the following:

```
310    IF (IABS(PNTSTR(J,1)-PNTWRK(1)) .LE. 5 .AND.
   #   IABS(PNTSTR(J,2)-PNTWRK(2)) .LE. 5) GOTO 390
```

In the BASIC version the test would be written as:

```
310 IF ABS(PNTSTR(J,1)-PNTWRK(1))<=5 AND
    ABS(PNTSTR(J,2)-PNTWRK(2))<=2 THEN GOTO 390
```

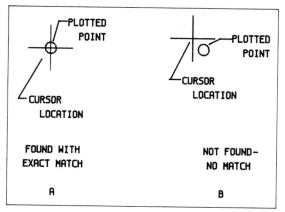

Figure 8-21.

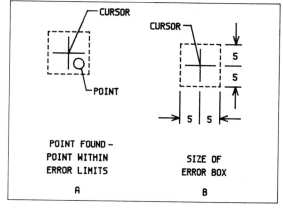

Figure 8-22.

Note the different error range for the Y coordinate. This is to allow for the nonsquare grid on our system (see Figure 8-22).

Now we can be a bit inaccurate in our definition of coordinate values. There are some limits on the amount of inaccuracy that can be tolerated, however. When a drawing is very dense—that is, when it contains a large number of points, lines, and polygons drawn close to one another—it is easy to get the wrong entity if the closeness factor is very large. It is a good idea to test several different values on your system to select the set that works best.

In some cases, the amount of imprecision allowed in the X and Y value may be different. For instance, on the IBM PC in high-resolution mode, the X values are somewhat less than half as far apart on the screen as the Y values. Therefore, a larger factor for X would be appropriate. In medium-resolution mode, however, the physical distance between X values is twice what it is in high-resolution mode, but the Y-value separations do not change. The closeness factor for X should be adjusted to take this into account. Many systems have grids that are not "square" and therefore may call for different closeness factors for X and Y.

Transferring data to the working array is accomplished with a loop in the manner that was discussed earlier (see Figure 8-20). Sometimes our purpose in locating the stored data is to redraw the figure in its original form. In other cases we may desire to change coordinates or dimensions and then redraw the figure. In still other cases we may change only the linetype or dot/cross mode. It might seem unnecessary to actually retrieve the data when only minor changes are to be made, since the data to be changed could simply be overwritten in the storage array. This approach can lead to trouble, however. The use of a closeness factor in the search may mean that the data being used for the search are not exact. Attempts to erase entities using inexact data will not be effective because parts of the figure will not be removed.

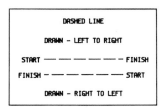

Figure 8-23.

Even if the data are exact, the order in which they are obtained is often important. For instance, a dashed line may be drawn on the screen from left to right. If, in selecting the end points for deletion, the rightmost point is selected first, the dashes and blanks will not line up when an attempt is made to erase the line going from right to left (see Figure 8-23). Consequently, it is best to retrieve the data, make any required modifications, use the modified data, and then resave them.

Deleting Data from Storage

When a graphics entity is erased from the screen, it is also necessary to remove the data for it from the storage array so that it will not get redrawn when those data are used to recreate the drawing. One way to delete the data from storage is simply to set the add/delete mode flag to delete and program the system to ignore any array data with a delete flag set. This approach has the advantage of not destroying the data. Recovery of the entity is thus possible if it is later found that it should not have been deleted. Another way to delete the data from the storage array is to physically remove it. Advantages to this approach are (1) the array space can be used for other data, (2) the search routines do not have to test the data, and (3) since all data in the array are add type, it is not necessary to store add/delete mode data, thus making the array one element smaller (another savings in space).

Techniques for data deletion and recovery will be discussed further in Chapter 9.

Tests with Multiple Data Points

The test procedures we have described for retrieving data from points storage arrays deal with only a single point (pair of coordinates); thus just one test is required. All entities other than points have multiple data values that must be tested in order to be sure that the correct entry has been found. For instance, any number of different lines can be drawn from the same starting point. However, given a single starting point and a single ending point, only one line can be drawn.

Tests for lines (except for advanced one-point tests, which will be discussed later) must, as a minimum, include testing both end points. In addition, it is often useful to test other features, such as line type, since the drafter may wish to overdraw a line in a different line type and then erase the original. Suppose a line has been drawn from (120,80) to (200,135) using dot mode and line type 1 (solid line) and the data stored in a storage array LINSTR. The working array is LINWRK. The arrays are dimensioned as:

```
DIMENSION LINWRK (7)
DIMENSION LINSTR (50,6)
```

The first two elements of LINWRK are used for the beginning point of the line, the next two elements for the ending-point coordinates, the fifth element for dot/cross mode flag, the sixth for line-type indicator, and the last for add/delete flag. The elements of LINSTR are the same except that it does not contain an element for ADDDEL. Suppose we wish to delete this line, having selected the end points and having entered all of the data in LINWRK. How do we make the tests?

A good procedure is to test only the coordinates of one end point until we find a match. When a match for this point is found, we proceed to test the coordinates of the other end point in the same row of data. If the coordinates of the second end point also match, we may test the dot/cross flag or the linetype flag. If everything matches, we have found the correct data. Otherwise, we go to the next row and start over with the first set of coordinates. If we are programming in FORTRAN, the code might look like the following (note that this code is not a complete subroutine; it shows only the portion of the routine that covers the actual search):

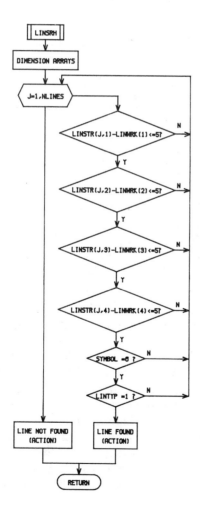

FORTRAN code:

```
C ** LINE SEARCH ROUTINE **
C ** NLINES IS NO. OF ROWS OF DATA **
C ** STORED IN LINSTR **
      SUBROUTINE LINSRH(LINSTR,LINWRK,NLINES)
      DIMENSION LINSTR(50,6),LINWRK(7)
      DO 2680 J=1,NLINES
        IF (IABS(LINSTR(J,1)-LINWRK(1)) .LE. 5 .AND.
   #    IABS(LINSTR(J,2)-LINWRK(2)) .LE. 5) THEN
          IF (IABS(LINSTR(J,3)-LINWRK(3)) .LE. 5 .AND.
   #      IABS(LINSTR(J,4)-LINWRK(4)) .LE. 5) THEN
            IF (LINSTR(J,5) .EQ. LINWRK(5) .AND.
   #        LINSTR((J,6) .EQ. LINWRK(6))THEN
              LINNUM=J
              GOTO 2730
            ENDIF
          ENDIF
        ENDIF
2680    CONTINUE
C ** NOT FOUND. TAKE APPROPRIATE ACTION **
      ** STATEMENT **
      ** STATEMENT **
C ** LINE FOUND. TAKE APPROPRIATE ACTION **
      ** STATEMENT **
      ** STATEMENT **
      RETURN
      END
```

The BASIC code may be written in a similar manner (note that this code is not a complete subroutine; it shows only the portion of the routine that covers the actual search):

```
2600 REM ** LINE SEARCH ROUTINE **
2602 REM ** NLINES IS NUMBER OF ROWS OF DATA **
2604 REM ** STORED IN LINSTR **
2610 FOR J=1 TO NLINES
2620   IF ABS(LINSTR(J,1)-LINWRK(1)) <=5 AND
       ABS(LINSTR(J,2)-LINWRK(2)) <=2 THEN
       IF ABS(LINSTR(J,3)-LINWRK(3)) <=5 AND
       ABS(LINSTR(J,4)-LINWRK(4)) <=2 THEN
       IF LINSTR(J,5)=LINWRK(5) AND
       LINSTR(J,6)=LINWRK(6) THEN
       LINNUM=J:GOTO 2730
2680   NEXT J
2690 REM ** NOT FOUND, TAKE APPROPRIATE ACTION **
2700 REM ** STATEMENT **
2710 REM ** STATEMENT **
2720 REM ** LINE FOUND, TAKE APPROPRIATE ACTION **
2730 ** STATEMENT **
2740 ** STATEMENT **
2750 RETURN
```

Let us now look at what this code does. The search loop begins at row 1 of LINSTR and will increment to NLINES, which is the pointer that tells us how many rows of the array currently contain data. This precludes searching empty, or garbage, data rows. The first test compares the X and Y coordinates of one end point to the stored data in the row being tested. If either coordinate does not match, the loop increments to the next row and the test is executed again. If the test is true, then the first point is found and the next test is executed to test the other end point. Again, if the test fails, the loop is incremented and the first test is executed to test the first point in the next row. However, if the second test is true, then the next statement is executed to test dot/cross mode and linetype.

Failure of this third test again increments the loop and the first test is executed on the next row of data. But, if the dot/cross-linetype test is true, then the right data have been found, because each test is run only if the preceding test was true. We then record the row number, exit the loop, and use the data as desired. Note that if all NLINES rows are tested and no match is found, then a different set of actions is taken. This usually amounts to notifying the user, setting a flag to notify the system, and returning to the calling segment.

While this search routine will work, it has a serious limitation. The line end points must be in the same order as when the line was drawn. If the line was drawn from left to right, for instance, a search using the rightmost end-point coordinates first will always fail. Modifying the code to test for lines drawn in the opposite direction will require more programming but is not difficult. Suppose we modify our previous search routine to the following.

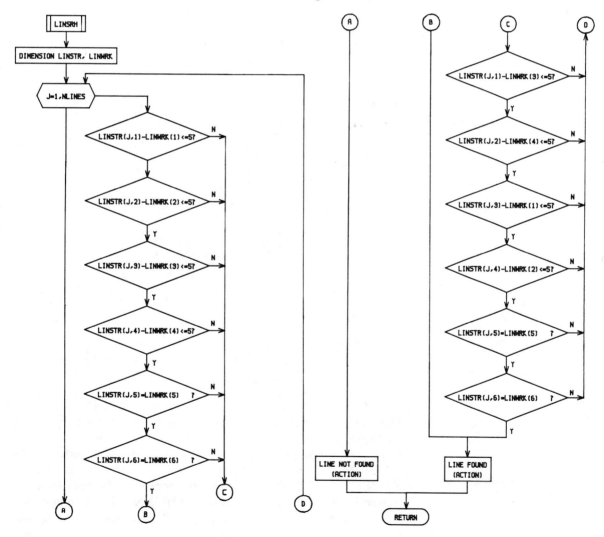

FORTRAN code:

```
C ** LINE SEARCH ROUTINE **
C ** NLINES IS NO. OF ROWS OF DATA **
C ** STORED IN LINSTR **
      SUBROUTINE LINSRH(LINSTR,LINWRK,NLINES)
      DIMENSION LINSTR(50,6),LINWRK(7)
      DO 2680 J=1,NLINES
        IF (IABS(LINSTR(J,1)-LINWRK(1)) .LE. 5 AND
     #  IABS(LINSTR(J,2)-LINWRK(2)) .LE. 5 AND
     #  IABS(LINSTR(J,3)-LINWRK(3)) .LE. 5 AND
     #  IABS(LINSTR(J,4)-LINWRK(4)) .LE. 5 AND
     #  LINSTR(J,5) .EQ. LINWRK(5) .AND.
     #  LINSTR((J,6) .EQ. LINWRK(6))THEN
     #  GOTO 2730
        IF (IABS(LINSTR(J,1)-LINWRK(3)) .LE. 5 AND
     #  IABS(LINSTR(J,2)-LINWRK(4)) .LE. 5 AND
     #  IABS(LINSTR(J,3)-LINWRK(1)) .LE. 5 AND
     #  IABS(LINSTR(J,4)-LINWRK(2)) .LE. 5 AND
     #  LINSTR(J,5) .EQ. LINWRK(5) .AND.
     #  LINSTR((J,6) .EQ. LINWRK(6))THEN
     #  GOTO 2730
2680    CONTINUE
C ** NOT FOUND. TAKE APPROPRIATE ACTION **
2700    ** STATEMENT **
        ** STATEMENT **
C ** LINE FOUND. TAKE APPROPRIATE ACTION **
2730  LINNUM=J
      ** STATEMENT **
      RETURN
      END
```

BASIC code:

```
2600 REM ** LINE SEARCH ROUTINE **
2602 REM ** NLINES IS NO. OF ROWS OF DATA **
2604 REM ** STORED IN LINSTR **
2610 FOR J=1 TO NLINES
2620    IF ABS(LINSTR(J,1)-LINWRK(1)) <=5 AND
        ABS(LINSTR(J,2)-LINWRK(2)) <=2 AND
        ABS(LINSTR(J,3)-LINWRK(3)) <=5 AND
        ABS(LINSTR(J,4)-LINWRK(4)) <=2 AND
        LINSTR(J,5)=LINWRK(5) AND
        LINSTR(J,6)=LINWRK(6) THEN
        GOTO 2730
2630    IF ABS(LINSTR(J,1)-LINWRK(3)) <=5 AND
        ABS(LINSTR(J,2)-LINWRK(4)) <=2 AND
        ABS(LINSTR(J,3)-LINWRK(1)) <=5 AND
        ABS(LINSTR(J,4)-LINWRK(2)) <=2 AND
        LINSTR(J,5)=LINWRK(5) AND
        LINSTR(J,6)=LINWRK(6) THEN
        GOTO 2730
2680    NEXT J
2690 REM ** NOT FOUND, TAKE APPROPRIATE ACTION **
2700 ** STATEMENT **
2710 ** STATEMENT **
2720 REM ** LINE FOUND, TAKE APPROPRIATE ACTION **
2730 LINNUM=J
2740 ** STATEMENT **
2750 ** STATEMENT **
2760 RETURN
```

Observe the difference: Now the first test combines all three tests from the previous code. If the test is true, the program executes exactly as it did before, but if it is false, a second test performs the previous set of three tests with the input coordinates in reverse order. If either of the two tests is true, control branches to 2730, which records the row number of the line (LINNUM) and then passes control on to following statements for further action. Thus, the test

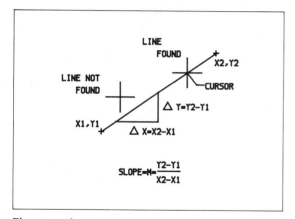

Figure 8-24A.

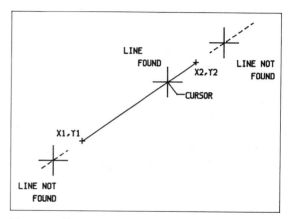

Figure 8-24B.

procedure will find the data no matter which end-point coordinates are entered first. This is not necessarily the most efficient testing procedure from a speed-of-execution standpoint. Can you rewrite it to execute more quickly?

One-Point Line Search

The search technique we have described requires that the user enter the coordinates of each end of the line. While this is an effective way of defining the line we want, it is somewhat slow. A faster method, used in many graphics packages, is to permit the user to select the desired line by touching one point on it. The search routine then has to find a line that contains that point (see Figure 8-24A). If the point selected is unique to that line, the search routine can go through the storage array row by row as before. This time the routine must formulate the equation of the line in the storage array and then test the selected coordinates to see whether they satisfy the equation. If they do, have we found the correct data? Not necessarily. One other condition must be met. The point must lie on the line that we found; that is, it must be between the end points (see Figure 8-24B). There may be several different collinear lines, and all will have the same equation, since all could be part of one line stretching from negative infinity to positive infinity. To make the last test we determine which of the two X values is smaller and then test to see that the X coordinate of our selected point is at least as large as the small X and not larger than the large X. Alternatively, we could use the Y coordinates for this test.

Referring back to our previous example, we had a line whose coordinates were (120,80) and (200,135). Suppose we have selected a point and want to find out if it is on that line. First we will develop the formula for the line. Remember that the general formula for a line is

$$Y = mX + b$$

where m is the slope of the line, b is its intercept on the Y axis when $X = 0$, and Y and X are a pair of coordinates. The slope is calculated as:

$$m = \frac{(Y2 - Y1)}{(X2 - Y1)}$$

$$m = \frac{(135 - 80)}{(200 - 120)} = 0.6875$$

Since we know two points on the line, we can write the two equations:

$$80 = 0.6875 \times 120 + b$$
$$135 = 0.6875 \times 200 + b$$

each of which is satisfied by a value of $b = -2.5$. Our equation now becomes:

$$Y = 0.6875X + (-2.5)$$

It is now a simple matter to evaluate the equation for the X coordinate of our test point and compare the calculated Y value with the Y coordinate of our test point. If they are equal, or if the difference is within an acceptable closeness factor, and if the X coordinate of the point is ≥ 135 and ≤ 200, then we have determined that the point does lie on the line. If these conditions are not met, the point does not lie on the line.

We now have a procedure for selecting a point or a line on the screen and searching the storage array to find the row in which the data is stored. We also have a method of copying that data from our storage array to our working array and returning it to the calling routine to be used to erase the point or line. Finally, we have a method for keeping track of the array row number if the data for the entity are to be erased. The logic is easily extended to provide search routines for polygons or other sets of data. However, the data have not yet been removed from the storage array nor has any means been provided to modify and replace the data. These tasks will be covered in Chapter 9.

Exercises

1. How many elements are required for a working array to describe a rectangle? What are they? Write a dimension statement for an array to STORE the data for 20 rectangles that will be drawn with their sides parallel to the X and Y axes.

2. How much memory does your system have available for each user? How many items of each type may be stored in memory if the limits on the dimension statement are the same for each entity? (Note: You have to determine the number of bytes required for integer and real numbers.)

3. Data for 50 points, 50 lines, and 30 polygons (circles and arcs) are to be stored and manipulated as arrays in memory. How many bytes of memory will be required if (a) the array elements are integer, (b) the array elements are real? Organize your answers as follows:

	Integer	Real
Points		
Lines		
Polygons		

4. Type in coded examples for (a) reserving memory space for storage arrays for lines and points and (b) drawing lines and points and storing the data. Verify that the routines work on your system. Use keyboard input and write the routines to call the examples for points only, for lines only, and for both lines and points.

5. Establish the closeness factors for your system. Do you use the same factor value for searching for coordinates for X and Y?

6. Write a search routine for circles.

7. Write a search routine for arcs.

8. Write a search routine for polygons.

9. Write two one-point search routines for lines, one to search on one end point and the other to search on any point on the line.

10. Write a routine that will blink the entity that has been found for user verification. (Hint: Alternately drawing and erasing the entity will cause it to appear to blink.)

Modification of the Drawing

Nothing can be more frustrating to a drafter than to have to redo an entire drawing because of some error or because of damage to the sheet. If every detail of a drawing had to be done exactly right the first time or the drawing started over from the beginning, the productivity of drafters would drop drastically. And even if the drawing were done perfectly the first time, future design or other changes could require that it be modified. In any case, it is important to be able to make the required modifications with a minimum of additional effort.

Reasons for Modifying a Drawing

Perhaps the most common reason for modifying a drawing is that a mistake has been found and must be corrected. The mistake may have been made by the drafter or it may be in the design or data that the drafter has been given.

Another common reason for modifying a drawing is to incorporate a design change. The engineer may find that the design can be improved with a relatively minor change, such as increasing the size of a bolt; a new model may require a slightly different configuration for styling, function, or safety reasons; or a drawing that is presenting data, such as a chart, may be changed to incorporate new data.

Engineers and other designers tend to think on paper. They commonly try out alternate ideas by sketching them and perhaps building models for testing and analysis. Their initial concept may go through many modifications before it is finalized.

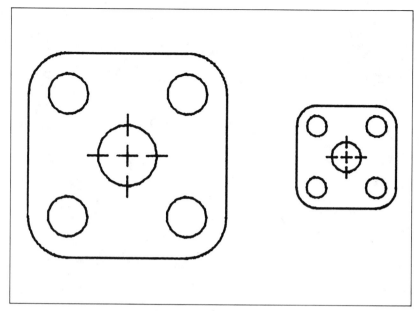

Figure 9-1. Bracket shown at full scale and at half scale.

Animation is becoming a very powerful way of analyzing the dynamic relationships of the many parts of a complex mechanical device. One way of studying the dynamic interactions of the parts is to build and test a physical model. Another way is to produce animated drawings that allow the operation of the device to be simulated. In this way, the interactions can be studied without the expense or time involved in making physical models. Clearly, frequent modification to the graphic images may be necessary when working with computer-animation simulations.

Still another reason for modifying a drawing is to change the scale. The same drawing may be needed for a number of different purposes. For instance, the drawing of a manufactured machine part may be used by Engineering, Estimating, Tool Design, and Manufacturing departments as well as by Sales, Inventory, Shipping, and possibly other departments. A very small version of a drawing could be used effectively in a catalog. Each area of a company has different uses for drawings and each may find that a different scale is appropriate. Each department may also want different details presented. Figure 9-1 shows a machine part at two different scales.

Deleting Details on Storage-Tube Devices

With minor exceptions, it is not possible to selectively delete details from a storage-tube display. Such displays retain everything that is created on them, whether it be drawing details, character information, or extraneous material.

The normal way you would delete a portion of a drawing on a

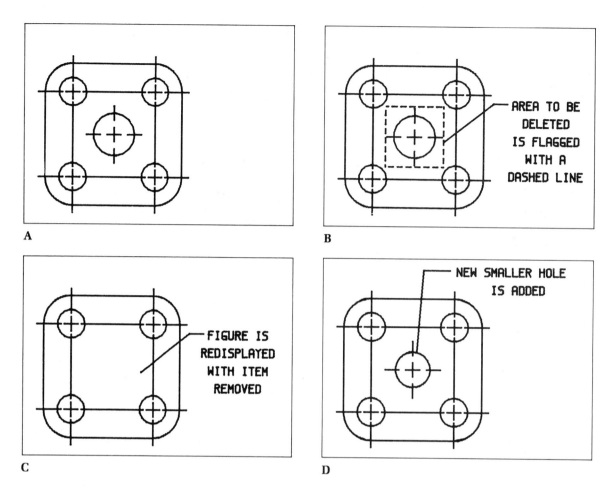

A

B — AREA TO BE DELETED IS FLAGGED WITH A DASHED LINE

C — FIGURE IS REDISPLAYED WITH ITEM REMOVED

D — NEW SMALLER HOLE IS ADDED

Figure 9-2. Deletion and replacement of a detail on a storage-tube display.

storage-tube display would be to first select and flag the details to be deleted, then erase the entire screen, and finally redraw all of the details that were not flagged for deletion (see Figures 9-2A, 9-2B, and 9-2C). Of course, the stored data are used to recreate the drawing, otherwise you would have to reenter everything from the start.

Deleting Details on Raster Displays

Since raster displays have the ability to turn any pixel on or off without disturbing the status of the others, individual drawing details can be erased without redrawing the entire display. Therefore, you could move from step A to step C in Figure 9-2 without the intermediate step of redrawing. Figure 9-2D carries the process one step further by drawing in a replacement feature.

Selective Erasing

The mechanics of selectively erasing or deleting unwanted drawing features may vary from system to system. On some systems the drawing details can be redone using dark vectors to draw over the

Table 9-1. LINSTR Array Contents.

		Column						
		1	2	3	4	5 Variable	6	7
		X1	Y1	X2	Y2	LINTYP	SYMBOL	A/D
Row	1	150	25	250	25	1	1	1
	2	250	25	200	75	1	1	1
	3	200	75	100	75	1	1	1
	4	100	75	150	25	1	1	1
	5	150	25	200	75	1	1	1
	6	200	75	200	125	1	1	1
	7	100	75	100	125	1	1	1
pointer	8	100	125	200	125	1	1	1
	9	200	125	250	75	1	1	1
→	10	250	75	250	25	1	1	1

light ones, thus effectively turning off the pixels at the affected locations. To use this technique you may call a routine that reverses the normal light-vector drawing mode. Many systems now have color capabilities and generally have a background or fill color specified. By setting the pen color to be the same as the fill color, or, if necessary, by swapping or toggling the pen and fill colors and then redrawing the details, you can effectively delete the details.

Updating Data Storage

When the drawing is modified, it is also necessary to update the stored data to record the changes. When a detail is deleted, the data for it must be removed from the data storage array. Since the information typically occupies one row of the array, we need a procedure for deleting the row.

One way to delete a row is to insert a flag that tells the system the row is not to be used. This flag is called an add/delete flag and is commonly used when it might be important to retain the data for future use or when the space is not needed for other data. Using add/delete flags is generally fast, since the array does not have to be restructured. The data of Table 9-1 were used to create Figure 9-3 on a system with 640 × 200 resolution and with the origin in the upper left corner. The data were previously entered and stored in an array named LINSTR, which was dimensioned to accept 50 rows of 7 columns each, as described in Chapter 8. Each row contains the information necessary to construct one line on the screen. A separate variable, NLINES, is being used to store the pointer that shows the number of rows of good data that the array contains. Note that some language versions start arrays with Column 0 and Row 0 instead of Column 1 and Row 1. Some provide an option allowing the programmer to select a minimum subscript value of either 0 or 1. We will assume here that the lower limit is 1.

The first two columns of Table 9-1 are the X and Y coordinates of

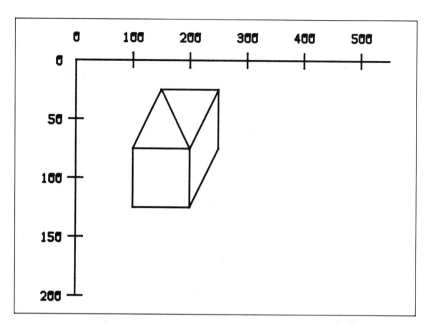

Figure 9-3. Drawing created from data given in Table 9-1.

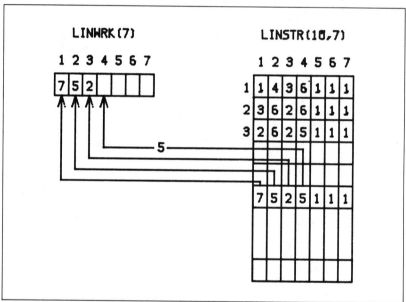

Figure 9-4. Transfer: LINSTR to LINWRK.

the beginning point and the next two columns are the X and Y coordinates of the ending point. Column 7 is reserved for the add/delete flag. If that column contains a 1, the line is to be drawn; if it contains a 0, the line is not to be drawn.

The following computer code was used to draw Figure 9-3. It uses a loop to copy each row of data from the storage array, LINSTR, to a singly subscripted array, LINWRK (see Figure 9-4), and send the data to the line-drawing routine (from Chapter 4) to draw the line. The loop increments from 1 to NLINES, since NLINES is the number of rows of data stored in the array. Note that the retrieval loop tests the add/delete flag and calls the drawing subroutine only if the flag is set (1). Alternatively, the retreival loop could call the drawing routine regardless of the row value and let the pen color be determined by the flag, but this is not recommended because it wastes time drawing invisible lines and because these lines will erase any drawing feature they cross at the points of intersection. Note also that the routine makes no use whatsoever of the line type or symbol information contained in the data. That sophistication could be added to the drawing routine if desired. It will be discussed later in this chapter.

Flow charts:

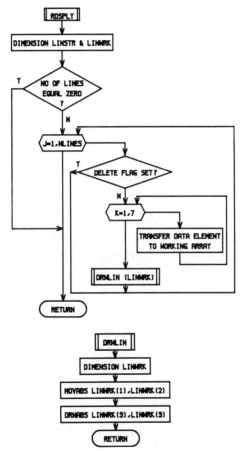

FORTRAN code:

```
C ** RETRIEVE DATA AND REDISPLAY DRAWING **
      SUBROUTINE RDSPLY (LINSTR,LINWRK,NLINES)
      DIMENSION LINSTR(50,7),LINWRK(7)
      IF (NLINES .EQ. 0) GOTO 999
C ** BEGIN LOOP **
      DO 100 J=1,NLINES
         IF (LINSTR(J,7) .EQ. 0) GOTO 100
         DO 50 K=1,7
            LINWRK(K)=LINSTR(J,K)
```

```
50        CONTINUE
          CALL DRWLIN (LINWRK)
100       CONTINUE
999   RETURN
      END


C ** DRAW LINE BETWEEN POINTS **
      SUBROUTINE DRWLIN (LINWRK)
      DIMENSION LINWRK(7)
      CALL MOVABS (LINWRK(1),LINWRK(2))
      CALL DRWABS (LINWRK(3),LINWRK(4))
      RETURN
      END
```

BASIC code:

```
6000 REM ** SUBROUTINE TO RETRIEVE DATA AND **
6010 REM ** REDISPLAY DRAWING **
6080 IF NLINES = 0 THEN GOTO 6400
6090 REM ** BEGIN LOOP **
6100 FOR J=1 TO NLINES
6110    IF LINSTR(J,7)=0 THEN GOTO 6160
6120    FOR K=1 TO 7
6130       LINWRK(K)=LINSTR(J,K)
6140    NEXT K
6150    GOSUB 2200:REM ** LINE DRAWING ROUTINE **
6160    NEXT J
6400 RETURN


2200 REM ** SUBROUTINE TO DRAW LINE BETWEEN POINTS **
2230 LINE (LINWRK(1),LINWRK(2))-(LINWRK(3),LINWRK(4)),1
2390 RETURN
```

Suppose we wish to delete the diagonal line in the top of the box. The data for that line would be located and retrieved using the procedures described in chapter 8, along with those covered later in this chapter. Note that it is Row 5 of the data in Table 9-1. If the system has selective removal capability, the line can be removed from the screen using the data retrieved from storage. To insure that the line is not redrawn, a 0 is inserted in Column 7 of the data row. Since the drawing routine has been written to ignore any data that are thus flagged, the line will not be redrawn. If, however, the system does not have selective erasure capability, the 0 can be inserted in the row as above, the entire screen erased, and the display recreated. As before, the system is programmed to ignore flagged data so the line will not be redrawn. Table 9-2 shows the revised data.

Another way to delete a row of data is to overwrite it with other data. As an example, the array of Table 9-3 contains the same ten rows of data as Table 9-1. However, the add/delete flag column has been left off. As before, we desire to delete Row 5. This time we will overwrite Row 5 with data from Row 10 and then reset the pointer NLINES to indicate that only nine rows of good data exist (see Figure 9-5). Since the pointer indicates that Row 10 does not exist, the data it contains will not be used. Our modified array will look like the one in Table 9-4, and the modified drawing is shown in Figure 9-6. The next addition to the array will be to Row 10, thus overwriting the

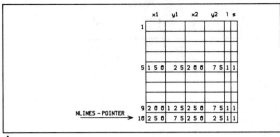

A

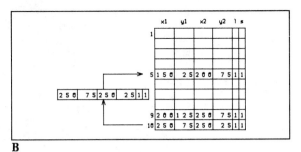

B

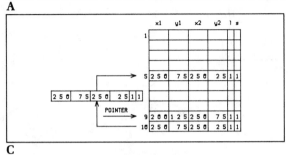

C

Figure 9-5. (A) LINSTR array with Rows 5, 9, and 10 shown. (B) Row 10 overwrites Row 5. (C) Pointer moves to Row 9.

Table 9-2.

		Column					
		1	2	3	4	5	6	7
						Variable		
		X1	Y1	X2	Y2	LINTYP	SYMBOL	A/D
Row	1	150	25	250	25	1	1	1
	2	250	25	200	75	1	1	1
	3	200	75	100	75	1	1	1
	4	100	75	150	25	1	1	1
	5	150	25	200	75	1	1	0
	6	200	75	200	125	1	1	1
	7	100	75	100	125	1	1	1
pointer	8	100	125	200	125	1	1	1
	9	200	125	250	75	1	1	1
→	10	250	75	250	25	1	1	1

Table 9-3.

		Column					
		1	2	3	4	5	6
					Variable		
		X1	Y1	X2	Y2	LINTYP	SYMBOL
Row	1	150	25	250	25	1	1
	2	250	25	200	75	1	1
	3	200	75	100	75	1	1
	4	100	75	150	25	1	1
	5	150	25	200	75	1	1
	6	200	75	200	125	1	1
	7	100	75	100	125	1	1
pointer	8	100	125	200	125	1	1
	9	200	125	250	75	1	1
→	10	250	75	250	25	1	1

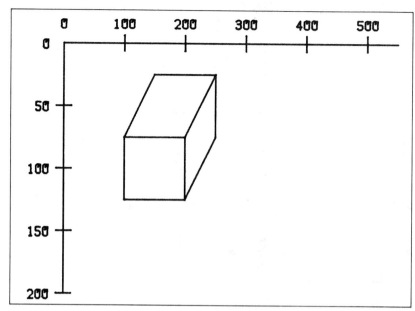

Figure 9-6. Drawing created from data given in Table 9-4.

Table 9-4.

					Column		
		1	2	3	4	5	6
					Variable		
		X1	Y1	X2	Y2	LINTYP	SYMBOL
Row	1	150	25	250	25	1	1
	2	250	25	200	75	1	1
	3	200	75	100	75	1	1
	4	100	75	150	25	1	1
	5	250	75	250	25	1	1
	6	200	75	200	125	1	1
	7	100	75	100	125	1	1
pointer	8	100	125	200	125	1	1
	9	200	125	250	75	1	1
→	10	250	75	250	25	1	1

duplicate row of data and eliminating it. In the meantime, Row 10 will not be recognized as containing valid information.

Of course, the program must be rewritten to use this data format. Our previous coded examples have been rewritten to read only Columns 1 through 6 of LINSTR. The add/delete flag test is not needed since there is no add/delete flag column. All data read are good data. The loops still increment the number of rows of data indicated by the pointer NLINES, which now calls for only nine rather than ten. The array LINSTR is, of course, dimensioned to LINSTR(50,6) so that it contains only six columns. LINWRK will retain its seventh column since, as explained in Chapter 8, the add/delete flag is used in other operations.

Flow charts:

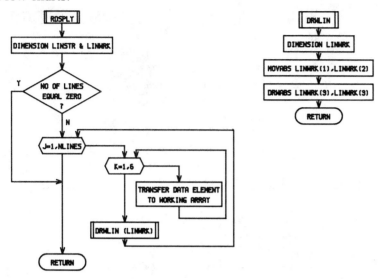

FORTRAN code:

```
C ** RETRIEVE DATA AND REDISPLAY DRAWING **
      SUBROUTINE RDSPLY (LINSTR,LINWRK,NLINES)
      DIMENSION LINSTR(50,6),LINWRK(7)
      IF (NLINES .EQ. 0) GOTO 999
C ** BEGIN LOOP **
      DO 100 J=1,NLINES
        DO 50 K=1,6
          LINWRK(K)=LINSTR(J,K)
 50     CONTINUE
        CALL DRWLIN (LINWRK)
100   CONTINUE
999   RETURN
      END


C ** DRAW LINE BETWEEN POINTS **
      SUBROUTINE DRWLIN (LINWRK)
      DIMENSION LINWRK(7)
      CALL MOVABS (LINWRK(1),LINWRK(2))
      CALL DRWABS (LINWRK(3),LINWRK(4))
      RETURN
      END
```

In the following BASIC version, LINSTR will be redimensioned to six columns, as in the FORTRAN version, and LINWRK will remain at seven columns. That is not obvious when looking at the code since the dimensioning is done in the main routine, which is not shown. Unlike FORTRAN, interpretive BASIC does not require redimensioning in every subroutine.

BASIC code:

```
6000 REM ** SUBROUTINE TO RETRIEVE DATA AND **
6010 REM ** REDISPLAY DRAWING **
6080 IF NLINES = 0 THEN GOTO 6400
6090 REM ** BEGIN LOOP **
```

Table 9-5.

		Column					
		1	2	3	4	5	6
					Variable		
		X1	Y1	X2	Y2	LINTYP	SYMBOL
Row	1	150	25	250	25	1	1
	2	250	25	200	75	1	1
	3	200	75	100	75	1	1
	4	100	75	150	25	1	1
	5	200	75	200	125	1	1
	6	100	75	100	125	1	1
	7	100	125	200	125	1	1
pointer	8	200	125	250	75	1	1
	9	250	75	250	25	1	1
→	10	250	75	250	25	1	1

```
6100 FOR J=1 TO NLINES
6120   FOR K=1 TO 6
6130     LINWRK(K)=LINSTR(J,K)
6140     NEXT K
6150   GOSUB 2200:REM ** LINE DRAWING ROUTINE **
6160   NEXT J
6400 RETURN


2200 REM ** SUBROUTINE TO DRAW LINE BETWEEN POINTS **
2230 LINE (LINWRK(1),LINWRK(2))-(LINWRK(3),LINWRK(4)),1
2390 RETURN
```

Suppose that the order in which the data appear in the array is important. In this case, moving the data from Row 10 to Row 5 will not be feasible. An alternative is to write the data from Row 6 to Row 5, then write the data from 7 to 6, from 8 to 7, from 9 to 8, and, finally, from 10 to 9. The pointer NLINES is then decremented as before. The modified array will look like Table 9-5. This process takes much longer than simply writing Row 10 to Row 5, so it should not be used unless it is necessary to protect the integrity of the data. The code for this routine is left as an exercise for the reader. The finished drawing should look the same as Figure 9-6. Figure 9-7 depicts the process.

Mechanics of Detail Deletion

The mechanics of deleting details consist of four separate steps: (1) entering the description of the detail to be deleted, (2) searching the storage array for matching data, (3) deleting the data from the storage array, and (4) erasing the detail from the display. These steps should be performed in that order.

Entering the Description

Entering the description of the detail to be deleted is generally accomplished in the same way that the description was entered to draw the detail. If the original coordinates were entered from the

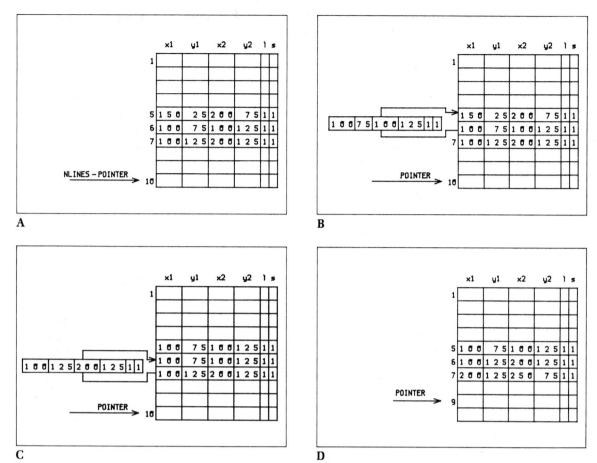

A

B

C

D

Figure 9-7. (A) LINSTR array with Rows 5, 6, and 7 shown. (B) Row 6 replaces Row 5. (C) Row 7 replaces Row 6. (D) Modified LINSTR array with Rows 5, 6, and 7 shown.

keyboard, those same coordinates can be entered from the keyboard again. Other ways the coordinates may have been entered include using a light pen, a joystick, programmed cursor control keys such as the arrow keys on the keyboard, or a digitizing tablet. While it is not necessary that the same input device be used for both creation and deletion, this is a common arrangement.

When entering data from the keyboard to delete a drawing detail, it is necessary that you know what values to use. You will not have ready access to the array data, as we did in the previous tables. Even if you did have such access, it might be difficult to relate a row of data in the table to a specific detail on the screen. That means that a record must be kept of the data and of the scale used to create the detail, or else there must be provision for interrogating the system to find the data and scale. For that reason, the keyboard approach is not an easy one.

The primary advantage of using a light pen, digitizing tablet, or controllable cross-hair cursor on the screen is that the device can be used to point at the feature to be deleted. The user does not need to know the numerical values of the coordinates involved. Some systems permit use of the arrow keys on the computer keyboard to drive a graphics cursor around the screen. The user positions the cross hair in the desired location and then strikes an alphanumeric key to select the coordinates of the chosen point. If desired, the ASCII value of the key that was hit can be used as a pointer to select the next action to be taken. Other systems permit similar control of the cross-hair cursor with a joystick, thumbwheels, or other devices. The IBM PC does not provide for cursor control with the arrow keys. However, a routine can be written by the programmer to accomplish this task. The technique is discussed in detail in Chapter 11.

Searching the Storage Array

When the entity to be removed has been selected and the data have been entered into the system, the next step is to search the storage array for data matching the entered values. The following code presents a search technique for lines data. In this example, the data are assumed to have been input in another routine (not shown) and passed to the search subroutine. The lines array is first searched, row by row, to find a set of data that matches the set entered for the line to be deleted. Since the user may not remember which end point was selected first to draw the line, the code tests the data as if the line were drawn in one direction; if that test fails, it retests the same data to determine whether the line was drawn in the opposite direction. When a row is found whose data match the entered data, then the data are retrieved from storage for return to the drawing routine to be used for deleting the detail. Finally, the row is deleted from storage and control is returned to the calling segment. This routine is an expansion of the code of Chapter 8 for retrieving data. The flow charts are shown on page 223.

FORTRAN code:

```
C ** LINE SEARCH ROUTINE **
C ** NLINES IS NO. OF ROWS OF DATA **
C ** STORED IN LINSTR **
      SUBROUTINE LINSRH(LINSTR,LINWRK,NLINES,NOTFND)
      DIMENSION LINSTR(50,6),LINWRK(7)
      DO 2680 J=1,NLINES
    #   IABS(LINSTR(J,2)-LINWRK(2)) .LE. 5 .AND.
    #   IABS(LINSTR(J,3)-LINWRK(3)) .LE. 5 .AND.
    #   IABS(LINSTR(J,4)-LINWRK(4)) .LE. 5 .AND.
    #   LINSTR(J,5) .EQ. LINWRK(5) .AND. LINSTR(J,
    #   6 .EQ. LINWRK(6)) GOTO 2730
        IF(IABS(LINSTR(J,1)-LINWRK(3)) .LE. 5 .AND.
    #   IABS(LINSTR(J,2)-LINWRK(4)) .LE. 5 .AND.
    #   IABS(LINSTR(J,3)-LINWRK(1)) .LE. 5 .AND.
    #   IABS(LINSTR(J,4)-LINWRK(2)) .LE. 5 .AND.
    #   LINSTR(J,5) .EQ. LINWRK(5) .AND. LINSTR(J,
    #   6 .EQ. LINWRK(6)) GOTO 2730
2680    CONTINUE
C ** NOT FOUND. SET FLAG, BEEP, EXIT **
2700  NOTFND=1
      CALL BELL
      GOTO 999
C ** LINE FOUND. TRANSFER DATA, DELETE FROM **
C ** ARRAY, AND RETURN TO CALLING ROUTINE   **
```

Continued on page 224

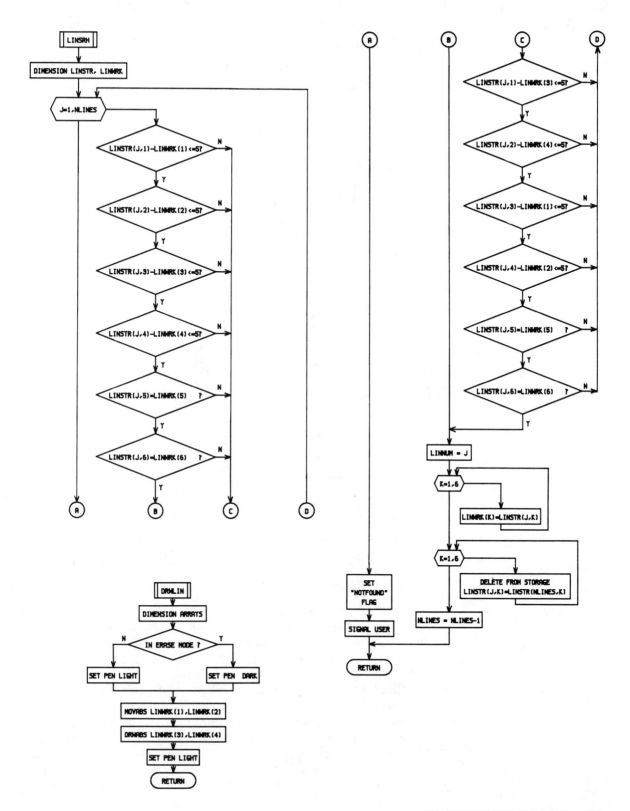

```
2730    NOTFND=0
        LINNUM=J
        DO 2780 K=1,6
          LINWRK(K)=LINSTR(LINNUM,K)
2780      CONTINUE
        DO 2810 K=1,6
          LINSTR(LINNUM,K)=LINSTR(NLINES,K)
2810      CONTINUE
        NLINES=NLINES-1
 999    RETURN
        END
```

The search technique coded below accomplishes the same task in BASIC. As with the FORTRAN code, this is an extension of the retrieval routine that was discussed in Chapter 8.

BASIC code:

```
2600 REM ** LINE SEARCH ROUTINE **
2602 REM ** NLINES IS NO. OF ROWS OF DATA **
2604 REM ** STORED IN LINSTR **
2610 FOR J=1 TO NLINES
2620    IF ABS(LINSTR(J,1)-LINWRK(1)) <=5 AND
        ABS(LINSTR(J,2)-LINWRK(2)) <=2 AND
        ABS(LINSTR(J,3)-LINWRK(3)) <=5 AND
        ABS(LINSTR(J,4)-LINWRK(4)) <=2 AND
        LINSTR(J,5)=LINWRK(5) AND LINSTR(J,6)
        LINWRK(6) THEN GOTO 2730
2630    IF ABS(LINSTR(J,1)-LINWRK(3)) <=5 AND
        ABS(LINSTR(J,2)-LINWRK(4)) <=2 AND
        ABS(LINSTR(J,3)-LINWRK(1)) <=5 AND
        ABS(LINSTR(J,4)-LINWRK(2)) <=2 AND
        LINSTR(J,5)=LINWRK(5) AND LINSTR(J,6)
        LINWRK(6) THEN GOTO 2730
2680    NEXT J
2690 REM ** DATA NOT FOUND. SET FLAG, BEEP, EXIT **
2700 NOTFOUND=1
2710 PRINT CHR$(7);
2715 GOTO 2790
2720 REM ** LINE FOUND. RETRIEVE DATA, DELETE FROM **
2725 REM ** ARRAY, AND RETURN TO CALLING ROUTINE **
2730 NOTFOUND=0
2750 LINNUM=J
2760 FOR K=1 TO 6
2770    LINWRK(K)=LINSTR(LINNUM,K)
2780    NEXT K
2790 FOR K=1 TO 6
2800    LINSTR(LINNUM,K)=LINSTR(NLINES,K)
2810    NEXT K
2820 NLINES=NLINES-1
2890 RETURN
```

Several important features of the search routine need to be discussed. One important feature is the use of a "closeness factor" or "proximity factor" in the search. The need for this factor was discussed in Chapter 8. (Refer to Figure 8-22.) When a detail is selected for deletion by pointing at it with a light pen or other device, it may be difficult to identify the exact pixel whose coordinates were used to create it. In order to make selection of the point easier, the search routine allows the coordinates of a point to be considered a match if they are reasonably close to the entered values. In our examples the X coordinate must be within 5 units and the Y value must be within 2 units. We have thus created an area 10 units wide and 5 units high (a total of 50 pixels) that we can select and still have the routine find the actual data. The proximity factors to be specified for a specific system will depend on the resolution of the system, the density of data to be drawn, and the desires of the programmer. If the factors are too small, it will be more difficult to delete details; if they are too large, the wrong points may be selected.

Another feature of the routine is that if the data are not identified in the storage array, the user is notified (by a beep) and the calling routine is also notified (by setting a flag) so the routine will not try to delete the detail. In some cases it may be desirable to display a message, either in addition to the beep or instead of it.

Deleting and Erasing

Deletion of the data from the storage array is accomplished by overwriting the row to be removed with data from the last row and then decrementing the pointer NLINES. Since the storage array does not contain a delete code, the data must be removed to prevent their being used when the drawing is redisplayed at a later time. Note that the data are not deleted until they have been copied to the working array LINWRK for use by the drawing routine. Also, no attempt to delete any data is made if the search fails. This precludes deleting the wrong data, such as the last row of data in the array.

Erasing the detail from the screen is done by the drawing routine. The routine actually redraws the detail using a pen color matching the background, black in our case. Of course, if the system does not allow selective erase, it will be necessary to redisplay the drawing in order to erase the detail. In this case, it may be desirable to wait until a number of changes have been made, since redisplay can be time consuming. Note that it is important to use the data returned from the storage array when deleting by redrawing with a dark pen, since the entered data may be inaccurate. The wisdom of doing so can be readily seen by drawing a line on a diagonal and then trying to erase it using slightly incorrect data. The usual result is that some of the pixels get turned off but that a large number do not. The difficulty is even more apparent when trying to erase a circle using a center point 1 or 2 pixels away from the real center.

The following FORTRAN code was written to work with a system that has library routines to set the pen color on a raster display terminal to LIGHT or DARK for drawing or erasing respectively. It is an extension of the routine developed in Chapter 4.

FORTRAN code:

```
C ** DRAW LINE BETWEEN POINTS **
      SUBROUTINE DRWLIN (LINWRK)
      DIMENSION LINWRK(7)
C ** SET DRAWING PEN COLOR TO LIGHT OR DARK **
      IF (LINWRK(7) .EQ. 1) CALL LIGHT
      IF (LINWRK(7) .EQ. 0) CALL DARK
      CALL MOVABS (LINWRK(1),LINWRK(2))
      CALL DRWABS (LINWRK(3),LINWRK(4))
```

```
C ** RESET PEN COLOR TO LIGHT (FOR USE BY
C ** OTHER ROUTINES) **
      CALL LIGHT
      RETURN
      END
```

The following BASIC code is also a modification of the line-drawing code developed in Chapter 4. It uses a pen color of 1 to draw a visible line (turn the pixels on) and a pen color of 0 to draw an invisible line, or to erase a visible line (turn the pixels off).

BASIC code:

```
2200 REM ** SUBROUTINE TO DRAW LINE BETWEEN POINTS **
2210 REM ** LINWRK(7) IS PENCOLOR TO BE USED. IT IS SET **
2220 REM ** BY THE CALLING ROUTINE. 1=LIGHT 0=DARK **
2230 LINE (LINWRK(1),LINWRK(2))-(LINWRK(3),LINWRK(4)),LINWRK(7)
2390 RETURN
```

Note that this code ignores the dot/cross symbol mode as well as line type. The dot/cross mode is easily added by writing a short subroutine to draw a cross using relative coordinates and then calling it whenever a cross is needed. The beam is positioned at the desired point with a MOVE or DRAW statement before calling the cross routine. The cross routine can be coded as follows. Note that the BASIC version assumes a nonsquare grid.

FORTRAN code:

```
C ** DRAW A CROSS AT PRESENT LOCATION OF BEAM **
      SUBROUTINE CROSS
      CALL MOVREL (-5,0)
      CALL DRWREL (10,0)
      CALL MOVREL (-5,5)
      CALL DRWREL (0,-10
C ** MOVE BEAM BACK TO STARTING POSITION **
      CALL MOVREL (0,5)
      RETURN
      END
```

BASIC code:

```
2800 REM ** SUBROUTINE TO DRAW A CROSS AT PRESENT **
2810 REM ** BEAM POSITION **
2820 PRESET -STEP (-5,0)
2830 LINE -STEP (10,0)
2840 PRESET -STEP (-5,-2)
2850 LINE -STEP (0,4)
2860 REM ** MOVE BEAM BACK TO STARTING POSITION **
2870 PRESET -STEP (0,-2)
2880 RETURN
```

The line type can be implemented by writing a subroutine to test the line type and then to access another subroutine that is programmed to draw a line of that type. PLOT10 contains library subroutines that will draw lines in dash patterns specified by the arguments of the subroutine call. Unfortunately, many versions of BASIC, including early releases of IBM DOS, do not have this capability, so the programmer must write his or her own routine. (Note that IBM's DOS 2.0 has limited dashed-line capability.) Chapter 15 presents a subroutine in BASIC to draw dashed lines. For the present we will assume that the line-type selections are either SOLID or DASH.

The following code presents subroutines for drawing solid or dashed lines. The FORTRAN version uses the PLOT10 subroutine calls and the BASIC version contains a GOSUB to an as-yet-unwritten dashed-line subroutine similar to the one in Chapter 15. Note that both subroutines will draw solid lines if the line type is other than 1 or 2.

FORTRAN code:

```
C ** DRAW LINE OF SELECTED TYPE (SOLID OR DASH) **
      SUBROUTINE MYDRAW (IX,IY,LINTYP)
      GOTO (10,20), LINTYP
 10   CALL DRWABS (IX,IY)
      GOTO 999
 20   CALL DSHABS (IX,IY,3)
999   RETURN
      END
```

BASIC code:

```
2900 REM ** SUBROUTINE TO DRAW LINE OF SELECTED **
2910 REM ** TYPE (SOLID OR DASH) **
2930 ON LINWRK(7) GOTO 2940,2960
2940 LINE -(LINWRK(3,LINWRK(4)),LINWRK(7)
2950 GOTO 2990
2960 GOSUB 12000:REM * DASH LINE SUBROUTINE *
2990 RETURN
```

We are now ready to modify our earlier line-drawing routines to make use of the new subroutines.

FORTRAN code:

```
C ** DRAW LINE BETWEEN POINTS **
      SUBROUTINE DRWLIN (LINWRK)
      DIMENSION LINWRK(7)
C ** SET DRAWING PEN COLOR TO LIGHT OR DARK **
      IF (LINWRK(7) .EQ. 1) CALL LIGHT
      IF (LINWRK(7) .EQ. 0) CALL DARK
      CALL MOVABS (LINWRK(1),LINWRK(2))
      IF (LINWRK(6) .EQ. 1) CALL CROSS
      CALL MYDRAW (LINWRK(3),LINWRK(4),LINWRK(5))
      IF (LINWRK(6) .EQ. 1) CALL CROSS
C ** RESET PEN COLOR TO LIGHT (FOR OTHER ROUTINES) **
      CALL LIGHT
      RETURN
      END
```

BASIC code:

```
2200 REM ** SUBROUTINE TO DRAW LINE BETWEEN POINTS **
2210 REM ** LINWRK(7) IS PENCOLOR TO BE USED. IT IS SET **
2220 REM ** BY THE CALLING ROUTINE. 1=LIGHT 0=DARK **
2230 PRESET (LINWRK(1),LINWRK(2))
2240 IF LINWRK(6)=1 THEN GOSUB 2800:REM * CALL CROSS
2250 GOSUB 2900:REM * DRAW LINE OF CHOSEN TYPE *
2260 IF LINWRK(6)=1 THEN GOSUB 2800:REM * CALL CROSS
2390 RETURN
```

Restoring Deleted Details

We have noted that the use of a delete code makes it easy to restore drawing details, since the data have not been erased, only the drawing. Sometimes a detail is erased by mistake or the drafter may want to remove a detail temporarily to determine the effect. In these cases it may only be necessary to keep the data for a short time. One way to do so is to set up temporary storage for the data. In the examples used in this chapter, the data for the deleted line would be copied into a seven-element array, TEMP, for temporary storage before flagging them for deletion or actually overwriting them. Then, if the operator wanted to restore the detail, the data from the temporary storage would be used to draw the detail and the storage array would be updated by removing the delete code or by writing a new line to the array. The actual data transfer to TEMP would be done with a loop, as were the other data transfers from one array to another. This will be left as an exercise for the reader (remember to dimension TEMP).

A common situation requiring restoration of details is deletion by mistake. The mistake is generally discovered as soon as it is made. In such a case recovery is easy, since the data still reside in the working array. A RESTORE LAST routine need only reset the pen color to LIGHT, redraw the figure, and store the data in the storage array just as was done originally. This, too, is left to the reader.

Remember that if the order of data storage in the array is important, and if the overwriting method of removal has been used, it will be necessary to "open up" a space in the array. In this case it may be desirable to dimension TEMP with an extra element (column) that will be employed to store the row number in which the data were stored.

Redisplaying (Redrawing) the Entire Display

The capability of redrawing the entire display is probably one of the most important features of a drafting package. As indicated previously, it is the only way to remove unwanted details from most storage tube systems. However, even those systems that have selective erasure capability make frequent use of REDISPLAY.

Systems that use keyboard entry techniques for data entry often erase the screen so that it can be used for data entry and then, when the data have been entered, redraw the entire graphics picture. Since data entry will occur many times during the creation of a large drawing, the REDISPLAY routine will get a lot of use.

During the process of creating a drawing and erasing details, unwanted extraneous marks will sometimes be retained because of failure to erase complete images or because of peculiarities of the system. Erasing the entire screen and redrawing all of the desired features will remove these blemishes, but REDISPLAY can also be used to restore detail lost by erasure of features. For instance, when two lines cross and one is erased, the erasure leaves a "hole" in the other line at the point of intersection. During the course of adding and removing several features, one may create a number of such holes. Figure 9-8 is a screen dump from the IBM PC showing some of these blemishes. Again, REDISPLAY is a convenient way to make repairs.

Using REDISPLAY to Verify Corrections

In some cases it may be convenient to mark features to be deleted rather than to remove them immediately. (This is especially true of

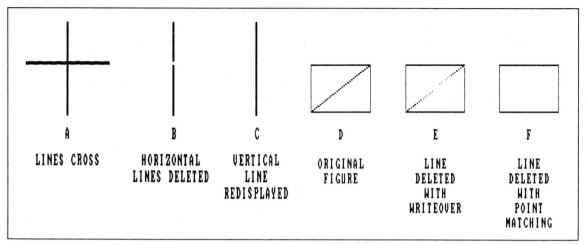

Figure 9-8.

storage-tube displays.) Then, when all corrections have been marked, the images can be erased and REDISPLAY used to redraw all retained features, thus verifying that the corrections have been made as desired. The usefulness of this approach is readily seen when a feature has been inadvertently drawn twice. Erasing it once will remove it from the screen but, since a duplicate set of data is still in the storage structure, redisplaying the drawing will reproduce the deleted feature.

The routines discussed in this chapter for modifying drawings have been illustrated for lines data. The techniques apply equally well to points, rectangles, polygons, circles, arcs, lettering, and all of the other graphic entities that make up a drawing. The code to modify these entities can be written as modifications of the code presented here. It is recommended that the reader write the code for other entities as exercises.

Exercises

1. The methods and code for deleting lines were shown in this chapter. Write the line-deletion routines and test them on your system.

2. Integrate the line-drawing and line-deleting routines with the point-drawing and point-deleting routines.

3. Modify the line-drawing and line-deleting routines in order to include dashed lines in addition to solid lines.

4. Modify the point-drawing and point-deleting routines in order to include points marked with a cross as well as points marked with a dot.

5. Write the routines necessary to redisplay the points and lines stored in the PNTSTR and LINSTR arrays.

6. Write the routine to search a polygon storage array for the data to match a given polygon, copy them to a working array, delete them from the storage array, and return to the calling routine.

7. Modify the polygon-drawing routine of Chapter 5 to draw polygons using either solid or dashed lines and store the information for redisplay.

8. Write a routine for points that stores the most recently deleted point in an array called PNTTMP and test it on your system.

9. Write a routine for lines that stores the most recently deleted line in an array called LINTMP and test it on your system.

10. Write a routine called RSTLST to restore the last detail deleted by retrieving the information from LINTMP, redrawing the detail, and inserting the data into the proper storage array.

11. Write a line-deletion routine that removes the deleted line from the storage array containing n lines and then moves the next line in the array into the vacant position. Each subsequent line should then move into the vacant space above it, as shown in Figure 9-7, until the pointer is indicating the nth $-$ 1 position in the array.

10

Scaling, Clipping, and Translation

In previous chapters we have dealt primarily with graphics that were created using screen coordinates; that is, the actual X and Y coordinates of the pixels that we wished to energize. We did not concern ourselves with drawings that might be too large for the screen or with the task of moving a drawing or portion of a drawing to a new location or duplicating it in a new location. True, we did some scaling of X values to make round circles and we did scaling and marking of axes in Chapter 7 when creating charts and graphs, but the subject was developed in only enough depth to solve the problems of the moment.

Chapter 4 described the CRT screen as being analogous to a sheet of graph paper. Each pixel on the screen was identified by specifying its X and Y coordinates. The origin was located in one corner of the screen, either the upper left or the lower left depending on the system being used, and all coordinates were positive integers. Lines were drawn by specifying the screen coordinates of the two end points.

Unfortunately, real-world values are not all positive integers. As we found in Chapters 5 and 6, when drawing polygons, circles, and curves, and again in Chapter 7, when plotting pie, bar, and other charts, we must deal not only with values that have decimal parts but also with negative values. In addition, we found that the distance between pixels in the X direction was generally not the same as the distance between pixels in the Y direction. When these distances are equal, the screen grid is said to be "square." When the grid is not square, pictures will appear distorted unless the values are adjusted to compensate for the screen's spacing difference. Cir-

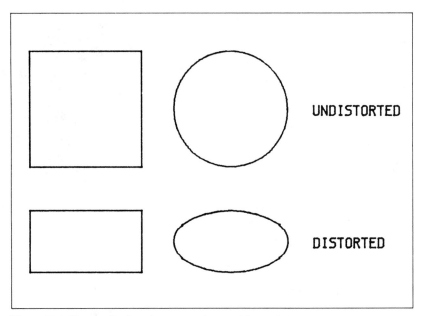

Figure 10-1. Figures displayed on computer graphics systems.

cles, for example, will look like ellipses and squares will look like rectangles with unequal side lengths or even like parallelograms. This effect is illustrated in Figure 10-1.

Adjusting to Get a Square Grid

In order to compensate for the screen distortion (lack of squareness) when drawing circles, we applied a factor to all X values so that units in the X and Y directions were the same size. We could have adjusted the Y values instead, but since the Y distances are greater than the X distances on most nonsquare systems, adjusting the X values was easier and more effective. With one system (see Figure 10-2) the Y distance between pixels was 2.5 times the X distance when using high-resolution mode, so when drawing a circle we calculated the X and Y distance of each needed point from the center and then multiplied each X distance by 2.5.

The technique we used consisted of two separate adjustments. First, we treated the center of the circle as the origin. Remember that the general equation for a circle is $(X - a)^2 + (Y - b)^2 = r^2$, where a and b are the coordinates of the center of the circle (see Figure 10-3A). Placing the origin at the center of the circle, as shown in Figure 10-3B, reduced a and b to 0 and thus simplified our equation. Another effect of moving the origin was that we were able to use negative values for X and Y as well as positive ones. Second, we multiplied the X values by 2.5, thus rescaling the screen. We also rounded all resulting X and Y coordinates to integers and then converted them back to screen coordinates by calculating their values relative to the origin in the corner of the screen. Finally, we used

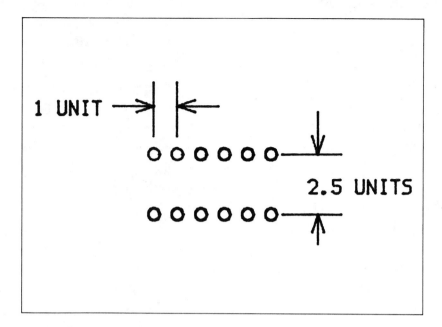

Figure 10-2. Distance between pixels on an example screen.

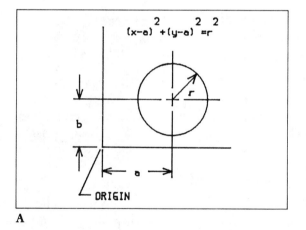

A

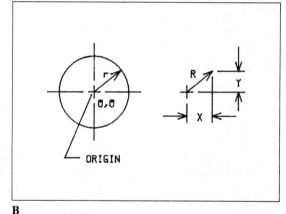

B

Figure 10-3. Circle drawn with origin in lower-left corner of screen. (B) Origin in center of circle.

these recalculated X and Y values as the arguments for the MOVE, POINT, and DRAW commands needed to create the circle.

The process of converting the values from one system to another—in our case, from the coordinate system whose origin is at the center of the circle to the coordinate system whose origin is in one corner of the screen—is known as "mapping." In our example we had only to add the constant value of a (from our general circle formula) to each X value and the constant value of b to each Y value, since the X values had already been adjusted to keep the range the same as the range of X screen coordinates and the number of units (range) in the Y direction had not been changed, only the location of the origin.

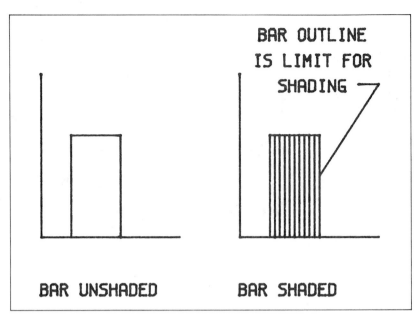

Figure 10-4.

Although it was not described as such, the process of scaling the axes and marking the data points in the charting exercises of Chapter 7 was a more complicated exercise in mapping. In this case, not only was the origin moved to the intersection of the abscissa and the ordinate, but the data range was adjusted to fit the range of the data being plotted. For instance, in Figure 7-15, 1 pixel vertically on the screen represented several units. Additionally, the chart's origin was placed at (150,129). The screen's origin was in the upper left corner, but all calculations converted to the chart origin and plotted positive values upward and to the right from that point rather than downward and to the right. Formulas for accomplishing this are presented later in this chapter.

Defining the Display Area as Other Than the Full Screen
In previous chapters we always used the full display screen as the display area. There are many times, however, when it is useful to be able to use only a part of the screen. One such case is when work is to be confined to a portion of the screen, such as in shading, cross-hatching, or otherwise detailing a feature, as illustrated in Figure 10-4. Some systems provide "fill" or "paint" commands that allow a specified area to be colored. This is very useful when creating bar charts, cutaway views of an object, or views where different areas are to be shaded to provide a feeling of perspective or depth.

Another reason for limiting the drawing area is to provide room on the screen for other drawing. Sometimes it is convenient to be able to create more than one drawing and to keep the visible parts of each drawing within predefined boundaries.

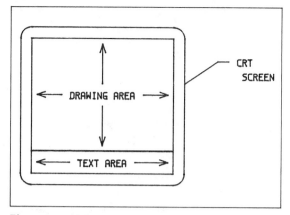

Figure 10-5. CRT screen with reserved text area.

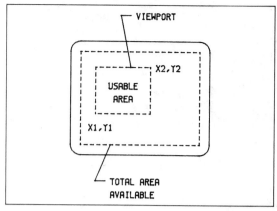

Figure 10-6.

Still a third reason for limiting the drawing area is to provide room for displaying text. It is common practice to display menus, prompts, and other messages on the screen to guide the user. A special area that cannot be drawn in should be reserved for this purpose. It is also common practice to place notes, bills of material, and title blocks on drawings. Again, the areas for these uses should be kept free of other drawing. Figure 10-5 illustrates a CRT screen with the lower area reserved for inputting text. This is a common practice with Apple II computers in graphics mode.

Techniques used to confine the work area to a part of the screen will vary depending on the system being used and the complexity of the area being defined. The most common practice is to confine drawing to a rectangular area that is defined by horizontal and vertical lines. Many graphics languages contain statements that will accomplish this task. PLOT10, for instance, has a VIEWPORT statement that allows you to specify the minimum and maximum X and Y coordinates for the drawing, as illustrated in Figure 10-6. The default is the full screen. If you wish to draw on only the left half of a screen with 1024 × 780 resolution, the minimum X value might be set at 0, the maximum X at 512, the minimum Y at 0, and the maximum Y at 779. Any drawing specified would then be confined to that area. A line to be drawn from (400,300) to (625,300), for example, would be visible only from (400,300) to (512,300). The other portion of the line would be outside the viewport area and would not be displayed (see Figure 10-7). Similarly, if a circle were drawn at (500,300) with radius 100, nearly half the circle would be outside the viewport and would not be displayed (see Figure 10-8). Even if the drawing were created using real (user-defined) coordinates, the system would not allow drawing outside the defined viewport.

To use real coordinates, you specify the minimum and maximum X and Y values that are to be displayed. The system then maps them to screen coordinates and displays only those that are within the viewport. The range of user-defined coordinates is generally called

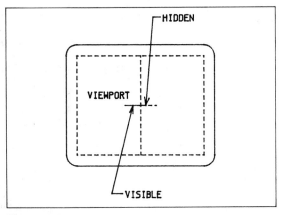

Figure 10-7.

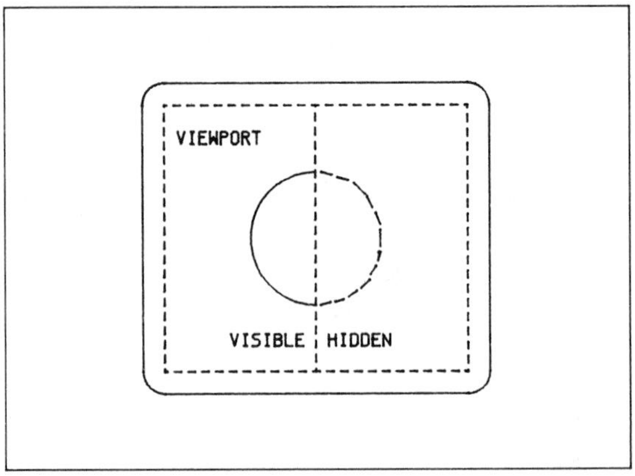

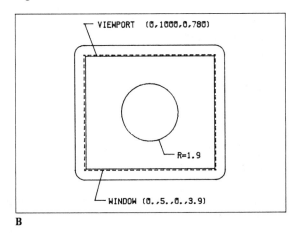

Figure 10-8.

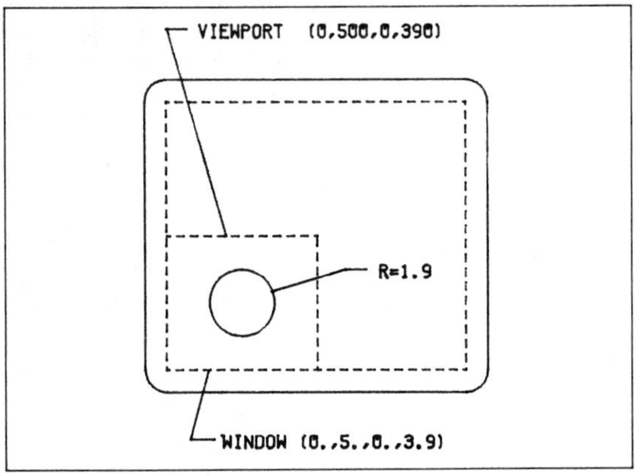

A

B

Figure 10-9. CRT screens showing same window displayed on two different viewports.

the "window," since it defines the range of data that are to be displayed. The viewport is the opening through which the selected data are seen. Figures 10-9A and 10-9B depict a circle with two different viewport specifications but the same window.

Apple III with BUSINESS BASIC contains a viewport routine that is called with the statement

```
PERFORM VIEWPORT(%LEFT,%RIGHT,%BOTTOM,%TOP)
```

The parameters refer to the left or minimum X, right or maximum X, bottom or minimum Y, and top or maximum Y, respectively. The percent signs tell the system to pass the parameters to the routine as integers. The origin on this system is in the lower left corner of the screen. As with PLOT10, the default is full screen. Unlike PLOT10, however, APPLE BUSINESS BASIC does not support user-defined real drawing coordinates.

IBM PC with BASICA does not contain a viewport statement in versions prior to 2.0, nor do a number of other systems. PAINT will restrict the fill to a defined enclosed area and CIRCLE will restrict the resulting circle to the full screen. Other attempts to draw beyond the screen boundaries may produce unexpected results. Coordinates that are outside the screen area may default to the limiting screen value, resulting in lines being drawn in the wrong place. Except for PAINT, no provision is made to limit drawing to less than a full screen. Consequently, it is up to the programmer to write the needed routines to provide viewport capability.

Clipping

Clipping is the name given to restricting the portion of the drawing that will be displayed. All portions of the drawing that are outside of the defined window are deleted (clipped), and the remainder of the drawing is displayed in the viewport. For systems that do not support coordinates other than screen coordinates or other than real values, such as the Tektronix 4051/52, the window and viewport are identical. Where real coordinates are supported, the drawing is clipped to the data window and the resultant drawing is scaled to fit the viewport. Thus, with different window specifications, various portions of the drawing can be presented in the same physical part of the display screen.

Systems that support VIEWPORT statements also contain routines that clip the image to the display viewport. Those that support WINDOW statements likewise clip to the window and also map from the window to the viewport. Other systems may contain certain drawing commands that clip. For instance, IBM PC, which does not support VIEWPORT in its earlier versions, will clip a circle created with the CIRCLE statement to the screen area as illustrated in Figure 10-10A. There is no provision, however, to clip the circle to any other viewport size. Consequently, it is up to the programmer to include a clipping algorithm in the drawing package if clipping capability is desired. While many systems that do not support clipping will default any out-of-range coordinates to the screen boundary value, some may provide very unexpected results, as shown by the circles in Figure 10-10B and 10-C.

Clipping is at best very time/resource consuming. The process requires a number of tests to determine what portion, if any, of a line is to be kept and what portion, if any, is to be deleted. To do this a number of tests need to be made. First, if both end points of the line are within the window, then the entire line lies within the window and it does not have to be clipped. If, however, one end lies within the window and the other end is outside the window, then the line definitely does need to be clipped. Suppose both ends lie outside the window. Figure 10-11 shows several such lines. Some of them pass through the window and some do not. Obviously, we cannot simply delete all lines whose end points lie outside the window. On the other hand, performing a complete sequence of tests on each of these lines will be a slow process. Can we establish any decision rules to reduce the number of these lines that must be tested? Referring to

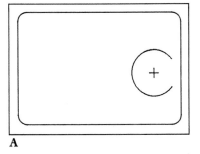
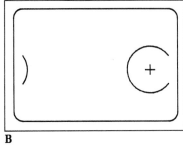
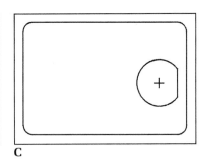

A   B   C

Figure 10-10. Circle drawn near the edge of the CRT screen. (A) The expected result. (B) A possible result. (C) Another possible result.

line A, we note that it lies completely to the right of the window. The X coordinate of each end point is greater than the X value of the window's right edge. Similarly, both end points of line B have Y coordinates that are greater than the window's top. Line B lies completely above the window.

By testing the X and Y coordinates of each line in Figure 10-11, we can eliminate four of the nine lines. The remaining five lines must be tested further to determine whether they intersect the window. One test that might be made would be to determine whether any of the lines are either horizontal or vertical and, if so, whether they lie entirely within the range of the window. A line is horizontal if both end points have the same Y coordinate. The line lies within the range of the window if the Y coordinate is greater than the window's bottom and less than the window's top. The test for a vertical line is similar. In our example, line E lies completely within the window and line F is identified as one that definitely must be clipped.

We now have three lines that are still in question and one that we know must be clipped. How do we proceed from here? We could go ahead and clip the vertical line to the maximum and minimum Y window extremes, but what about the other lines? One way to proceed would be to formulate the equation of each line, calculate its intersection with each of the edges of the window, and, when an intersection is found that lies within the range of the window boundaries, clip to that point. Any line whose intersections with the window edges are all outside the window boundaries will not intersect the window and can be rejected. This approach appears workable but is obviously very cumbersome and time consuming.

In our approach to the clipping problem in Figure 10-11, we first determined whether the line was entirely within the window. Referring to our routine for drawing lines, we might make this test with the following BASIC code:

```
2211 REM ** CODE TO CALL CLIPPING ROUTINE IF ANY ONE OF
     THE COORDINATES IS OUTSIDE THE WINDOW **
2212 IF X1<XMIN OR X1>XMAX OR Y1<YMIN OR Y1>YMAX OR
     X2<XMIN OR X2>XMAX OR Y2<YMIN OR Y2>YMAX
     THEN GOSUB 9000
2213 * statement *
```

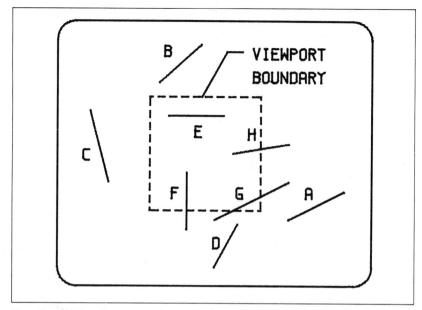

Figure 10-11. Lines in various relations to the viewport.

Note that the code sends the line data to the clipping routine (sub-routine 9000) *only* if a portion is outside the window. That way the program is not slowed down unnecessarily. When it is determined that a portion of the line does lie outside the window, the problem is turned over to the subroutine. We had decided that the first action of the subroutine should be to process vertical and horizontal lines. Clipping vertical and horizontal lines to horizontal and vertical window boundaries is a relatively simple process. Furthermore, these lines do not lend themselves to processing with the standard equation of a line. The slope of a vertical line is not defined, so the equation cannot be used. The slope of a horizontal line is 0, so $Y = b$ regardless of the value of X.

In the following BASIC code, the reject flag has been set (statement 9040). If the line is to be clipped (not rejected in its entirety), the flag will be taken down when the clipping is accomplished. Statements 9060 and 9070 test the line to determine if it lies entirely to one side of the window and can thus be rejected immediately.

```
9000 REM *********** CLIPPING ROUTINE ************
9010 REM ** XMIN,XMAX,YMIN,YMAX ARE WINDOW/VIEWPORT
     BOUNDARIES
9020 REM ** XP1,YP1,XP2,YP2  ARE ENDPOINT COORDINATES
9030 REM
9040 REJECT = 1
9050 REM **** TEST LINE FOR IMMEDIATE REJECTION ****
9060 IF XP1<XMIN AND XP2<XMIN OR XP1>XMAX AND XP2>XMAX
     THEN GOTO 9900
9070 IF YP1<YMIN AND YP2<YMIN OR YP1>YMAX AND YP2>YMAX
     THEN GOTO 9900
9090 REM ** PROGRAM GOES TO 9100 **
```

If the line is not rejected by the above code it is tested by the following code:

```
9100 REM ****** TEST FOR AND CLIP VERTICAL LINE ******
9110 REM
9120 IF NOT XP1=XP2 THEN 9200
9130 IF YP1>YMAX THEN YP1=YMAX:REJECT=0:GOTO 9150
9140 IF YP1<YMIN THEN YP1=YMIN:REJECT=0
9150 IF YP2>YMAX THEN YP2=YMAX:REJECT=0:GOTO 9170
9160 IF YP2<YMIN THEN YP2=YMIN:REJECT=0
9170 GOTO 9900
9180 REM ** PROGRAM GOES TO 9200 OR 9900 **
```

This code accomplishes three tasks. First, it determines whether the line is vertical. If so, then each end point is tested against the maximum and minimum window limits in turn and, if the end point is found to be outside the window, it is clipped to the window. Note that an end point clipped to one window edge is not tested against the other boundary. Why? Statement 9170 returns to the calling routine (via 9900), since any lines processed as vertical are now either clipped or rejected. Statement 9120 passes any nonvertical lines to the horizontal line test.

Any line that was not processed as a vertical line is tested and processed through the horizontal-line portion of the clipping routine in the same manner. The BASIC code is identical to the code for the vertical test except that X references have been replaced with Y references and Y references have been replaced with X references:

```
9200 REM ********* TEST FOR AND CLIP HORIZONTAL LINE
9210 REM
9220 IF NOT YP1=YP2 THEN 9300
9230 IF XP1>XMAX THEN XP1=XMAX:REJECT=0:GOTO 9250
9240 IF XP1<XMIN THEN XP1=XMIN:REJECT=0
9250 IF XP2>XMAX THEN XP2=XMAX:REJECT=0:GOTO 9270
9260 IF XP2<XMIN THEN XP2=XMIN:REJECT=0
9270 GOTO 9900
9280 REM ** PROGRAM GOES TO 9300 OR 9900 **
```

Any line that was found to be neither vertical nor horizontal must now be processed by testing it against each of the window boundaries in turn. We do not know at this point whether the lines are partially outside the window or totally outside the window. Remember that both ends of the line can be outside and the line can still intersect the window. To determine how to clip the line, we will first determine its equation. That can be accomplished with the following BASIC code, which calculates the line's slope and intercept:

```
9300 REM **** CALCULATE SLOPE AND INTERCEPT OF LINE ****
9310 REM
9320 SLOPE=(YP2-YP1)/(XP2-XP1):INTERCEPT=YP2-(SLOPE * XP2)
9330 REM ** PROGRAM CONTINUES AT 9400 **
```

We are now ready to calculate the intersection of this line with the window edges. The following BASIC code first determines the intersection of the line with the window boundary. It then tests each line end in turn to find out whether that end is outside the window. If it is, then the intersection is tested to see if it is within the range of the window boundary. Remember that the intersection calculation assumed an infinitely long line and as infinitely long window boundary (refer to Figure 10-2). If the intersection does fall between the minimum and maximum window values, then the line end is clipped to that intersection.

```
9400 REM ******** CLIP LINE TO MINIMUM X BOUNDARY
9410 REM
9420 YSECT=XMIN * SLOPE + INTERCEPT
9430 IF NOT XP1<XMIN THEN 9450
9440 IF YSECT>YMIN AND YSECT<YMAX THEN XP1=XMIN:
     YP1=YSECT:REJECT=0:GOTO 9500
9450 IF NOT XP2<XMIN THEN GOTO 9500
9460 IF YSECT>YMIN AND YSECT<YMAX THEN XP2=XMIN:
     YP2=YSECT:REJECT=0
9470 REM
9500 REM ******** CLIP LINE TO MINIMUM Y BOUNDARY
9510 REM
9520 XSECT=(YMIN - INTERCEPT)/SLOPE
9530 IF NOT YP1<YMIN THEN 9550
9540 IF XSECT>XMIN AND XSECT<XMAX THEN YP1=YMIN:
     XP1=XSECT:REJECT=0:GOTO 9600
9550 IF NOT YP2<YMIN THEN GOTO 9600
9560 IF XSECT>XMIN AND XSECT<XMAX THEN YP2=YMIN:
     XP2=XSECT:REJECT=0
9570 REM
9600 REM ******** CLIP LINE TO MAXIMUM X BOUNDARY
9610 REM
9620 YSECT=XMAX * SLOPE + INTERCEPT
9630 IF NOT XP1>XMAX THEN 9650
9640 IF YSECT>YMIN AND YSECT<YMAX THEN XP1=XMAX:
     YP1=YSECT:REJECT=0:GOTO 9700
9650 IF NOT XP2>XMAX THEN GOTO 9700
9660 IF YSECT>YMIN AND YSECT<YMAX THEN XP2=XMAX:
     YP2=YSECT:REJECT=0
9670 REM
9700 REM ******** CLIP LINE TO MAXIMUM Y BOUNDARY
9710 REM
9720 XSECT=(YMAX - INTERCEPT)/SLOPE
9730 IF NOT YP1>YMAX THEN 9750
9740 IF XSECT>XMIN AND XSECT<XMAX THEN YP1=YMAX:
     XP1=XSECT:REJECT=0:GOTO 9900
9750 IF NOT YP2>YMAX THEN GOTO 9900
9760 IF XSECT>XMIN AND XSECT<XMAX THEN YP2=YMAX:
     XP2=XSECT:REJECT=0
9770 REM
9900 RETURN
```

Note that clipping involves changing both the X and the Y coordinates of the line end. Each of the line ends is tested in turn against each of the window edges.

Several modifications might be made to improve the efficiency of the routine. For instance, if one line end point is found to be inside the window, no additional work need be done on that end point. It would not need to be repeatedly tested against all boundaries. Similarly, once each end of the line has been clipped, further testing is unnecessary. Each line cannot intersect more than two window edges. These improvements in the routine are left to the reader.

Obviously, clipping is a time-consuming process. When a large number of lines must be tested and clipped, as in a complex drawing, the time required becomes of major importance. A number of

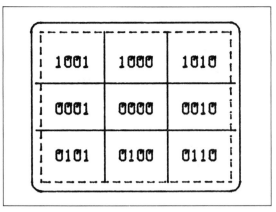

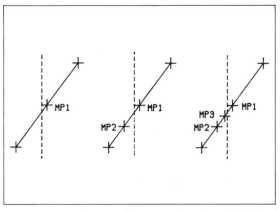

Figure 10-12. OUTCODEs used with the Cohen-Sutherland clipping algorithm.

Figure 10-13. Midpoint subdivision algorithm. The dashed line indicates the edge where the solid line is to be clipped.

clipping algorithms have been developed to improve the efficiency of the process. One of the best known is the *Cohen-Sutherland clipping algorithm*. This algorithm is very efficient for cases where most of the lines are either totally within the window or totally to one side of the window. The display area is divided into nine regions, as shown in Figure 10-12. The central region is the window that is to be clipped to. Each end point of the line is examined and assigned a 4-bit OUTCODE that identifies which of the nine regions it is in. The first bit tells whether the end point is above the window, the second bit tells whether it is below the window, the third bit tells whether it is to the right of the window, and the fourth bit tells whether it is to the left of the window. If the condition is TRUE, then the bit is assigned a 1. If FALSE, it is assigned a 0. Thus, a point within the window would have a bitcode of 0000, indicating that it is not above, below, to the right, or to the left of the window. If any of the four bits of the bitcode is 1 and the corresponding bit of the bitcode for the other end point is also 1, then the line lies wholly to one side of the window and is immediately rejected. This bitcode makes the algorithm very efficient for rejecting lines that lie to one side of the window. The remaining lines, those that have one end in the window and those that might cross the window, are then processed by the clipping routine.

Another type of clipping algorithm is known as the *midpoint subdivision algorithm*. Its operation is as follows. The midpoint of the line is calculated and is tested to see whether it is a point at which the line intersects the window. If the midpoint does not lie on a window boundary and neither half can be rejected as lying to one side of the window, then both halves are subdivided and tested. The process continues until the two points of intersection are located or, if the line does not intersect the window, until all line segments are rejected. Figure 10-13 illustrates the process. This algorithm requires many more iterations than the Cohen-Sutherland algorithm but it can be done in integer arithemetic, which is much faster for many processors than the floating-point method that must be used for the Cohen-Sutherland algorithm.

Defining the Data Range as Other Than the Viewport Range

For most of our work to this point, the data range and the viewport range have been identical. The one major area where this was not true was drawing charts and graphs (Chapter 7). There are many instances in which it is desirable to be able to "map" one value range to another. *Mapping* is the process by which data points from one coordinate system are plotted or positioned in another. For instance, in Chapter 7 we drew charts whose abscissa and ordinate scales had to be related (mapped) to the CRT screen so that the data could be plotted with screen coordinates. We may also need to handle negative data values—as when drawing a circle with the origin assumed to be at the center, or when charting negative data—or we may need to handle values that are larger than the screen limits, which often happens when creating charts and graphs. Mapping is necessary in each of these situations.

Some other uses for mapping are(1) to relate the coordinates from a digitizing tablet to screen coordinates and (2) to relate the screen coordinates to the coordinates used by a pen plotter. We will discuss these uses in more detail in Chapter 11, when we begin using these devices.

Sometimes we want to be able to enlarge or shrink the drawing. Suppose you were working on a small detail of a large drawing. If the entire drawing were on the screen, the detail might be too small to work with easily. By mapping only the portion of the drawing containing the detail onto the full screen, the task of modifying the detail could be made much easier. Of course, the completed detail must be reduced and made a part of the overall drawing.

When working with large drawings, it may be difficult or impossible to display the entire drawing at one time. Various portions of the drawing, each corresponding to the display area, might be displayed and worked on in succession. In this way the entire drawing could be worked a portion at a time.

Mapping Techniques

Sometimes when mapping, the range—that is, the difference between the maximum and minimum values—is not changed and only the origin, or zero point, is relocated. Other times only the range is changed, while the origin remains fixed. In still other cases both the origin and the range are changed. When drawing circles, we assumed that the origin was located at the center of the circle. The Y coordinate range was not changed. The X values, however, were all multiplied by 2.5, effectively reducing the range of X values from 640 to 256. Thus, a circle with its center at the middle of the screen and with a radius of 128 would occupy the entire width of the screen. It would, of course, have to be clipped to the top and the bottom of the screen.

When using PLOT10, Apple III, IBM BASIC beginning with DOS version 2.0, and other graphics languages that support both WINDOW and VIEWPORT, the task of mapping is quite easy. The desired viewport is specified in screen coordinates, which, of course, must lie in the range of the screen. The command is of the general form

VIEWPORT (XSMIN,XSMAX,YSMIN,YSMAX)

where the argument XSMIN is the minimum X boundary value of the viewport in screen coordinates and the following three arguments are the maximum X, the minimum Y, and the maximum Y viewport boundary values, respectively. Similarly, the window is specified by a command of the general form

WINDOW (XWMIN,XWMAX,YWMIN,YWMAX)

where the arguments are the same as the ones above except in real user-defined value ranges that are not restricted by the screen resolution. Thus, for example, a user-defined coordinate range of XWMIN = -6000, XWMAX = 6000, YWMIN = -2000, YWMAX = 7000 could be mapped to a viewport with 640 × 200 resolution. If the entire screen were to be used, then, the VIEWPORT arguments would be XSMIN = 0, XSMAX = 639, YSMIN = 0, YSMAX = 199. Any portion of the screen could be used. Either the VIEWPORT or the WINDOW specification, or both, can be changed at will throughout the program.

When a system does not support VIEWPORT or WINDOW, or when one is mapping from an input device such as a digitizer, it is necessary to provide a mapping routine. Three factors must normally be considered when mapping. The first is *translation*. An example of translation would be moving or duplicating a figure on a different portion of the display screen. Referring to Figure 10-14A, suppose we are redesigning the plate to have four bolts in the upper-right corner instead of two. Instead of drawing two more bolt heads from scratch, we could duplicate the area containing the two bolt heads, as shown in Figure 10-14B. To accomplish this task, we would define the area to be duplicated, identify one point as temporary origin(1), and duplicate the area by specifying the new location, origin(2). All other points could be located by determining their position relative to origin(1) and duplicating them in the same location relative to origin(2).

The second consideration in mapping is *scale* or *value range*. Suppose a plate similar to the one shown in Figure 10-14A is to be modified as above, but in order to more accurately place the duplicated area we desire to work at a larger scale. We might identify an area, as in Figure 10-15A, and then enlarge it to fill the screen, as in Figure 10-15B. Working at this scale, it is much easier to position the objects exactly (see Figure 10-15C). When the modification is com-

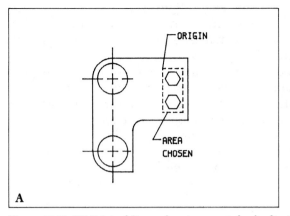

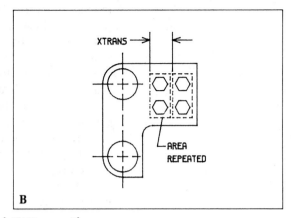

Figure 10-14. (A) Original figure showing area to be duplicated. (B) Figure with defined area repeated through translation.

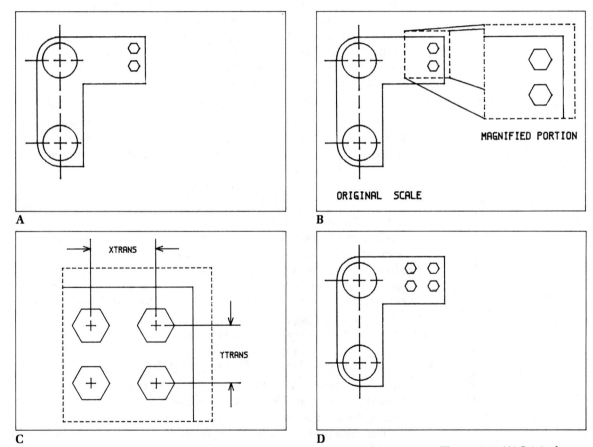

plete, it is used to update the original drawing at the original scale (Figure 10-15D).

The first step in this process is to enlarge the portion of the drawing we wish to modify. A corner of the selected area (the origin)

Figure 10-15. (A) Original figure to be modified. (B) Magnification of area to be modified. (C) Magnified area showing precise duplication of detail. (D) Modified figure.

is located on the screen at a new location, as before. Then, all other points are located relative to this origin. This time, however, their distance from the original origin must be multiplied by a scale factor to get the distance from the new origin.

Once the area to be worked is mapped to the screen at the larger scale, the modification takes place as before. Origin(1) is defined for the area to be duplicated and the area is duplicated starting at origin(2). Of course, all values will reflect the larger scale.

When the modification is complete, remapping to the original drawing is the reverse of the process used to create the work area. The work-area origin is mapped to the original origin and then all points are mapped relative to that point, using the reciprocal of the multiplier to calculate their location (the distances have to be scaled back down).

The third consideration in mapping is that, when working to the screen from another device, the screen and the input or output device may establish their origins in different corners. For instance, if the screen origin is in the upper-left corner and a drawing is being digitized from a pad whose origin is in the lower-left corner, the image will appear on the screen upside down. This is easily corrected by setting the Y coordinate to

$$Y = (Ymax - Y)$$

A straightforward way to accomplish scaling is to change the ratio of viewport-to-window value ranges. Suppose that the square we discussed earlier in the chapter were drawn using the following 1:1 ratio of window-to-viewport values:

```
VIEWPORT (0,0,200,100)
WINDOW (0.0,0.0,200.0,100.0)
```

To draw the second, enlarged square the viewport could be defined as being in the new location and the window ratio of window-to-viewport data ranges changed to two-to-one. Now if the square is redrawn with user coordinates, the values will be mapped to the viewport at double size. In general, to map our figure from one coordinate system to another, the following formula would apply:

```
Y(A.new)=Y(A.old)+Y.trans
Y(C.new)=Y(A.new)+MULTIPLIER*(Y(C.old)-Y(A.old))

X(A.new)=X(A.old)+X.trans
X(C.new)=X(A.new)+MULTIPLIER*(X(C.old)-X(A.old))
```

where X(A) and Y(A) are the X and Y coordinates of the origin we selected and X(C) and Y(C) are the X and Y coordinates of any other point in the area being duplicated.

If our viewport and window specifications are the same for both the old and new area, the MULTIPLIER will be unity (one). The MULTIPLIER is obtained by dividing the range of viewport values by the range of window values. If the X limits of the viewport are called X(V.min) and X(V.max) and those of the window are X(W.min) and X(W.max), then

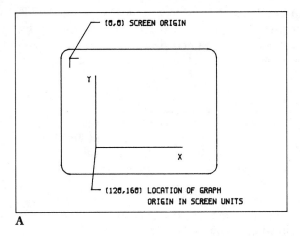

A

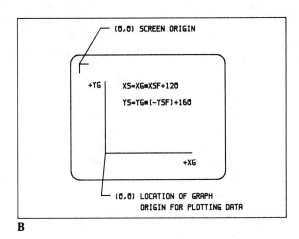

B

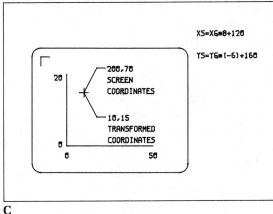

C

Figure 10-16. CRT screen showing an example of mapping and scaling.

$$\text{MULTIPLIER} = \frac{X(V.MAX) - X(V.MIN)}{X(W.MAX) - X(W.MIN)}$$

$$\text{MULTIPLIER} = \frac{Y(V.MAX) - Y(V.MIN)}{X(W.MAX) - X(W.MIN)}$$

We are using the same multiplier for both the X and Y dimensions. Note that changing the shape of the viewport relative to the window will distort the image. Sometimes this is desirable, or even necessary, as when mapping from a "square" system such as a digitizer tablet to a nonsquare system such as the typical microcomputer display screen. However, changing the shape of the viewport should be done with great care and a full understanding of the consequences.

Figure 10-16 shows an example of mapping and scaling on an IBM PC screen. The screen origin is in the upper-left corner and the graph origin is located in the lower-left quadrant of the screen. Note that Y screen values increase from top to bottom and Y graph values increase from bottom to top. Verify that the equations shown in the figure are consistent with the general form of the equations previously shown.

In this chapter we have learned to create our own VIEWPORTS and clip drawings to them. We have also learned to create WINDOWS and to map values from one coordinate system to another. These mapping techniques will be used extensively in the following chapters.

Exercises

1. Write a short program that draws a square box on your CRT. Does the box appear square? If not, determine what the mapping value or ratio should be to produce a square when you use sides of equal length.

2. Does the system provide an origin in the upper-left corner or the lower-right corner of the CRT screen? If the origin is in the upper-left corner, write an equation for the plotted Y values that will allow you to use the lower-left corner of the screen as the origin. If your system uses the lower-left corner of the screen as the origin, then write the equation to convert the origin to the upper-left corner.

3. Does your system provide a VIEWPORT statement or its equivalent? If so, what is it called? What information or arguments are required? Are these integers or real numbers? Is it possible to have more than one viewport active at the same time?

4. Does your system provide the ability to PAINT or FILL as an integral part of the graphics statements? What are the statements or subroutine calls that allow you to fill shapes on the screen? How many colors or shades of gray are available? Does your system allow items or areas to be drawn with blinking colors as well as with nonblinking colors? Is this a separate program statement or is it part of the PAINT or FILL statement?

5. If your system does not provide clipping through a VIEWPORT statement, then write a routine that will clip on your system.

6. Use the VIEWPORT statement, its equivalent, or the routine written in Exercise 5 to clip to the left half of your screen. Demonstrate that the routine works by drawing horizontal, vertical, and inclined lines on the screen.

7. Does your system have a WINDOW statement that works in conjunction with the VIEWPORT statement? If so, list the statement or subroutine call and the arguments required. Are they integer or real?

8. Determine the scaling factors that must be used to put a 500 mm × 750 mm (20 inch × 30 inch) drawing on your full CRT screen without distortion. If your system provides the WINDOW statement or its equivalent, write the statement(s) that would map the drawing to your full CRT screen.

9. Write the code to move (translate) an object from the lower-left corner of the CRT screen to the middle of the CRT screen. Test your code by first drawing a circle about the origin (lower-left or upper-left corner) and then about the center of the screen. If your system provides this capability through the VIEWPORT or WINDOW statements, then write the statements or subroutine calls with the proper arguments to accomplish this task.

10. Does your system provide a statement, subroutine, or function that draws a circle undistorted, even though the screen pixel grid is not "square"? If a circle statement or its equivalent is provided, test it by using it to draw a circle and then draw one of equal radius using the circle routine you wrote for Chapter 6.

11. Does your system have any statements that provide display of objects other than circles?

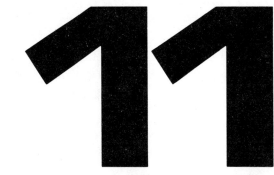

Input/Output Devices

p to this point, we have assumed that all data input would come from the alphanumeric keys on the keyboard and that all output, both character and graphics, would be to the display screen. We also assumed that all data storage would be in main memory. Those assumptions simplified our presentation of techniques for creating graphics. However, while keyboard input and screen output are important parts of a computer graphics package, they are totally inadequate to serve many of the needs of the user. In this chapter we will study a variety of other input/output (I/O) devices that form a part of computer graphics systems, including permanent storage of data on disk in various types of files and retrieval of the data for further use. Figure 11-1 shows a workstation that includes (1) for input, a digitizing tablet, a joystick, and a keyboard; (2) for output, a pen plotter and a printer with print-plot capability; and (3) for both input and output, floppy disk drives.

The alphanumeric keys will continue to be a source of input for text and, in many cases, for other data. However, most users favor a controllable graphics cursor for locating points and other details on the screen. The cursor is manipulated by (1) cursor control (arrow) keys either on the keyboard or, in some cases, on a separate keypad; (2) a joystick; (3) thumbwheels; (4) the puck on a digitizing tablet; or (5) other devices such as a "mouse."

Other popular devices for inputting data include a light pen and a digitizing tablet, which can be used to digitize drawings or used as a menu board. Light pens interact directly with the screen. The user

Figure 11-1. Computer graphics workstation.

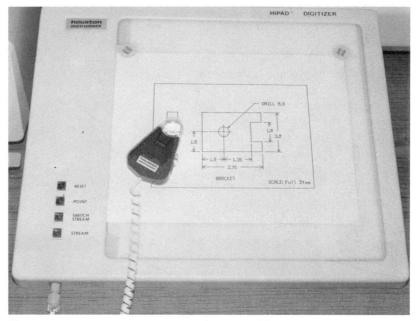

Figure 11-2. Houston Instruments HIPAD digitizing tablet.

points with the pen to a location on the screen and the system returns the coordinates of the location. Digitizing tablets are separate devices with their own coordinate systems. The user typically selects a location on the digitizing tablet with a "puck" containing cross hairs and then presses a button that causes the coordinates of the selected location to be transmitted to the system. The selected coordinates may be mapped to a menu selection grid or they may be mapped to the screen coordinate system to cause an action to occur on the screen. Figure 11-2 is a Houston Instruments HIPAD digitizing tablet.

Undoubtedly, the most important output device on a computer

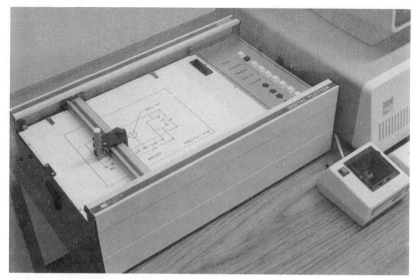
Figure 11-3. Houston Instruments HIPLOT digital plotter.

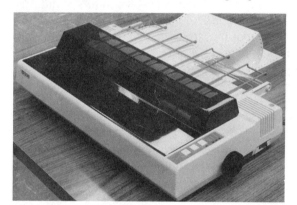
Figure 11-4. Epson MX-100 dot matrix printer-plotter.

Figure 11-5. Tektronix 4611 electrostatic plotter.

graphics system is the display screen. In many cases it is the only device that will be used. From time to time, however, most users will want to be able to make a permanent hardcopy of their drawing. The three most common devices for making hardcopies are (1) a pen-type plotter (Figure 11-3), (2) a printer that can create dot-resolution graphics (print-plot—see Figure 11-4), and (3) a xerographic hardcopy device (Figure 11-5).

Permanent storage of drawings is generally done on disk or tape. The data may be stored, thus allowing the system to redraw the picture, or the picture itself may be stored. In the latter case it is not easy to change any details of the picture since the data used to create it are not stored (only the bit pattern required to display it on the screen). The user can, however, add more details to the picture.

External I/O devices are typically connected to the system in one

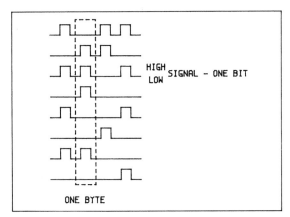

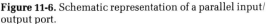

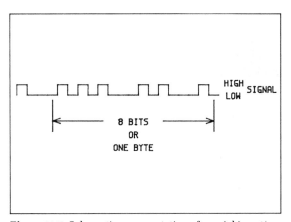

Figure 11-6. Schematic representation of a parallel input/output port.

Figure 11-7. Schematic representation of a serial input/output port.

of two ways. The connection may be serial or it may be parallel. *Serial connection* means that data are transmitted one bit at a time over one wire. *Parallel connection* means that several bits of data are transmitted at one time over multiple wires that are running in parallel. A separate wire is required for each bit. Thus, if a byte were to be transmitted as 8 bits in parallel, eight transmission wires would be required. The connecting cable might have many more wires than that, since separate sets may be provided for sending and receiving and additional wires may be required for parity checks, grounds, and the like. Figure 11-6 shows the schematic representation of the eight lines of a parallel I/O port.

Serial connections have the advantage of simplicity. The number of wires required is small and, since they are generally used when speed is not an important factor, the data can be sent long distances with a minimum of errors. Figure 11-7 shows a schematic representation of a serial I/O port. Connections over telephone lines are made with a device called a MODEM, which stands for modulator/demodulator. MODEMs are serial devices so that they can operate over the phone line, which has only one transmission path. Figure 11-8 is a picture of a popular MODEM. Obviously, a primary disadvantage of serial connections is that they are relatively slow.

Parallel connections have speed as their primary advantage. The speed at which they can be operated is the product of the number of parallel paths (wires) used and the speed of transmission over the wires. Parallel connections are almost always used for disks and tape drives and are often used for printers. Their main disadvantage is the number of wires required. They cannot be used for telephone hookups since the phone lines do not provide enough parallel paths. Parallel connections to devices such as disk drives are typically very high speed. Consequently, they are distance limited. High-speed lines typically create the potential for more transmission errors than

Figure 11-8. A popular modem.

do low-speed lines, and long lines are more susceptible to transmission errors than short lines.

Input Devices

Alphanumeric data are generally input from the keyboard, and each character or operation requires a separate keystroke. Virtually all I/O is controlled with ASCII control characters. For example, the cursor or beam is moved back to the beginning of the line with a carriage return (ASCII control character 13), a new line is obtained with a line feed (ASCII control character 10), and a new page is obtained with a form feed (ASCII control character 12). ASCII 32, a space, is the first printable character. ASCII characters 33 through 122 are the letters of the alphabet (uppercase and lowercase) and a variety of punctuation marks and math symbols. In all, there are 256 different ASCII values (0 through 255), some of which are listed in Table 11-1.

Cursors

When the alphanumeric data are to be placed in a user-selected position on the screen, or when a specific location is to be selected, it is common practice to provide a user-controlled cursor to aid in selecting the spot. The two types of cursors in general use are alphanumeric cursors and graphics cursors. The alphanumeric cursor is the one that is provided by the text editor or, under program control, by the INPUT statement (BASIC) or READ statement (FORTRAN). The alphanumeric cursor can sometimes be used to locate text on a graphics screen as well as on an alphanumeric screen. Typically, it can move on a grid of 24 rows and 80 columns.

Table 11-1. Decimal to ASCII Conversion

Decimal	ASCII	Decimal	ASCII	Decimal	ASCII	Decimal	ASCII
0	NUL	32	SP	64	@	96	`
1	SOH	33	!	65	A	97	a
2	STX	34	"	66	B	98	b
3	ETX	35	#	67	C	99	c
4	EOT	36	$	68	D	100	d
5	ENQ	37	%	69	E	101	e
6	ACK	38	&	70	F	102	f
7	BEL	39	'	71	G	103	g
8	BS	40	(	72	H	104	h
9	HT	41	)	73	I	105	i
10	LF	42	*	74	J	106	j
11	VT	43	+	75	K	107	k
12	FF	44	,	76	L	108	l
13	CR	45	-	77	M	109	m
14	SO	46	.	78	N	110	n
15	SI	47	/	79	O	111	o
16	DLE	48	0	80	P	112	p
17	DC1	49	1	81	Q	113	q
18	DC2	50	2	82	R	114	r
19	DC3	51	3	83	S	115	s
20	DC4	52	4	84	T	116	t
21	NAK	53	5	85	U	117	u
22	SYN	54	6	86	V	118	v
23	ETB	55	7	87	W	119	w
24	CAN	56	8	88	X	120	x
25	EM	57	9	89	Y	121	y
26	SUB	58	:	90	Z	122	z
27	ESC	59	;	91	[		
28	FS	60	<	92	\		
29	GS	61	=	93	]		
30	RS	62	>	94	^		
31	US	63	?	95	_		

The graphics cursor is typically a cross hair that is displayed on the screen. The intersection of the horizontal and vertical lines "marks" the pixel that is being "pointed to" by the cursor.

Hardware cursors are graphics cursors that are supported by the terminal being used and thus do not require an applications program to operate them. They are standard on many graphics terminals and are often "Tektronix compatible"; that is, they support the same calls used to manipulate Tektronix graphics cursors. They are often manipulated with arrow keys on a built-in or separate keypad but are sometimes manipulated with thumbwheels, joysticks, or other devices.

The hardware cursors are put up (displayed) by calling a subroutine or a function. While the cursor is up it can be moved about the screen by means of the manipulation device (keypad, joystick, thumbwheel) supplied with the system. A typical subroutine to activate a Tektronix compatible cursor from FORTRAN is

```
CALL SCURSR (ICHAR,IX,IY)
```

This call places the cursor on the screen. The user can then move it to the desired position and strike any keyboard character. The subroutine will then return the ASCII value of the key that was struck along with the X and Y screen coordinates of the position of the cursor. The user may choose to ignore the value of ICHAR and simply act on the coordinates IX and IY. However, there are many cases where a specific point (such as an origin) may need to be identified, and there are also cases where the user may wish to use the information as to which key was struck as the basis for further action.

Many microcomputers do not provide graphics cursors. Consequently, it is up to the programmer to create the cursor and to provide a method of controlling it (driving it around the screen).

IBM and other personal computers that use Microsoft BASIC have the statements GET and PUT included in the BASIC instruction set. These two statements can be used to create and display a cursor, as will be shown. Programmable function keys can then be used to manipulate the cursor. On the IBM PC we will use the arrow keys on the numeric keypad for this purpose, although we could use other programmable keys if we so desired. Alternatively, the cursor can be manipulated by a joystick or by the puck on a digitizing pad. We will discuss use of all of these devices in this chapter.

Apple II provides a means of creating a cursor using a shape table. The cursor can then be displayed on the screen using XDRAW. Again, the use of programmable keys will provide the means of manipulating the cursor.

PUT and XDRAW both have a special feature that make them especially useful for cursor display. When PUT or XDRAW is used to place a design on the screen twice in the same location, the second PUT or XDRAW erases the image and restores the background to what it was before the image (cursor) was displayed. Consequently, the cursor can be moved over the drawing without destroying any details or adding any unwanted details.

CREATING A CURSOR WITH GET The BASIC statement GET is used to create a cursor as follows. A cross hair of the desired size is created on the screen using line-drawing statements. An integer array is dimensioned to store the image. GET is used to capture the image and store it in the array. (Figure 11-9 illustrates this process.) Note that GET uses two pairs of coordinate values as arguments. These arguments define diagonally opposite corners of a rectangular portion of the screen containing the image. This method of defining the

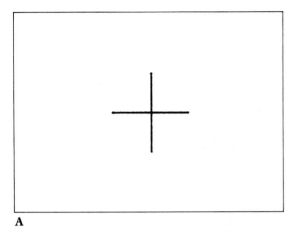

A

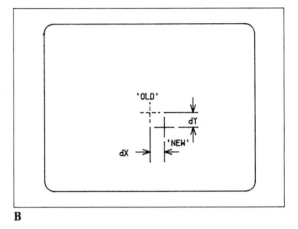

B

Figure 11-9. (A) Cursor drawn with lines. (B) Cursor captured with GET (X1,Y1) − (X2,Y2), CURSOR%.

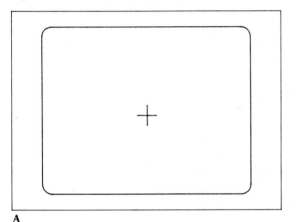

A

B

Figure 11-10. (A) Cursor drawn in middle of screen. (B) Cursor moved with PUT command.

area to be captured is the same as we used earlier to draw rectangles. The BASIC code to draw and capture a cursor on the IBM PC is shown below. Note that this is intended as a subroutine, not a complete program. The screen is assumed to be in 640 × 200 (screen 2) resolution mode and the cursor is drawn in the center of the screen (see Figure 11-10A).

```
7000 REM ** SUBROUTINE TO CREATE AND CAPTURE **
7010 REM ** GRAPHICS CURSOR FOR IBM PC **
7020 PSET (309,100)
7030 LINE -STEP (20,0)
7040 PSET (319,95)
7050 LINE -STEP (0,10)
7060 GET (309,95)-(329,105),CURSOR%
7065 XG%=309:YG%=95
7070 PUT (XG%,YG%),CURSOR%:REM ERASES CURSOR
7190 RETURN
```

The array CURSOR% was previously dimensioned as

```
10 DIM CURSOR%(30)
```

The size of the array needed is calculated by a formula found in the BASIC manual. It must contain four elements plus one additional element for each group of 8 pixels in each row of the screen area to be captured. Any partially filled group (even 1 pixel) will require an array element. Line 7065 is used to define the location of the upper-left corner of the rectangular area containing the cursor. All subsequent PUTs will reference that corner to locate the image on the screen. Of course, the actual coordinates used will depend on where the image is to be PUT. Line 7070 is the first use of PUT. Since the image is already on the screen in that location, this PUT erases it and restores the background. Putting the image at any other location would have duplicated it rather than erasing the original (try it). Only the cross hair itself affects the area where it is drawn, even though the rectangle includes many more pixels.

DISPLAYING AND MOVING THE CURSOR Displaying and moving the cursor is relatively easy. The coordinates of a point where the cursor is to be displayed are determined. Since that point is the center of the cross hair and the PUT statement uses the corner of the rectangle containing the cross hair, the coordinates (XG%,YG%) for the PUT statement are calculated by subtracting 10 from the X coordinate and subtracting 5 from the Y coordinate of the center. Alternatively, the cross hair is PUT on the screen and its center is calculated by adding 10 to XG% and adding 5 to YG%. Since we erased the cursor after creating it, this PUT will display it again.

```
7200 REM ********** GRAPHICS CURSOR **********
7220 PUT (XG%,YG%),CURSOR%
7530 RETURN
```

The Apple II can be programmed to display a cursor in the same way by creating the cursor with a shape table and then moving it with XDRAW. Repeated XDRAWs perform like repeated PUTs. Routines for the Apple II will be found in Appendix A.

Moving the cursor is a three-step process. First, the cursor is erased from its present location with a PUT. Then the coordinates of the desired location are determined and mapped to the coordinates for the required PUT. Finally, the cursor is displayed (PUT) in the new location (see Figure 11-10B). For instance, suppose that the cursor is currently displayed at (130,65). Then XG% = 120 and YG% = 60. If we desire to move the cursor to (140,65), the distance to be moved is dX = 10, dY = 0. The following subroutine will accomplish the task:

```
7200 REM ********** GRAPHICS CURSOR **********
7210 REM
7220 DX%=10
7230 DY%=0
7340 PUT (XG%,YG%),CURSOR%
7341 XG%=XG%+dX%
7345 PUT (XG%,YG%),CURSOR%
7580 RETURN
```

Of course, this routine will only move the cursor a fixed distance in a single direction. To be truly useful the routine will need to be modified to permit moving in any of four directions (up, down, left, or right). Incremental moves of user-selectable sizes are also desirable. The choice of direction can be obtained by writing four move routines, each to be implemented by pressing a separate function (arrow) key. The incremental move distance can be controlled by incorporating a routine to change the value of DX% and DY%. For instance, function key F10 can be employed as follows:

```
7075 REM ** THIS STATEMENT DEFINES KEY FUNCTION
     AND ACTIVATES IT (TURNS IT ON) **
7080 KEY 10,"":KEY (10) ON


7231 REM ** THIS STATEMENT CAUSES THE ACTION **
7237 ON KEY (10) GOSUB 7500


7490 REM ** THIS STATEMENT TOGGLES THE dX AND dY
     VALUES BETWEEN (dX=1,dY=1) AND (dX=10,dY=4) **
7500 IF IFLG<1 THEN IFLG=IFLG+1:DX%=10*IFLG:DY%=4*
     IFLG:RETURN ELSE IFLG=0:DX%=1:DY%=1:RETURN
```

Statement 7080 "cleans out" the default function BASIC gives to this key and turns the key on so that trapping can take place. Statement 7237 traps (acts on) the pressing of key F10 by the user. When a KEY (10) ON statement has been executed by the program, execution of statement 7237 activates the trapping. Each time BASIC starts a new statement it will check whether F10 has been pressed. If F10 has been pressed, then subroutine 7500 is called. Action on the key can be suspended by executing the statement KEY (10) STOP. If the key is pressed while STOP is in effect, the event is remembered and the system will perform a trap as soon as KEY (10) ON is executed again. Trapping can be eliminated by executing KEY (10) OFF. If the key is pressed while it is OFF, no trap will take place and the event will not be remembered by the system.

Note that statement 7500 can be used to create multiple sets of DX%, DY% values. For instance, if the upper test limit on IFLG were 2 instead of 1, and the multipliers were set at 5 and 2, then DX% could take on values of 1, 5, and 10 with corresponding values of DY% of 1, 2, and 4. A 2.5:1 ratio between the DX% and DY% moves is desirable when they are other than 1, since the screen scale factor for a nondistorted image is 2.5:1.

When the cursor has been displayed and moved to the desired spot, selection of that screen position can be recorded by executing an INKEY$ statement. For instance, the program can be put into an endless loop with the statement

```
7630 IK$ = INKEY$: IF IK$="" THEN GOTO 7630
```

We have used this technique in previous chapters to create a pause in program execution. This statement, when encountered, will execute over and over until a key is struck. Even though the program is "hung" on this line of code, pressing the coded function key (F10 in our example) will cause a trap to take place. The subroutine specified (7500 in our example) will execute, and the return from the subroutine will be to statement 7630. Of course, F10 counts as a key, so 7630 will now transfer control to the next statement. The code in line 7630 could be rewritten to recognize only certain keys. For example, the following statement would keep executing 7630 until the space bar was pressed (pressing F10 would still perform a trap and subroutine 7500 would execute before returning to 7630):

```
7630 IK$ = INKEY$: IF IK$<>" " THEN GOTO 7630
```

Let us now experiment with use of an arrow key to move the cursor. We will rewrite the previous cursor-control code to include activation of the UP ARROW (function key 11) and the DOWN ARROW (function key 14) to move the cursor vertically on the screen. Following is the revised BASIC code.

```
7200 REM ********* GRAPHICS CURSOR ***********
7210 PUT(XG%,YG%),CURSOR%
7220 DX=1:DY=1:IFLG=0
7225 KEY(10)ON:KEY(11)ON:KEY(14)ON
7237 ON KEY(10) GOSUB 7500
7240 ON KEY(11) GOSUB 7300
7270 ON KEY(14) GOSUB 7360
7280 GOTO 7237
7290 REM ** SUBROUTINE TO MOVE CURSOR UP **
7300 PUT(XG%,YG%),CURSOR%:YG%=YG%-DY:PUT (XG%,YG%),
     CURSOR%:RETURN
7350 REM ** SUBROUTINE TO MOVE CURSOR DOWN **
7360 PUT(XG%,YG%),CURSOR%:YG%=YG%+DY:PUT (XG%,YG%),
     CURSOR%:RETURN
7490 REM ** THIS STATEMENT TOGGLES THE dX AND dY
     VALUES BETWEEN (dX=1,dY=1) AND (dX=10,dY=4) **
7500 IF IFLG<1 THEN IFLG=IFLG+1:DX%=10*IFLG:DY%=4*
     IFLG:RETURN ELSE IFLG=0:DX%=1:DY%=1:RETURN
```

In this code, statement 7224 cleans out the default values for the two keys and 7225 activates (enables) trapping with them. Subroutine 7300 erases the cursor, calculates a new position by subtracting DY% from the old value (remember, up is a move in the negative Y direction) and redisplays the cursor at the new location. Similarly, subroutine 7360 moves the cursor down. Similar statements can be added to control right-left movement of the cursor.

Note that these routines need considerable error trapping to be truly usable. For instance, the user should guard against any attempt to move the cursor beyond the limits of the screen, since this action will cause a serious error. No attempt is made here to include error trapping, since it would obscure the main purpose and operation of the code.

Cursor-moving routines for the Apple II are similar to those above and will be found in Appendix A.

Joysticks

Joysticks are popular devices for controlling events on the graphics screen. Their advantages include ease and speed of cursor movement and ease of programming for use. Because of this speed they are used with many fast-action games. They are not used as frequently for computer-aided drawing because they are not as precise as cursors controlled by keypads, thumbwheels, or mouselike devices. Also, the drafter or designer is not interested in high-speed selection of points and thus does not need the manipulative capabilities of the joystick. Therefore, its use tends to be limited to relatively low-precision work where speed and ease of use are important.

On large systems, joysticks are normally supported by the system and their use requires only a call to a system subroutine or function, but this is generally not true with microcomputers. Therefore, the microcomputer user program must include any needed joystick control routines. The following paragraphs describe the implementation of joystick cursor control on an IBM PC. The routines use the cursor that was created earlier in this chapter.

In the previous discussion of cursor control by arrow keys, new location coordinates were calculated every time an arrow key was depressed. The cursor was then erased from its old location and redrawn at the new location. Holding the arrow key down would cause the trap to repeat, so the cursor could be made to move in a jerky fashion at a fixed speed. The joystick, on the other hand, provides continuous signals to the computer indicating the position of the stick. Those signals can be read and converted to X-Y coordinates with the BASIC statements

```
X% = STICK(0)
Y% = STICK(1)
```

and the X-Y values can then be used in a PUT statement to display the previously created cursor at the appropriate location on the screen as follows:

```
PUT (X%,Y%),CURSOR%
```

In order to move the cursor, it must first be erased from its old location. The following statement obtains the coordinates, displays the cursor, and then erases it:

```
16040   X%=STICK(0):Y%=STICK(1):PUT(X%,Y%),CURSOR%:
        PUT(X%,Y%),CURSOR%
```

Placed in a continuous loop, this statement will create a blinking cursor that can be manipulated by simply moving the joystick handle.

It may be necessary to "adjust" the range of the joystick to fit the screen. The stick used by the authors covered only a small part of the screen, as shown in Figure 11-11. The adjustment consisted of mapping the cursor to the screen by first translating the minimum stick values to the screen origin and then applying a scale factor to the translated stick values so that the maximum values matched the screen's maximums (639 and 199). In practice, the scale was reduced

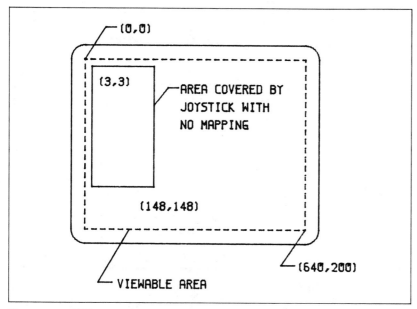

Figure 11-11. CRT screen showing area covered by joystick prior to mapping.

somewhat to prevent getting an out-of-range error and to allow room at the bottom of the screen for menu and prompts. The final coordinate calculations were

```
X% = 3.8 * (STICK(0) - 3)
Y% = 1.2 * (STICK(1) - 3)
```

Another adjustment the authors made was to introduce a delay loop to reduce the blink rate of the cursor. The finished routine became:

```
16000 REM ** CONTINUOUS CURSOR LOOP **
16040 X%=3.8*(STICK(0)-3):Y%=1.2*(STICK(1)-3):
      PUT(X%,Y%),CURSOR%:FOR K=1 TO 200:NEXT:
      PUT (X%,Y%),CURSOR%
16060 GOTO 16040
```

Selection of a point on the screen was done under the previous (keypad) routine by pressing the space bar. The joystick has a trappable KEY function that is supported by BASIC. This trap is more easily used. The joystick button is activated by

```
16020 STRIG(0) ON
```

and is trapped by

```
16030 ON STRIG(0) GOSUB 16070
```

The argument (0) simply tells the system which button to trap on which joystick (more than one joystick can be used at a time).

The following subroutine turns the trapping function OFF, uses a delay loop to guard against multiple hits (the joystick button may send several signals before the user releases the button), sets a flag to

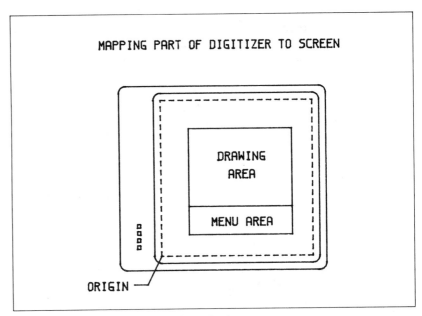

Figure 11-12. A digitizing tablet showing the drawing area and the menu area.

signal the system to return to the appropriate routine, and then returns to the point in the program where execution was taking place when the trap occurred (in this case, the continuous cursor loop). The test

```
16050 IF STIKFLAG = 1 THEN RETURN
```

has been inserted in the loop to return control to the calling task routine when the trap has been acted upon. Of course, STIKFLAG must be reinitialized each time the cursor routine is called.

The completed cursor control module is

```
16000 REM ** CONTINUOUS CURSOR LOOP **
16010 STIKFLAG=0
16020 STRIG(0) ON
16030 ON STRIG(0) GOSUB 16070
16040 X%=3.8*(STICK(0)-3):YK%=1.2*(STICK(1)-3):
      PUT(X%,Y%),CURSOR%:FOR K=1 TO 200:NEXT:
      PUT (X%,Y%),CURSOR%
16050 IF STIKFLAG=1 THEN RETURN
16060 GOTO 16040
16070 REM ** TRAP PROCESSING ROUTINE **
16080 STRIG(0) OFF
16090 FOR J=1 TO 200:NEXT
16100 STIKFLAG=1
16110 RETURN
```

Digitizing Tablets

Digitizing tablets find their major use as menu boards. That is, the menu of tasks and modes available to the user is displayed in boxes on the tablet. Figure 11-12 is a computer-generated drawing of a digitizing tablet showing the drawing area and the menu area. The user selects from the menu by placing the selection device (often a "puck" with cross hairs) over the box containing the desired task or mode and pressing a button on the selection device. The digitizing tablet sends a character string to the system. The string contains information regarding the device, the mode it is set in, and the coordinates of the point on the tablet that was selected. The tablets typically have 1100 × 1100 resolutions or about 100 points per inch in both X and Y directions. Some, such as the HIPAD, can be set up for resolution of either 100 or 200 points per inch. The lower resolution matches closely with that of the Tektronix 4010 graphics terminals. The coordinates of the selected point are then mapped to a menu selection routine that determines what task or mode was selected and then acts on the selection.

The following BASIC code will open the digitizer port as a communication file, input a character string from the tablet, close the port, and return to the calling routine. Note that this was written to work on an IBM PC with a Houston Instruments HIPAD digitizer. Other hosts or digitizers may require different codes. Later in this section we will discuss methods of extracting the needed data from the input string.

```
17000 REM ** DIGITIZER INPUT ROUTINE **
17020 OPEN "COM1:2400,S,7,2" AS #1
17040 INPUT#1,A$
17060 CLOSE #1
17080 RETURN
```

Digitizing tablets generally have several modes of operation. Typically, they can operate in point mode, stream mode, and switched-stream mode. When the digitizing tablet is in point mode, no information is sent to the system until the button is pressed, at which time one character string is sent. In stream mode, however, the tablet sends character strings repeatedly on a preset interval. In switched-stream mode, the tablet is in stream mode as long as the button is depressed but quits sending as soon as it is released.

The task of mapping the tablet to the screen consists of (1) determining the origin on both the tablet and the screen and determining the range of coordinates that can be addressed on each; (2) calculating the necessary conversion factors; and, (3) as coordinates are received from the tablet, converting them to comparable screen coordinates. For instance, if the tablet has 1000 points per inch and the screen has 100 points per inch in the X direction and 40 points per inch in the Y direction, then an X scale factor of 10:1 an a Y scale factor of 25:1 would be used to create the same size and shape drawing on the screen as is on the tablet. Other scale factors could be used to intentionally enlarge or reduce, or even distort, the drawing.

Many digitizing tablets have user-selectable origins, a convenient feature that allows the origin to be in the upper-left or lower-left corner to match the system with which it is used, or to allow the origin to be other than in a corner. This capability is handy when the user wants to digitize only a part of a picture or drawing or wishes to place it in a different place on the screen than it is on the tablet. Depending on the tablet, the first point chosen after the system is turned on may be interpreted as being the origin. In this case, the user should be prompted to establish the origin before beginning to work; otherwise the results may be unexpected.

The HIPAD tablet sends the following character string to the computer:

```
"M+-XXXXX+-YYYYY<CR><LF>"
```

where M is the mode as follows:

M = 0	First coordinate of switched stream.
1	Successive coordinate of switched stream.
2	A coordinate of point mode.
3	A coordinate of stream mode with cursor (puck) button released.
4	A coordinate of stream mode with the cursor (puck) button depressed.

A typical string when the tablet is in point mode might be

```
"2+06220+04345<CR><LF>"
```

which would indicate that the digitizer cursor is at an X coordinate of $+6.220$ inches from the origin and a Y coordinate of $+4.345$ inches from the origin. These coordinates can be compared to the known boundaries of the various menu boxes on the tablet to determine which box was selected, and the system can then act on the selection.

A second popular use for digitizing tablets is to digitize pictures or drawings. Sometimes users have a picture or drawing that they would like to modify but they have only a hardcopy. With a digitizing tablet they can recreate the drawing on the system without having to draw it from scratch. The drawing is placed on the digitizing tablet and the points and lines used to create it are transferred to the system by selecting them one at a time with the puck. Each coordinate is mapped to the proper screen location as described above. If the tablet is set to stream mode or switch-stream mode, the user may simply "trace" the outline of the figure with the puck, thus sending a large number of point coordinates to the system. This technique is useful for digitizing photographs. Line drawings, which contain more lines than individual points, may be digitized with the tablet in point mode. In this case the user would select the task just as he or she would for drawing on the screen and would then select the appropriate line end points or other appropriate coordinates from the drawing on the tablet, and the system would create the figure on the screen. Of course, it is necessary to map the coordinate system of the tablet to that of the screen.

The following BASIC code will open the digitizing tablet as a communications file, input a character string, evaluate it to obtain the coordinates of the puck location, map them to the screen, plot the point, and then loop back to input the character string for the next point. This is written as a subroutine to be used with the IBM PC and a HIPAD digitizer in stream mode. Return to the calling routine is accomplished by pressing function key F9. Note that the program reads two string values and then uses the second one. This was found in practice to work better than using every string value. Note also that an error trap has been added to guard against overflow of the input buffer. The trap simply closes COM1, reopens it, and resumes. Remember that the BASIC statement

$$LEFT\$(A\$,n)$$

returns the first n characters of the character string A$ while the BASIC statement

$$MID\$(A\$,m,n)$$

returns n characters from the string A$ beginning with the mth character.

```
17200 REM *** POINT PLOTTING ROUTINE FOR DIGITIZING
      TABLET OPERATING IN STREAM MODE **
17210 RTNFLG=0:KEY 9,"":KEY(9) ON:ON KEY(9) GOSUB 17290
17220 OPEN "COM1:2400,S,7,2" AS #1
17230 ON ERROR GOTO 17290
17240 FOR J=1 TO 2:INPUT#1,A$:NEXT
17250 X1=VAL(MID$(A$,3,5))/17:Y1=199-VAL(MID$(A$,9,5))/40
17260 IF RTNFLG=1 THEN RETURN
17270 PSET (X1,Y1),PPEN
17280 GOTO 17240
17290 CLOSE #1:OPEN "COM1:2400,S,7,2" AS #1:RESUME
17390 RTNFLG=1:RETURN
```

A third use of the digitizing tablet is to move a graphics cursor on the screen. The tablet can be placed in stream mode and the stream of coordinates can be used to continually update the location of the cursor by having them provide the values for the PUT statement. In this method of operation, the screen cursor would appear to "follow" the movement of the digitizer puck. Pressing the button on the puck would change the first character in the string from a 3 to a 4. Thus, a test of the first character, LEFT$(A$,1), signals that the button has been pressed. This information could be processed in the same way that the joystick-button information was used.

The following BASIC code takes the previous routine and adds mapping the puck position to the screen and moving the screen cursor. In this routine the coordinates are used to calculate a cursor position. Unlike the previous routine it is designed for the HIPAD in stream mode. Pressing the button on the puck will set the first character of A$ to 4, which will cause the routine to close the port and return to the calling routine, which can then act on the coordinates X1%,Y1% (just as previous routines have acted on cursor coordinates to draw the required item).

```
17400 REM *** CURSOR ROUTINE
17420 ON ERROR GOTO 17480
17430 OPEN "COM1:2400,S,7,2" AS #1
```

```
17440 FOR J=1 TO 2:INPUT#1,A$:NEXT
17450 X1%=VAL(MID$(A$,3,5))/17:Y1%=199-VAL(MID$(A$,9,5))/40
17460 PUT (X1%,Y1%),CURSOR%:FOR K=1 TO 30:NEXT:PUT (X1%,Y1%),
      CURSOR%:IF LEFT$(A$,1)="4" THEN CLOSE #1:RETURN
17470 GOTO 17440
17480 CLOSE #1:OPEN "COM1:2400,S,7,2" AS #1:RESUME 130
```

Light Pens

Light pens are generally used in a somewhat different fashion than are the arrow keys, joysticks, and digitizing tablets we have discussed so far. Unlike these devices, the light pen is used on the screen itself. The user points the pen at a location on the screen and activates a selection device by pressing the tip of the pen to the screen or by pressing a switch on the side of the pen. The BASIC statements used to activate the pen are similar to the KEY and STRIG statements used for arrow keys and joysticks respectively. For instance, on the IBM PC, a PEN ON statement enables the pen, a PEN OFF statement disables it, and a PEN STOP statement suspends trapping.

A pen function, PEN (n), can be used with a statement of the type

```
17620  x = PEN (n)
```

to read the light pen coordinates. The value assigned to n can range from 0 through 9 and is used to specify the type of data that are to be returned. The following pair of statements will return the X and Y coordinates of the point where the pen was last activated. X will range from 0 to 639 for high-resolution graphics and Y will range from 0 to 199.

```
17620 X = PEN (1)
17630 Y = PEN (2)
```

Another pair of pen values will return the last known valid X and Y coordinates. They are

```
17640 X = PEN (4)
17650 Y = PEN (5)
```

The primary difference between these two sets of functions is that PEN (1) and PEN (2) operate like the digitizing tablet in point mode; that is, the pen switch must be activated each time a new pair of values is desired. PEN (4) and PEN (5), however, are similar to the digitizing tablet in switch-stream mode: As long as the pen button is held down, new coordinates are sent continuously.

Similarly, the following statement pair will return the character row and column where the pen was last activated. The row can range from 1 to 24 and the column from 1 to 40 or 1 to 80 depending on the width specified at the time.

```
17660 CHRROW = PEN (6)
17670 CHRCOL = PEN (7)
```

PEN (8) and PEN (9) return the last known valid character row and column. Two more functions, PEN (0) and PEN (3), return information about the pen's switch. PEN (0) tells whether the switch has been pressed since the last poll, while PEN (3) tells whether the switch is currently down.

Because the light pen requires light from the screen in order to operate, and because selecting a specific pixel with a pen is difficult, pens are not normally used for drawing original figures. A much more common use is to select menu items to control program execution. The operator will typically point the pen to a lighted portion of the screen to make a selection. Another common use of the light pen is to manipulate previously drawn figures.

It is possible, however, to drive the graphics cursor around the screen and draw lines using the light pen if the screen is first flooded with sufficient light. Depending on the sensitivity of the particular light pen and the type of monitor being used, it may be necessary to operate with dark lines on a light background (reverse video). The following BASIC code for the IBM PC assumes that the cursor has been created in a previous routine, that the screen is in mode 2, that this routine has been called from a drawing routine, and that coordinate selection will be made by pressing the space bar:

```
17600 REM ** GRAPHICS CURSOR ROUTINE FOR LIGHT PEN **
17610 PEN ON
17625 PUT (X1,Y1),CURSOR%:FOR K=1 TO 50:NEXT:PUT
      (X1,Y1),CURSOR%
17640 X = PEN (4): Y = PEN (5)
17655 IF X>619 OR Y>189 OR X<0 OR Y<0 THEN 17640
17665 RNT$=INKEY$IF RTN$=" " THEN PEN OFF:RETURN
      ELSE 17625
```

The points selected may be used by the calling routine to create points, lines, complex figures, or text on the screen.

If the screen must be flooded with light in a reverse video fashion, the following (or an equivalent) statement should work:

```
115 LINE (0,0)-(639,200),1,BF
```

Points and lines can then be drawn with pen color 0 and erased with pen color 1.

As with the KEY and STRIG statements, there is a PEN statement to access subroutines. It is of the form

```
17680 ON PEN GOSUB 17750
```

where the line number and the subroutine to be accessed are defined by the programmer. This statement can be used to provide selective use of the light pen. The subroutine (17750 in this case) will then be called every time the light pen switch is pressed.

Disk Drives as Input/Output Devices

Most devices used with computers are either input devices or output devices. However, there are two devices that are designed for both input and output. One of these is the console—the combination of keyboard and CRT—that we have been using since Chapter 1. The other device, which we have also been using all along, is the disk drive. Most computers store all of their instructions on disks: operating system, languages, programs, and data. So far we have limited our use to the first three of these. In the following paragraphs we will discuss using the disk drive to store and retrieve our own data.

Disk files are a very important part of any computer program. For many systems they represent the only permanent storage and retrieval capability for program data. They also provide storage for the programs being used. A third use for disk files is temporary storage of large amounts of data that cannot be accommodated in main memory.

Disk data files are categorized as either sequential or random-access. In *sequential files*, the first access to the file for input reads data starting at the beginning of the file, and each successive input access reads data starting where the last read left off. The user may specify that the file be reset before each read, which means that the read will always start at the beginning. Since the read always starts either at the beginning of the file or where the last read left off, selective retrieval of data is difficult. Similarly, each access for output (WRITE) to the file adds the data to the end of the file. There is no way to selectively overwrite data. As with input, the user can usually specify that the output is to begin at the beginning of the file, but that action destroys the other data that were in the file.

Sequential files are efficient and should be used when practical. One use is to save all of the data used to create an entire drawing. The contents of all of the storage arrays, pointers, and flags can be written to the file. Then, when the data are needed, the entire contents of the file are read into memory for processing. If the data are changed, the entire file can be rewritten with the modified data, thus effectively updating the file. See Figures 11-13A and 11-13B for an illustration of sequential access.

Random-access files are so named because they can be accessed at multiple points, generally every record, for either input or output. If an item of information is needed from record 27, for instance, that record, or, in some cases just the desired part of that record, can be read without having to work through records 1 through 26 to reach that point. Similarly, if the record is to be changed, just that record can be rewritten without disturbing the rest of the file. Figure 11-13C illustrates the operation of random-access files.

There are various ways of addressing the record that is to be read or written to by the system. The most obvious is to specify the record number. Thus, in the example above, the READ or WRITE statement would specify record 27.

Many systems support *key-access files*. When using key access, the user specifies a character string to look for and the system searches a specific portion of each record (the key field) to find a matching string. When the string is found, the input or output is accomplished on that record. In practice, the system will probably

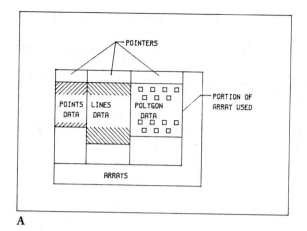

A

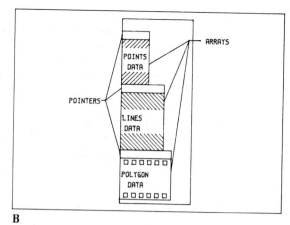

B

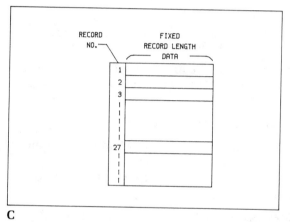

C

Figure 11-13. (A) Total memory available. (B) Sequential disk file (only filled portions of arrays are saved). (C) Random-access file.

maintain a separate key file containing the key and the number of the record that has that key. Then when the user specifies the character string to key on, the key file is searched to obtain the record number. Access to the main file is via this record number. This is a fast process, since the key file is relatively small and easy to search. Also, the key file can be sorted without disturbing the main file. The sorted key file can be searched using binary search techniques, which further speed up the process.

Another type of record access is obtained through the process of "hashing." The technique used is to relate the data of a key field in the random-data file to a record number by means of an algorithm. This is tricky because the data generate their own record number, so more than one record will often have the same number. This problem is resolved by creating a linked list of all the records that have the same record number. The system accesses the first record in the list and, if that is not the one that is wanted, the link pointer directs the system to the next record in the list. The scan continues until either the desired record is found or the list is exhausted. All records beyond the first one in the list for any one record number are kept in an overflow area. An advantage of this type of access is that the user does not need to specify either record number or key. Another advantage is that access is extremely fast. This technique is used by many data-base programs.

The type of file to be used is specified when the file is opened. The file must be opened before it can be used. After the user has finished with the file it should be closed. Most systems perform automatic closing of all files when the program ends. However, if the program terminates abnormally, as when an untrapped program error or hardware malfunction is detected, the files may not be closed. That can cause them to be locked, causing problems the next time the program is run.

To open a sequential-access data file in a FORTRAN program running under RSX11M (a DEC 11 series computer operating system), the following statement might be used:

```
OPEN (UNIT=1,NAME='MYDATA.DAT',TYPE='NEW',ACCESS=
* 'SEQUENTIAL',FORM='FORMATTED')
```

This statement assigns UNIT 1 to the file and specifies that it is to be a new, formatted, sequential file. Subsequent writes to the file could be of the form

```
WRITE (1,30) FRST,SCND,THRD
```

where (30) specifies a format statement number to be used and, of course, (1) says to write to the file that is opened.

A sequential file would be opened for output on the IBM PC with the following statement:

```
10240 OPEN "MYDATA.DAT" FOR OUTPUT AS #1
```

As with the FORTRAN example above, this statement assigns UNIT 1 to the file and specifies that it is to be a new, sequential file. It is not necessary, however, to format the WRITE statements used to write data to it. Writes would be of the form

```
10300 WRITE #1, FRST,SCND,THRD
```

As another example, an existing random-data file with record access could be opened on the DEC 11 system as follows:

```
OPEN (UNIT=3,NAME='RNDDTA.DAT',TYPE='OLD',ACCESS=
* 'DIRECT',FORM='FORMATTED',RECORDTYPE='FIXED',
* RECORDSIZE=71)
```

This FORTRAN statement assigns UNIT 3 to the file and specifies that it is an existing record (direct) access formatted file with a fixed record length of 71 characters/record. A subsequent read of a record (say record 27) from this file would be specified as follows:

```
READ (3'27,30) FRST,SCND,THRD
```

where (3'27) specifies record number 27 from unit 3 and (30) again specifies the format statement to be used.

The corresponding statements in BASIC for the IBM PC would be as follows. First, the OPEN statement would be

```
10800 OPEN R,#3,"RNDDTA.DAT",71
```

where R specifies a random I/O file, #3 is the assigned file number, "RNDDTA.DAT" is the file name, and 71 is the record length in bytes. The default record length is 128.

Reading from the file for the IBM PC is accomplished with the following statements:

```
10810 FIELD #3,4 AS FRST$,4 AS SCND$,4 AS THRD$
10820 RECRD%=27
10830 GET #3,RECRD%
10840 FRST=CVS(FRST$)
10850 SCND=CVS(SCND$)
10860 THRD=CVS(THRD$)
```

The reason for this rather complex set of statements is that all data are stored in the file as ASCII strings. Since our data are single-precision numeric, they must be converted to their numeric type upon retrieval. The FIELD statement tells the system where to look in the string for the data. In this case the first four characters are the 4 bytes needed to store the real data value FRST, the next four characters are for SCND, and the third four are for THRD. Statement 10820 simply specifies which record is to be retrieved (number 27, just as in the FORTRAN version). The GET statement says "get the data from record 27 according to the FIELD specification and store it in the buffer." Statements 10840, 10850, and 10860 convert the data to single-precision real.

Sequential files are an effective way to store and retrieve the storage arrays we have used for our data. Suppose that we have an array for lines data that has six elements per line and is dimensioned to store 100 lines. We could store this entire array in a sequential file by simply writing it to the file element by element, but that would be wasteful of space if the array contains only the data for a few lines.

We have been using a variable NLINES as a pointer to record the number of lines stored in the array. Suppose we write it to the file first and then write only the good lines of data. Then, when we retrieve the file, we will read NLINES first and know how many lines of data to retrieve. Recording NLINES in the file may seem unnecessary, since an end-of-file condition can be tested for instead, but if we store all of our arrays in the same file, the pointers act as separators to allow us to assign the correct data to each array.

The following code might be used to write the data to the file. We assume here that the array has already been dimensioned and filled in another part of the program. (Note that this is not intended to be a complete subroutine.)

FORTRAN code:

```
C ** PORTION OF ROUTINE TO WRITE TO ALREADY OPEN
C ** UNFORMATTED SEQUENTIAL FILE (UNIT #1)
      WRITE (1,*) NLINES
      DO 30 J=1,NLINES
```

```
                    DO 20 K=1,6
                    WRITE (1,*) LINES(J,K)
        20          CONTINUE
        30      CONTINUE
```

BASIC code:

```
10400 REM ** PORTION OF ROUTINE TO WRITE TO ALREADY
                OPEN SEQUENTIAL OUTPUT FILE (UNIT #1)
10410 WRITE #1, NLINES
10420 FOR J=1 TO NLINES
10430   FOR K=1 TO 6
10440     WRITE #1, LINES(J,K)
10450     NEXT K
10460   NEXT J
```

Reading the data from the file at a later date is a matter of using the same technique. We would read NLINES and then use it in the loop to specify how many rows of data to retrieve.

Output Devices

Printers can be thought of as output-only files. In fact, some systems define them as such. The user can open the printer as a sequential output file and then write to it as he or she would to a disk. The ASCII control characters discussed earlier in this chapter can be used to control the appearance of the printed output.

Printers can also be used as the target of a copy command. For instance, a file can be copied from one disk to another. It can also, in many cases, be copied to the printer. That is not always advisable since the needed ASCII print control may not be available to provide the correct format for the printer. For instance, the record length in the file may be different from the length of one line on the printer. Since the copy command does not know about the special needs of the printer, the file will not be reformatted.

Printer-Plotters

Printer-plotters are printers that are capable of dot graphics resolution and are thus capable of printing an image of the screen. Printers operating in their normal mode are sent data a character at a time. One byte of data corresponds to one ASCII character. If this character is a printable character, then it is printed. If it is a control character, then the printer treats it as such and does a carriage return, line feed, or whatever is being asked for by the system.

In dot-graphics mode, 1 byte of data corresponds to eight binary digits, each of which controls one wire in the print head of the printer. Thus, instead of the byte specifying an ASCII character, it specifies whether a dot is to be printed in each of eight dot positions on the paper. Figure 11-14 shows the relationship between the normal character specifications in ASCII and the character that is printed. Figure 11-15 shows how a byte of data is interpreted when the printer is in graphics mode for an Epson MX-80 dot matrix printer.

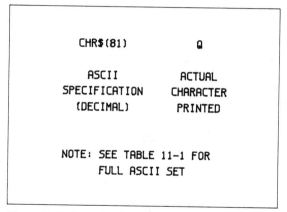

Figure 11-14. Example of character specification in ASCII and actual character printed.

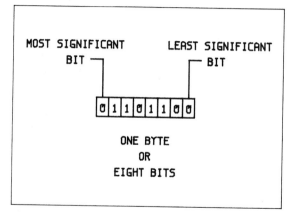

Figure 11-15. Interpretation of a byte of data by the Epson MX-80 dot matrix printer in graphics mode.

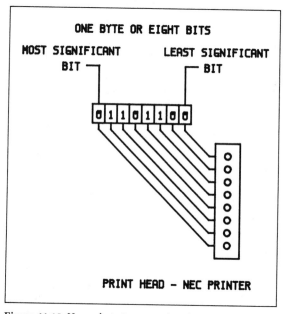

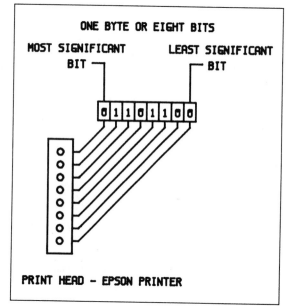

Figure 11-16. How a byte is mapped to the printer head by the NEC 8023 A-C (*left*) and Epson (*right*) dot matrix printer.

Since different printers operate in different ways, it is difficult to generalize. For instance the Epson MX-80 and MX-100 use the most significant bit in the byte to control the top wire in the print head, the next most significant bit to control the second wire, and so on. The NEC 8023A-C dot matrix printer, on the other hand, uses the least significant bit to control the top wire, the next least significant bit to control the second wire, and so on (just the reverse of the Epson approach). Figure 11-16 is a diagram of the way a byte is mapped to the printer head.

Screen dumps are accomplished by bit-mapping the screen to a data array that is formatted in the form that the printer can use and then sending the data from the array to the printer 1 byte (8 binary bits) at a time. With single-user systems such as microcomputers the data may be sent to the printer as they are read and formatted, thus bypassing the array step. Multi-user systems, however, tend to build a print file that is spooled to the printer when it is completed. This is so that the printer is not tied up while the data are being formatted. This also allows the user to build the screen-dump array even if the printer is busy.

A screen dump for the IBM PC is relatively easy to write. It relies on the fact that a byte of information in memory records the on/off condition of 8 consecutive pixels on the screen (in high-resolution mode). Consequently, if the screen buffer memory is accessed in the proper fashion, each byte can be sent directly to the printer to control the eight wires in the print head. The following BASIC code accomplishes this for the Epson MX-80 with dot graphics capability or for the Epson MX-100. Note that the screen image is printed sideways on the page (why?) and that each byte is printed twice. The double printing is to "adjust" for the fact that neither the screen grid nor the printer grid is square.

```
12000 REM ********** SCREEN DUMP SUBROUTINE ************
12010 REM ******** SET UP PRINTER FOR GRAPHICS *********
12020 WIDTH "LPT1:",255
12030 OPEN "LPT1:"FOR OUTPUT AS #1
12040 LPRINT CHR$(27);CHR$(65);CHR$(8);
12050 REM ** RETRIEVE SCREEN DATA AND SEND TO PRINTER **
12060 DEF SEG=&HB800:'DEFINE SCREEN BUFFER LOCATION
12070 FOR X=0 TO 79
12080 LPRINT CHR$(27);"K";CHR$(144);CHR$(1);
12090 FOR Y=7920+X TO 0+X STEP -80
12100 D=PEEK (Y)
12110 Z=Y+8192
12120 E=PEEK (Z)
12130 PRINT#1,CHR$(E);
12140 PRINT#1,CHR$(E);
12150 PRINT#1,CHR$(D);
12160 PRINT#1,CHR$(D);
12170 NEXT Y
12180 PRINT#1,CHR$(10);
12190 NEXT X
12200 CLOSE #1
12210 RETURN
```

Pen Plotters

Pen plotters are devices that draw the picture on paper using a mechanically driven ink pen. The lines are created by specifying end points and are continuous, as opposed to the dot representation created by printer-plotters. Pen plotters typically use stepper motors to drive the pens, thus producing a "line" that is not truly uniform. The incremental steps, however, are usually 0.005 inch or less (200 steps per inch). Consequently, the quality is very good. By way of contrast, in high-resolution mode the display on the IBM PC provides only 640 steps over the entire width of the screen and only 200 steps over the entire height of the screen. The Tektronix 4010 terminal's screen is approximately 10 inches by 8 inches and has a resolu-

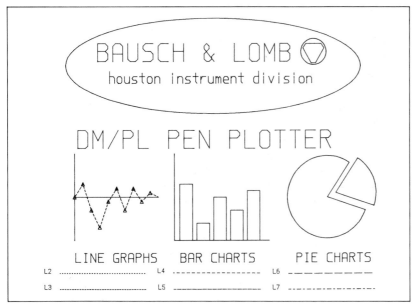

Figure 11-17. Examples of the variety of lines and characters
available on a flat-bed plotter.

tion of 1024 × 780 points. Therefore, an 8 inch by 10 inch plotter
with a stepsize of 0.01 inch will map 1:1 with the Tektronix screen.

Unlike printer-plotters, which produce a bit-image representation
of the screen, the pen plotter output may be quite different in appearance than what is on the screen. There are several aspects in
which the two may differ. First, the lines will be much more uniform
on the pen plotter. Second, the pen plotter may have its own set of
dotted- or dashed-line styles that can be used. Third, the character
set on the pen plotter will probably produce a different style of
character than is on the screen. Fourth, the character size is usually
adjustable over a fairly broad range. Fifth, the characters can probably be rotated into various orientations on the plot even though
they may all be in the same orientation on the screen. Sixth,
multiple-color plots can be achieved with pen plotters by providing
a manual or, with the more sophisticated plotters, automatic change
of pens at user-specified points (though some printers also have
multicolor capability).

Another difference between printer-plotters and pen plotters is
that large pen plotters can create drawings that would fill several
screens and thus require many separate screen dumps. A final possible difference is that, since the pen-plotter actually draws the picture
rather than just copying it from the screen, the methods and results
of clipping and scaling may be different and so may the placement of
individual entities such as text characters. Figure 11-17 illustrates
the line quality, line types, character style, character sizes, and character orientations available on one small flat-bed plotter.

Creation of a drawing on the screen requires that the coordinates of each point and of the beginning and end of each line be calculated. These coordinates are then sent to the system as the arguments of MOVE, POINT, and DRAW statements. Similarly, creation of a drawing on a pen plotter requires that the coordinates of each point and the beginning and end of each line be sent to the plotter. A MOVE is differentiated from a DRAW by specifying PEN UP before performing the move and PEN DOWN before performing the draw. A PEN DOWN followed immediately by a PEN UP might be used to create a point, as might a very short DRAW (remember that the system can draw a line as short as 0.005 inch).

Characters are plotted by (1) specifying a MOVE to the desired location, (2) specifying that a character string is to be plotted, (3) specifying the orientation of the string, (4) specifying the size of character to be produced, and (5) specifying the actual characters to be plotted. While this appears to be a big job, the entire task may be completed in one statement.

Most multi-user systems require that the user create a plot file that is then dumped to the plotter. This is done for the same reasons that a print-plot file is created and then dumped to the printer-plotter. If the data that were used to create the drawing were saved as a series of individual lines and points, then all that might be necessary would be to rescale the data coordinates to fit the plotter's coordinate range, add the plotter control codes, and send the data to the plotter. The approach we have used for data storage and retrieval, however, has been to store only the values the user has entered. Our program then takes these data and calculates all of the coordinates needed to draw the figure. A major reason for our approach is that the amount of memory space required to store all of the coordinates needed to draw such figures as circles, arcs, and other complex entities would overtax most systems. Our redisplay procedures simply retrieve the stored data and send them to the same drawing routine that used them to draw the figure in the first place.

Obviously, we cannot use the drawing routines for plotting. We can, however, modify them with minimum rewriting so that they can be used for this purpose. The major change would be to replace the MOVE, DRAW, and POINT statements with plotting statements containing the same coordinates.

Let us now open a Houston Instruments DMP4 plotter on the IBM PC as COM1 and draw a line on it from (100,100) to (500,500). Remember that the plotter has 200 points per inch, so our line is at a 45 degree angle and is 2.8 inches long.

```
13000 REM ** ROUTINE FOR HI DMP4 PEN PLOTTER **
13020 OPEN "COM1:4800,N,8,2"AS #3
13031 DATA ";: I 0D 001 U H A 225,125, 0 "
13040 READ HIPLOT$
13050 PRINT #3, HIPLOT$
13060 B1$="100":B2$="100"
13070 HIPLOT$="U "+B1$+","+B2$+" "+"D"+" "
13080 PRINT #3 HIPLOT$
```

```
13090 B3$="500":B4$="500"
13100 HIPLOT$=B3$+","+B4$+" "
13110 PRINT #3, HIPLOT$
13120 CLOSE #3
```

Several comments are in order here. First, the plotter is being treated as a standard communications device. Second, all data sent to the plotter must be in the form of character strings with delimiters (spaces and commas) to separate the parts. Third, the plotter must be initialized. Statements 13040 and 13050 read the data needed to initialize the plotter and send this information to the plotter. Statements 13060, 13070, and 13080 convert the starting point to a character string and send it to the plotter. Statements 13090, 13100, and 13110 do the same for the ending point. The "U" and "D" tell the plotter whether the pen is to be up or down (move or draw).

Exercises

1. Using the information given on screen cursors, (a) write a subroutine to activate the built-in cursor, read several chosen coordinates, and print their X and Y values on the screen; (b) write the code to create a cross-hair cursor, move it to known screen locations, and print out the coordinates (X and Y) of each location. (Can you do this on your system without switching between character and graphics modes? Can you print to the printer instead of the screen?)

2. Write a program to call the cursor (bring it up on the screen), read its location coordinates, move it to a new location (by using the controls), and connect the two locations with a solid line.

3. Write the code to take the input from one of the following devices and print the information on the screen: (a) digitizer, (b) light pen, (c) joystick, (d) track ball. Test all modes available and when the code is working properly, send the information to the printer.

4. When the code from Exercise 3 is working correctly, modify it to (a) place dots on the screen; (b) place crosses on the screen; and (c) connect the locations with solid lines.

5. What is the resolution of the plotter or printer-plotter provided with your system? Are these hardcopy devices usable without writing a plotting routine as part of your programs?

6. Write a subroutine for your plotter to take the end points of a line typed in from the keyboard and plot the line. When this works, modify the routine so that it plots the line on the CRT screen just before it is plotted on the plotter. Do the lines appear the same on both output devices?

7. On a sheet of paper draw the menu shown below, tape it to your digitizer, and write a menu-select routine that allows you to select the mode and element and prints the selection on the CRT screen.

8. Write the code to display the menu of Exercise 7 on the CRT screen. Write a separate routine to use the (a) light pen or to use the cursor controlled either by the (b) thumbwheels, (c) cursor keys (arrow keys), (d) digitizer-tablet puck, (e) track ball, or (f) mouse to select the mode and element and print the selected items on the screen.

9. What statements are required to open, to read from, to write to, and to close files on your system? Can a file be opened for both reading and writing without closing and reopening it? If not, list the sequence of statements that would allow the contents of a file to be read into an array and then written back out to the file.

10. How does your plotter draw characters? Is this done by sending the character string and specifications for plotting or is it done by plotting each character as a set of lines? Must each line be sent to the plotter in order to create a character?

11. Write a subroutine that draws the letters A, B, and C 2 inches (50 mm) high on the CRT screen. How many moves and draws are required to produce each letter? Modify your subroutine to send the moves and draws to your plotter as well as to plot them on the screen.

Drawing
in Three
Dimensions

The previous chapters have shown methods for creating two-dimensional images on the CRT. This chapter is dedicated to showing the mathematics necessary for creating two-dimensional images from three-dimensional objects. There are many ways of modeling three-dimensional objects, but the one we have chosen is the wire-frame technique, which means that the edges of the object have been defined. The power of this technique is the easy creation of all two-dimensional images.

Only orthographic, oblique, and isometric drawings will be covered in this chapter. These drawings require an understanding of algebra and trigonometry and an understanding of the mechanisms of translation and scaling. Axonometric and perspective pictorial drawings will be covered in Chapter 13.

Orthographic Projection

Engineers often use a form of two-dimensional drawing called *orthographic projection*. An orthographic projection of a bracket is shown in Figure 12-1. (The same bracket is also shown in an oblique drawing in Figure 12-2 and in an isometric drawing in Figure 12-3.) We will provide only a brief explanation of orthographic projection here. If you wish further explanation or review, we suggest that you read *Graphic Science* by French and Vierck, *Engineering Design Graphics* by Earle, *Engineering Drawing* by Giesecke, Mitchell, Spencer, Hill, et al., or another standard graphics text.

Orthographic projection assumes that the viewer of an object is at a fixed distance from the object and

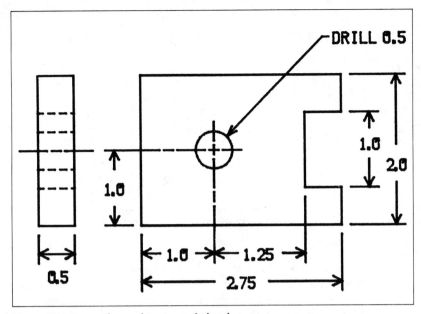

Figure 12-1. Two orthographic views of a bracket.

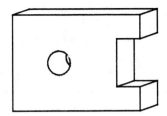

Figure 12-2. Oblique drawing of a bracket.

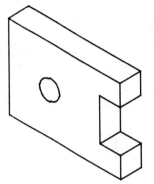

Figure 12-3. Isometric drawing of a bracket.

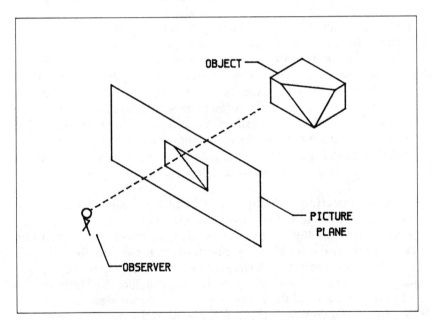

Figure 12-4. Orthographic projection.

that all lines of sight are parallel or perpendicular to the plane of projection (see Figure 12-4). Another way to think about this type of projection is to picture a glass box surrounding the object. Each of the box's surfaces is a plane parallel to one face of the object. Thus, when the object is projected to a surface of the box, the viewer sees a

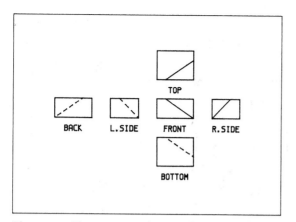

Figure 12-5. The six principal views of an object.

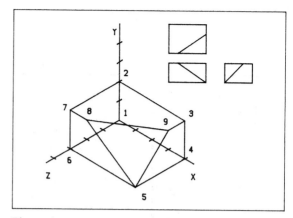

Figure 12-6.

three-dimensional representation of the corresponding face of the three-dimensional object.

Figure 12-4 shows the method for projecting to get the front view of the object. Projecting the object in a similar manner to all six planes of an imaginary cube surrounding the object provides the six principal views of that object. These views are identified as the top, front, right, bottom, left, and back (see Figure 12-5).

Normally, however, an orthographic projection of an object consists of only three views, since three views are generally sufficient to describe any object. The views generally chosen are the top, front, and either the left or right side (see Figure 12-6). The engineer draws these views showing visible surfaces as solid lines and hidden surfaces as dashed lines. Normally, the drawing is dimensioned so that the manufacturing personnel can produce the part to the correct size. (Refer again to Figure 12-1, which shows two orthographic views of an object with dimensions so that the part can be produced to the proper scale.)

The engineering drawings must have a reference point, or an origin, for each view. Measurements are made from this reference point. In creating the figure to be used by the system there must also be an origin and a set of axes for each of the three directions. Figure 12-7 shows four origins. The one in the lower-left corner is the origin for the paper or CRT screen. The origins for each of the views are the intersection points of the X and Y axes in the front view, the X and Z axes in the top view, and the Y and Z axes in the right-side view.

The axes in an orthographic projection must be mutually perpendicular, as shown in Figure 12-8. This means that the angles between the X and the Y axes, the X and the Z axes, and the Y and the Z axes are all 90 degrees. However, Figure 12-8 shows the axes in an isometric drawing, whereas we need to see their position on the CRT in relation to the principal orthographic views.

The origin is taken to be the left rear corner of the object, to

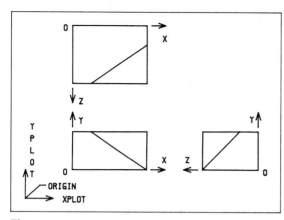

Figure 12-7.

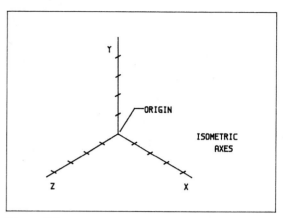

Figure 12-8.

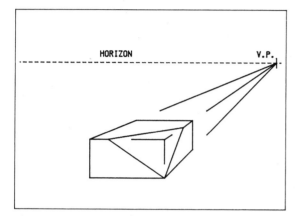

Figure 12-9. One-point perspective.

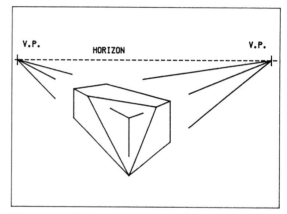

Figure 12-10. Two-point perspective.

conform to the standards of the machine tool industry and to conform to mathematical practice when plotting information. Note that this means that the Z axis comes out toward the viewer in the front view (thus appearing as a point) while the X and Y axes are shown true length. However, the X and Y axes appear as points in the right-side and top views respectively (see Figure 12-7). Observe also that the origin has been translated from the edges of the CRT or piece of drawing paper so that dimensions and notes can be added to the drawing.

When starting to lay out a drawing, the drafter chooses the scale and the size of the paper, and the same thing must be done when using a computer graphics system as well. Screen coordinates (pixels) are almost never used for creating working drawings.

Pictorial Drawings

There are several types of pictorial drawings available for use by the engineer. The most realistic is the *perspective drawing*, which, if done carefully, duplicates a photograph. Figures 12-9, 12-10, and

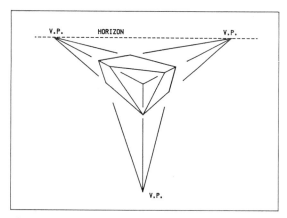

Figure 12-11. Three-point perspective.

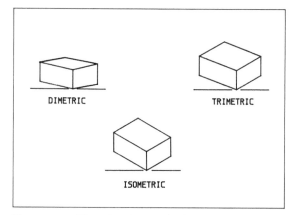

Figure 12-12. Dimetric, trimetric, and isometric projections.

12-11 show three types of perspective drawings. Other common types of pictorial drawing are the axonometric projection, the oblique drawing, and the isometric drawing. With the proper subroutines, each of these types of drawing can be created from the information for a three-dimensional figure.

Perspectives and Axonometric Projections

Both perspectives and axonometric projections are created by rotating the object around two of its three sets of axes. These axes, in order of rotation, are the Y and X axes. The two rotations can move the object to any position desired by the system operator, though many systems provide rotation about the third axis as well.

If the axes are oriented so that the angle between the sets of two axes is equal or appears to be 120 degrees, the projection is said to be *isometric*. If the angles between the X and Y and the Y and Z axes are equal but the angle between the X and Z is not, the projection is said to be *dimetric*. A *trimetric* projection is created when the angles between the sets of two axes are not equal. (See Figure 12-12 for examples of isometric, dimetric, and trimetric projections.) The development of perspective and axonometric projections will be presented in detail in Chapter 13.

Oblique Drawings

Oblique drawings (see Figure 12-2) are produced to help cabinet makers, who find most of the detail on one face of the objects that they construct. Given that the three-dimensional information is available, the oblique drawing is easy to create on the CRT.

Isometric Drawings

Isometric drawings (see Figure 12-3) are used for assembly drawings. They are good two-dimensional representations of the three-dimensional object. Isometric drawings are created by laying off true

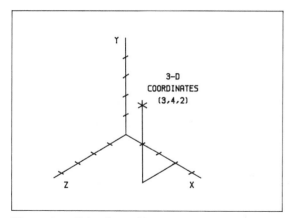

Figure 12-13. Points located in space.

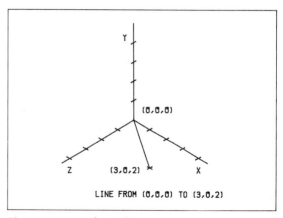

Figure 12-14. Line located in space.

length distances along the three axes and thus can be dimensioned. Isometric drawings can also be sectioned and exploded.

Three-Dimensional Representations

Three-dimensional objects can be represented by wire-frame models, by geometric modeling using solids, and by using planes. Each of these methods has its advantages and disadvantages. This text uses the wire-frame model most extensively because it is easy to understand and to use for creating subroutines.

Wire-Frame Modeling

The wire-frame concept is that each definable edge of an object can be represented by a line. These lines are determined by corners or vertices on the object. Each corner can be positioned and noted by the X, Y, and Z coordinates for that corner. Figure 12-13 shows a point located in space by an X, a Y, and a Z value. Figure 12-14 shows a line in the X-Z plane created by connecting two points.

Three methods can be used to connect the corners or vertices of an object. The first method is to assume that a pen is being used to draw from the first corner to the last corner. In this technique, the pen is either up and moving to a new point or it is down and is drawing to a new point. This information can be stored, along with the vertex coordinates, as X-coordinate, Y-coordinate, Z-coordinate, and pen position or value. This technique is known as the *line method*. A sample object drawn with the line method, is shown in Figure 12-15, and its accompanying data are given in Table 12-1.

The second method, known as the *face method*, is based on the surfaces that make up a figure. Each surface or face is drawn by moving to one vertex and then drawing to each of the other vertices. Figure 12-16 shows our sample object with its vertices and faces numbered. Tables 12-2 and 12-3 show the seven sets of face and vertex information that make up our sample object.

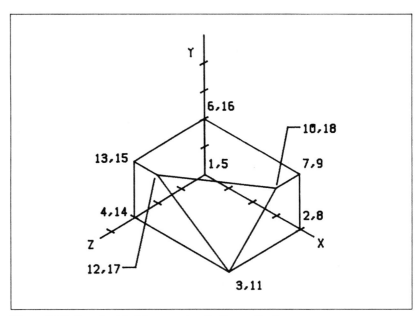

Figure 12-15. Sample object drawn using the line method.

Table 12-1. Line-Method Data for Sample Object in Figure 12-15
(PEN = 3, move to point; PEN = 2, draw to point)

Point No.	X	Y	Z	PEN
1	0	0	0	3
2	4	0	0	2
3	4	0	3	2
4	0	0	3	2
5	0	0	0	2
6	0	2	0	2
7	4	2	0	2
8	4	0	0	2
9	4	2	0	3
10	4	2	1	2
11	4	0	3	2
12	1	2	3	2
13	0	2	3	2
14	0	0	3	2
15	0	2	3	3
16	0	2	0	2
17	1	2	3	3
18	4	2	1	2

The third method for dealing with wire-frame modeling is to
again record all of the vertex coordinates but also to create a second
file that lists all of the connections or lines from each vertex to all of
the other vertices where there are lines. This technique is called the

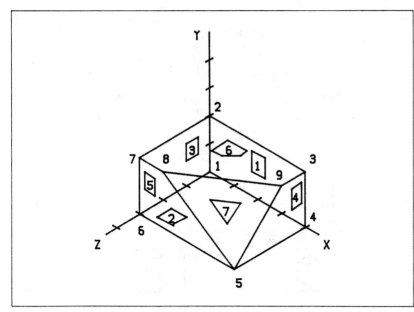

Figure 12-16. Sample object drawn using the face method.

Table 12-2. Vertices and Coordinates for Sample Object in Figure 12-16

Vertex No.	X	Y	Z
1	0	0	0
2	0	2	0
3	4	2	0
4	4	0	0
5	4	0	3
6	0	0	3
7	0	2	3
8	1	2	3
9	4	2	1

Table 12-3. Faces and Order of Vertices to be Connected for Sample Object in Figure 12-16

Face No.	Order of Vertices
1	1-2-3-4-1
2	1-4-5-6-1
3	1-6-7-2-1
4	3-9-5-4-3
5	5-8-7-6-5
6	2-7-8-9-3-2
7	5-8-9-5

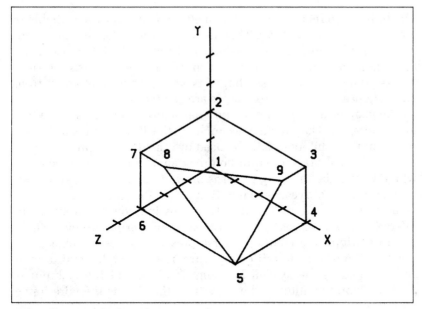

Figure 12-17. Sample object drawn using the connected-vertex method.

connected-vertex method. Figure 12-17 shows our sample object with the vertices numbered. The data set that must be created for this method will be given later in the chapter.

Geometric Modeling: Primitives
A method that will probably be adopted widely when computer

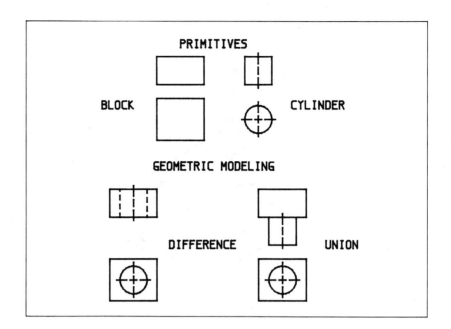

Figure 12-18. Geometric modeling using primitives.

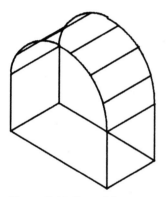

Figure 12-19. Geometric modeling using surfaces.

capabilities are increased and when efficient software is available is that of *geometric modeling*. This method assumes that all objects are created from simple, primitive shapes. "Primitive" in this case refers to rectangular, cylindrical, and conical blocks or parts of such blocks. When one of these shapes is added to or subtracted from other shapes, new, complex shapes are created (see Figure 12-18).

The geometric-modeling method has many advantages and a few disadvantages. The advantages include the three-dimensional description that can potentially be used by machine tool programmers and the logical breakdown of complex shapes into simple shapes, which copies the thinking patterns of drafters, designers, and engineers. If the primitive can be identified, then the entire primitive can be moved or removed. The disadvantages include the problems of intersection of surfaces, the identification of a primitive by a single point or origin, the technique for representation of the objects on the CRT, and the data-file structure that must be maintained and updated as the system is being used. One of the techniques used for representation of the objects on the CRT is the wire-frame technique.

Geometric Modeling: Surfaces

Another approach to working with solids and computer graphics is to define surfaces. Figure 12-19 shows the half cylinder that is the top of the object as a series of planar faces or facets rather than as a smooth curve. A rather complex data base is required to maintain the necessary information for this object in the system. This technique

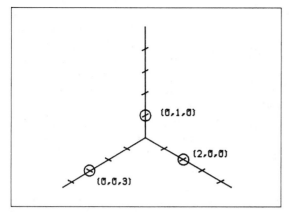

Figure 12-20. Points located on axes.

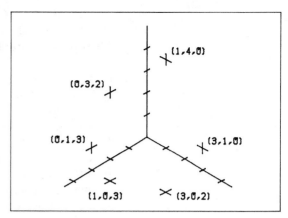

Figure 12-21. Points located on planes.

offers the advantage that, as planes are added to a picture to create a solid object, they can be added from back to front. Each added surface can be filled, thus effectively taking care of the problem of hidden lines in a particular drawing. The color or gray scale used to fill the surface can be a problem if colors are not complementary or if the gray scale is not carefully chosen to eliminate the previously drawn lines.

Constructing the Wire-Frame Model

The premises for constructing a wire-frame model include the following: The object is transparent, there are no hidden lines (unless one line is in front of another), and collections of lines are used to represent planes and surfaces. There is also the implicit assumption that any curved surface can be broken into a series of planar surfaces as shown in Figure 12-19.

Locating Points in Three-Dimensional Space

Points for the data file are identified by their X, Y, and Z coordinates. In order to facilitate this process a set of isometric axes is drawn on isometric grid paper. This allows the points be positioned easily and accurately. Figure 12-20 shows three points, one located on each of the three axes. The coordinates of the points are shown next to their locations. Note that when points are located on an axis, the other two coordinates are 0.

Points can also be located on one of the principal planes. Figure 12-21 shows six different points located on the X-Y, Y-Z, and Z-X planes. Note that when the points are located on a plane, one of the coordinates is always 0.

Points can also be located in space by moving along one axis, then moving away from it and parallel to the other two axes. Figure 12-13 shows a point located in the positive octant, the portion of space where all coordinates are positive.

Creating the Data File

The storage of the coordinates requires three arrays; one for each of the axes. Recall that when plotting is done by an ink pen plotter, the concept is pen up, move to a new coordinate, and pen down to draw a line. If pen up is given a value of 3 and pen down is given a value of 2, as was the case in Figure 12-15, then a fourth array in the storage array can be used to take care of the connection of points. This set of arrays then provides enough information for the three-dimensional object to be drawn as an orthographic drawing or a pictorial. We will use this concept for development of the equations for orthographic and pictorial drawings.

There are problems with this concept in that working with the points defined uniquely with pen up and pen down means that deletion of lines requires deletion of two points and redefinition of the pen up, pen down array. In spite of these problems, this method allows us to develop the drawing and to understand the display and rotation/translation algorithms.

Figure 12-22 shows the MOVEs and DRAWs required to construct our sample three-dimensional object. Remember that a MOVE represents a pen up and a DRAW represents a pen down. The object drawn in Figure 12-22 is the sample object that we will be using for the rest of the algorithmic development.

Once the data set has been developed it must be stored in the computer so that it can be used for calculations and manipulations. This procedure should be set up to read the information from DATA statements or a DATA file.

The reading/storing procedure should be a subroutine. The subroutine should read the point values into arrays and should be set up so that virtually any number of points can be used. In our case, we will limit the size of the storage arrays to 50 points, and the FORTRAN read/store subroutine will be written with an option to stop reading when the end of the data or when the end of the file is reached. The subroutine can also be set up to use a signal value at the end of the data, which, when reached, terminates the reading loop. This is the approach that will be used in BASIC. The subroutine should also be capable of counting the number of data points used so that the number can be used in the other subroutine for display.

The subroutine for reading and storing the data is shown below. Note in the FORTRAN version that the argument list contains only the data counter, NDATA, and that the information stored is transmitted from the subroutine to the main program and the other subroutines via the COMMON statement.

FORTRAN code:

```
      SUBROUTINE READIN(NDATA)
      COMMON X(50),Y(50),Z(50),PEN(50)
C ** INSERT A FILE OPEN STATEMENT HERE IF USING
C ** FILES RATHER THAN DATA CARDS OR STATEMENTS
      NDATA = 1
      DO 60 K = 1,50
```

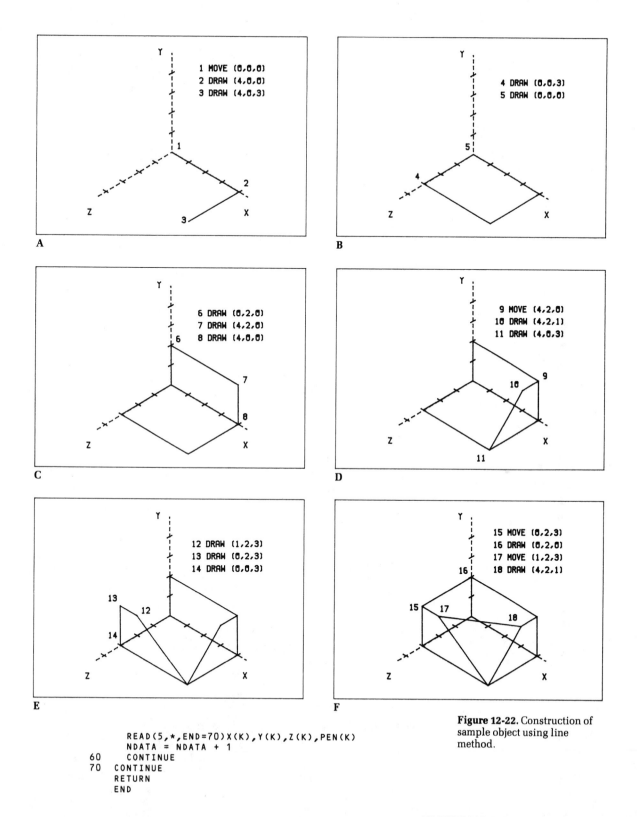

```
        READ(5,*,END=70)X(K),Y(K),Z(K),PEN(K)
        NDATA = NDATA + 1
60      CONTINUE
70   CONTINUE
        RETURN
        END
```

Figure 12-22. Construction of sample object using line method.

Table 12-4.

Vertex No.	X	Y	Z
1	0	0	0
2	0	2	0
3	4	2	0
4	4	0	0
5	4	0	3
6	0	0	3
7	0	2	3
8	1	2	3
9	4	2	1

Table 12-5. Face Information

Face No.	Number of Vertices	Order of Vertices
1	5	1-2-3-4-1
2	5	1-4-5-6-1
3	5	1-6-7-2-1
4	5	3-9-5-4-3
5	5	5-8-7-6-5
6	6	2-7-8-9-3-2
7	4	5-9-8-5

The BASIC routine is shown below. Note that the main program calling this subroutine should have a dimension statement to request the storage of the variables.

BASIC code:

```
 5 DIM X(50),Y(50),Z(50),P(50)

21000 REM ** THIS SUBROUTINE READS, COUNTS, AND
21012 REM ** STORES DATA FOR USE IN THE 3 DIMEN-
21014 REM ** SIONAL DISPLAY ROUTINES - LINE METHOD.
21016 NDATA = 0
21018 FOR J = 1 TO 50
21020    READ X(J),Y(J),Z(J),P(J)
21021    IF X(J)=999 GOTO 21026
21022    NDATA = NDATA + 1
21024    NEXT J
21026 RETURN
```

The Face Method

The first step in using the face method of drawing three-dimensional objects is to identify the vertices and their X, Y, and Z coordinates. In our sample object there are nine vertices, numbered as shown in Figure 12-23. The vertex numbers and coordinates are shown in Table 12-4.

The data for this sample program are provided here in data statements for the BASIC version and can be put on data cards or in a data file in the same order for the FORTRAN version. The DATA statements for the vertex coordinate information are as follows:

```
22100 DATA 9
22102 DATA 0,0,0
22104 DATA 0,2,0
22106 DATA 4,2,0
22108 DATA 4,0,0
22110 DATA 4,0,3
22112 DATA 0,0,3
22114 DATA 0,2,3
22116 DATA 1,2,3
22118 DATA 4,2,1
```

The second step in the face method is identifying the faces by number and by their accompanying number of vertices and vertex order. In this case we are recording the vertex numbers in counterclockwise order so that we can easily determine mathematically whether the face is visible or hidden. Table 12-5 shows the face

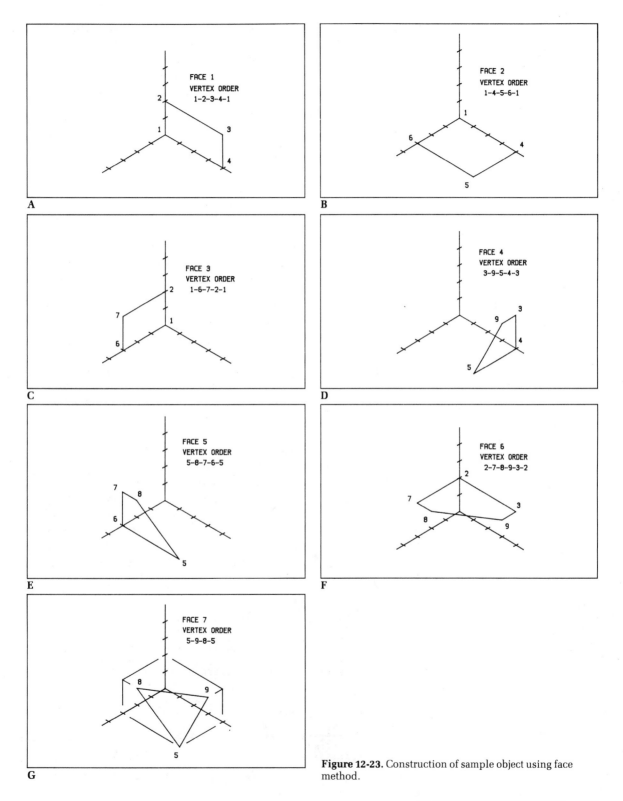

Figure 12-23. Construction of sample object using face method.

number, the number of vertices on the face, and the counterclockwise order of the vertices. Note that there will be a MOVE to the first vertex and then a DRAW to each subsequent vertex and that the lines must be closed by returning to the first vertex on the face.

The data statements for the face information are as follows:

```
22148 DATA 7
22150 DATA 5
22152 DATA 1,2,3,4,1,0
22154 DATA 5
22156 DATA 1,4,5,6,1,0
22158 DATA 5
22160 DATA 1,6,7,2,2,0
22162 DATA 5
22164 DATA 3,9,5,4,3,0
22166 DATA 5
22168 DATA 5,8,7,6,5,0
22170 DATA 6
22172 DATA 2,7,8,9,3,2
22174 DATA 4
22176 DATA 5,9,8,5,0,0
```

These data must be read into arrays so that the information can be used. The array for the vertices is set up as a two-dimensional array where the first subscript represents the vertex number and the second subscript represents the X, Y, or Z coordinate.

The arrays for the number of vertices per face and vertex order on each individual face are dimensioned as singly subscripted and doubly subscripted, respectively. The subscript on the number of vertices per face array indicates the face number. The first subscript on the vertex order array indicates the face number and the second indicates the first through nth vertex that is part of the face.

The subroutines have been written to be as straightforward as possible. Note that the data have been set up to keep the second subroutine limited to one reading loop rather than a nested loop. This requires some dummy numbers in the data to match the READ statement. The FORTRAN and BASIC subroutines have been organized in the same fashion and are shown below. The data to be placed in a file or on data cards for FORTRAN would be placed in the same order as the information in the DATA statements for the BASIC version.

FORTRAN code:

```
      SUBROUTINE READFC (NUMFCE,NUMVRT)
C ** THIS SUBROUTINE READS IN INFORMATION ABOUT A 3-D
C ** FIGURE USING THE FACE METHOD. THE NO. OF VERTICES
C ** AND X,Y,Z COORD. INFORMATION IS READ FIRST. THE NO.
C ** OF FACES IS READ NEXT FOLLOWED BY THE NO. OF
C ** VERTICES/FACE AND THE ORDER OF THE VERTICES ON THAT
C ** FACE.
      INTEGER FCEVRT,VN
      COMMON VERT(20,3),FCEVRT(10),VN(20,10)
      READ(5,*)NUMVRT
      DO 80 K = 1,NUMVRT
        READ VERT(K,1),VERT(K,2),VERT(K,3)
   80   CONTINUE
      READ(5,*)NUMFCE
      DO 90 M = 1,NUMFCE
        READ(5,*)FCEVRT(M)
```

```
        READ(5,*)VN(M,1),VN(M,2),VN(M,3),VN(M,4),VN(M,5)
      * VN(M,6)
 90     CONTINUE
      RETURN
      END
```

The FORTRAN example requires one routine with two loops to read in the data. The BASIC example, shown below, uses two subroutines. One is for the vertices while the other is for the information about the vertices that form the face.

BASIC code:

```
22000 REM ** THIS SUBROUTINE READS IN THE INFORMATION
22002 REM ** FOR THE VERTICES TO BE USED WITH THE FACE
22004 REM ** METHOD. VERT - VERTEX COORD.,NUMVERT - NO.
22006 REM ** OF VERTICES.
22008 DIM VERT(20,3)
22010 READ NUMVERT
22012 FOR K = 1 TO NUMVERT
22014   READ VERT(K,1),VERT(K,2),VERT(K,3)
22016   NEXT K
22018 RETURN

22050 REM ** THIS SUBROUTINE READS IN THE INFORMATION
22052 REM ** FOR THE FACES TO BE USED WITH THE FACE
22054 REM ** METHOD. NUMFCE - FACE NUMBER, FCEVRT -
22056 REM ** NO. VERTICES/FACE,VN - VERTEX NUMBER
22058 DIM FCEVRT(10),VN(20,10)
22060 READ NUMFCE
22062 FOR M = 1 TO NUMFCE
22064   READ FCEVRT(M)
22066   READ VN(M,1),VN(M,2),VN(M,3),VN(M,4),VN(M,5),
        VN(M,6)
22068   NEXT M
22070 RETURN
```

Table 12-6.

Vertex No.	X	Y	Z
1	0	0	0
2	0	2	0
3	4	2	0
4	4	0	0
5	4	0	3
6	0	0	3
7	0	2	3
8	1	2	3
9	4	2	1

Table 12-7.

Vertex No.	Connected Vertices
1	2-4-6
2	1-3-7
3	2-4-9
4	1-3-5
5	4-6-8-9
6	1-5-7
7	2-6-8
8	5-7-9
9	3-5-8

The Linked-Point Concept

The linked-point concept requires that each point defining a corner of the object, a point on the edge of the object, or a point on the surface of the object be stored in arrays of X, Y, and Z data. This concept requires that connections of each point to all other points be defined.

Tables 12-6 and 12-7 show the data for the two arrays necessary to use the linked-point concept. The first array is the same as the vertex array for the face method. Note that the vertices are labeled again by numbers and that the numbers provide the data. Take a moment to verify that at least the first three or four points and their connections are valid.

Note that in the linked-point concept it is very easy to remove a point and all of its connecting lines without disturbing the data, with the exception that there will be a missing element in the vertex array.

Converting the Data

Now that we have the data to use for sample figures, we will develop the equations for the conversion of the three-dimensional data to two-dimensional representations. A separate alogrithm is required

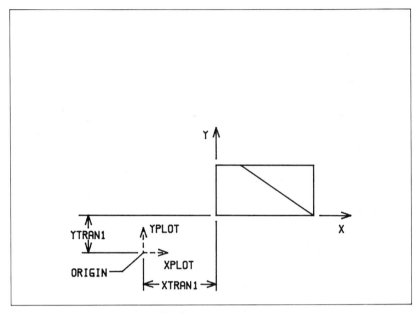

Figure 12-24. Front view of sample object.

for each representation, and each of these will be treated as a subroutine.

Orthographic Views

The concept of orthographic representation requires that the viewer be looking perpendicular to each of the various planes of an object. Refer again to Figure 12-4, which shows the observer looking at the object through the picture plane. The observer is looking down the Z axis and sees the front view. If we assume that we are looking at an object projected on the picture plane so that the Z axis becomes a point, then the Z values disappear from the representation that we perceive.

Figure 12-24 shows the front view of our sample object. The origin of the screen is shown in the lower-left corner of the figure, representing the lower-left corner of the CRT screen. Now we must develop the subroutine that will reduce the sample data to that front view. The coordinates that will be sent to the screen for display or to the plotter for display will be called XPLOT and YPLOT. Remember that we want to look down the Z axis, so the Z axis will appear as a point. Mathematically this can be represented by saying that the XPLOT value is equal to the X array value and that the YPLOT value is equal to the Y array value. The equations are

```
XPLOT = X(J)
YPLOT = Y(J)
```

Take the data for the sample figure and plot it by hand on a piece of rectangular grid paper to verify that plotting just the X and Y values does indeed produce the front view.

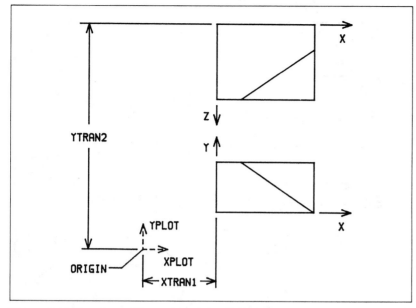

Figure 12-25. Top view and front view of sample object in relation to screen or page origin.

Now further development of the equations for the front view in orthographic projection are required. We assume that the lower-left corner of the page is considered to be the origin for drawing pictures. If we were to plot the X value as XPLOT without any translation, we would always find the front view in the lower-left corner of the page or the lower-left corner of the screen. This is not acceptable for engineering drawings, so the origin of the sample object must be moved away from the page origin. This requires two translations, one in the X direction and one in the Y direction. In order to distinguish the translation values we will call them XTRAN1 and YTRAN1. The equations with the addition of the translation values are

```
XPLOT = X(J) + XTRAN1
YPLOT = Y(J) + YTRAN1
```

Using these equations, again plot by hand the sample figure on a piece of orthographic grid paper using values of 1 or 2 units for the translation distances.

The equations for the other five views that constitute the principal views in orthographic projection are left to you as exercises. Remember that in some cases we are using the values as positive values and in other cases we are using normally positive values as negative values. Figure 12-25 shows the relationship between the top view and front view and the screen or page origin. Figure 12-26 shows the six principal views and the view-origin location for each of the views.

If we always pick small items to be displayed, then the orthographic views will always fit on a single sheet of 8½ by 11 paper. If,

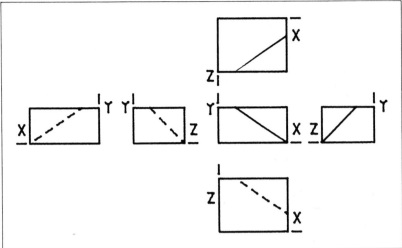

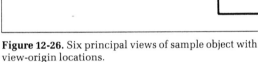

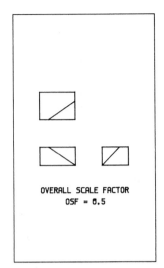

OVERALL SCALE FACTOR
OSF = 0.5

Figure 12-26. Six principal views of sample object with view-origin locations.

Figure 12-27. Three views of sample object at half scale.

however, we want to have equations that will work with all sizes of figures, then we must provide some way of shrinking large figures and expanding the size of very small figures. Both of these operations can be accomplished by using a scale factor (SF). The X and Y coordinates can be multiplied by the scale factor to either shrink or expand the three-dimensional object. Figure 12-25 shows the top and front views of our sample object at full scale (SF = 1.0) while Figure 12-27 shows three views at half scale (SF = 0.5). If the object were to be displayed at twice its original size, the scale factor would be 2.0. Our equations must now be modified to accommodate the scale factor. They become

```
XPLOT = X(J)*SF + XTRAN1
YPLOT = Y(J)*SF + YTRAN1
```

These equations will work on the Tektronix terminals or on most plotters because the distance between plotted points is the same in both the vertical and horizontal directions. A reasonable scale factor to be used with the Tektronix CRT is SF = 50. (This assumes that screen coordinates are used.) The IBM PC screen is not "square," and a multiplying factor must be used on the X coordinates to get an accurately proportioned object. This factor is approximately 2.5. The equations for the IBM PC are shown here with the proper scale factor to allow the three orthographic views to be displayed on the CRT screen:

```
SF = 30
XPLOT = X(J)*2.5*SF + XTRANF
YPLOT = -Y(J)*SF + YTRANF
```

Take three or four of the data points and plot them using both the translation values and the appropriate scale factor for your system. Verify that this procedure works.

The subroutines for the front view are presented in both FOR-TRAN and BASIC for the MOVE/DRAW method of display. When reading these subroutines, look back at the read/store subroutine to see the connection between the storage and data counter. Also study these routines and use them as the pattern for developing the other subroutines for the standard three-view orthographic projection, namely the top and right side views.

FORTRAN code:

```
SUBROUTINE FRONT(NDATA)
INTEGER XPLOT,YPLOT
COMMON X(50),Y(50),Z(50),PEN(50)
SF = 50
XTRAN1 = 100
YTRAN1 = 100
DO 80 J = 1,NDATA
  XPLOT = X(J)*SF + XTRAN1
  YPLOT = Y(J)*SF + YTRAN1
  IF(PEN(J).EQ.3)THEN
      CALL MOVABS(XPLOT,YPLOT)
    ELSE
      CALL DRWABS(XPLOT,YPLOT)
    END IF
80    CONTINUE
RETURN
END
```

BASIC code:

```
23100 REM ** THIS IS THE FRONT VIEW  SUBROUTINE -
23102 REM ** LINE METHOD. IT REQUIRES THE READ/STORE
23104 REM ** SUBROUTINE FOR THE DATA AND NUMBER OF
23106 REM ** COORDINATE POINTS.
23108 SF = 30:XTRAN1=20:YTRAN1=190
23110 FOR J = 1 TO NDATA
23112   XPLOT = X(J)*2.5*SF + XTRAN1
23114   YPLOT = -Y(J)*SF + YTRAN1
23116   IF (P(J)=3) THEN PSET(XPLOT,YPLOT)
        ELSE LINE- (XPLOT,YPLOT)
23118   NEXT J
23120 RETURN
```

When utilizing the face method to develop orthographic views, a double loop must be used, with the outside loop taking each face in order and the inside loop cycling through the vertices that make up the face. Note that in this method the procedure for drawing each face has two features. The first feature is that if each edge of each face is drawn, each edge of the figure will be drawn twice. This is certainly inefficient in comparison to our previous method, but it is essential when we attempt to eliminate faces or to shade faces. The second feature is that our vertex data for each face show each vertex and allow for drawing the last line to connect the last vertex to the first vertex.

FORTRAN code:

```
SUBROUTINE FRNTFC (NUMFCE,NUMVRT)
INTEGER FCEVRT,VN,V,XPLOT,YPLOT
COMMON VERT(20,3),FCEVRT(10),VN(20,10)
SF = 50
XTRAN1 = 100
YTRAN1 = 100
DO 60 K = 1,NUMFCE
  LMAX = FCEVRT(K)
  DO 50 L = 1,LMAX
```

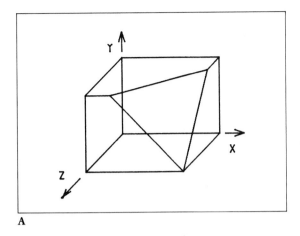

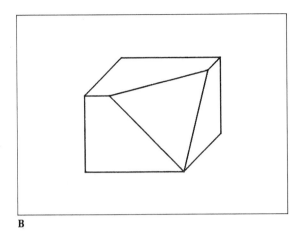

A

B

Figure 12-28. (A) Oblique wire-frame drawing with axes shown. (B) Oblique pictorial with hidden lines eliminated.

```
          V = VN(K,L)
          XPLOT = SF*VERT(V,1) + XTRAN1
          YPLOT = SF*VERT(V,2) + YTRAN1
          IF (L = 1) THEN
              CALL MOVABS(XPLOT,YPLOT)
            ELSE
              CALL DRWABS(XPLOT,YPLOT)
            END IF
50        CONTINUE
60      CONTINUE
        RETURN
        END
```

BASIC code:

```
24000 REM ** THE ORTHOGRAPHIC PLOTTING ROUTINES
24002 REM ** USING THE FACE METHOD.
24100 REM ** THE FRONT VIEW
24102 SCREEN 2
24104 XTRAN1 = 20
24106 YTRAN1 = 190
24108 FOR K = 1 TO NUMFACE
24110    LMAX = FCEVRT(K)
24112    FOR L = 1 TO LMAX
24114       V = VN(K,L)
24116       XPLOT = SF*VERT(V,1)+XTRAN1
24118       YPLOT = -SF/2.5*VERT(V,2)+YTRAN1
24120       IF (L=1) THEN PSET(XPLOT,YPLOT)
24122       LINE -(XPLOT,YPLOT)
24124    NEXT L
24126    NEXT K
24128 RETURN
```

Oblique Pictorials

The oblique pictorial is not used nearly as often as isometric, axonometric, or perspective pictorials. However, it will provide a good place to start the more complicated reduction of three-dimensional data to two-dimensional display. Figure 12-28 shows a wire-frame oblique drawing with the X, Y, and Z axes and an oblique pictorial with the hidden lines eliminated.

The development of equations can be aided by the proper mental picture of the display desired. Figure 12-29 shows a single point in the positive octant (the portion of space where the X, Y, and Z values are all positive).

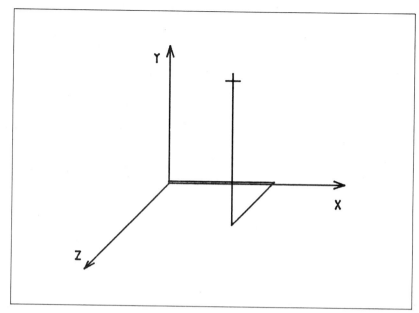

Figure 12-29.

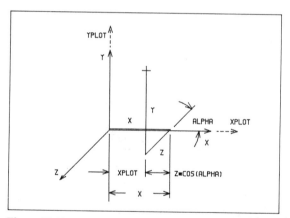

Figure 12-30.

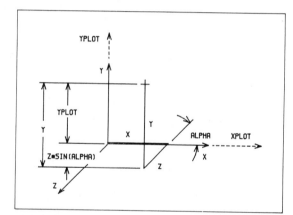

Figure 12-31.

There are three items that must be taken into account as we look at oblique figures. Figure 12-30 illustrates the first of these. Study this figure carefully and note that the angle that the negative Z axis makes with the X axis is critical. The XPLOT value depends on the X and Z coordinates of a point. The YPLOT value depends on the Y and Z coordinates of the point. Figure 12-31 shows the derivation of the YPLOT values. Study this figure and compare the figures with the unmodified equations shown here:

```
XPLOT = X(J) - Z(J)*COS(ALPHA)
YPLOT = Y(J) - Z(J)*SIN(ALPHA)
```

The other two items that must be taken into account with oblique figures are the scale factor for the Z-axis values and the overall scale

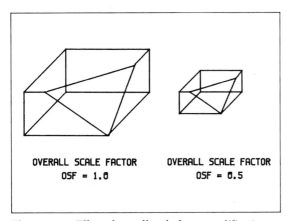

Figure 12-32. Effect of overall scale-factor modification on an oblique figure.

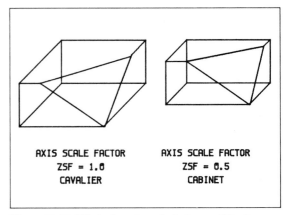

Figure 12-33. Effect of z-axis scale-factor modification on an oblique figure.

factor for the figure. The two scale factors can be added to the equations by remembering that the Z values can be shortened without the X and Y values being modified. All of the coordinates must be multiplied by the overall scale factor prior to the Z-axis scale factor being taken into account.

The following set of equations shows the overall scale factor modifying the initial equations, and Figure 12-32 shows the effect of the overall scale factor on the sample object.

```
XPLOT = (X(J) - Z(J)*COS(ALPHA))*SF
YPLOT = (Y(J) - Z(J)*SIN(ALPHA))*SF
```

This set of equations contains the Z-axis scale-factor modifications:

```
XPLOT = (X(J) - Z(J)*ZSF*COS(ALPHA))*SF
YPLOT = (Y(J) - Z(J)*ZSF*SIN(ALPHA))*SF
```

Figure 12-33 shows the sample object with the Z-axis scale factor equal to 0.5. When the Z-axis scale factor is 1.0, the oblique drawing is referred to as a *cavalier* drawing. When the Z-axis scale factor is 0.5, the oblique drawing is referred to as a *cabinet* drawing.

The final modification to the equations is to add in the X and Y translation values so that the object can be moved from the origin of the sheet or CRT (lower-left corner) to the middle of the page:

```
XPLOT = (X(J) - Z(J)*ZSF*COS(APLHA))*SF + XTRAN1
YPLOT = (Y(J) - Z(J)*ZSF*SIN(ALPHA))*SF + YTRAN1
```

Here is the subroutine for oblique pictorials, shown in both FORTRAN and BASIC.

FORTRAN code:

```
SUBROUTINE OBLIQ(ALPHA,ZSF,SF,XTRAN1,YTRAN1,NDATA)
INTEGER P,XPLOT,YPLOT
COMMON X(50),Y(50),Z(50),P(50)
CA = COS(ALPHA)
SA = SIN(ALPHA)
DO 60 J = 1,NDATA
   XPLOT = (X(J) - Z(J)*ZSF*CA)*SF + XTRAN1
   YPLOT = (Y(J) - Z(J)*ZSF*SA)*SF + YTRAN1
```

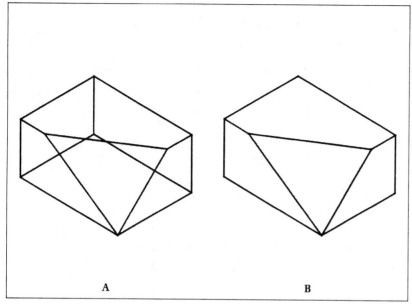

Figure 12-34. (A) Isometric wire-frame drawing. (B) Isometric pictorial with hidden lines eliminated.

```
            IF (P(J).EQ.3) THEN
                CALL MOVABS(XPLOT,YPLOT)
            ELSE
                CALL DRWABS(XPLOT,YPLOT)
            END IF
    60      CONTINUE
        RETURN
        END
```

BASIC code:

```
25150 REM ** THIS IS THE OBLIQUE SUBROUTINE - LINE
25152 REM ** METHOD. IT REQUIRES THE READ/STORE
25154 REM ** SUBROUTINE AND VALUES FOR SCALE FACTORS,
25156 REM ** SF AND ZSF, AND Z AXIS ANGLE, ALPHA.
25158 CA = COS(ALPHA)
25160 SA = SIN(ALPHA)
25162 FOR J = 1 TO NDATA
25164   XPLOT = (X(J) - Z(J)*ZSF*CA)*SF + XTRAN1
25166   YPLOT = -(Y(J) - Z(J)*ZSF*SA)*SF + YTRAN1
25168   IF P(J) = 3 THEN PSET(XPLOT,YPLOT)
        ELSE LINE -(XPLOT,YPLOT)
25170   NEXT J
25178 RETURN
```

Isometric Pictorials

Isometric pictorials are desirable because they look like a picture of a real object. They can be developed by using only the trigonometric values of one angle and the scale factor. One of the prime advantages of isometric pictorials is that their coordinates are plotted true size parallel to each of the axes. Figure 12-34 shows an isometric wire-frame drawing and an isometric drawing with the hidden lines eliminated.

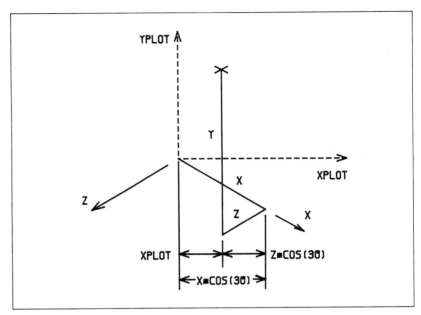

Figure 12-35.

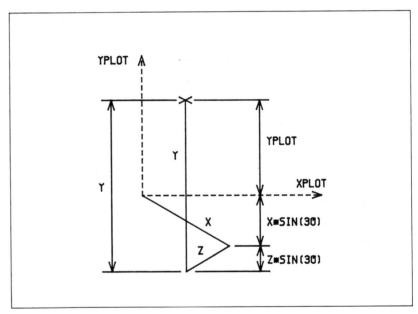

Figure 12-36.

The picture of a point in space must be created with the point in the positive octant and in the positive quadrant (both XPLOT and YPLOT positive; see Figure 12-35). As we did in the development of the oblique drawing, we must move parallel to each of the axes to locate the point. Figures 12-35 and 12-36 show the XPLOT and

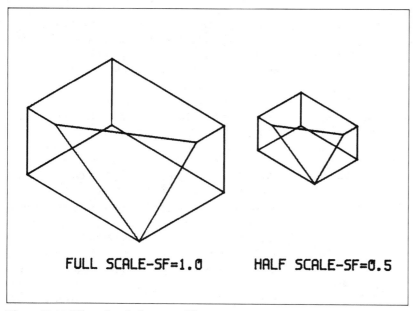

FULL SCALE-SF=1.0   HALF SCALE-SF=0.5

Figure 12-37. Effect of scale-factor modification on an
isometric drawing.

YPLOT values as they are derived from the X, Y, and Z coordinate
values. The equations are

```
XPLOT = X(J)*COS(30) - Z(J)*COS(30)
YPLOT = Y(J) - (X(J) + Z(J))*SIN(30)
```

In order to complete the isometric-drawing subroutine, you must
include the scale factors and the X and Y translation distances from
the corner of the screen. The actual writing of the subroutines, using
both the line method and the face method, is left to you as an
exercise. Figure 12-37 shows the effect of the scale factor on the
isometric wire-frame drawing of the sample object.

This chapter has provided two methods (line and face) for displaying three-dimensional figures as two-dimensional drawings.
Either of these methods provides a useful approach to the material
that will be presented in Chapter 13. The material covered in this
chapter makes use of translation and scaling in screen coordinates.
Many systems today provide for more sophisticated methods of
scaling and translating figures, but these methods still require the
calculations shown here.

The orthographic, oblique, and isometric subroutines presented
in this chapter provide you with effective methods for displaying a
variety of figures. The addition of rotation, as presented in Chapter
13, will complete the fundamental operations of displaying two- and
three-dimensional figures.

Exercises

1. Use a piece of isometric grid paper to plot a sample figure that you can use in the three-dimensional exercises. The maximum values on each of the axes (X, Y, and Z) should be 10 units. This will allow you to plot relatively complicated figures and use integer values for your data set.

2. Make up a table of values for your figure that includes the values for X, Y, Z and the pen value to indicate whether the points are connected by a line or whether there is a move that connects the points. Use a value of 3 to indicate that the pen is up and a value of 2 to indicate that the pen is down and that a line should be drawn between succeeding points.

3. Key in the subprogram given for drawing the front view. Check the program to see if it works properly on your system using the following set of data:

Point No.	X(J)	Y(J)	Z(J)	PEN(J)
1	0	0	0	3
2	1	0	0	2
3	1	2	0	2
4	0	2	0	2
5	0	0	0	2
6	0	0	3	2
7	0	2	3	2
8	0	2	0	2
9	1	0	0	3
10	1	0	3	2
11	0	0	3	2
12	0	2	3	3
13	1	2	3	2
14	1	0	3	2
15	1	2	3	3
16	1	2	0	2

4. Convert the data from Exercise 3 so that they provide the needed information for using the face method rather than the line method. Key in the subroutines for reading/storing the information and for displaying the front view using the face method.

5. Convert the data from Exercise 3 so that they provide the needed information for using the connected-vertex method rather than the line method. Write the flow charts for, and develop the subroutines for, reading/storing and for displaying the front view using the connected-vertex method.

6. Write the subroutine for drawing the top view of an object given the three-dimensional data shown in Exercise 3. Use (a) the line method, (b) the face method, and (c) the connected-vertex method.

7. Write the following subroutines using either the line method, the face method, or the connected-vertex method, as assigned by your instructor: (a) right side view, (b) left side view, (c) back view, (d) bottom view.

8. Draw the flow chart and key the oblique subroutine (line method) shown in the chapter and test it using the data given in Exercise 3. Develop the oblique subroutine using the face method (draw the flow chart first) and test it using the data given in Exercise 3.

9. Draw the flow chart for the isometric subroutine, write the subroutine, and test it using the data given in Exercise 3. Use (a) the line method, (b) the face method, and (c) the connected-vertex method.

In Chapter 12 we discussed the creation of three-dimensional wire-frame drawings. We created a sample three-dimensional object and displayed it as an orthographic drawing with three views. We also developed two pictorial views of the object: the oblique drawing and the isometric drawing. In all three cases we presented the figure with all edges drawn as visible lines.

In this chapter we will create two types of pictorials, the axonometric projection and the perspective drawing. The axonometric projection is produced by rotation of the figure first around the Y axis and then around the X axis. The perspective drawing is created by including the distance of the viewer from the object in the calculations of the positions of features in the rotated figure.

In both axonometric and perspective drawings it is possible to eliminate hidden lines or surfaces of the displayed object if the object is a convex polyhedron. The term *convex polyhedron* means that the object has no notches or cuts. The sample object that we used in Chapter 12 was a convex polyhedron. Figure 13-1 shows two cut blocks. The block on the left is a convex polyhedron and the other block, with the notch, is not a convex polyhedron.

In order to do hidden-line removal and shading or lighting, we must use the face method rather than the vertex method to display the object. Both the vertex-to-vertex method and the face method, presented in Chapter 12, were utilized to do the orthographic and pictorial projections. In this chapter, both approaches will be used for the axonometric and perspective projections, but only the face approach will be used for hidden-line removal and

13

Rotation, Perspective, Hidden-Line Elimination, and Lighting

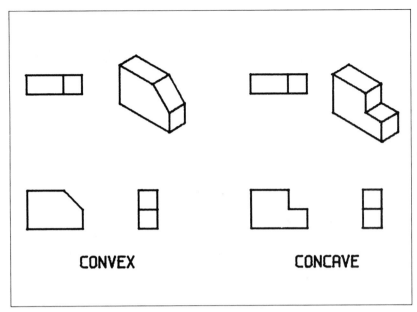

Figure 13-1. Polyhedrons.

for shading or lighting. Our method is a very simple form of hidden-line elimination through the elimination of hidden surfaces, showing that apparently complicated procedures can be relatively simple to accomplish if the problem is approached systematically and is subdivided into small parts.

Axonometric Projections

Axonometric projections are created by rotating the object to be drawn around any two of its three axes. The two axes that will be used for our presentation are the Y axis and the X axis. Figure 13-2 shows a sample object as an orthographic drawing with no rotation around either axis. Note that no corner has been removed, as was the case with the sample object used in Chapter 12. There are two reasons for this. The first is that, as rotations are made, it becomes more difficult to see what is happening to complicated objects. The second is that the upper-right corner closest to the observer will be used for deriving the equations for rotation, which we will present later in this chapter.

The rotation around the Y axis is performed first and produces Figure 13-3. The second rotation is around the X axis and produces Figure 13-4. Note that, although each of the three orthographic views that are produced after the two rotations provides a different view of the object, the front view is the most desirable.

When the object is seen by the observer, all of the lines are foreshortened; that is, they become less than true length. However, this foreshortening is only apparent when the isometric projection of the sample object produced by the axonometric rotations is com-

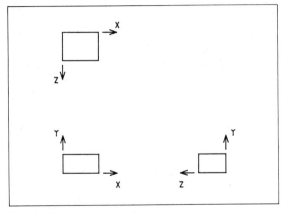

Figure 13-2.

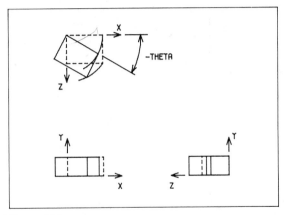

Figure 13-3.

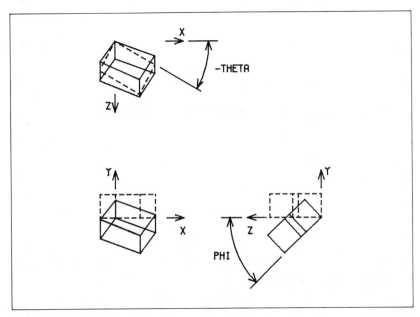

Figure 13-4.

pared with the isometric drawing. In our example, the axonometric view was produced by rotating the object about the Y axis by −45 degrees and about the X axis by 35 degrees, 16 minutes.

Once you have completed the coding of either the face or vertex method for the axonometric projection (see the exercises at the end of the chapter), compare it against the isometric projection from Chapter 12.

Y-Axis Rotation

Figure 13-5A shows a sample point in the unrotated position and Figure 13-5B shows the same point after a clockwise rotation (negative angle) around the Y axis. Note the positions of the sample point

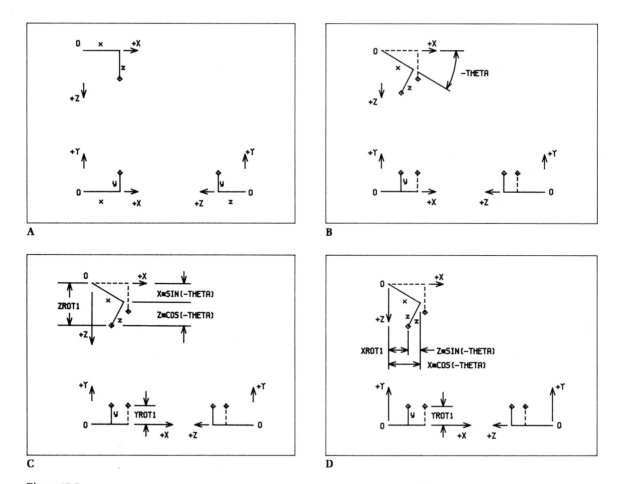

A

B

C

D

Figure 13-5.

in each view. In this example the vertex is located where the X, Y, and Z coordinates are all positive.

Figure 13-5C shows the components of the equations that can be used to calculate the position of the vertex after one rotation. The equations are

```
XROT1 = X*COS(-THETA) - Z*SIN(-THETA)
YROT1 = Y
ZROT1 = X*SIN(-THETA) + Z*COS(-THETA)
```

These equations are written for the negative Y-axis rotation. If the equations are rewritten so that they are defined in terms of a positive angle, they become

```
XROT1 = X*COS(THETA) + Z*SIN(THETA)
YROT1 = Y
ZROT1 = -X*SIN(THETA) + Z*COS(THETA)
```

The equations must be calculated for each vertex that forms part of the sample figure. In order to accomplish this, the equations should be contained in a loop, as were the equations for the orthographic

A   B

Figure 13-6.

and pictorial drawings in Chapter 12. The development of the sub-routine to do this for the vertex method and the face method are the first two exercises at the end of this chapter.

Note that a rotated value has been calculated for Z. This value is not needed for displaying the front view of our rotated figure but would be needed for displaying the right-side, top, bottom, or left-side views. It will also be needed when the calculations for the perspective projections are performed. This will be discussed later but you should study the equations dealing with the rotated Z values while studying the equations dealing with rotated X and Y values.

X-Axis Rotation

In order to produce the pictorial projections that are familiar to most observers, we assume that the Y rotation always takes place first and then the X rotation. This is done to preserve all of the vertical lines in the front view as vertical even though they may be foreshortened. In order to justify this approach you may need to study the room in which you are sitting or a nearby building to ascertain that vertical lines do remain vertical. The photographs in Figure 13-6 show a front view of a building and a view that would correspond to an axonometric projection. Study these photographs as well.

If we assume that the Y rotation has taken place, then the rotation about the X axis is done using the XROT1, YROT1, and ZROT1 values. The rotation about the X axis is counterclockwise (positive). The position of the vertex for which the equations are developed is kept within the octant where the X, Y, and Z values are positive.

The equations can be derived by studying Figure 13-7. Verify that the equations shown here are correct for the X axis rotation:

```
XROT2 = XROT1
YROT2 = -YROT1*COS(PHI) + ZROT1*SIN(PHI)
ZROT2 = YROT1*SIN(PHI) + ZROT1*COS(PHI)
```

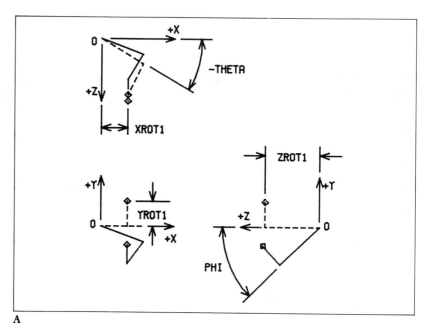

Figure 13-7.

A

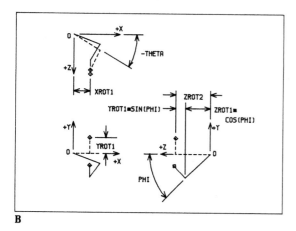

B

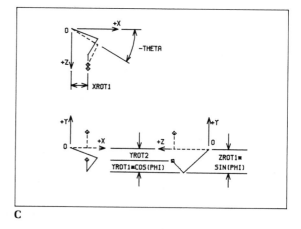

C

Substitution of the XROT1, YROT1, and ZROT1 values into the first two equations is left as an exercise. The derivation for ZROT2 by substitution is

```
ZROT2 = (Y)*SIN(PHI) + (-X*SIN(THETA) + Z*COS(THETA))*COS(PHI)

ZROT2 = -X*SIN(THETA)*COS(PHI) + Y*SIN(PHI) +
              Z*COS(THETA)*COS(PHI)
```

The equation is set in this form so that the original X value comes first, then the Y value, and then the Z value. This is done to correspond to mathematical practices in the use of matrices.

Classification of Projections

Axonometric projections are classified according to the apparent

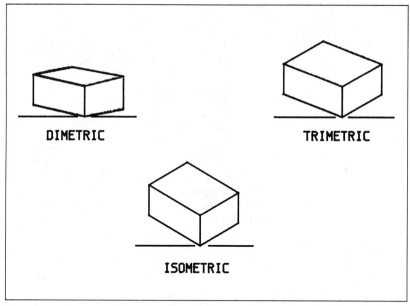

Figure 13-8. Dimetric, trimetric, and isometric projections of the same object.

Table 13-1.

Projection	Y rotation	X rotation
Isometric	−45°	35°16′
Dimetric	−45°	any
Trimetric	any	any

relationship of the axes in the projection. If the angle between each pair of projected axes is 120 degrees, then an isometric projection has been created. If angles between two pairs of axes are equal but are not equal to the third, then a dimetric projection is created. If none of the angles between any pairs of axes is equal, then a trimetric projection is created. Figure 13-8 shows the isometric, dimetric, and trimetric projections.

In order to create these projections using the axonometric subroutine, the X and Y rotations shown in Table 13-1 must be used.

Three-Point Perspective

In Chapter 12 three different types of perspective were shown. In this chapter, we will be developing the three-point perspective, or the perspective that appears to have three vanishing points (see Figure 13-9). As we did with axonometric projection, we are going to develop the perspective as seen in the front view. In other words, we are concerned about the X and Y plotted values.

In the previous section we developed the rotated values for Z as well as for X and Y. The perspective projection needs the Z value to establish the distance from the observer to various parts of the object.

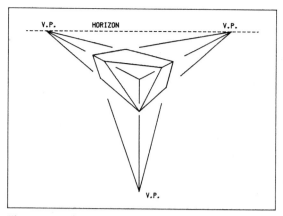

Figure 13-9. Three-point perspective.

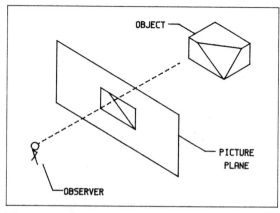

Figure 13-10.

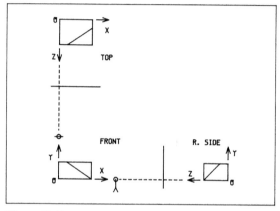

Figure 13-11.

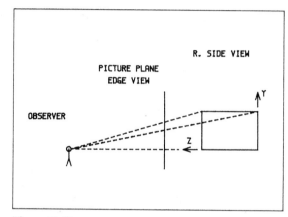

Figure 13-12.

Figure 13-10 shows the relation of the observer, the picture plane, and the object, while Figure 13-11 shows the front, top, and right-side views of the object considered in Figure 13-10. The top and right-side views will be enlarged to show the details for developing the perspective equations. Note that the observer's eye is located on the positive Z axis.

Figure 13-12 is an enlargement of the right-side view, where it is possible to see that various points are projected onto the picture plane. You can see that vertical lines closer to the observer and the picture plane will be projected as longer than the vertical lines that are further away.

Figure 13-13 takes a typical point on the object and shows the similar triangles that allow development of the equation for calculating the Y-perspective value. From the figure, you can see that the equation would be

$$\text{YPERS} = \text{YROT2} * (\text{PPLANE} / (\text{OBS} - \text{ZROT2}))$$

The development of the X-perspective value is left as an exercise.

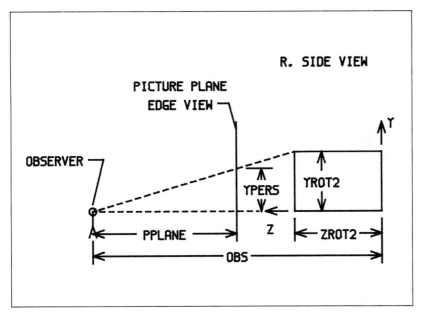

Figure 13-13.

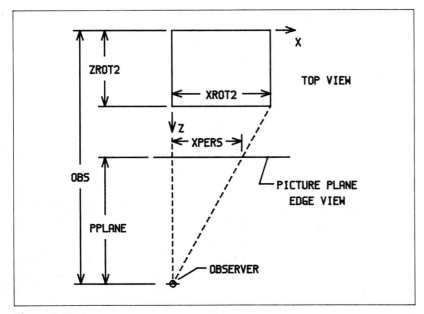

Figure 13-14.

(Use Figure 13-14, which shows the top view of the object.)

The equation for the Y-perspective value, along with that for the XPERS value, can be used to modify both versions of the axonometric routine that were developed earlier in this chapter. It is also possible to provide the perspective view as an option for the program user through the use of conditional statements.

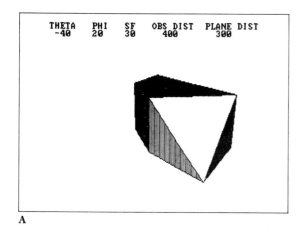

A

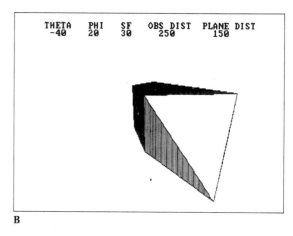

B

Figure 13-15.

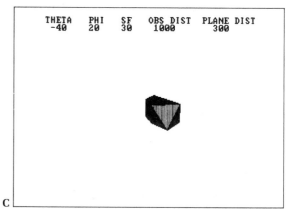

C

Note that when developing a perspective drawing, it is possible for the observer to move close to the origin of the object and even to be inside the object, but this does not lend itself to good pictorial drawings. The picture plane and the observer should not be so close to the object that the object appears greatly distorted. Similarly, it is not good practice to place the observer so far away that the object appears very small (see Figure 13-15). Your input should be checked so that you get an acceptable picture for each set of input values. Determination of the limiting values will be part of the exercises for this chapter.

Hidden-Line Algorithm for Convex Objects

This section will deal with the display of wire-frame objects with only lines normally visible in a pictorial shown. This is a simple form of the hidden-line elimination technique that can be used with the face method only. The concept here will be to test the planes that make up the figure to determine whether they are visible to the observer.

The line of sight for the hidden-surface elimination process will

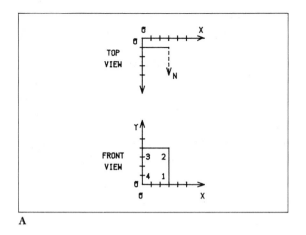

A

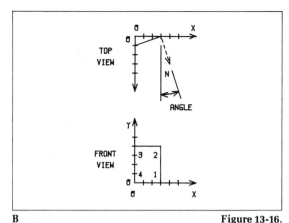

B

Figure 13-16.

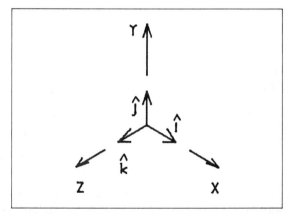

Figure 13-17.

be the observer looking down the Z axis. Vectors will be used to determine the visibility of surfaces. The vectors that will be most important to us in this process are the vector representing the Z axis and the vector that is perpendicular to each of the surfaces, or the normal vector. Figure 13-16A and 13-16B show views of two planes with the normal vector. The first plane is parallel to the X-Y plane and the second is parallel to the Y axis. The arrows that appear perpendicular to the edge views of the planes in the top view are the normal vectors. The top view of each figure will be used to develop and check the equations for doing the hidden-surface elimination.

In science and engineering, vectors are created by assuming that there are three vectors, each 1 unit long, beginning at the origin and coincident with the X, Y, and Z axes. Any other vector in three-dimensional space can be made up of combinations of unit vectors. These three vectors are called **i, j,** and **k.** Figure 13-17 shows the axes and the three unit vectors. In this representation, the Z axis could be considered a vector one unit long pointing in the Z direction and would be written as $0 \times \mathbf{i} + 0 \times \mathbf{j} + 1 \times \mathbf{k}$. It can also be written as (0,0,1), which is a little easier to use.

In Figure 13-16A, the normal vector to the X-Y plane shown is parallel to the Z axis. Figure 13-16B shows the normal vector at an angle to the Z axis.

Two vector operations must be used to determine the vector direction or parameters. The first is the vector cross product, which will provide the normal vector. The second is the vector dot product, which will yield the cosine of the angle between the normal vector to the X-Y plane and the Z-axis vector.

If we have two vectors, **A** and **B**, their vector equations are ax**i** + ay**j** + az**k** and bx**i** + by**j** + bz**k**. The cross product (**A** × **B**) for these two vectors is

$$[(ay \times bz) - (az \times by)]\mathbf{i} + [(az \times bx) - (ax \times bz)]\mathbf{j} + [(ax \times by) - (ay \times bx)]\mathbf{k}$$

The dot product is

$$ax \times bx\mathbf{i} + ay \times by\mathbf{j} + az \times bz\mathbf{k}$$

which is equal to

$$|\mathbf{A}| \times |\mathbf{B}| \times \cos(angle)$$

The item of concern here is the cos(angle). We need the cosine of the angle to provide information about visibility and to determine the lighting of the face.

Development of Procedures

We will work through two examples in order to show the procedures necessary for incorporating the vector manipulations. Referring again to Figure 13-16A, you can see that the plane is defined by lines connecting the four vertices. In order to have two vectors in the plane to provide a cross product, we will connect the first vertex to the second vertex and the first vertex to the third vertex (see Figure 13-18). In Chapter 12 we established the face method, with the vertices stored in a counterclockwise order. If the line connecting the first vertex and the second vertex is vector **A** and the line connecting the first vertex and the third vertex is vector **B**, then the cross product **A** × **B** is the normal vector and points to the outside of the figure.

Vector **A** and vector **B** are determined by subtracting the coordinates of vertex 1 from those of vertex 2. Vertex 1 has coordinates 3,0,1, vertex 2 has coordinates 3,4,1, and vertex 3 has coordinates 0,4,1. Vector **A** is $(3 - 3)\mathbf{i} + (4 - 0)\mathbf{j} + (1 - 1)\mathbf{k}$. Vector **B** is $(0 - 3)\mathbf{i} + (4 - 0)\mathbf{j} + (1 - 1)\mathbf{k}$. Therefore **A** and **B** are represented as $0\mathbf{i} + 4\mathbf{j} + 0\mathbf{k}$ and $-3\mathbf{i} + 4\mathbf{j} + 0\mathbf{k}$, respectively. Substituting into the equation given above for the cross product gives the normal vector:

$$\mathbf{N} = [(4 \times 0) - (0 \times 4)]\mathbf{i} + [(0 \times -3) - (0 \times 1)]\mathbf{j} + [(0 \times 4) - (4 \times -3)]\mathbf{k}$$

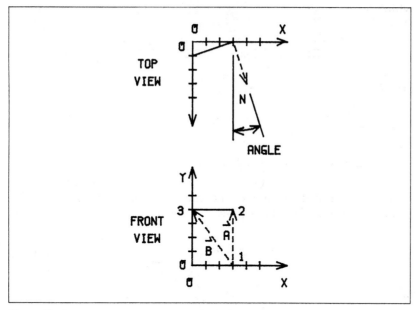

Figure 13-18.

which becomes $N = 0i + 0j + 12k$. Thus, N is a vector pointing down the Z axis.

Let us now determine vectors A and B for the plane shown in Figure 13-16B. Vertices 1, 2, and 3 are (3,0,0), (3,4,0), and (0,4,1). Vector A is vertex 1 minus vertex 2, or $0i + 4j + 0k$, and vector B is vertex 3 minus vertex 1, or $-3i + 4j + 1k$. Their normal vector or cross product is

$$N = [(4 \times 1) - (0 \times 4)]i + [(0 \times -3) - (0 \times 1)]j \\ + [(0 \times 4) - (4 \times -3)]k$$

which becomes $N = 4i + 0j + 12k$. Note that this vector has no component in the Y direction, which is correct when the plane is drawn parallel to the Y axis.

The next step is to compute the values of the cosine for the angles that the normal vectors make with the Z axis. It should be obvious that the normal vector for the first plane is parallel to the Z axis and the cosine of the angle between the normal vector and the Z axis would be unity. The angle for our second example plane in Figure 13-16B appears to be approximately 20 degrees.

Calculation of the cosine of the angle between the normal vector and the Z axis for the plane shown in Figure 13-16A is

$$NZ = |N| \times |Z| \times \cos(angle)$$

or

$$\cos(angle) = \frac{NZ}{|N| \times |Z|}$$

which becomes

$$(0 \times 0 \times \mathbf{i})^2 + (0 \times 0 \times \mathbf{j})^2 + (12 \times 1 \times \mathbf{k})^2$$
$$= \sqrt{0^2 + 0^2 + 12^2} \times \sqrt{0^2 + 0^2 + 1^2} \times \cos(angle)$$

or

$$\cos(angle) = \frac{12}{12} = 1$$

Therefore, the angle between the normal vector and the Z axis is 0 degrees.

Calculation of the cosine of the angle between the normal vector and the Z axis for the plane shown in Figure 13-16B is

$$(4 \times 0 \times \mathbf{i})^2 + (0 \times 0 \times \mathbf{j})^2 + (12 \times 1 \times \mathbf{k})^2$$
$$= \sqrt{4^2 + 0^2 + 12^2} \times \sqrt{0^2 + 0^2 + 1^2} \times \cos(angle)$$

or

$$\cos(angle) = \frac{12}{12.65} = 0.949$$

Therefore, the angle between the normal vector and the Z axis is 18.43 degrees. This value is close to the estimate that we made based on our examination of Figure 13-16B.

The axonometric and perspective subroutines developed earlier must be modified to process this additional information and the rotated vertices must be stored as they are calculated. Then the visibility of the plane is determined and, if visible, the plane is plotted. Note that the criterion for the plane to be plotted is that the cosine of the angle that the plane normally makes with the Z axis must be positive.

The following is a "verbal" flow chart for the axonometric subroutines:

```
SUBROUTINE AXONOMETRIC(THETA,PHI,SF)
COMMON arrays
Calculate sine/cosine for THETA and PHI
Loop to cycle through the faces
    Loop to calculate the rotated values of
          the face vertices and assign them
          to a new array
    Call the subroutine (DOTCRS) that
          calculates the normal vector
          for the plane and the cosine
          of the angle between the normal
          and the Z axis
          (information needed - 1st 3 rotated
          vertices, information returned -
          value of cosine)
    If cosine > 0 plot lines forming face
          Loop to move to first vertex and
                draw to other vertices
          End loop
```

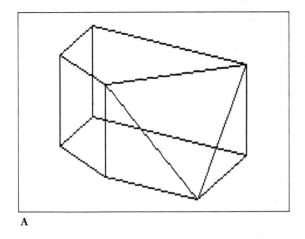

A

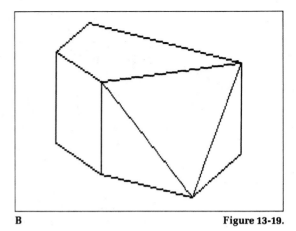

B

Figure 13-19.

```
                        Draw to first vertex
                    Else finish loop
                    End loop
              End loop
        RETURN

        SUBROUTINE DOTCRS(ROTVER1,ROTVER2,ROTVER3,COSINE)
        Calculate ax,ay,az and bx,by,bz
        Calculate Nx,Ny,Nz (cross procuct for A X B)
        Calculate the cosine of angle between N and Z axis
        RETURN
```

Although the rotated vertex values for the first three vertices are represented as three singly subscripted arrays in SUBROUTINE DOTCRS, they could be stored in a doubly subscripted array where the first subscript is the face number and the second represents X, Y, and Z. Having all of the rotated vertices stored for each face will be helpful in the next section, where lighting is addressed. Figure 13-19A is an axonometric projection with all lines showing. Figure 13-19B shows the same figure with the hidden lines removed.

Shading or Lighting

Many terminals now have the ability to display color and different degrees of brightness (called grayscale). We will discuss these two topics briefly before we put them to use making better pictures of our axonometric and perspective pictorials.

Terminals that can display only one intensity of dot to form pictures require less memory than those that can display different colors or different dot intensities. On/off requires 1 bit. Two bits can provide four colors or shades of gray (0,1,2,3) and 3 bits can provide eight colors or shades of gray. The IBM PC in SCREEN 1 mode (320 × 200) allows the use of two different sets (palettes) of colors. One set is black(0), green(1), red(2), and brown(3). The other is black(0), cyan(1), magenta(2), and white(3). When these are used with a monochrome CRT, the difference between green and red or between cyan and magenta is not distinguishable. Therefore, only three shades of gray are available. It is easiest to use the second set, where we have black, white, and either cyan or magenta, though the picture will appear a little less real than it might if more shades were available.

The commands that deal with color for the IBM PC include:

- COLOR background,palette;
- PSET x1,y1,color;
- LINE x1,y1-x2,y2,color;
- PAINT x,y,color,boundary color;
- SCREEN number

The screen number determines the resolution and therefore the number of available colors.

In addition to the IBM PC, we have also used an ID 100 terminal, from ID Systems, which provides eight shades of gray or eight colors when working at a resolution of 512×250. The colors this terminal provided were black, red, green, blue, cyan, magenta, yellow, and white. In this case only five of the shades of gray were distinguishable but the pictures showed marked improvement over those using just three shades.

The ID 100 terminal also required escape (ESC) sequences to set the foreground and background colors, to fill areas, and to blink colors. FORTRAN subroutines were written to send these sequences to the terminal. Examples of these subroutines are CALL PCOLOR(color number,blink) and CALL IDFILL(color number,blink). Once a color was set, it was used to draw all vectors. This particular terminal had enough display memory to allow all eight colors or eight levels of grayscale, blinking, and filling at the 512×250 resolution.

For a truly universal set of perspective subroutines, both the observer and the light source should be movable to any location. Thus far we have fixed the observer on the Z axis because we can rotate the object into any position. We will continue to do so. We will also put the light source on the Z axis. This simplifies the calculations required to determine the grayscale value or color for each face. Once the algorithms have been developed for the cross and dot products, it will be relatively easy to establish the light source in another location and obtain the amount of light reflected to the observer. If the light source and the observer are both in the same location on the Z axis, then the amount of light reflected to the observer is in proportion to the cosine of the angle between the surface normal vector and the Z axis.

Each terminal or microcomputer provides different methods for filling or painting surfaces. In general, the approach is to surround the area to be painted in some value of grayscale or color and then fill the area with the desired grayscale or color. The IBM PC requires the area to be defined or surrounded by the color to be filled. In order to shade a face with black, three steps are required. First the face must be surrounded with black, then it must be filled, and then it must be surrounded with white.

The ID 100 terminal required each face to be surrounded with blinking black vectors and then filled with any color. In this case, as with the IBM PC, the vertices had to be connected with white lines so as to display all faces once each face had been filled. An effective method for ensuring that the face edges are visible on terminals with many levels of grayscale is to reserve the brightest level only for drawing edges. This is particularly important if black is one of the colors used for the faces. If all faces are lit with a visible level of grayscale, then it may be more effective to draw the edges in black.

The verbal flow chart given previously will now have to be modified to draw the vectors connecting the vertices in more than one grayscale value or color. It will also have to be modified to draw the vectors at least twice if the faces are to be surrounded with the brightest grayscale or white after they have been filled. Use the IF–END IF section given here to replace the IF–END IF section in the flow chart given previously:

```
If cosine > 0 plot lines forming face
      Check value of cosine - choose color
      Loop  to do fill limiter(1) and white(2)
         Loop to move to first vertex and
            plot to other vertices and back
            to first vertex
         End loop
      If first time through loop then
         Move to center of area and fill
         Else end if
      End loop
   Else end if
```

Both the connected-vertex method and the face method will work for displaying axonometric and perspective drawings. The heart of both of these pictorial drawing subroutines is the double rotation required to place the object as the viewer wants to see it. The perspective drawing developed is a three-point perspective and requires the program user to choose the distances between the object, the picture plane, and the observer. One or two new subroutines must be written in either method to draw these two pictorials, depending on the approach chosen by the programmer.

Only the method of drawing faces visible by the observer provides the easy removal of hidden lines, and this method works only for convex polyhedrons. Once the hidden-face method has been programmed, it requires only drawing the edges or outline of the visible faces in the fill limiting color, filling the face, and drawing the edges again in white to create a shaded or lighted object.

One of the problems in working with the face method is that of closing the face or drawing from the last vertex to the first vertex. While there may be several methods to accomplish this, the one that we recommended is to store the location of the first vertex in temporary variables or in an array. When the loop to calculate and to

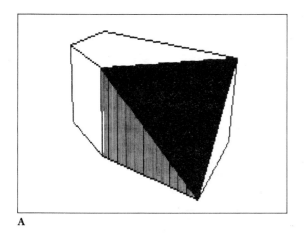

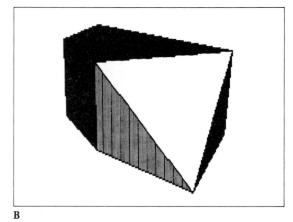

A   B

Figure 13-20.

draw the first through last vertex is completed, the first vertex can
then be drawn to close the face.

The routines used with the hidden-face elimination technique
should employ the storage of the rotated points in arrays, particularly for the lighting of the faces. The rotated points are needed in
four routines. The first routine is the calculation of the cosine of the
angle between the normal vector and the Z axis. (In this case the first
three points are needed for the calculation of the cross product.) The
second routine is for the drawing of the vectors that make up the
edges of the faces. The third routine is for calculating the centroid of
the faces, and the last is for drawing white or brightest vectors
around the edges of the visible faces.

Note that the image produced on the screen using these routines is
the correct one as far as lighting is concerned, but is not the correct
one if the picture is sent directly to a dot matrix printer. If this is
done the image produced is the negative of the desired picture. In
order to get the correct printed picture the program can be modified
to reverse the order of lighting assignments for the faces. Obviously,
this will not appear correct on the screen and you may wish to give
the user of your program the option to use either display algorithm.
Figure 13-20A shows a printer plot of a figure that appeared properly
lighted on the screen and Figure 13-20B shows the printer plot from
a figure that has had its lighting reversed on the screen.

Another problem that can occur when using these routines is
filling not only a single face but having the fill "escape" and fill the
entire screen, covering lines that have already been drawn. This is
caused by failure to close the face (not drawing back to the original
vertex).

Geometric Modeling

In this chapter and Chapter 12 we have dealt with three-dimensional
figures by surrounding them with a wire frame. We have dealt with
them by methods of lines and faces and thus have provided methods

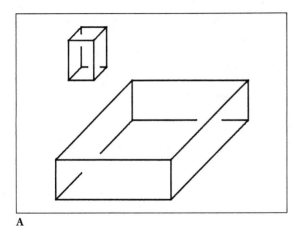

A

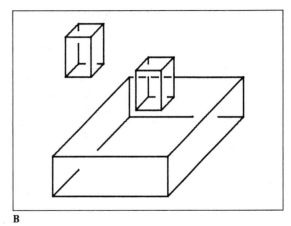

B

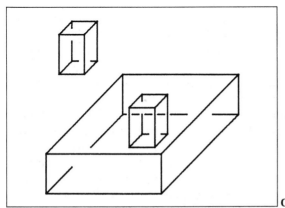

C

Figure 13-21. Geometric modeling. (A) Two rectangular blocks. (B) The two blocks united. (C) The smaller block subtracted from the larger block.

for pictorial display. With the addition of the lighting algorithm, the figures appear realistic. These are efficient methods for figures with limited complexity.

Different methods must be employed when objects with more complexity are required. One of the best methods for dealing with shapes of any complexity is geometric modeling. Geometric modeling builds complex objects from simple three-dimensional shapes. These three-dimensional shapes can include rectangular solids, cylinders, cones, spheres, and any part of these shapes, such as hemispheres or quarter-cylinders.

Geometric modeling provides methods for adding parts together (union), such as the two rectangular blocks shown in Figure 13-21A (Figure 13-21B shows the union). Geometric modeling also allows the user to subtract out a shape (difference) so that material can be removed, as shown in Figure 13-21C.

The objects in Figure 13-21 appear to be standard wire-frame drawings and in a sense they are. The difference, however, is that, to generate these objects, the user simply specified the desired shape, size (height, width, depth, diameter, and so on), and orientation, and the system produced the picture of the shape. There was no need to specify each vertex and each face.

Geometric modeling is particularly effective when used for parts being designed for manufacturing. Manufacturing processes frequently include the adding together of shapes (which may be a metal-joining process such as welding) or the subtracting of shapes (which may be the removal of metal by drilling holes or by milling to achieve a desired thickness).

When designers begin defining parts in geometric-modeling terms, the preparation of manufacturing processes will be made simpler. Far more important for large corporations, however, is the classification and storage of parts by their geometric shapes and their manufacturing processes. When new parts are to be designed and produced, the designers and manufacturing engineers can look at drawings of similar parts stored on the computer and, where possible, adapt or modify an existing part, which can reduce the time from product specification to finished part.

One geometric-modeling system is PADL, which has been developed by, and is being refined by, the Production Automation Project at the University of Rochester. PADL stands for the Part Application and Description Language. PADL I provided methods for defining parts, for drawing them as wire-frame images, and for producing dimensioned drawings. PADL II provides methods for producing colored or shaded images of parts so that they appear more realistic.

One of the limitations of geometric-modeling systems is that they demand enormous computer resources. For example, a minicomputer with 4 megabytes of random-access memory can support 20 to 25 students writing, compiling, and running programs. This same minicomputer can support only 3 to 5 experienced PADL users. Distributed processing can be part of the answer to this problem. In addition, as the price of sophisticated microprocessors decreases, and as their capabilities increase, much of the burden will be removed from the minicomputer.

Battelle Laboratories is providing another geometric-modeling package that runs on distributed and networked microprocessor-based workstations that include the CRT, the CPU, and the disk storage. With this system each user will have his or her own computer and will not be confronted with system degradation when other users are working.

This chapter has presented the concept of rotation about two axes to produce axonometric projections. It has also presented a method to produce a three-point perspective. In both of these types of pictorial, hidden lines can be eliminated by omitting faces that cannot be seen by an observer. (This method will only work for convex polyhedrons, however.) The determination of which surfaces can be seen by an observer require the calculation of normal vectors to faces and the angle between the normal vector and the observer's line of sight. This information also allows us to provide a method to light the faces and produce better pictorials.

Exercises

Note: Before writing any code for these exercises, write out or draw the flow charts for the programs to be developed. Include the scale factors or adjustment of window size in each routine developed. Also include the proper X and Y translation values to locate the figure in the center of the screen. These programs should be interactive and, where possible, you should allow the user to choose values for rotation angles, scale factors, X and Y translation distances, and observer and picture-plane distances.

1. Axonometric projections require two rotations. Refer to the first set of equations given in this chapter for rotation about the Y axis, and write a subroutine for the three-dimensional figure you used in Chapter 12 that will provide rotation about the Y axis. Use the vertex method or the face method, as assigned by your instructor.

2. (a) Develop the equations for rotation about the other axes (X and Z). (b) Write subroutines to do these rotations. Use the vertex method or the face method, as assigned by your instructor.

3. (a) Develop the equations XROT2 and YROT2 for the Y rotation followed by the X rotation, using the derivation of ZROT2 as an example. (b) Write the subroutine that will provide rotation about both axes when the user supplies the angles, the starting point, and the scale factor (if necessary). Use the vertex method or the face method, as assigned by your instructor. (Note that this subroutine produces figures with the vertical lines shown in the vertical position.)

4. (a) Use equal scale factors for your isometric-drawing routine developed in Chapter 12 and your axonometric-projection routine developed in Exercise 3 and compare the sizes of the images. (In order to produce an isometric projection with your axonometric routine you will have to use $\theta = -45°$ and ϕ = approximately 35°.) (b) Use equal values for the scale factors but vary the sizes of θ and ϕ to produce isometric, dimetric, and trimetric projections. Verify that you have produced each of these by measuring the angles between the X, Y, and Z axes.

5. (a) Develop the equations for a rotation about the X axis followed by a rotation about the Y axis. (b) Write the subroutine to provide these rotations with the same input information that was supplied in Exercise 4. Use the vertex method or the face method, as assigned by your instructor.

6. Modify the axonometric-display routine developed in Exercise 4 so that the user has the option of displaying the three-dimensional figure as either an axonometric drawing or a perspective drawing. Use the vertex method or the face method, as assigned by your instructor.

Note: For Exercises 7 through 12 you may have to reset the screen/window size for doing lighted faces in order to be able to display the grayscale or color for your system.

7. Modify the axonometric subroutine developed in Exercise 4 for the face method so that it will display only the visible faces. You will need to develop a subroutine or subroutines to calculate the cross product to establish the plane normal and the dot product to determine the cosine of the angle between the plane's normal and the Z axis. Review the discussion in the chapter before starting the exercise.

8. Modify the program developed in Exercise 7 so that it will light the faces that are visible. (This assumes that you are working on a black background.) Refer to the discussion in the chapter before starting this exercise. You will need to write a subroutine for determining the centroid of the face. You may also need to write a modification to the drawing routine to change to a specified color and draw the face outline before moving to the face centroid. You should use at least three colors or levels of grayscale.

9. Modify the program developed in Exercise 8 so that it will provide either shading or reverse shading.

10. Modify the routines of Exercises 7, 8, and 9 so that they can draw either axonometric or perspective projections. For the perspective plotting you must develop the equation for XPERS, using Figure 13-14. What are the limiting values for the observer and picture-plane distances that produce good perspectives with a minimum of distortion? Provide this information in your prompts to the user and write your programs so that the user cannot pick inappropriate values.

11. Develop a program to display either axonometric or perspective projections with the following options: (a) all lines shown, (b) only visible lines shown, (c) shaded faces, (d) faces with reverse shading.

12. Modify Exercise 11 to allow any of from four to six three-dimensional figures to be read from disk

files and displayed. Allow the user to pick the desired figure by displaying isometric drawings of all the figures on the screen and by prompting for selection.

13. Modify Exercise 12 to include the orthographic, oblique, and isometric drawings as choices for the user.

14. Write a program that will display the axonometric drawing using the front view as its initial position and then will rotate the figure to the user's input values of θ and ϕ in ten steps. After each projection is displayed, erase it and display the next projection using the new angles. This is a simulation of dynamic rotation.

14

The User Interface

Up to this point, we have concentrated on learning to write the individual routines that make up a drawing package. In the next chapter, we will assemble our routines into a menu-driven user-oriented drawing program that a nonprogrammer can use. To do this we need to create a *user interface*; that is, a means of communication between user and machine. The requirements of a good user interface are the subject of this chapter.

The Importance of Good Documentation

Assuming that a program runs and does pretty much what it was intended to do, the two biggest criticisms that are often expressed are, "The program is too hard to use; it has confusing and awkward commands," and "The documentation is absolutely awful; I can never find what I need to know." Indeed, good documentation and ease of use often make a less capable program more popular than those that are much more powerful but less well documented.

As examples of software documentation, consider the manuals that are available for your system. Look them over and think about what is good or bad about them as you read this chapter.

The Relationship Between User and Machine

Any device or system designed for people to use must provide them with something that will help them do their job. They should be better off with it than without it. The device or machine must increase their potential to do more things faster, better, or at least easier. A partnership of sorts must be formed, with the users doing what they do best while the machine does what it does best.

A shovel is an example of a very simple tool that allows a worker to do a better job. The shovel provides a hard, sharp edge and a relatively broad "hand" for lifting the earth. It also provides a method for people to use their weight to cut the sod and dig into the earth.

When people choose to use a computer system to aid them in their work, they must make sure that the system does the repetitious work, allowing them to be more creative and to make decisions based on the system's accumulation and display of facts. In this division of work the users and the system form a partnership, and the partnership must provide a smooth working relationship. The system must also be designed for the users to input the minimum amount of information to accomplish the task efficiently. In addition, the system must be able to display the amount of information desired by the users at any time and with the minimum number of prompts. In other words, the system must provide a natural extension of the resources the users have to assist them in their work.

Importance of Communication

The input and output of information is called *communication*. Communication capability must be carefully designed into a computer system, and the actual application must be researched and studied at length. If the users are people who traditionally stay in a particular job for long or relatively long periods of time, then the number of commands they have available for directing the computer and, consequently, the depth of knowledge they will need to acquire for efficient system use, can be greater. If the users are relatively transient, the system must sacrifice some types of performance in exchange for rapid learning and quick attainment of a reasonable skill level.

The Link Between Users and the System

Communication begins when a computer system is turned on. The users must know what commands to issue to the system and the system must provide them with the information as to what commands it understands. It is not unusual to see users sitting in frustration in front of a computer trying to get it to do something, only to have it repeat "Syntax Error" or "OK" no matter what they do. The computer system programmer probably assumed that the users would have some experience in using the machine or that they would obtain help from the manuals or from another person. Eventually, these users are forced to turn to the manuals or to seek help from someone with more experience, or even to give up, but in the interim they are wasting their time and probably lose some of their interest in the computer.

The system these users are trying to operate includes not only the software and the prompts that appear on the screen but also the written documentation or oral instruction provided for the system. The commands that they are expected to use should be easy to understand and easy to execute and the system's response must be clear, concise, and, most of all, helpful. Unfortunately, the type of response that is most helpful may vary as individuals gain experience with the program. One way to deal with this situation is to provide a range of response levels. One popular menu-driven microcomputer program with multiple menus provides several levels of "help." Novice users may elect a very complete set of menus and prompts and then, as they gain experience, gradually reduce them to suit their needs. Another well-known program provides a choice of either "verbose" responses and prompts or "brief" ones. Generally speaking, users will choose the lowest or briefest level that is satisfactory, because the response is faster and the screen is less cluttered.

The Result of Poor Communication

Poor communication or, worse yet, no communication can make an otherwise powerful program impossible to use. Commands that consist of several words that must be input in a precise sequence can frustrate users when they desire only to get on with the task at hand. For example, the system used to write the manuscript version of this book provided a four-keystroke sequence to set a margin. The sequence was to press the CONTROL key and then, while holding it down, to press 0, followed by L or R (for left or right margin) and, finally, to press the ESCAPE key. The program provided a one-keystroke alternative, which was to simply press function key F3 (for left margin) or F4 (for right margin). Guess which sequence got the most use!

Uses of Defaults to Aid Communication

If a machine requires a string of words for it to understand what it must do, then the software in the command structure must be written so that a few English words are equivalent to many words for the computer. This can be accomplished through a *default structure* or through a series of questions or prompts that provide either a menu of choices or examples of typical commands or both.

Many systems provide as defaults the most popular choices that the users must select. The users then need only to change those choices that are not correct for their purposes rather than to input all of the responses from the keyboard. One popular way to do this is to walk the users through all the choices but to require only that ENTER be pressed for each choice unless the default is to be overridden, in which case the user types in the desired choice and then presses ENTER.

Figure 14-1 is an example of a set of options for printing a document file. Each of the options has a default that can be overridden or can be accepted by simply pressing the return. The user may accept

```
                         PRINT A FILE
    To accept all print options press ESCAPE after typing filename
    To edit options press RETURN after typing filename

    NAME OF FILE TO PRINT?

    For default press RETURN for each question
        DISK FILE OUTPUT (Y/N): N
        START AT PAGE NUMBER (press RETURN for beginning)?
        STOP AFTER PAGE NUMBER (press RETURN for end)?
        USE FORM FEEDS (Y/N): N
        SUPPRESS PAGE FORMATTING (Y/N): N
        PAUSE FOR PAPER CHANGE BETWEEN PAGES (Y/N): N
    Get printer ready, then press RETURN:
```

Figure 14-1. An example of using defaults for making choices (adapted from WordStar).

```
                         SETUP PROGRAM
                   SETUP PARAMETERS UPDATE

    Configuration name:    VT_PRT__    Break key? (Y/N):             Y
    Com line (1/2):        1           UK character set? (Y/N):      N
    Baud rate:             1200        Screen background (D/L):      D
    Bits/character-parity: 8N          Cursor type (B/U):            B
    Stop bits (1/2):       1           Margin bell? (Y/N):           N
    Online or Local (O/L): O           Device attributes:            1;11
    ANSI or VT52 (A/V):    A           Status line (N/L/S):          S
    Newline? (Y/N):        Y           Backspace/delete swap? (Y/N): N
    Wraparound? (Y/N):     Y           Disconnect on EXIT? (Y/N):    Y
    Local echo? (Y/N):     N           Print termination char (N/F): N
    Auto xon/xoff? (Y/N):  Y           Print extent (S/F):           F

    Answerback message: <13>_____

    Tab settings:
        T       T       T       T       T       T       T       T       T
    123456789012345678901234567890123456789012345678901234567890123456789012345678901234567890

    DY,=nxt field  =prev fld  HOME=1st fld  END=last fld  ESC=del fld  del chr
```

Figure 14-2. Use of a table for setting defaults (adapted from TE 100-FT by Persoft).

all of the defaults with one keystroke by pressing the ESCAPE key or may go through the list line by line.

Another popular way to deal with defaults, particularly when there is a long list of parameters that may be set the same way every time the program is run, is to create a table of questions and responses. The users can then edit the table and, when it is correct, can save the edited version. Then each time the program is run, it is necessary only to review the table and either approve it as a whole with one response or make the necessary changes before approving it. Figure 14-2 shows such a table for a commercially available terminal emulation program. When the users have set the parameters to suit their needs, it is not necessary to call up the table again until a change is desired. Even when the system is rebooted (restarted), the users need only respond that the desired mode is as defined by the table.

Error-Handling Procedures

When users make mistakes, then the system must tell them so and must provide a clear response indicating the error type and location. The system must also give users a way to correct the error or to abort the command without exiting the program. This latter is often done via the ESCAPE key. Without this type of communication, the users can move from frustration to anger in a matter of minutes. If there is frustration, there may also be intimidation, which can be just as devastating to users. Intimidation can be overcome with carefully designed instruction, even when the system is complicated.

You may be familiar with a common response from the system when the door of the disk drive is not closed. It may take a form similar to one of the following:

```
Disk not Ready
```

or

```
Not ready error reading drive B
Abort, Retry, Ignore?
```

Obviously, the second form of the response provides more complete information than the first. It also gives the user a list of choices for aborting the command, correcting the mistake and trying again, or ignoring the error. It does not, however, state the consequences of ignoring the error, which might be to abort the entire program. In addition, first-time users might like more information regarding the specific source of the error or possible moves to correct it, such as "Close Drive Door" or "Bad Disk." The program, however, often has very little memory space available to provide error messages and must be as concise as possible.

The costs of mistakes in system design that result in poor communication between system and user are obvious. Lost time, lost work, and lost revenues can never be regained. If the machine's use does not result in gains in efficiency or production, then it is very possible that the new users will return to the old ways of doing things and will not try to solve their problems with computer systems, even though their competitors use them. Most computer systems are sold by individuals to other individuals (this is true even within the corporate structure of a large company), and it is important that the people doing the selling also provide system-operation training for the new users as well as help in getting the system to work correctly.

User Interface

The operators who use a computer graphics system must be able to understand several different sets of information. First of all, the operators must understand the task that they and the system are to perform. Next, they should have a mental picture or concept of the things that the system will do for them. This includes a concept of how the system functions and the purpose of each part of the system. Only then will the operators feel really comfortable using the system.

The Users' Model

The operators must visualize the parts of the system and be able to understand the role that each part plays in the operation of the system. Once the operators watch the system run, they can more easily understand the function of such components as the plotter, digitizer, keyboard, and CRT. It can be much more difficult to understand the role of the central processing unit and the mass storage devices, however, since their functions generally do not result in visible output. The computer can be presented as a device that takes the operator's commands and the information being processed and serves in the role of a person who does repetitious things without being bored. This concept may make it easier for inexperienced persons to use the system and to understand why there sometimes appear to be time delays in responding to requests.

The Real-World Model

If possible, it is advantageous to have operators or users who have a basic understanding of how computers work, but the time that must be invested in training operators to develop this depth of understanding seldom pays back dividends for a system designed to be used rather than programmed. Most employers will only invest in the amount of training that is absolutely necessary to operate the system efficiently. Therefore, the programmer should not assume that the operator will have any significant amount of experience beyond the training course that is offered with the system.

It is important for users to realize both the system's limits and the opportunities for their own creativity to be put to work. For instance, a particular application may lend itself to use of standard symbols or "parts." Libraries of parts and the menus needed to access them can be created by the operators as well as purchased from the system vendor. As the operators gain experience on the system, they may learn to break down the drawings that they prepare into modules that can be used over and over. Then they can prepare a menu of these modules, which can be used to quickly create the framework for new drawings. Having such modules at their disposal frees the operators to concentrate on fitting the parts together and providing notes and dimensions.

A simple example of this procedure is drawing a border and title block, which will probably be needed on each drawing. Other examples are creating standard circuit elements for electrical drawings or creating valves and fittings for plumbing drawings. Still another example is drawing a floor-plan outline for a high-rise building where the size, shape, column locations, and other general features are the same for each floor.

Commands Available to Users

Users may communicate with the system by typing on a keyboard, by selecting items from a menu on a digitizing tablet, or by selecting from a menu on the CRT screen with a light pen or with a cursor that may be controlled with a variety of devices. The commands and the manner in which they are assembled to get the required actions from the system are critical.

The commands must be related to the users' tasks. As an example, if a line is to be drawn, the command should be DRAW. However, if the users are moving to a new point as they get ready to draw a new line, the command should be MOVE. If the line to be drawn is to be a red line or a blue line, a thick line or a thin line, the structure of the command should provide a relatively easy-to-learn system that relates to the type of line being drawn. Use of single letters or numbers to select the mode for drawing is preferred if the keyboard is being used for input. The object is to minimize the number of keystrokes required to enter the command. If the instruction requires a long string of commands, then it is usually possible to put these commands into a subroutine that is accessed by entering a simple one-keystroke command or, if the system has programmable function keys, to program the command string into one of the function keys. In either case, the users are freed from a complicated and error-prone command routine.

If a digitizer menu is being used, the mode selections should all be in the same physical area of the menu. If a screen menu is being used and there is a series of hierarchical menus, the modes should all be on a single menu or else each menu should have the appropriate modes for its own tasks. An alternative is to have a prompt string for each task and to allow mode selection while the task is active. Examples of screen-based and digitizer-based menus are presented later in this chapter, as are prompt strings that allow mode selection.

Feedback

Feedback is essential to the operation of any interactive computer system. Without feedback, there would be no way for the user to know what instructions to enter or when to enter them. Just as dialogue between two humans is necessary when they are working together on a common task, so dialogue is necessary when a human and a machine are working together. We are not strangers to the concept of feedback. The speedometer and other gauges and warning lights on an automobile provide feedback to the drivers. Similarly, indicator lights, dials, audible signals (bells), and the like provide feedback to the users of home appliances. Feedback, then, lets the users know what is happening, shows them the results of actions that have been taken, and provides them with the basis for further actions.

Feedback consists of the instructions, prompts, error messages, and status reports that the system gives to the users to inform them of the progress of the task and to let them know when their input is needed. An example of feedback when a particular user is drawing a regular polygon might be as follows:

First, the user selects the task POLYGON from the menu. Then the system prompts

ENTER NUMBER OF SIDES DESIRED

When the user has provided the answer, say 6, the system prompts

POLYGON (6) Enter CENTER   menu/abort(F9) ADD(F1)

When the user has entered the desired location of the polygon's center, the system prompts

POLYGON (6) Enter STARTING VERTEX menu/abort(F9) ADD(F1)

Finally, when the starting vertex has been entered, the polygon is drawn and the system prepares for the next six-sided polygon by prompting

POLYGON (6) Enter CENTER   menu/abort(F9) ADD(F1)

Note that the user always knows that the active task is a six-sided polygon, that the system is in ADD mode (which can be changed by pressing function key F1), that the task can be aborted and the menu redisplayed by pressing function key F9, and that the next action required to perform the task is to enter the location of the CENTER or a STARTING VERTEX.

The Concept of a Workstation

We generally call the equipment available to the users of an interactive computing system a *workstation*. Workstations vary in makeup depending on the tasks that are to be performed, but they should contain all of the devices the users will need to perform their tasks.

Some components are common to nearly all workstations, including an information display (CRT or equivalent), a keyboard for entering information and commands, and the necessary furniture (desk, chair, lighting). Other components that are generally found at a workstation for graphics use are a digitizing tablet and, often, a light pen or joystick (or both). Many workstations now use track balls or mouse devices instead of a joystick.

Still other components that are necessary but that may be shared by two or more workstations are a printer, a pen plotter, storage devices (disk drives, tape drives), and, of course, the host computer.

We will discuss selection of furniture and equipment and the layout of a workstation later in this chapter.

What Can Go Wrong

Good programmers will anticipate potential problems and will write their codes to avoid such problems or to deal with them. A difficulty faced by programmers in this regard is that they know how the program should work, so it is difficult for them to make the same mistakes in running the program that novice users might make. Therefore, programmers should make a list of all the hardware problems that they can think of, simulate each problem, and test their program's recovery capability. Programmers should also make a list of all the things users might do wrong, intentionally make these mistakes themselves, and see what happens. Alternatively, programmers may ask a friend or colleague to test the program and try to make it fail.

Overly Complex Procedures

Among potential problems with the user interface are overly complex procedures. The users may be required to enter a long string of commands in a specific order to accomplish even the simplest task. The sequence of commands may be very complicated, containing many steps that must be memorized, and the syntax may be inconsistent from one command string to another.

Procedures that are inconsistent from command to command, or verification procedures that change from command to command, can destroy the ability of the users to memorize the needed commands. A program that requires the operators to look up commands on a regular basis will be abandoned in short order in favor of one that is easier to use. In the previous example of a prompt routine for polygons, use of function key F9 aborted the task and returned to the menu. Suppose that a different function key were used to abort the lines task, and a third to abort circles. Further, suppose that inputting a capital M was required to abort the points task and return to the menu. Obviously, the user would have difficulty remembering which key to use to abort any given task. Of course, the prompt says which key to press, but the prompts should be there for help when needed, rather than being required reading.

Poor Cancellation or Recovery Capability

One of the most sickening feelings users can experience is the realization that they have just hit a key that deleted the drawing or file they have been creating. Such potentially disasterous commands must be protected with cancellation or recovery procedures. One common technique is to ask the users to verify each entered command. An example from the IBM disk operating system (DOS) occurs when the users are deleting files. If the command

```
DEL *.*
```

which means to delete all file names with all extensions, is entered, the system responds with

```
ARE YOU SURE (Y/N)?
```

and the users must verify or deny that all files on the disk are to be deleted. Unfortunately, this protection is offered only when the users specify that *all* files are to be deleted.

Another protection technique is to "back up" the deleted material so that it can be recovered should it be deleted in error or lost due to a system crash. Many editors automatically make a backup copy of any file that is to be edited so that it can be restored if something happens to the version that is being edited. Some drawing programs write the data for a deleted primitive (point, line, polygon, or other figure) to a buffer. Then the data can be recovered with a command of the type

RESTORE LAST

A protection feature used by IBM PC DOS to prevent inadvertent rebooting of the system (which would clear the memory and destroy everything that was not saved on disk or tape) is to require that three keys be pressed in a specific sequence in order to reboot. Furthermore, the spacing of the keys is such that both hands are needed to do the job. Note, however, that this can make system use difficult for handicapped people.

Uncomfortable Working Conditions

A major complaint heard from users who are required to work with a system for several hours at a time is that the working conditions are uncomfortable. Uncomfortable working conditions can take many forms. The workplace layout may be cramped or the various components of the workstation may be poorly placed. For instance, the CRT screen may be too high or too low, or at the wrong distance from the operator's eye. Similarly, the keyboard may be too high or too low. The digitizing tablet may be difficult to use because it is on the wrong side of the workstation for, say, the left-handed user. Or there may not be enough leg room under the desk or table.

The solution to CRT problems can take the form of CRT stands that swivel, tilt, move laterally, and maybe even adjust in height. Similarly, adjustable furniture for both left-handed and right-handed people is available.

Sometimes the components themselves are poorly designed. Keyboards that are laid out with keys in unusual locations or with poor key action (tactile feel is a form of feedback) can be very tiring. Often, keys that toggle between states, such as the shift lock, have no indicator to inform the user as to which state they are in. (Such indicators could be in the form of a light, or the key could remain depressed in one state and up when in the other.)

Light pens are unpopular with some users because it is necessary to hold them up to point at the screen. If the pens are used continually over the course of a work day, the effort required for prolonged pointing at the screen can result in arm fatigue.

Display screens that are poorly designed can cause eye fatigue. Potential screen problems include poor color rendition, glare, distortion, flicker, and poor resolution (fuzzy or indistinct image). Considerable study has been done to determine the best phosphor colors to use for monochrome screens. Black and white has given way to green screens and green is now giving way to amber. The search for the color that is easiest on the eyes will continue. A related issue is the persistence of the phosphor. Long-lasting phosphors are more flicker resistant and tend to give a steadier image, but they smear more when an image is moved and are thus not as good for animation or moving images. Even the cursor may cause undesirable smearing with some phosphors.

Software Bugs

Software bugs are a fact of life with computer programs. In spite of the most careful planning and writing, followed by hours of testing, the typical new program will contain one or more software bugs that will show up only after it is in use. Sometimes the bugs are not discovered for months or even years. Other times, however, they will show up right away and may be so serious as to render the program unusable.

Perhaps the most serious type of bug is one that causes the system to crash. The end result of a system crash is usually loss of a lot of time, loss of a lot of work, and loss of confidence in the program. This type of problem is usually the result of inadequate or no error trapping. Both hardware-related errors and software-related errors should be handled by error-trapping routines to prevent system crashes.

Another type of software bug is one that will cause the system to "hang," that is, to go into an endless loop or other form of apparent suspension of operation that users can only get out of by shutting the system off and rebooting it. The end result is very much like that of a spontaneous system crash.

Designing an Effective User Program

The first thing you must do when designing a program is to develop a plan. The plan should provide for *top down* design of the program. "Top down" means that the overall objectives are laid out first and then additional levels of detail are added until the design is complete. For example, your program design could start with a description of the program's objectives and a listing of the tasks that it is to perform. You could then supplement this description with listings of the drawing aids that need to be provided, the various modes that need to be supported, and the I/O devices that will be used. You can continue to add levels of detail until the verbal description is complete.

This program description should enable you to begin defining the routines that will be needed for your program and to begin designing the program itself. However, you are not ready to write code yet. The step that you should be taking at this point is to create the structure of the program, not the details.

Design in Modules

Your program should be designed in a modular fashion. Each module should be a complete but simple routine that is callable from other routines when needed and should perform a single task or group of tasks that are always done as a unit. In that way, the module can be called whenever it is needed and there will be no problem with its performing unwanted operations. The module should have a clear set of input requirements (parameters that are passed to it when it is invoked), its execution should not adversely affect any other part of the program (loop counters, pointers, flags, and variables that it was not designed to modify should remain unchanged), and its output should be in a form that is usable by any routine that might call it.

Start with the Menu

If your program will be menu driven, you should start by designing the menu layout and deciding which routines will be accessed from the menu. If the menu is to be on the same screen as the drawing, perhaps a multiple-level menu will be needed. Multilevel menus on the screen are generally hierarchical in design; that is, there is a main menu and there are one or more levels of submenus. Multilevel menus must be carefully designed to reduce the time users must spend going from one menu to another as well as to keep the portion of the screen occupied by the menu to a minimum.

Figure 14-3 shows a multilevel hierarchical menu layout with a main menu and eight submenus. Figure 14-4 is a treelike diagram that depicts the relationship between the main menu and the submenus. The main menu can be thought of as the trunk and the submenus as branches. Note that there is no direct communication between submenus. All paths are through the main menu. As a result, it is sometimes awkward to make such changes as selecting a different line type or putting up a dot grid. For example, to change line type while doing a six-sided polygon, it is necessary for users to return to the main menu and select the line-type submenu. When the submenu comes up, the users select the new line type and then return to the main menu and select the polygons submenu. Finally, after a six-sided polygon is selected from the polygons submenu, the users are ready to draw the figure. To help you understand the strengths and weaknesses of this particular menu design and what changes might be made to improve it, you should work through a number of other examples of selecting and changing tasks and modes.

Menus displayed on digitizing tablets do not suffer from the space limitations that screen-based menus do. Consequently, they can be displayed on a single level, which reduces the problems we have mentioned. Figure 14-5 shows a menu for a digitizing tablet that is similar to that of Figure 14-3, although there are fewer options. Using the examples that you worked through for the menu of Figure 14-3, make task and mode selections and changes from the digitizing tablet menu and observe the difference. Which examples were easier

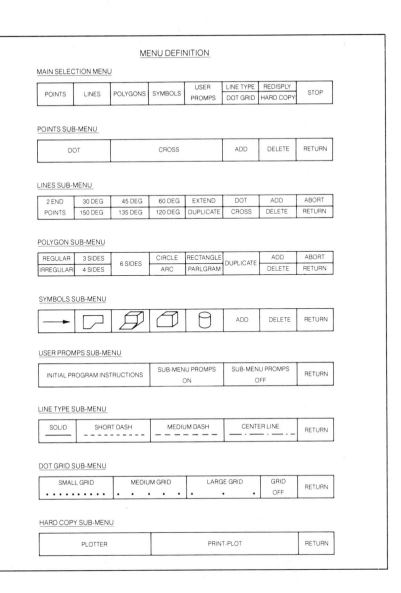

Figure 14-3. Hierarchical menu layout.

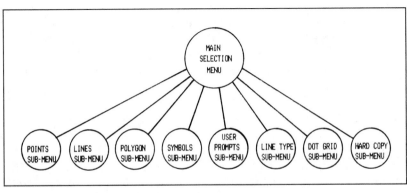

Figure 14-4. Diagram of hierarchical menu.

POINT	LINE 2 END PT.	LINE N DEGREES	RECTANGLE	N-SIDED REGULAR POLYGONS		CIRCLE	ARC	⟶		
ADD MODE	DELETE MODE	DOT MODE	CROSS MODE	LINE TYPE 1,2,3, OR 4		DOT GRID	REDISPLAY	STOP		
	1	2	3	4	5	6	7	8	9	0	•	END DIGITS	RETURN TO TERMINAL

Figure 14-5. Menu for digitizing tablet.

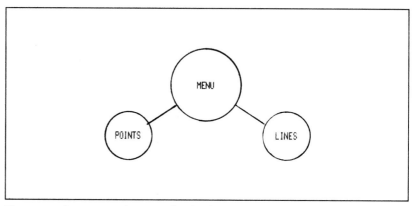

Figure 14-6. Interaction of menu and task subroutines.

to make from the digitizer menu? Were any easier from the screen menu?

Use Prompts

Earlier in this chapter we talked about prompts and presented a set of sample prompts for drawing a polygon. The add/delete mode selection could be made by pressing a function key and did not require exiting the task. Changing the number of sides, however, did require returning to the menu. The ability to make changes, such as line type changes or drawing mode changes, or to put up or remove a dot grid, without exiting the task tends to make a program more user friendly. In the case of the IBM PC, these changes are made by pressing a function key that has been programmed to provide an interrupt, perform the desired function, and return to the point in the program where the interrupt took place. This same capability can be provided for other systems and languages either as a part of the operating-system/language package that comes with the system or through additional programming.

Add the Main Tasks

Figure 14-6 depicts the interaction of the menu and the routines it accesses. Note that this figure is, again, a treelike diagram, with the menu being the trunk and the routines it accesses branching off from it. For simplicity of illustration, this program has only two main tasks, drawing points and drawing lines.

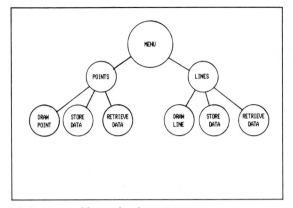

Figure 14-7. Adding subtask routines.

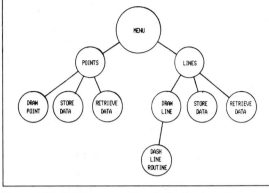

Figure 14-8. Adding second level of subtask routines.

Add the Subtasks

The routines that will be accessed from the main task routines shown in Figure 14-6 can be added to the diagram. These routines provide a further branching of the tree. Figure 14-7 shows subtasks for each of the two main tasks. Note that the lines connecting the routines define the communications paths from one routine to another. It is now clear that the menu routine calls a drawing task (say lines) and that this task may call any of three subtasks. The subtasks cannot communicate with each other except through the task routine, nor can the task routines communicate with each other except through the menu. To create a line, then, users select the appropriate routine from the menu and the lines subroutine is called. When the data have been input via this routine, the subroutine calls another routine to store the data. The return from the storage routine is to the lines routine, which then calls the drawing routine to draw the line. The return path is back to the lines routine, then to the menu. Trace this path on Figure 14-5.

Suppose that an alternate line type (dashed line) is to be supported. This may be provided as a separate routine, called from the line-drawing routine, thus adding another level to the diagram, as shown in Figure 14-8.

Write the Code

Only when the entire program has been laid out in proper fashion is it time to begin writing code. The first routine you need to write is the menu routine. You can completely write and test this routine by simply providing dummy subroutines for the tasks. A typical dummy subroutine might be as follows.

FORTRAN code:

```
C ** DUMMY SUBROUTINE FOR USE WITH MENU ROUTINE **
      SUBROUTINE LINES (LINSTR,LINWRK)
      DIMENSION LINSTR (100,6), LINWRK (7)
      CALL BELL
      RETURN
      END
```

BASIC code:

```
2000 REM ** DUMMY LINES SUBROUTINE FOR USE WITH
     MENU ROUTINE **
2010 REM INPUT PARAMETERS ARE LINSTR AND LINWRK
2020 REM DIM LINSTR (100,6), LINWRK (7)
2030 BEEP
2040 RETURN
```

Note that this subroutine simply gives an audible signal to the users and then returns to the calling routine. Alternatively, this subroutine could print a message saying which routine it is representing. Note also that the required input parameters—that is, the values to be provided by the calling routine—are shown. In the case of the BASIC version the parameters are shown as REMARK statements and are for reference only, since all variables are global (they are the same throughout the program).

When you have completely written and debugged the menu routine, you can begin to write the task routines. Again, you can simulate the subtasks with dummy routines, and you should complete each task routine before going on to the next one. An important feature here is that you have a complete working program at every step, even though many of the details have not been completed. You also have a complete diagram of the entire program and all of the communications paths. This is invaluable, especially when writing a large program that may have 50 to 100 separate routines on several levels.

Make Sure Your Program Has Good Structure

Structured programming is considered by most professionals to be the only type of programming worth doing. A program that is not well structured is very difficult to debug, modify, and maintain. All of the new languages that are being developed are highly structured and tend to force the programmer to proceed in a structured fashion. Older languages, such as FORTRAN and BASIC, are being revised to include more structure. The old, less-structured programming techniques will still work, however, and it is possible for the programmer to generally ignore the constructs and other aids to structured programming that are being added. This is *not* recommended.

Design for the Users

A very important concept, too often forgotten, is that a program should be designed for the *users*, not the programmer. Ease of use is very important and will often carry more weight than additional power or more features when the users are choosing between alternative programs. Their main purpose in choosing a program in the first place is to help them get their job done faster and easier. If two different programs will both do the job, then the one that is easier to use will be a better choice, even if the other is more powerful. Unfortunately, ease of use and ease of implementation do not go hand in hand. You may need to spend many extra hours to make a program truly easy to use. Consequently, you will always face the temptation of stopping short of creating the ultimate user program. This is a temptation you must overcome.

Keep the Approach Consistent

All of us have had the experience of switching from one program to another or from one operating system to another and suddenly finding that the entire command syntax has changed. For instance, to delete a file, one system may use DEL while another may use KILL. DELETE may mean something entirely different on this second system. As another example, the functions of certain keys, such as backspace, delete, insert, or others, may vary from program to program or from operating system to operating system. As difficult as this is to deal with, a much more difficult situation is one where the command syntax changes within the same program! It can be devastating to users to have to use a particular set of keystrokes in one part of a program to accomplish a given task and then to have to use a different set of keystrokes to accomplish the same task in another part of the same program. While this situation may sound unlikely, it occurs with surprising frequency.

Try to keep execution and recovery procedures as consistent as possible throughout the program. Users will automatically apply a technique that has worked in another part of the program and, if it fails, they will waste valuable time trying to recover and may lose all of their work.

Provide Feedback

Feedback is one of the most important parts of any program. Users must be kept informed of the program's progress at all times and must always know what steps are at their disposal to alter the progress of program execution. The feedback that you can build into a program includes instructions, prompts, help routines, status messages, and display updates. These should be used wherever they will be truly helpful. However, you should avoid the temptation to overdo it. Auditory feedback—beeps, buzzes, and the like—can be very annoying if used to excess. Similarly, users may ignore printed prompts and messages if your program includes more than are needed or if you have made them too elaborate to be easily read. Such prompts can also be annoying if they intrude on the information that the users are attempting to obtain from the running of the program.

Include Effective Error Processing

Errors will occur in the running of any program. Errors can be made by the users (such as incorrect input in response to a prompt, failure to insert a data disk or to close the door on the disk drive, failure to turn the printer on, or a variety of other mistakes) or they can exist in the program. A system's normal error-processing routine is to inform the users that there is an error and to terminate execution of the program. The result can be loss of hours of work. Your program must provide an effective alternative to normal error processing if it is to be truly usable. Good error processing includes trapping the error and notifying the users, just as normal system processing does, and then giving users a way to recover from the error without starting over.

Most systems provide easy ways to trap I/O errors. For instance, FORTRAN includes an ERR= specification that you can use to specify a statement number to which the system is to branch if an error occurs. You can then create a procedure for determining the nature of the error and for specifying a recovery procedure. BASIC provides similar capability with an ON ERROR GOTO statement. A simple example of the use of these statements in conjunction with input from the keyboard is given in the following code. This simple example does not check to determine what the error was, it just says, "Go back and try again."

FORTRAN code:

```
C ** EXAMPLE OF USING ERR= FOR ERROR TRAPPING **
      SUBROUTINE VALUIN
130   READ (5,*,ERR=160) AVALUE
      RETURN
160   WRITE (6,*) 'Value not usable, please reenter'
      GOTO 130
      END
```

BASIC code:

```
100 REM ** EXAMPLE OF USING ON ERROR FOR ERROR
    TRAPPING **
110 REM ** SUBROUTINE TO ENTER VALUE **
120 ON ERROR GOTO 160
130 INPUT AVALUE
140 ON ERROR GOTO 0
150 RETURN
160 PRINT "Value not usable, please reenter"
170 GOTO 130
180 END
```

Note that the BASIC code includes a statement that says ON ERROR GOTO 0. This statement cancels the special error processing specified in line 120. Without this statement, the program would branch to line 160 anytime an error was encountered, not just in line 130. The FORTRAN code doesn't need a comparable statement because the error specification applies only to the READ statement (130).

Allow for Mistakes

In an interactive program, mistakes by users are a certainty. Some of these mistakes will be seen as errors by the system and can be processed as discussed above. Others will be perfectly legitimate as far as the system is concerned but may not be what users want. One common mistake of this type is overwriting an existing file with new material, thus destroying the old file. This is perfectly acceptable to

Figure 14-9. A small system workstation.

the system but may be disasterous to the users. Another common mistake is to select a task that was not wanted and then need to abort it and recover to the previous position. Your program will need confirmation routines, exit routines, and restore features to handle these situations. Still another common error occurs when the system tries to divide using a divisor of 0. This can occur when incorrect data are entered. It can also occur during normal processing through no fault of the users or the program. One solution is to always test divisors before using them.

Equipment Selection and Layout

Selection of furniture can be very important. The comfort and convenience of the furniture can have a dramatic effect on the quantity and quality of the work that is produced at the workstation. Even its appearance can affect worker morale and, consequently, production.

Chairs should be comfortable and adjustable to suit the users. Generally, secretarial or clerical type chairs without arms are preferred because they place the users in a better position relative to the equipment (they are designed for working at typewriters or other office machines), and the lack of arms leaves the users able to move close to the desk or table and to turn the chair to reach another area.

The work surface should be large enough to hold all of the equipment (CRT, keyboard, light pen, digitizing tablet, joystick, mouse, and so on) plus manuals and other needed materials. It should not be so large, however, as to make it difficult to reach needed items without excessive moving about. Many workstations have multiple levels, with some items suspended above the work surface and some below. Others are designed in L or even U configurations in order to put more work surface close to the operator. This can be particularly important with systems that use two CRT screens, one for graphics display and the other for alphanumeric I/O. Figures 14-9 through 14-11 show several arrangements that have been used both commercially and in educational labs.

Figure 14-10. A medium-sized system.

Figure 14-11. Line drawing of a multiple-screen system with large digitizer and drum plotter.

CRT screens should have adequate resolution for their tasks (drafting tasks require higher resolutions—640 × 480 or 1000 × 800—than some other graphics tasks) and should provide viewing ease through choice of phosphor color, antiglare treatment, and positioning. The keyboard should be well laid out (as to positions of keys) and should have good tactile feedback.

Digitizing tablets are available in a variety of sizes. Tablets used only for menus are generally quite small and portable so that they can be moved about and even placed in the lap if desired. Those used for digitizing drawings must be large enough to accommodate the drawing to be digitized. They are frequently as large as a drafting table and are, in fact, separate tables that require the users to stand up or to use a drafting-type stool. Digitizing tablets should be located in such a manner that users can view the CRT screen while using them.

There are many other peripherals that may be chosen to complete the workstation. Plotters, printers, and other peripherals must be compatible with the system and must be located so as to be convenient to the users. While this may seem like a simple problem, it can turn out to be quite complex. Many times the control functions required by the peripheral are different than those provided by the operating system or the applications package. As a result, it may be necessary to write a custom "driver" software package to translate what one device is sending into statements the other device understands. Other problems include type of interfacing (serial or parallel) and communications rates.

In this chapter we have discussed what is needed to provide an effective user interface, and we have explored techniques for creating a friendly environment for the user. The user-friendly environment we have used as an example is the creation of a simple turnkey drawing package, which will be more fully developed in Chapter 15. Our discussion has included the items that are of importance when creating a program for users. Chapter 15 will review some of these concepts and apply them to creation of the turnkey drawing program.

Exercises

1. Make a list of the manuals that are provided for your system. Which ones were provided by the manufacturer of the computer? Which ones were supplied by manufacturers of peripherals? Were any provided by software suppliers?

2. Rank the manuals you listed in Exercise #1, starting with the best one(s). What factors did you use in deciding their rank order?

3. Name three different ways a user might communicate with a computer graphics system.

4. Name three different ways a computer graphics system might communicate with its user.

5. What is meant by "defaults"? How are they used in an interactive program?

6. What is meant by "error trapping"? Name three different errors that may occur when trying to read data from a disk. Name an error that may occur in

doing mathematical calculations. How would you trap these errors?

7. Name some standard symbols or "parts" that might be included in a computer graphics system library that you might use in your chosen field.

8. Define "top down" as it applies to writing computer programs.

9. Describe what is meant by "modular" programming. What are the advantages of modular programming techniques for writing large programs?

10. What is a "construct"? Does the programming language you are using have any constructs? If so, name them.

11. Why do some computer graphics systems have more than one CRT screen? What is the function of each screen? What advantages does a dual-screen system have over a single-screen system?

12. Name four hardware components other than the computer that might be found at a typical computer graphics workstation.

13. A dummy subroutine was presented in this chapter to allow a program to be complete and operable at each stage of development. Modify the dummy subroutine for your system to print out a message stating which subroutine it represents, to wait for a response from the user, then to erase the message and return to the calling routine.

14. What is "feedback" as applied to the operation of a computer system? Your system may provide feedback that is detected by at least three of the five human senses. Name the three and give an example of feedback your system provides for each one.

15

Turnkey Drawing and Graphing Programs

This chapter will present the development of a simple two-dimensional drawing program. For the most part, the routines presented here have been discussed in previous chapters and have either been presented as examples or recommended as exercises. In this chapter we will combine these routines into a single program with a suitable menu. Our approach will be as follows: First, we will pose the questions that the programmer must answer; second, we will establish the specifications for the program to be developed; third, we will develop the communications-path (tree) diagrams; fourth, we will present any programming examples that have not been presented in previous chapters. You are encouraged to create flow charts for the example code as an aid to understanding its functions.

If you have a copy of the program that is available for use with this text, run it now several times to familiarize yourself with it. If you have already done this, proceed through the chapter. Note, however, that as questions are presented regarding features to be employed in this program, you may wish to scan ahead to the second section so that you can see the items that are being chosen for menus and tasks. The exercises for this chapter will lead you through the steps of program creation.

The Concept of a Turnkey Program

Unlike many computer programs that are written by programmers and used by the writer or by another programmer, turnkey programs are intended for people who are using the computer as a machine or a tool.

				N-SIDED REGULAR POLYGONS			
POINT	LINE 2 END PT.	LINE N DEGREES	RECTANGLE	N-SIDED REGULAR POLYGONS	CIRCLE	ARC	⟶
ADD MODE	DELETE MODE	DOT MODE	CROSS MODE	LINE TYPE 1,2,3, OR 4	DOT GRID	REDISPLAY	STOP
1	2	3	4	5	6	7	8	9	0	•	END DIGITS	RETURN TO TERMINAL

Figure 15-1. Digitizing tablet menu.

These people may have neither programming background nor programming aptitude. To them the computer is just another device to help them get their job done. With this in mind, let us examine the requirements for a good turnkey program.

Ease of Starting

First, and foremost, the program must be easy to start up. No matter how many help routines have been built in, none of them function until the program is running on the machine. Many microcomputer operating systems support "auto execute" files that will automatically load and run when the system is booted. In some cases these are program files, while in other cases they are batch-execution files. In either case, these files can be used to start the program running and to display the first instructions and prompts for the users. On larger, shared systems it is often possible to load and run a program with a one-word command. That command may be an easily remembered English word such as "draw."

Initial instructions are a must. The first thing the users should see on the screen is an identification of the program, so that there is no question whether the right program is being run. The next thing the users should see are instructions for use. It is important to remember that these instructions must stand on their own. You will not be there to help if they are not understood. Not only must they be clear and complete, but there also should be provision for repeating them if the users wish. One reading may not be sufficient for first-time users. On the other hand, people who have been using the program for some time will become impatient at having to wade through the instructions every time the program is run. Therefore, provision should be made to allow the users to bypass the instructions if they so desire.

In addition to on-screen instructions, most programs come with written documentation that includes instructions for use and, frequently, some training exercises. These are typically example problems that contain step-by-step instructions for execution.

Menu-driven programs are nearly universal. Menus tend to be awkward, especially if they are multilevel, but very few acceptable large programs have been written without a menu. Figure 15-1 is a menu that was designed for use on a digitizing tablet for a program written in FORTRAN to run on a DEC PDP 11/44 using PLOT10 graphics calls. Note that this menu contains mode selections as well as task selections and also provides a way of specifying an input value for line angle, line type, or number of polygon sides by selecting individual digits to build the number.

Ease of Understanding

Remember that you will not be there to interpret the instructions and iron out the rough spots when people are using your program. That job must be accomplished by the program documentation. The documentation must cover the capabilities of the program so that the users or potential users know what the program will do and what it will not do. Knowing the program's capabilities is of little use if the procedures required to unlock and use those capabilities are not understood by the users. Therefore, documentation of the procedures is of utmost importance. Finally, the command structure should be well documented so that it can be readily learned and fully understood. The commands available to the users to implement the procedures are the basis of the entire program. If they are not well documented so that the users can learn them easily, the program will suffer.

Ease of Use

A program that is not easy to use will fall into disrepute and disuse regardless of its capabilities. People are not willing to struggle with cumbersome software. But what makes a program easy to use?

MENUS Menu-driven programs are generally easier to use than non-menu programs, but menus tend to become long and complex if they are not created with great care, in which case they can be more of a problem than a help. However, no satisfactory substitute for menus exists for any but the smallest of programs.

The menu may be displayed on the graphics screen either with the drawing or on a separate "page" that can be displayed alternately with the drawing. On some systems the "menu" consists of a number of well-marked function keys on the keyboard or, frequently, on a separate keypad. Figure 15-2 is a multilevel menu that consists of a main menu and eight subsidiary menus that are displayed alternately at the bottom of the screen. The return from any subsidiary menu is always to the main menu. An interesting feature of this menu is that initial program instructions are selected from one of the submenus. This means that users must have at least a rudimentary knowledge of how to use the program in order to get any instructions!

Another approach is to display the menu on a separate alphanumeric screen. This two-screen approach is more costly but has the advantage that not only does the menu not conflict with the drawing, but the alphanumeric screen can be used as a data-input device without disturbing the drawing.

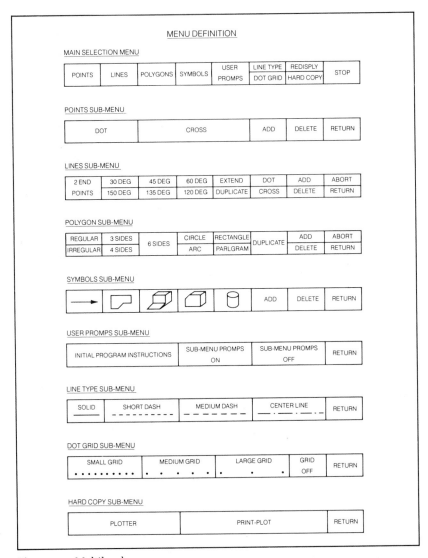

Figure 15-2. Multilevel menu.

Menus are often displayed on a digitizing tablet or other peripheral device (as shown in Figure 15-1). This approach has the advantage that the entire menu can be displayed at one time. Menus that must be displayed in several different parts, such as the one shown in Figure 15-2, will force users to be constantly switching from menu to menu while using the program. Another advantage of using the digitizing tablet for the menu is that, as with the two-screen approach, the drawing is not disturbed by the menu input and nearly the entire screen is available for drawing. (Some sort of prompt and program-status feedback are needed, so a portion of the screen is normally reserved for that purpose. Of course, with the two-screen approach, the alphanumeric screen is used for prompts and status messages.)

Users can select from the menu in several ways. A common method, when the menu is displayed on the screen, is for the users to enter a letter or number from the keyboard corresponding to the code shown for the menu item. This works best when the selection can be made with a single keystroke.

The graphics cursor that is used to select points for creating drawing features can also be used to select tasks and modes from a menu or a prompt line. This is the technique used for selecting from the menu shown in Figure 15-2. If the cursor is over a menu item when the point is selected, a menu choice is being made; otherwise, drawing data are being input. The cursor may be driven by arrow keys on the keyboard (or on a separate pad) or by a joystick or even the digitizing-tablet control. A similar and often used approach is to make the selection with a light pen. Systems using light pens may not have a controllable cross-hair cursor.

When the digitizing tablet is used for the menu, as is the case in Figure 15-1, selection is made with the device supplied with the tablet. Normally, this is a cross-hair locating device called a puck, with a button-selection entry. Sometimes, however, it is a penlike device with a button or switch that is depressed to make the selection.

COMMAND STRUCTURE Good command structure is very important to ease of use of the program. Too often, the commands available from the menu are ambiguous or vague. Users are not sure what the commands will do—and what side effects the commands may create. Commands must be clear, easily understood, and easily implemented. Frequently, the same command will mean different things, depending on which of the many submenus happens to be active at the time the command is input. Another weakness often found in command structures is that a complex sequence of entries is required to activate a command. A command that requires four or five keystrokes in a specific manner, such as, "Hold down the control key and, while holding it down, press O, then release the control key and press S, then press ESC" is difficult to implement. How much easier it is for the users if this sequence has been encoded into one keystroke!

FEEDBACK Good feedback is critical to any operation, whether it be walking, operating a machine tool, or running a computer program. Feedback is simply keeping the users informed of the results of their actions and the current status and direction of program execution. When we think of feedback we visualize messages appearing on the screen. Actually, feedback includes everything that is done to let the users know what has happened. Movement of the cursor or drawing

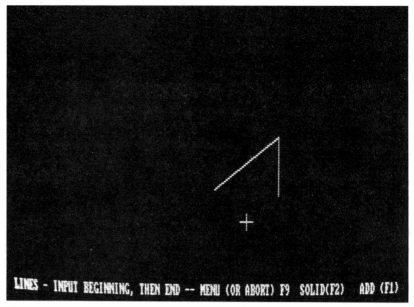

Figure 15-3. IBM PC screen displaying user prompt.

a line or object on the screen in response to operator input are both forms of feedback.

A form of feedback that the programmer must provide is *user prompts*. Prompts provide the answer to the question, "What do I do now?" It *is* possible to include too many prompts, but more programs err on the side of having too few prompts than of having too many. A program should contain an adequate number of prompts to guide the users through all phases of program operation. What that number is and where the prompts should be provided will vary from program to program. If in doubt, ask a friend or colleague to run your program and tell you where prompts are needed.

A common difficulty with prompts is that they must be presented in limited space and therefore must be cryptic and, often, abbreviated. Your challenge as a programmer is to make them clear and understandable. Actually, lack of space for prompts may be an advantage, since it will force you to be concise. A major factor in writing good prompts is consistency. The same prompt should mean the same thing in all parts of the program; it should be phrased in the same way and displayed in the same place. Figure 15-3 shows the screen of an IBM PC displaying a user prompt for drawing lines by picking two end points. Note that the status of the ADD/DEL and LINE TYPE modes is also displayed, along with an indication of the function key to press to change them.

Another important form of feedback is *status messages*. Status messages range from the red light on the disk drive indicating that it is storing or retrieving data, to messages on the screen, to sounds produced by the system. The status messages over which you have control when programming usually fall into the screen-message category, supplemented by beeps or other programmable sounds. When the system is prompting users to do something, it might not be clear which of several possible actions should be taken, so status messages provide the base from which the users can make their decisions. As with prompts, status messages must be adequate in number and clearly and concisely presented.

The third form of feedback is *help routines*. Most commercially available programs contain help routines. Unfortunately, only a small percentage of these routines are truly helpful. Too often they are written from the programmer's vantage point and do not tell the users what they need to know. One problem with help routines is that they take up space, which is often at a premium. Some help routines are too verbose, requiring users to suffer through a vast amount of text before finally coming to the information they want. Even then there may be no escape. The users may have to go through the rest of the help package before being released. Good help routines should be easily accessed, easily exited, and truly helpful.

When considering modes of feedback, you must take care to accommodate the physically handicapped. You might, for example, supplement audible feedback with tactile or visual feedback to help the hearing impaired, or you might avoid input routines that require two hands for execution.

Task Appropriateness

Saying that your program must be appropriate for the task may sound like stating the obvious. Many people, however, are trying to use programs that are totally inappropriate for the task they are trying to perform. It is not uncommon to see people trying to do word processing with a text editor intended to be used for writing source code. The program may do the job, but not easily, since it is being used to accomplish a task for which it was not intended. Perhaps a more common occurrence is to see people trying to perform complicated tasks with unsophisticated programs, or, at the other end of the spectrum, trying to do simple jobs with highly sophisticated, very complex programs. Managers who only want to create a bar or pie chart from time to time do not want to struggle with the complexities of full-fledged CAD/CAM systems any more than the designers of circuit boards want to work with low-resolution systems running simple programs that require them to create the symbol for each circuit element from scratch each time it is to be used.

A good program should provide enough features to enable the users to conveniently perform all of their required tasks on a regular basis. Such a program should include all of the necessary basic routines and, in addition, one-step routines for frequently performed complex tasks. Circuit designers, for example, would need prewritten routines to draw all of the circuit elements needed to create a normal design. These routines should all be one-step; that is, the circuit element should be placeable with one or two commands.

Overcomplexity for the intended job must be avoided. It is easy to get caught in the trap of building in features that are of marginal utility at best. This tendency is often called the "if only" syndrome (or, in some circles, the "creeping feature creature"). The problem here is that with every choice given the users there is also the requirement that a decision be made. A program may have so many user-selected parameters that the users will grow weary and give up before accomplishing the required task. Features to avoid include never-used or seldom-used capabilities, needless duplication of capabilities, and overly complex procedures for utilizing the necessary capabilities. Complex systems should provide a set of default choices for the users while they are learning the system. These defaults should be easy to change when the users become more experienced.

Equipment Support

Your program should be designed and written to run on the intended users' CPUs and to operate correctly and effectively with the users' I/O devices. Users should not be expected to purchase a new operating system to run your program. In addition, the systems on which your program will run will have memory limits (RAM) that may be a function of the CPU or of the operating system and language address capabilities. For instance, BASIC will often address only 64K, although the CPU it is running on may have several times that much memory installed. Finally, your program should operate on whatever number, type, and size of disk drives the users will have available.

Support of the users' I/O devices includes the ability to communicate with printers, plotters, digitizing tablets, and various communications channels. Printers vary in the type of control codes they support and even in the specific code required to activate a particular capability. Plotters require drivers and, even if the drivers are built-in to the computer's language or operating system, the data will need to be formatted to match the device's input requirements. Digitizing tablets also require software interfaces. Many commercial programs are provided with configuration packages that allow the program to be installed to match the parameters of the specific equipment the users possess.

Creating a Turnkey Drawing Package

Now that we have described the pitfalls to be avoided in creating a turnkey drafting package, let us turn our attention to the decision processes involved in actually creating such a package. We will not attempt to cover every nuance of the process—that could take many volumes and still not be complete. Instead, we will confine our attention to the main points about which decisions must be made.

Defining Intended Use

Before you can begin to develop the parameters within which your program will be written, you need to know how it will be used. Not only do you need to know the general discipline within which it will be used, you also need to know specifically how it will be used within the discipline.

Perhaps your package will be used to create engineering drawings. Your first questions might be, "What kind of drawings? Are they going to be two dimensional? three dimensional? Will color, grayscale, or other types of shading be required? In what engineering discipline will the program be used?" Electrical engineers designing circuit boards would need precreated electrical symbols and a layered, two-dimensional approach, while mechanical engineers doing machine design would have entirely different needs, including three-dimensional capability.

Maybe your package will be used for the creation of architectural drawings. In this case, some possible uses would include drawing plans, doing renderings, and mapping. Each of these uses places different requirements on your drawing package.

Another possible use for your package is to create business charts and graphs. These drawings might be used in conjunction with oral presentations to management, for internal-planning purposes, or for inclusion in written reports. The type, form, and quality of the drawings would depend on their intended use.

Still another possible use for your package is creation of art. Computer-generated art is being used increasingly in the motion-picture industry as well as in advertising. Color and animation would probably be of paramount importance in such a package.

Deciding What Features Are Needed

When you have defined the intended use of your program, you must begin the task of selecting the needed features. Certainly it will be necessary to be able to draw points, lines, and simple shapes. If three-dimensional drawing is required, will hidden-line and hidden-surface suppression be needed? Will the users be creating isometric drawings? oblique drawings? some other type? What about perspective drawings? two-point perspectives?

What shading and filling capabilities will be needed? Is color a requirement? Is grayscale? Will cross-hatching be needed (as when doing cutaway views of assembly drawings)? What other shading/filling patterns will be needed?

Creating a Menu

Now that you have established the intended use of your program and you have decided on the features it must have, you can proceed to design a menu. It is important to create the menu before proceeding with the subroutines that will actually accomplish the tasks, because the menu provides the framework within which all of the routines operate. A well-thought-out and well-designed menu will make the rest of the programming much easier.

The location of the menu will depend on the configuration of the systems your program will be run on as well as on the size and complexity of the menu itself. If the program is small and the menu brief, your best approach might be to display the menu directly on the screen. If your program will be used on systems having two screens, one for graphics and another for alphanumerics, you should locate the menu on the alphanumeric screen. The large menus associated with the many menu items of a sophisticated package may make a digitizing tablet the best choice, even if the system has two screens. Of course, the display screen may be the only choice available, in which case it must be used regardless of other considerations.

You must also decide on the means by which users will select from the menu. Possible choices in the case of a menu displayed on the screen might be (1) to key in the choices from the keyboard; (2) to make selections with a cursor controlled by arrow keys, thumbwheels, joystick, mouse, or other control device; or (3) to use a light pen. If the menu is on a digitizing tablet, the input device would probably be the digitizer cursor or pen device.

An important consideration in planning menu layout is whether the menu will be displayed as one unit or in several parts. Screen-located menus are typically divided into main menu and several submenus, due to space limitations. The menus on digitizing tablets are typically single-level; that is, the entire menu is displayed and available at all times. Multilevel menus require careful design to reduce the need to move from menu to menu while using the program. Of course, some swapping of menus is unavoidable, but it should be minimized. The key is to keep related tasks on the same menu. Some duplication of menu items is preferable to requiring the users constantly to go from one menu page to another to set up one task.

Selecting the items to be offered on the menu and determining which items to put on each of the levels of multilevel menus are important parts of the menu design. When laying out the menu, you must consider the tasks that can be selected, the modes to be used, any needed instructions, HELP routines, and, in the case of multilevel menus, a way of going to other menus.

Diagramming the Communications Paths

Any program that contains even one subroutine must have a way for the main program segment to communicate with the subprograms. If your program contains many subprograms that are accessed from many points in the main segment and in other subprograms, the paths of communication become very complex. If all parts of your program are to work together as one cohesive whole, you must work out all the paths of communication. If you do this before you write the various parts of the program, you will save a lot of rewriting later on.

Communication takes place between the main menu and the submenus and sometimes between two submenus, between the main menu and each action module, and among the many action modules. A good way to diagram the communications paths is to start with the main program segment, show which subprograms it calls, which subprograms (if any) each of these subprograms calls, and so on down to the last subprogram that does not call any others. All paths of communication will be along the lines from calling routine to called routine through the various levels of subprograms. The return paths are the same as the calling paths except that they are traveled in reverse.

Neither FORTRAN nor BASIC allows recursiveness; that is, a subroutine in these languages cannot call itself. Consequently, a communications path cannot be a closed loop. Figure 15-8 diagrams the communications paths for the routines of the program you will be developing. Look ahead to it now and keep it in mind as you develop it step by step. Note that many of the routines are shown at more than one location in the diagram. That is because these routines can be called from more than one location in the program. Of course, it is necessary that the proper values be input to the routine for the task it is to perform. This is done with argument and parameter lists in FORTRAN or, in BASIC, with a separate set of variables whose only purpose is to transfer data to and from the subroutine.

Writing the Program for the Menus

Once you have completely diagrammed the program, you can begin writing the code. Start with the initialization section and then the menus—main menu first followed by the submenus. Use dummy modules for all unwritten subroutines and complete and test *all* menu code before starting on the subroutines. The subroutine calls in the menu should contain all needed arguments.

Dummy subroutines are easy to write since they need contain nothing more than a beginning statement (the subroutine name and parameter list, or a COMMON statement in the case of FORTRAN programs) and a return statement. A "beep," printed message, or other indication that the menu really did access the subroutine is helpful. The message can take the form "Now in subroutine A."

Writing Action Subroutines

Writing action (task and mode) subroutines is the final step in creating your program and is accomplished only after all parts of the menu modules are working properly. Modules called by the menu should be written first. If they, in turn, call another level of subroutines, more dummy modules can be inserted until the additional layers of subroutines are written. Your program should be complete and operable at all times, even though many of the routines may not yet do anything but provide a response message and a return. In other words, you should write the program in layers so that only one or two modules are being written and debugged at any one time. Once a module is completely operable, your attention can be directed to completing another part of the program.

A Sample Drawing Program

To aid you in developing your programming abilities, we are now going to create a sample drawing program following the procedures we have just discussed. The program will be used to create two-dimensional line drawings of the type used by engineers and architects. The users of the program need to be able to store and retrieve the data as well as to plot the results. We will assume that the users have moderate knowledge of computers, including some use of interactive systems, but no programming experience or ability. We will also assume that the users are very knowledgeable regarding conventional drawing techniques and the function of the object being drawn.

Our program will be coded in two versions. One version will be coded in FORTRAN with PLOT10 graphics subroutine calls to run on DEC 11 series computers under the RSX11M or VMS operating system using Tektronix-compatible raster terminals. The second version will be coded in MicroSoft Advanced BASIC to run on an IBM PC or compatible computer under PC DOS or MS DOS.

Our program will be menu-driven, with the menus appearing at the bottom of the screen. It should be possible to select from the menu without disturbing the drawing. Alternate menus and prompts are to share the same display space on the bottom of the screen. Figure 15-4 is a representation of the screen showing the area to be used for drawing and the area to be used for the menu.

Selection from the menu is to be made by entering the appropriate number with the numeric keys at the top of the keyboard. An acceptable alternative approach would be to use the cursor to make the selection. In this case, the graphics cursor would be moved to some specified location within the menu area to select the desired task, and the actual selection would be made by pressing the space bar or other appropriate key when the cursor is properly positioned. The program could then compare the coordinates of the selected location with the known boundaries of the menu to determine whether the cursor was within the menu and, if so, which menu item was being selected.

Some tasks, such as saving or retrieving drawing files, may require directories that will not fit conveniently in the menu/prompts space. In this case, it will be permissible to erase the drawing and then redisplay it when the task is completed.

The tasks that are to be supported by the program are the creation and deletion of points, lines, rectangles in standard position, regular

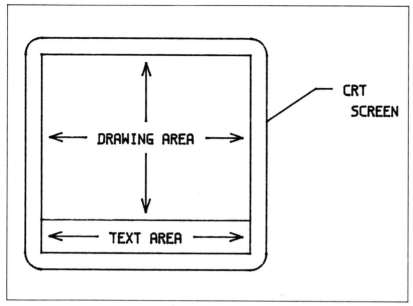

Figure 15-4. CRT screen showing drawing area and menu area.

polygons, circles, arcs, and text. Modes to be supported are ADD and DELETE for all drawing and text, and a choice of line type (solid or dashed) for the line task only. The DELETE routines are to be of the "proximity" type; that is, they should allow a margin of error in selection of the object to be deleted and should use the original input data to make the actual erasure from the screen. Data for deleted items are to be removed from the data storage so as to preclude redrawing the items when the drawing is redisplayed or plotted.

Drawing aids to be provided, in addition to prompts, are two styles of dot grid: square and isometric. It is desirable, but not necessary, to allow a choice of grid sizes (distance between dots). Input/output devices to be supported are the system's disk drives, a pen plotter, and a dot matrix printer-plotter.

Cursor control shall be by arrow keys on the keyboard or on a separate keypad. Function keys shall be used, if available, for selection of modes. Otherwise, mode change shall be provided by single keystroke of designated keys on the keyboard.

The following is an outline of the drawing-package specifications described above:

   I. Menu driven: menus on the screen
 II. Tasks supported
     A. Points
     B. Lines
     C. Rectangles
     D. Circles
     E. Arcs

F. Regular polygons

G. Text (uppercase and lowercase)

III. Modes supported

A. Add

B. Delete

C. Alternate (dash) line type (lines task only)

IV. Drawing aids

A. Grid

1. Square (rectangular)

2. Isometric

B. Prompts

1. For tasks

2. For modes

3. For menus

V. Input/output

A. Disk

1. Store and retrieve data files

2. Store and retrieve image (picture) files

B. Printer-plotter

C. Pen Plotter

VI. Cursor control

A. Arrow keys on keyboard

B. Separate keypad

VII. Function (or designated) keys

A. ADD/DELETE selection

B. Line type selection

C. Cursor "speed" control

D. Abort task/return to menu

E. Arrow keys for cursor control

VIII. Menu selections

A. Primary drawing tasks

1. Points

2. Lines

3. Rectangles

4. Regular polygons

5. Circles

6. Arcs

B. Other tasks

1. Plot drawing

2. Dot grid

3. Text

4. Redisplay drawing

5. Save drawing

6. Retrieve drawing

7. Switch menus

8. End program

IX. Selection subtask details

    A. For all drawing tasks and text task

        1. Add

        2. Delete

    B. For text

        1. Uppercase

        2. Lowercase

    C. For lines: line type

    D. For polygons: number of sides

    E. For dot grid: grid spacing and type (square or isometric)

    F. For data storage/retrieval

        1. Disk drive to use

        2. Display directory of files on disk

        3. File name to use

    G. For plotting

        1. Pen plot

        2. Printer plot

        3. Save in picture file for later use

            a) Disk drive to use

            b) Display directory

            c) File name to use

    H. Prompts

        1. Active task

        2. Active modes

            a) ADD/DELETE (drawing features or text)

            b) Line type (line)

            c) Number of sides (polygon)

            d) Type and size of grid (grid)

        3. Directions for accomplishing task (all tasks)

        4. Directions for abort/return to menu (all tasks)

Now that the requirements for the program have been defined, we can proceed to design its structure. Perhaps the easiest way to do this is to think about the program from a user's point of view.

If you were to run the program, how would you expect it to work, and what would you want to see on the screen? Perhaps the first thing novice users want is some instructions. After users have run the program several times, they will want to skip the instructions and get on with the work. Therefore, we should include instructions as part of the start-up routine, but we should make them optional by permitting the users to bypass them.

When the users have gone through the instructions and are ready to begin using the program, it is time for the menu to be displayed. If there is more than one menu, one should be designated as the main menu and the others as subsidiary menus. In order to reduce the amount of time users must spend going from menu to menu, the

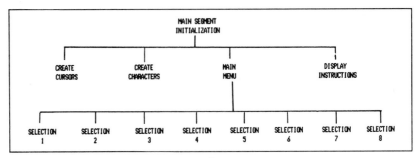

Figure 15-5. Preliminary communications diagram.

most used selections—that is, the main tasks—should be on the main menu and the other menus should be supporting menus (for less used features).

Another consideration in menu design is what features to include as menu items and what features to put elsewhere. For instance, suppose a user is drawing lines and has selected the LINES task from the menu. After drawing several lines, he or she may wish to draw a line in a different line type. Should it be necessary for the user to go back to the main menu (and maybe from there to a subsidiary menu), change the line type, and then return to the task? From the user's point of view, it would be nice to be able to change line type without exiting the task. The same would hold true for deleting and redrawing a line. Exiting the task and going to one or more menus to reset the mode, returning to the task, deleting the line, exiting the task to reset the mode to ADD, and reselecting the task seems unnecessarily cumbersome. Therefore, we will make mode selections available at the task level, not at the menu level.

With this much initial planning, let us construct a diagram of the features and communications paths that we have considered so far. Figure 15-5 is such a diagram, showing the program structure as we now know it. Note that the root of the diagram is devoted to program initialization and initial instructions to the users and communicates only with the menu routine. The third level of the diagram contains task routines that are individually accessible from the menu but that do not communicate with each other. Thus, to access a task from start-up, the initialization/instructions routine passes control to the menu routine, which, in turn, passes control to the user-selected task routine. When that task is exited, control returns to the menu routine. From there another task can be selected, or control might return to the initialization/instructions routine for more instructions or to end the program.

Note that the program could probably be ended at any point by including the necessary END statements in a particular routine. Most programmers prefer, however, to have only one starting point and one ending point in a program. With this approach, the procedures required for those tasks need not be replicated, and it is easier to manage the flow of control in the program. The wisdom of this is very apparent when the steps required to end a program must be modified. How much easier it is to make the modifications in the one module that handles that task than to try to find every place in the program where an END routine has been included and to modify them all.

So far, we have not put any task names in the task-level nodes of our diagram. Referring back to our outline specifications (under heading VIII, Menu selections), we see that there are 14 different selections to be made from the menu. Should we try to include them all in one menu or do we need one or more subsidiary menus? We know that the menu area is to be confined to the bottom text line of the screen, which has space for, at most, 80 characters. This would give us about five spaces per menu item, which would make for a very congested and cryptic menu.

Some programs attempt to deal with this situation by making the menu a listing of single character mnemonics such as

ACDEGLOPQRST

where A is understood to stand for Arcs, C for Circles, D for reDis-play, E for rEtrieve, G for dotGrid, L for Lines, O for Output (plot and so forth), P for Points, Q for Quit (end), R for Rectangles, S for Save, and T for Text. This approach requires memorization of the mnemonics by the users and/or for a good set of HELP routines. However, it is difficult to come up with a good set of mnemonics for a long list of menu items because of duplication of sounds (retrieve, rectangles, and redisplay might all be represented by R). An advantage of this approach, in addition to keeping everything on one menu, is that selection is made with a single keystroke.

Our approach will be to use the name of the task (abbreviated if it is very long) and a single numeric key to strike to select the task. Since there are only ten numeric keys (0 through 9) and since 0 may not seem like an appropriate number to assign to a task, we will limit ourselves to nine selections per menu. Consequently, we will need at least two menus.

The decision to use multiple menus forces us to decide which items to put on which menu and which items, if any, to include on more than one menu. Certainly the drawing tasks (points, lines, rectangles, polygons, circles, arcs) could go on one menu. SWITCH MENUS and, perhaps, END PROGRAM should go on each menu. (Note that the users would probably find it convenient to end from any menu, even though the program itself would always return to a single module for the END routine.) If we include these eight selection items on the first menu, we have six selection items (plot drawing, dot grid, text, redisplay drawing, save drawing, retrieve drawing) left for the second, or subsidiary, menu. Adding SWITCH MENUS and END PROGRAM to the second menu leaves it with eight selection items as well. The two menus might appear as follows.

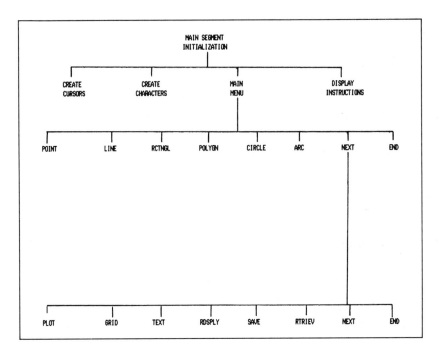

Figure 15-6. Communications diagram incorporating first and second menus.

First menu:

```
POINT=1  LINE=2  RECTANGLE=3  POLYGON=4
    CIRCLE=5  ARC=6  NEXT-M=7  END=8
```

Second menu:

```
PLOT=1  GRID=2  TEXT=3  REDISPLAY=4
SAVE=5  RETRIEVE=6  NEXT-M=7  END=8
```

We can now put task names in the boxes (nodes) of level three of our diagram. We can also add another level of menu and put names in the nodes for the routines for this second menu. Our new version of the tree is shown in Figure 15-6. This version shows all routines that are called from the menus. At this point it might seem that we are finished with the program structure design and ready to write code. This is not true, however, since each of the tasks will be calling subtasks (subroutines) to perform specific functions. These subtasks should be added to our tree, as has been done for LINES in Figure 15-7, and the entire program should be laid out before coding begins.

The final tree diagram is shown in Figure 15-8. Much of the design work from here on out is repetitive from task to task, and, while we will present and comment on the FORTRAN and BASIC code for the task LINES, completion of the code for the other tasks will be left to you.

In previous chapters we have depicted a drawing task as being composed of several subtasks, one of which was the INPUT task for the values needed to draw the entity. A second subtask STORED the

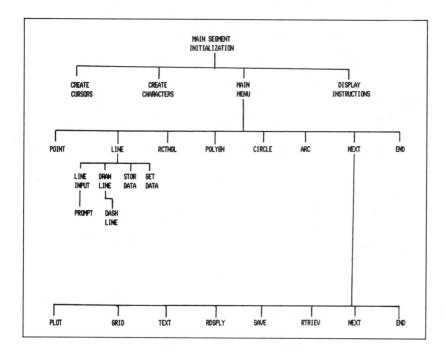

Figure 15-7. Communications diagram with sample subtask (LINES) shown.

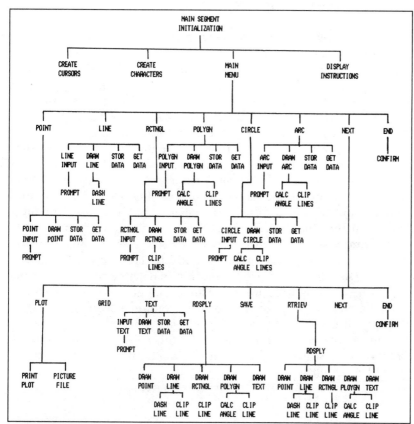

Figure 15-8. Completed communications diagram.

data, and a third subtask did the actual DRAWING. A fourth subtask was employed to retrieve data for DELETE and to remove them from the storage array. Each of these subtasks was called from the INPUT task and each returned control to the INPUT task when it had finished its assignment. Another subtask that must be called from the INPUT task is the CURSOR routine. INPUT may also call mode-selection routines such as ADD/DELETE and LINE TYPE. Depending on the functions supported by the system, these mode-selection routines may also be called directly from the CURSOR routine. We will show them as being called from the INPUT routine. Finally, the DRAWING routine may call another subtask routine to draw the line. This last routine is especially useful if a number of line types will be supported by each of the DRAWING routines (lines, rectangles, polygons, circle, arcs), since the code necessary to create the special line styles need only be written once.

Writing the Initialization Routine

We are now ready to begin writing the actual routines represented by the nodes on our tree diagram. As usual, the first step in writing a routine should be to draw a flow chart for it. You should draw a preliminary flow chart of the program initialization routine at this time, then compare your flow chart with the sample code that follows.

With the flow chart as a guide we can now create the code for the modules in FORTRAN and BASIC. The code for the initialization module is shown below. Note that it calls subroutines that are not yet written. To allow us to test the module, we have included dummy subroutines for INSTR (instructions) and MENU, plus two others for the BASIC version only. SUBROUTINE INSTR (29000 in the BASIC version) prints a message and beeps the terminal then waits for the operator to press a key before returning to the calling routine. SUB-ROUTINE MENU (100 in the BASIC version) and two other sub-routines found only in the BASIC version only beep the terminal and return. These subroutines are presented as alternate forms of dummy routines and can be modified to serve any dummy subroutine need. Note also that the FORTRAN version of the instructions dummy subroutine assumes a terminal with selective-erase capability and system library subroutines (DARK and LIGHT) to provide the pen-color toggle. ERASE, if used on a terminal without selective-erase capability, may be used to erase the screen after printing the mes-sage. Remember that we now have a complete working program, although it does not do anything. At each stage of development of the entire program we should maintain this working-program status. In this way we can always test each new module as it is written.

FORTRAN code:

```
C ** MAIN PROGRAM (INITIALIZATION ROUTINE)
      CALL ATTACH
      CALL INITT (960)
      CALL TERM (1,1024)
```

```
        CALL INSTR
        CALL MENU
        CALL FINITT(0,0)
        END


C ** INSTRUCTIONS SUBROUTINE (DUMMY VERSION)
        SUBROUTINE INSTR
        CALL MOVABS (5,720)
        CALL ANMODE
        WRITE (6,5) 'SUBROUTINE INSTR -- HIT RETURN'
    5   FORMAT ('+',A30)
        CALL BELL
        READ (5,10) ANS
   10   FORMAT (A10)
        CALL MOVABS (5,720)
        CALL ANMODE
        CALL DARK
        WRITE (6,5) 'SUBROUTINE INSTR -- HIT RETURN'
        CALL LIGHT
        RETURN
        END


C ** MENU SUBROUTINE (DUMMY VERSION)
        SUBROUTINE MENU
        CALL BELL
        RETURN
        END
```

BASIC code:

```
10 REM **** MAIN PROGRAM (INITIALIZATION ROUTINE) ****
20 DIM POINTS%(100,2),LINES%(100,4),RCTNGLS%(20,8),
   CIRCLES%(50,7),CURSOR%(30),TXTCRS%(20),ICHAR%(12,95),
   TCHAR%(12),TXTSTR%(100,3),T%(3),P%(2),L%(4),R%(10),
   C%(7),ADD$(2),TYP$(2)
30 CLS:KEY OFF:SCREEN 2
40 FACTOR=2.5:DX=1:DY=1:ADD$(0)="DEL":ADD$(1)="ADD":
   TYP$(0)="DASH":TYP$(1)="SOLID"
45 GOSUB 29000:    'calls instruction subroutine
50 GOSUB 7000:     'calls subroutine to create cursors
60 GOSUB 8800:     'calls subroutine to create text chracters
70 GOSUB 100:      'calls menu subroutine
80 SCREEN 0
90 END


100 REM ** MENU SUBROUTINE (DUMMY VERSION) **
110 BEEP
120 RETURN


7000 REM ** CURSOR SUBROUTINE (DUMMY VERSION) **
7010 BEEP
7020 RETURN


8800 REM ** TEXT CHARACTER SUBROUTINE (DUMMY VERSION) **
8810 BEEP
8820 RETURN


29000 REM ** INSTRUCTIONS SUBROUTINE (DUMMY VERSION #1) **
29010 LOCATE 20,5:PRINT "INSTRUCTIONS SUBROUTINE --HIT";
      " ANY KEY"
29020 BEEP
29030 IK$=INKEY$:IF IK$="" THEN 29030
29040 LOCATE 20,5:PRINT "                                ";
      "        "
29050 RETURN
```

Some comments are in order regarding the BASIC version of the initialization routine. This routine contains a DIMENSION statement, a statement to initialize values that will be used in prompts in other routines, and subroutine calls to create cursors and text characters. None of these are present in the FORTRAN version, since a hardware cursor is available and the subprogram ANMODE allows accurate placement of the normal character set. Also, variables are all local in FORTRAN so there is no need to initilize values or dimension arrays at this point.

Writing the Instructions Subroutine

Now that the initialization module is completed, we can turn our attention to the subroutines. We will begin with INSTR, the first subroutine. You should construct a preliminary flow chart of an INSTR subroutine that will give users the option of bypassing the instructions and then compare your solution with the sample code that follows. Do not feel that your algorithm (flow chart) must match the sample code. There can be several good solutions. In fact, the FORTRAN and BASIC versions shown here use different methods of printing the paging prompt on the screen and a slightly different paging procedure.

The following FORTRAN code contains some system-specific calls to library routines, namely, ADMMOD, VMODE, and ERSADM, which are library functions to switch the terminal to alphanumeric mode, to switch it to vector (graphics) mode, and to erase the alphanumeric screen (buffer). If your system has similar built-in or library routines, they can be substituted. Otherwise, you may need to print a screen at a time in graphics mode and then use CALL ERASE to clear the screen between each page of instructions.

FORTRAN code:

```
C ** INSTRUCTIONS SUBROUTINE **
        SUBROUTINE INSTR
        BYTE TEXT(71)
        CALL ADMMOD
   10   WRITE (6,20) 'DO YOU WANT INSTRUCTIONS ?'
   20   FORMAT('1',A30)
        READ (5,30) ANS
   30   FORMAT (A1)
        IF (ANS .EQ. 'N' .OR. ANS .EQ. 'n') GOTO 999
        IF (ANS .NE. 'Y' .AND. ANS .NE. 'y') GOTO 10
        OPEN(UNIT=1,NAME='INSTRCTNS.DAT',TYPE='OLD',READONLY)
        CALL ADMMOD
C       >>>>>BEGIN READ-WRITE LOOP<<<<<
    5   DO 70 I=1,20
        READ(1,40,END=999) TEXT
        WRITE(6,50) TEXT
C       >>>>>TEST FOR END-OF-PAGE (>) INDICATOR<<<<<
        IF(TEXT(1) .EQ. '>') GO TO 15
   70   CONTINUE
   40   FORMAT(71A1)
   50   FORMAT(' ',71A1)
C       >>>>>PAUSE FOR OPERATOR READ, THEN ERASE AND
C            OUTPUT NEXT PAGE<<<<<
   15   READ (5,31) ANS
   31   FORMAT (A1)
        WRITE (5,35)
```

```
   35      FORMAT ('1')
           GO TO 5
   C    >>>>>CLOSE INPUT FILE,ERASE SCREEN,RESET TO
   C        GRAPHICS MODE, AND RETURN TO CALLING ROUTINE<<<<
   999     CLOSE (UNIT=1)
           CALL ERSADM
           CALL VMODE
           RETURN
           END
```

The BASIC code that follows contains the user prompt. In the FORTRAN version, the prompt was in the instructions data file. The BASIC version prints to the screen while in graphics mode (the FORTRAN version switched to alphanumeric mode). Also, the BASIC version looks for the word PAGE as the signal to end a page of instructions, while the FORTRAN version looked for a >.

BASIC code:

```
29000 REM ** INSTRUCTIONS SUBROUTINE **
29010 AA$="   ****** DO YOU WANT INSTRUCTIONS? (Y/N) ******"
29020 GOSUB 29170
29030 IK$=LEFT$(IK$,1):IF IK$="Y" OR IK$="y" THEN 29050
      ELSE IF IK$="N" OR IK$="n" THEN 29140 ELSE 29020
29040 REM ** READ FROM INSTRUCTION FILE **
29050 OPEN "INSTR.TXT" FOR INPUT AS #1
29060 AA$="      ****** PRESS ANY KEY TO CONTINUE ******"
29070 FOR K=1 TO 200
29080 IF EOF(1) THEN 29130
29090 INPUT #1, INSTRUCTION$
29100 IF INSTRUCTION$="PAGE" THEN GOSUB 29160:GOTO 29120
29110 PRINT "      ";INSTRUCTION$
29120 NEXT
29130 GOSUB 29170
29140 CLOSE #1
29150 RETURN
29160 REM ** PAGING ROUTINE **
29170 LOCATE 25,15:PRINT AA$;
29180 IK$=INKEY$:IF IK$="" THEN 29180 ELSE CLS:RETURN
```

You should complete the writing and testing of your instructions module before continuing with other modules. The instructions themselves are contained in a text file that can be created and changed at will using your system's text editor. You should write at least two pages of instructions so that the paging portion of your code can be tested.

Writing the Menu Subroutine

The menu routine is somewhat more complex than the initialization and instruction routines but can still be a very straightforward program. The key to an easily written menu subroutine is to use a computed GOTO statement for the transfer of control to the correct routine. A computed GOTO has the following form in FORTRAN:

```
GOTO (statement,statement,statement), L
```

and in BASIC it has the form

```
300  ON L GOSUB line,line,line
```

In both versions L is a positive integer. The statement tests the value of L and, if it is 1, control transfers to the first statement (line) on the list. If the value is 2, control passes to the second statement (line), if it is 3, control passes to the third statement (line), and so on. If the value of L is outside the range of the statement (either 0 or greater than the number of items in the list), control passes to the next executable statement following the computed GOTO. A negative value for L may cause an error. In our program, L will be the numeric value typed in to select from the menu and will thus range from 1 to 8.

You can create the flow chart for the menu subroutine by referring to the communications-tree diagram. Note that the menu subroutine will use two computed GOTOs, one for the main menu and another for the subsidiary menu. You should prepare a preliminary flow chart and then compare it to the sample codes shown below in FORTRAN and BASIC. We have made the two versions as similar as possible, but some differences are unavoidable because of dissimilarities in the two languages. For example, the FORTRAN version requires a carriage return after entering the menu selection, while the BASIC version takes advantage of INKEY$, which does not require a carriage return to be keyed in. Note that the FORTRAN version uses the library function ICHAR in the error-trapping routine to test for a usable input from the keyboard, while the BASIC version uses the function VAL. Also, the FORTRAN version uses a subroutine WIPE to clean off the old menu before placing the new one. This is an alternate approach to reprinting the old menu in DARK mode. BASIC allows cleaning off the old menu by overprinting it with spaces. Note that the FORTRAN version has a DIMENSION statement and that it also has a COMMON statement to pass values to other subroutines.

FORTRAN code:

```
C *** MENU SUBROUTINE ***
        SUBROUTINE MENU
        CHARACTER*1 ANS
        DIMENSION PNTSTR(100,2),LINSTR(100,5),
      1 RCTSTR(20,8),POLSTR(50,8),PNTWRK(2),LINWRK(5),
      2 RCTWRK(10),POLWRK(8)
  120   CALL WIPE (1,1022)
        CALL MOVABS (1,1)
        CALL ANMODE
        WRITE (6,10) 'POINT=1 LINE=2 RECTANGLE=3 POLYGON=4',
      1 ' CIRCLE=5 ARC=6 NEXT-M=7',' END=8'
   10   FORMAT ('+',A36,A24,A7)
        CALL MOVABS (1000,1)
        CALL ANMODE
        READ (5,15) ANS
   15   FORMAT (A1)
        IANS=ICHAR(ANS)-48
        GOTO (250,300,350,400,450,500,180,900),IANS
        GOTO 120
  180   CALL WIPE (1,1022)
        CALL MOVABS (1,1)
        CALL ANMODE
        WRITE (6,30) 'PLOT=1 GRID=2 TEXT=3 REDISPLAY=4 SAVE=5',
      1 ' RETRIEVE=6 NEXT-M=7 END=8'
   30   FORMAT ('+',A39,A26)
        CALL MOVABS (1000,1)
```

```
        CALL ANMODE
        READ (5,15) ANS
        IANS=ICHAR(ANS)-48
        GOTO (600,700,750,550,800,850,120,900),IANS
        GOTO 180
250     CALL POINT
260     GOTO 120
300     CALL LINE(LINSTR,LINWRK)
        GOTO 120
350     CALL RCTNGL
        GOTO 120
400     CALL POLYGN
        GOTO 120
450     CALL CIRCLE
        GOTO 120
500     CALL ARC
        GOTO 120
550     CALL RDSPLY
        GOTO 120
600     CALL PLOT
        GOTO 120
700     CALL GRID
        GOTO 120
750     CALL TEXT
        GOTO 120
800     CALL SAVE
        GOTO 120
850     CALL RETRIV
        GOTO 120
900     RETURN
999     END

C ** SUBROUTINE TO ERASE PORTION OF MENU/PROMPT LINE
C ** ERASES FROM X=L TO X=M
        SUBROUTINE WIPE (L,M)
        CALL DARK
        DO 10 K=1,35
          CALL MOVABS (L,K)
          CALL DRWABS (M,K)
10        CONTINUE
        CALL LIGHT
        RETURN
        END
```

BASIC code:

```
100 *** MENU SUBROUTINE ***
110 CLS
120 LOCATE 25,1:PRINT"POINT=1  LINE=2  RECTANGLE=3";
    "POLYGON=4  CIRCLE=5  ARC=6  NEXT-M=7  END=8  ";
140 M$=INKEY$:IF M$="" THEN 140 ELSE TASK=VAL(M$)
150 ON TASK GOTO 250,300,350,400,450,500,180,900
160 GOTO 120
180 LOCATE 25,1:PRINT"PLOT=1  GRID=2  TEXT=3  REDISPLAY";
    "=4  SAVE=5  RETRIEVE=6  NEXT-M=7  END=8         ";
200 M$=INKEY$:IF M$="" THEN 200 ELSE TASK=VAL(M$)
210 ON TASK GOTO 600,700,750,550,800,850,120,900
220 GOTO 180
250 GOSUB 1000:       'calls points input routine
260 GOTO 120
300 GOSUB 2000:       'calls lines input routine
310 GOTO 120
350 GOSUB 3000:       'calls rectangles input routine
360 GOTO 120
400 GOSUB 4600:       'calls polygons input routine
410 GOTO 120
450 GOSUB 4000:       'calls circles input routine
460 GOTO 120
500 GOSUB 4800:       'calls arcs input routine
510 GOTO 120
550 GOSUB 6000:       'calls redisplay routine
```

```
560 GOTO 120
600 GOSUB 12600:    'calls print-plot routine
610 GOTO 120
700 GOSUB 10800:    'calls dot grid routine
710 GOTO 120
750 GOSUB 8000:     'calls text input routine
760 GOTO 120
800 GOSUB 10200:    'calls data disk storage routine
810 GOTO 120
850 GOSUB 10400:    'calls data disk retrieval routine
860 GOTO 120
900 RETURN:         'return to main module to end program
```

We have now provided sample code for an initialization routine, an instructions subroutine, a menu subroutine, and dummy subroutines for all other subroutine calls. Assuming that all of the dummy subroutines are written, we still have a complete, operating menu-driven program, even though it cannot yet do any tasks. You should reproduce this code on your system, debug it, and verify correct operation. Then you can write the required subroutines one at a time, add them to the program to replace their dummy subroutines, and test each one. In this way, you only need to work with one short subroutine at any time.

Each of the subroutines required for this program has been discussed in a previous chapter. You should refer to the appropriate chapter while writing the code for each subroutine. During this process, remember to make a variable list either as part of the program file or in a separate file. In a long program you should not trust your memory, especially in BASIC, where the variables are global. To aid you in writing your code, we will present sample code for the LINES group, including line-input, line-drawing, line-data-storage, and line-data-retrieval routines.

LINES Sample Code

Note that the FORTRAN line-input routine calls a prompt routine that is not shown. This routine can be written to replace the mode prompts in the same manner that the menus replace each other. Subroutine WIPE, called by subroutine PROMPT with proper arguments, will erase the old mode designation before displaying the new one. The WIPE subroutine is not as efficient as the technique used in the dummy instructions module. Another technique used with the storage-tube terminals is to erase the entire screen, but this requires redrawing the picture as well as the menu. The arguments in the FORTRAN call are to identify the particular message to be displayed.

Return to the menu or selection of a different mode is triggered by pressing the M, P, or L key. The CURSOR subroutine records the action and returns the ASCII value of the key, in decimal form, as the value of ICHAR (see Table 11-1 in Chapter 11). The program then determines whether M, P, L, or the space bar was pressed and takes appropriate action. The FORTRAN code also includes a subroutine named TOGGLE that toggles the mode values between 1 and 2.

FORTRAN code:

```
C ** LINE INPUT SUBROUTINE **
      SUBROUTINE LINE (LINSTR,NLIN)
      DIMENSION LINSTR(25,5),LINWRK(5)
      LINWRK(5)=LINTYP
      IDARK=1
      LINWRK(5)=1
      CALL WIPE (1,1022)
      CALL MOVABS (1,1)
      CALL ANMODE
      WRITE (6,5) 'LINES - INPUT START, THEN END MENU(M)',
    1 'SOLID(L)    ADD(P)'
    5 FORMAT ('+',A40,A25)
   10 CALL SCURSR(ICHAR,LINWRK(1),LINWRK(2))
      NOT=0
      IF(ICHAR .EQ. 77) GOTO 999
      IF(ICHAR .NE. 80) GOTO 11
      CALL TOGGLE (IDARK)
      CALL PROMP (IDARK)
      GOTO 10
   11 IF(ICHAR .NE. 76) GOTO 12
      CALL TOGGLE (LINWRK(5))
      IL=LINWRK(5)+2
      CALL PROMP (IL)
      GOTO 10
   12 IF(ICHAR .EQ. 32) GOTO 15
      CALL BELL
      GO TO 10
   15 CONTINUE
      IF (IDARK .EQ. 1) CALL PNTABS(LINWRK(1),LINWRK(2))
   22 CALL SCURSR(ICHAR,LINWRK(3),LINWRK(4))
      IF(ICHAR .EQ. 77) GO TO 999
      IF(ICHAR .NE. 80) GOTO 23
      CALL TOGGLE (IDARK)
      CALL PROMP (IDARK)
      GOTO 22
   23 IF(ICHAR .NE. 76) GOTO 25
      CALL TOGGLE (LINWRK(5))
      IL=LINWRK(5)+2
      CALL PROMP (IL)
      GOTO 22
   25 IF(ICHAR .EQ. 32) GOTO 27
      CALL BELL
      GO TO 22
   27 CONTINUE
      IF (IDARK .EQ. 2) CALL SRHLIN(LINWRK,NLIN,LINSTR,NOT)
      IF (IDARK .EQ. 2) GO TO 100
      CALL SAVLIN(LINWRK,NLIN,LINSTR)
  100 IF(NOT .EQ. 1) GO TO 5
      CALL DRWLIN(LINWRK,IDARK)
      GO TO 5
  999 RETURN
      END


C ** LINE DRAWING SUBROUTINE **
      SUBROUTINE DRWLIN(LINWRK,IDARK)
      DIMENSION LINWRK(5)
      LINTYP=LINWRK(5)
      IF(IDARK .EQ. 2) CALL DARK
      CALL MOVABS(LINWRK(1),LINWRK(2))
      IF(LINTYP .EQ. 1) CALL DRWABS(LINWRK(3),LINWRK(4))
      IF(LINTYP .EQ. 2) CALL DSHLIN(LINWRK(3),LINWRK(4),3)
      IF(IDARK .EQ. 2) CALL LIGHT
      RETURN
      END


C ** SUBROUTINE TO SAVE LINE DATA IN ARRAY **
      SUBROUTINE SAVLIN(LINWRK,NLIN,LINSTR)
      DIMENSION LINWRK(5),LINSTR(25,5)
```

```
     5     NLIN=NLIN+1
           DO 10 J=1,5
             LINSTR(NLIN,J)=LINWRK(J)
    10       CONTINUE
   999     RETURN
           END


C ** SUBROUTINE TO RETRIEVE DATA FOR DELETE **
           SUBROUTINE SRHLIN(LINWRK,NLIN,LINSTR,NOT)
           DIMENSION LINWRK(5),LINSTR(25,5)
           NOT=0
           DO 40 J=1,NLIN
             DO 10 K=1,3,2
               IF (ABS(LINSTR(J,K)-LINWRK(1)) .LE. 6. .AND.
         *       ABS(LINSTR(J,K+1)-LINWRK(2)) .LE. 10.) GO TO 20
    10         CONTINUE
             GO TO 40
    20       DO 30 L=1,3,2
               IF (ABS(LINSTR(J,L)-LINWRK(3)) .LE. 6. .AND.
         *       ABS(LINSTR(J,L+1)-LINWRK(4)) .LE. 10.) GO TO 60
    30         CONTINUE
    40       CONTINUE
    50     CALL BELL
           NOT=1
           GO TO 999
    60     DO 70 M=1,5
             LINWRK(M)=LINSTR(J,M)
    70       CONTINUE
           DO 80 M=1,5
             LINSTR(J,M)=LINSTR(NLIN,M)
    80       CONTINUE
           NLIN=NLIN-1
   999     RETURN
           END


           SUBROUTINE TOGGLE(K)
           IF (K .EQ. 2) GOTO 20
           K=2
           GOTO 40
    20     K=1
    40     RETURN
           END


           SUBROUTINE DSHLIN(LX,LY,K)
           CALL DSHABS (LX,LY,K)
           RETURN
           END
```

The BASIC code for the LINES group is very similar in form to the
FORTRAN code. However, some differences are unavoidable. For
instance, the CURSOR routine is not a hardware cursor but one
written by the programmer. (Chapter 11 shows example code for a
graphics cursor.) Also, the BASIC code takes advantage of both the
availability of function keys polled by the ON KEY(n) statement (the
code for this would be in the CURSOR routine) and the fact that
printing a character will replace the previous one (not just overprint
it as the PLOT10 code does). Finally, the BASIC code contains a
rather elaborate dashed-line subroutine, since there is not one available as a system subroutine. The IBM PC DOS 2.0 has a dashed line,
but it creates different length dashes for lines drawn at different
angles.

Default typing in FORTRAN types all variables beginning with I, J, K, L, M, or N as integers and all others as real unless declared otherwise. Character strings must be input or printed using an A format, and the character string names should be declared at the beginning of each module. BASIC default typing is as follows: Character string names end with $, integers end with %, and all others are considered to be real numbers. BASIC code accepts and sometimes requires more than one statement per line number. Multiple statements are separated by colons and execute faster than code written with one statement per line number.

BASIC code:

```
2000 ** INPUT ROUTINE FOR LINES **
2010 REM
2020 IK$="":ADDDEL=1:NOTFOUND=0:SOLDSH=1:LPEN=1
2030 LOCATE 25,1:PRINT"LINES - INPUT BEGINNING, THEN";
     "END -- MENU (OR ABORT) F9  SOLID(F2)   ADD (F1)  ";
2032 GOSUB 7200
2033 IF IK$="M" THEN GOTO 2080
2040 LINWRK%(1)=XG%+10:LINWRK%(2)=YG%+5
2041 PSET(LINWRK%(1),LINWRK%(2)),LPEN
2045 GOSUB 7200
2046 IF IK$="M" THEN GOTO 2080
2047 LINWRK%(3)=XG%+10:LINWRK%(4)=YG%+5
2050 IF ADDDEL=1 THEN GOSUB 2400
2060 IF ADDDEL=0 THEN GOSUB 2600
2070 IF NOTFOUND=0 THEN GOSUB 2200
2075 NOTFOUND=0:GOTO 2032
2080 REM
2090 RETURN


2200 REM ******** LINE DRAWING SUBROUTINE **********
2210 REM
2220 LPEN=ADDDEL
2230 IF LINWRK%(5)=2 THEN GOSUB 11000:GOTO 2260
2231 LPEN=ADDDEL
2238 IF LINWRK%(5)=2 THEN GOSUB 11000:GOTO 2260
2240 LINE(LINWRK%(1),LINWRK%(2))-(LINWRK%(3),
     LINWRK%(4)),LPEN
2250 REM
2260 RETURN


2400 REM ****** LINE DATA STORAGE SUBROUTINE *******
2410 NLIN%=NLIN%+1
2415 LINWRK%(5)=SOLDSH
2420 FOR J=1 TO 5
2430 LINSTR%(NLIN%,J)=LINWRK%(J)
2440 NEXT J
2450 REM
2460 RETURN


2600 REM **** LINE DATA RETRIEVAL FOR DELETE *******
2610 REM
2620 IF NLIN%=0 THEN 2690
2630 FOR I=1 TO NLIN%
2640    IF ABS(LINSTR%(I,1)-LINWRK%(1))<6 AND
        ABS(LINSTR%(I,2)-LINWRK%(2))<3 AND ABS(LINSTR%(I,3)
        -LINWRK%(3))<6 AND ABS(LINSTR%(I,4)-LINWRK%(4))<3
        THEN ROW=I:NOTFOUND=0:GOTO 2700
2650    IF ABS(LINSTR%(I,1)-LINWRK%(3))<6 AND
        ABS(LINSTR%(I,2)-LINWRK%(4))<3 AND ABS(LINSTR%(I,3)
        -LINWRK%(1))<6 AND ABS(LINSTR%(I,4)-LINWRK%(2))<3
        THEN ROW=I:NOTFOUND=0:GOTO 2700
2680    NEXT I
```

```
2690 NOTFOUND=1:PRINT CHR$(7);:GOTO 2750
2700 FOR J=1 TO 5:LINWRK%(J)=LINSTR%(ROW,J):NEXT J
2710 FOR J=1 TO 5:LINSTR%(ROW,J)=LINSTR%(NLIN%,J):NEXT J
2720 NLIN%=NLIN%-1
2730 REM
2750 RETURN


11000 ** DASH LINE SUBROUTINE ***
11020 XP1=LINWRK%(1):YP1=LINWRK%(2):XP2=LINWRK%(3):
      YP2=LINWRK%(4)
11030 R=SQR(((XP2-XP1)/2.5)^2+(YP2-YP1)^2)
11040 SINTHA= (YP2-YP1)/R
11050 COSTHA= (XP2-XP1)/2.5/R
11060 PRESET (XP1,YP1)
11070 X=XP1:Y=YP1
11080 FOR K= 4 TO R STEP  4
11090    X=X+5*COSTHA:Y=Y+2*SINTHA
11100    LINE -(X,Y),LPEN
11110    X=X+5*COSTHA:Y=Y+2*SINTHA
11120    LINE -(X,Y),0
11130    NEXT K
11140 LINE -(XP2,YP2),LPEN
11150 RETURN
```

Creation of this drawing package utilizes most of the information and procedures that we have presented in this book. Two types of drawings that we have discussed but that are not included in this package are graphs and three-dimensional representations. However, upon successful completion of this program, you should have no difficulty creating menu-driven programs for graphing and for displaying three-dimensional figures.

Exercises

1. Using the LINES communications path diagram as an example, draw the communications paths for (a) points, (b) rectangles, (c) polygons, (d) circles, (e) arcs, (f) plot, (g) grid, (h) text, (i) redisplay, (j) save, and (k) retrieve.

2. Write the initialization routines for your drawing package. Be sure to include the DIMENSION (or COMMON) statements for storing the information, set any initial values for variables, and do the initialization for the correct screen/window size. Also, include the necessary statements for program termination.

3. (a) Write the instructions for using your program. Use complete sentences. The instructions should include the keys to use (or not to use), the options that are available to the user along with directions for using each option, what feedback to expect, and any program limitations. (b) Write these instructions as a text file to be read by the instructions subroutine when the program is run, and write an instructions subroutine that gives the user the option of reading this file when the program begins executing. (c) Rewrite the instructions subroutine so that it can be used as a HELP file at any point during program execution.

4. If you are writing your program for a system that does not have a hardware cursor, then (a) write a routine to create cross-hair and text cursors (as was described in Chapter 11) and add this routine to your program as a subroutine to be executed as part of the initialization routine; (b) write routines to control (display and move) these cursors, and add these routines to your program as subroutines to be called from task routines that require the cursors.

5. Write the menu subroutine with subroutine calls to dummy subroutines for all of the options specified in the drawing-program description.

6. Write the dummy subroutines that are to be called by the menu subroutine. Each of these should provide both visible and audible feedback (a screen message and a tone or buzz) and should wait for a keystroke, then they should erase the message and return to the calling routine. Remember that program termination has already been written as part of the initialization routine.

7. Assemble your program, which is composed of the initialization routine, the instructions subroutine, the cursor subroutines (if required), the menu subroutine, and all of the dummy subroutines. Test your program to verify that all routines are functional. At this point you should have a complete operational program. Do not move on to the remaining exercises until you have completed this exercise.

8. Modify the data entry, draw, store, and retrieve subroutines for LINES that you developed as exercises in Chapters 4, 8, and 9. Incorporate them into your working program and verify that they function correctly. Include the ADD/DEL mode with these routines.

9. Modify the data entry, draw, store, and retrieve subroutines that you developed as exercises in Chapters 4, 5, 6, 7, 8, 9, and 11 for the following menu items (as assigned by your instructor): (a) points, (b) rectangles, (c) polygons, (d) circles, (e) arcs. Incorporate these routines into your program and verify that they function correctly. Include the ADD/DEL mode with these routines.

10. (a) Write a subroutine to display a rectangular dot grid with a spacing of 0.25 inches (6 mm) in both the horizontal and vertical directions. (b) Include an option for other grid sizes as specified by your instructor. Incorporate this routine into your program and verify that it functions correctly.

11. Modify the text entry, display, store, and retrieve subroutines described in Chapters 7 and 11, and incorporate them into your program. Verify that they will place text at any desired location on the screen using the hardware cursor or the text cursor developed in Exercise 4.

12. Modify the disk input/output routines described in Chapter 11 to store and retrieve your data using a single data file for each drawing. These routines should store the data used to create all drawing and text, whether the subroutines to create the entities have been written or not. Any empty storage array should be stored as having no elements. The grid does not have to be stored.

13. Write the necessary routines to create either a printer plot or a pen plot of your drawing, as appropriate for your system.

14. Write a user's manual for your program. Include the specification of the program applications, provide detailed descriptions of the operation of all function keys, and provide example drawings for the user with step by step instructions for their creation. The example drawings can be used for training purposes.

15. Write a technical reference manual for the programmers who will be maintaining your program and creating more functions. This manual should include a documented listing of the currently functioning code along with a discussion of each routine. The discussions should include the routine's function, a variables list, input and output requirements, and communications with other routines that call or are called by this routine.

Glossary

ALGORITHM A complete, step-by-step procedure for solving a problem. The algorithm may be presented in the form of written instructions, in the form of a flow chart or diagram, or even in the form of a computer program.

ALPHANUMERICS ASCII characters such as letters, punctuation marks, and numeric digits.

ANALOG Operating over a continuous range of values. The hand on a clock is an analog device.

ARRAY A set of data, each element of which has the same name but a different subscript to differentiate it from the other elements.

ASCII A commonly used coding system for data. The term is an acronym for "American standard code for information interchange." Each number that can be represented by the 8 bits in a byte (0 to 255) represents a different character. The ASCII for capital A, for instance, is 65.

BASIC A high-level computer language that is in common use for microcomputers. BASIC stands for "beginner's algebraic symbolic instruction code."

BAUD A measure of the speed with which data are transmitted from one device to another. One baud is about 1 bit per second. Correspondingly, 10 baud is about 1 character per second (thus, the popular 300 baud modem can transmit about 30 characters per second).

BINARY SYSTEM A system of numbers whose base is two. Each digit in the system has only two possible states (0 and 1), as opposed to decimal numbers, whose digits have ten possible states (0 through 9). Binary numbers are the basis of the internal language of computers because the two states are easy to represent electrically.

BIT The smallest amount of information a computer can handle. A bit is one binary digit that can take on one of two values, 0 or 1.

BUFFER A data-holding device that provides temporary storage of data being transmitted between two other devices. This temporary storage permits variations between send and receive rates and smooths (buffers) the data transfer.

BYTE Eight binary digits. A byte can take on values from 0 (00000000) to 255 (11111111) and can store one ASCII character.

CAD/CAM An acronym for "computer aided design/computer aided manufacturing."

CODE A computer program that is written in computer-language form. Before a program is coded, it is generally described in the form of a flow chart or other algorithm. Programs are generally written in high-level language, such as BASIC or FORTRAN, known as "source code." If the program is compiled, the resultant machine-language version is called "object code." In order to be runable, the object code must normally be combined (linked) with additional object code that provides built-in routines the program will need. The linked version of the code is known as "executable code."

COMPILING The process of converting a computer program from the high-level language in which it was written into the native machine language that the computer understands. FORTRAN is normally compiled before the program can be run. BASIC, on the other hand, is normally interpreted on a line by line basis while the program is being run.

CPU Central processing unit. This is the heart of the computer.

CRT A name used for computer terminals and monitors that display the image by means of cathode ray tubes. A television picture tube is a cathode ray tube.

CURSOR A marker that appears on the screen of the CRT to inform the user where the next character or graphics entity will be placed. The standard text cursor on many systems is either a flashing underline or a lighted rectangle. Graphics cursors are generally cross hairs.

DATA Information provided to a program. Data may be numeric values, character information such as names and addresses, status (on/off) information relating to devices or program modes, or logical information such as true/false results of IF-THEN tests.

DIGITAL Using discrete numerical values to represent quantities.

DOCUMENTATION The manuals and other instructional materials that are provided with a program.

DOS An acronym for "disk operating system." Most computers, except for the very smallest, use some form of disk operating system—that is, the program that forms the basis of their operation is read from a disk into memory each time the computer is started up.

DOT MATRIX The gridlike pattern of dots by which raster CRTs and dot matrix printers produce an image.

DUMP Transfer of a block of data to another location or device. For instance, a screen dump transfers the image on the screen to the printer by dumping the contents of the screen buffer.

EDITOR A special program that allows the user to write or modify programs or other text. Some editors, such as the BASIC editor, have only one function. Others, such as EDLIN, are general purpose and allow the user to create programs in various languages or even to create documents or data files.

FILE A block of information that is organized in a specific way. Files are usually stored on disk or tape but may be in main memory.

FLAG A binary (yes/no or on/off) indicator that is used to keep track of the status of a device or a mode of operation. Generally, the yes (or on) status is indicated when the flag is set. Conversely, the no (or off) status is indicated when the flag is not set.

FORTRAN A high-level language that was designed for scientific computing use. The name was derived from "formula transmutation." The language has been very popular on mainframe computers and minicomputers, but it has been less popular on microcomputers due to space requirements and the fact that, in most implementations, it must be compiled before being run.

GLOBAL Having the same meaning and values everywhere in a program. In BASIC, all variables are global. In FORTRAN, however, variables are local and must be redefined in each subroutine.

HOME The upper-left corner of a video display. Some languages, such as Applesoft, use the statement HOME to clear the screen and move the cursor into the home position.

I/O An abbreviation for "input/output" that refers to the communication between the computer and the peripherals or other devices.

INTERPRETER A device that converts each line of program code from source to machine language each time the line is encountered during the execution of the program. BASIC normally runs under an interpreter but is sometimes compiled.

LIBRARY Collection of subroutines that are stored in machine language (object) code and combined with a program as needed when the program has been compiled and is being linked.

LINKING The process of combining a compiled program with built-in libraries and any user libraries to create an executable (runable) program.

MODEM Modulator/demodulator. A device that permits communication between computers and peripherals over telephone lines.

MONITOR A CRT that is designed specifically for use with a computer or other nonradio-frequency device. Televisions are sometimes used as monitors but must be modified or connected to the computer through an interface device.

OPERATING SYSTEM A group of programs that provide the instructions for operating the computer. These programs provide instructions that control such functions as reading from a disk, writing to a printer, clearing the screen, and loading and running programs.

PARALLEL METHOD A method of transferring data from one device to another. When data transfer is parallel, the entire byte of information is transferred at one time, with each bit travelling over a separate path (wire). All of the wires are run in parallel, often in the familiar ribbon cable.

PIXEL A picture element, sometimes called a PEL. A pixel is a single addressable point on the screen—that is, it can be uniquely defined with an X coordinate and a Y coordinate.

POINTER A variable that keeps track of the status of operations within the program. For instance, a pointer would be used to record the next data to be read from a data statement so that no data would be duplicated or skipped.

RASTER A refresh type of CRT display that is similar in operation to a television set. The entire screen is refreshed (redisplayed) 30 to 60 times per second. This type of display allows selective replacement of any portion of the picture and is thus very versatile. The raster's main disadvantages are that it has limited resolution and that it requires relatively large amounts of memory to store the data needed to refresh the image.

RESOLUTION   A measure of the accuracy with which a graphics image can be reproduced (usually on the CRT). Resolution refers to the number of individual points or picture elements that are available to create the picture. Resolution is usually stated as the number of columns of pixels by the number of rows of pixels (for example 640 × 200), which is the same as the number of pixels in the X direction by the number of pixels in the Y direction.

SERIAL METHOD   A method of data transfer in which the transfer of a byte takes place one bit at a time over a single wire. This method is used for transfer in situations where multiple wires do not exist (for instance over the telephone) and in other cases where extremely high data-transfer rates are not required. Serial data transfer can generally be performed reliably over short distances at up to 9600 baud and over longer distances at 1200 to 2400 baud.

SOURCE CODE   The version of a program that is in the high-level language (BASIC, FORTRAN, Pascal) in which it was originally written.

STORAGE TUBE   A type of CRT display that retains everything printed or drawn on it until the entire screen is erased. Storage-tube displays have the advantage of offering very high resolution (as much as 4096 × 4096 pixels). Their main disadvantage is their lack of selective erase capability.

UTILITIES   Special programs, usually provided with the operating system of the computer, that provide the capability to format disks and to do a variety of other chores.

WORD   The number of bits a computer's processor can work with simultaneously. Micro-computers typically have 8 bit (1 byte) words or 16 bit (2 byte) words.

Coded Routines for Apple II+ and IIe

This appendix contains coded routines for the Apple II series computers. Code is presented for each of the routines covered in Chapters 4, 5, 6, 7, 12, and 15. In addition, some routines are presented for Chapter 11. The code in Chapters 8, 9, and 10 is very similar to the corresponding Apple code and is not repeated here.

The code segments are organized by chapter, and each segment is keyed to the page of text where corresponding IBM-PC code appears. Some of the segments are complete runable routines, but many are subroutines that depend on other program segments for variable values and device status.

The Applesoft BASIC code has been written to be as similar to the corresponding IBM-PC BASIC code as possible. Some differences are unavoidable. For example, the graphics statements are different in Applesoft BASIC. Second, the Apple II screen resolution is different (280×192 compared to 640×200). Third, the Apple II does not have programmable functions keys and, except for the IIe, does not have up or down arrow keys for cursor control, so some things must be done differently. The fourth and perhaps most obvious difference is in the variable names used. Applesoft recognizes only the first two characters of a variable name (for example, DX1 and DX2 are both DX to Applesoft) and will not accept variable names that contain a reserved word (for example, the Apple sees the variable name FAC-TOR as FAC TO R), so many of the variable names had to be changed to provide usable code. Fifth, the Apple II and II+ only display 40 characters per line (the IBM-PC displays 80). Sixth, the Apple in graphics mode will not mix graphics and text on the graphics screen (HGR splits the screen into a graphics portion and a text portion). Consequently, it is necessary to plot the characters on the screen (we use a shape table containing shapes for all of the characters).

You should read the material in the indicated chapters including the flow charts and the example routines before studying the routines shown here.

Chapter 4

Example 4-1, Page 84

```
10   REM ** DRAWING PROGRAM **
20   HOME : HGR : VTAB (21)
30   GOSUB 1000
40   HOME : TEXT
50   END
1000   REM  ** SUBROUTINE TO INPUT COORDINATES **
1010   REM  ** OF SIX POINTS **
1020   REM  ** COORDINATES ENTERED FROM KEYBOARD **
1030   REM  ** NO VISIBLE ACTION ON SCREEN **
1040   FOR K = 1 TO 6
1050   INPUT "ENTER COORDINATES OF POINT (X,Y) ";X,Y
1110   GOSUB 1200
1120   NEXT K
1130   HOME : VTAB (22): GET A$: REM CREATES A PAUSE
1190   RETURN
1200   REM  ** SUBROUTINE TO MOVE BEAM TO POINTS **
1230   HCOLOR= 0: HPLOT X,Y
1390   RETURN
```

Example 4-2, Page 87

```
10 REM ** DRAWING PROGRAM **
20   HOME : HGR : VTAB (21)
40   GOSUB 1000: HOME
60   TEXT
70   END
1000   REM  ** SUBROUTINE TO INPUT COORDINATES **
1010   REM  ** OF SIX POINTS FOR PLOTTING **
1020   REM  ** COORDINATES ENTERED FROM KEYBOARD **
1030   REM  ** POINTS PLOTTED ON SCREEN **
1040   FOR K = 1 TO 6
1050   INPUT "ENTER COORDINATES OF POINT (X,Y) ";X,Y
1110   GOSUB 1200
1120   NEXT K
1130   HOME : VTAB (22): GET A$: REM  CREATES A PAUSE
1190   RETURN
1200   REM  ** SUBROUTINE TO MOVE BEAM TO POINTS **
1230   HCOLOR= 7: HPLOT X,Y
1390   RETURN
```

Example 4-3, Page 90

```
10 REM ** DRAWING PROGRAM **
20   HGR : HOME : VTAB (21)
40   GOSUB 2000
50   TEXT
60   END
2000   REM  ** SUBROUTINE TO INPUT COORDINATES **
2010   REM  ** OF SIX POINTS FOR LINE DRAWING **
2020   REM  ** COORDINATES ENTERED FROM KEYBOARD **
2025   REM  ** LINES DRAW ON SCREEN **
2030   INPUT "ENTER COORDINATES OF FIRST POINT (X,Y)";X1,Y1
2040   FOR K = 1 TO 5
2050   INPUT "ENTER COORDINATES OF NEXT POINT (X,Y)";X2,Y2
2110   GOSUB 2200
2115   X1 = X2
2116   Y1 = Y2
2120   NEXT K
2130   HOME : VTAB (22): GET A$: REM  CREATES A PAUSE
2190   RETURN
2200   REM  ** SUBROUTINE TO DRAW LINE BETWEEN POINTS **
2230   HCOLOR= 7: HPLOT X1,Y1: HPLOT  TO X2,Y2
2390   RETURN
```

Example 4-4, Page 92

```
10   REM ** DRAWING PROGRAM **
20   HOME : HGR : VTAB (21)
40   GOSUB 2000
50   TEXT
60   END
2000   REM  ** SUBROUTINE TO INPUT COORDINATES **
2010   REM  ** OF SIX POINTS FOR LINE DRAWING **
2020   REM  ** COORDINATES ENTERED FROM KEYBOARD **
2025   REM  ** LINES DRAWN ON SCREEN **
2030   INPUT "ENTER COORDINATES OF FIRST POINT (X,Y) ";X1,Y1
2035   HCOLOR= 7: HPLOT X1,Y1
2040   FOR K = 1 TO 5
2050   INPUT "ENTER COORDINATES OF NEXT POINT (X,Y) ";X2,Y2
2110   HCOLOR= 7: HPLOT  TO X2,Y2
2120   NEXT K
2130   HOME : VTAB (22): GET A$: REM     CREATES A PAUSE
2190   RETURN
```

Example 4-5, Page 96

```
10   REM ** DRAWING PROGRAM **
20   HOME : HGR : VTAB (21)
40   GOSUB 1000
50   TEXT
60   END
1000   REM  ** SUBROUTINE TO INPUT COORDINATES **
1010   REM  ** OF SIX POINTS FOR PLOTTING **
1020   REM  ** COORDINATES ENTERED FROM KEYBOARD **
1030 X0 = 0:Y0 = 0
1040   FOR K = 1 TO 6
1050   INPUT "ENTER DISTANCE TO POINT (X,Y) ";X,Y
1060 X0 = X0 + X:Y0 = Y0 + Y
1110   HCOLOR= 7: HPLOT X0,Y0
1120   NEXT K
1130   HOME : VTAB (22): GET A$: REM  CREATE PAUSE
1190   RETURN
```

Chapter 5 _____

Example 5-1, Page 105

```
10   REM ** DRAWING PROGRAM **
20   HGR : HOME : VTAB (21)
30   HCOLOR= 7
40   GOSUB 3000
50   TEXT
60   END
3000   REM  ** SUBROUTINE TO INPUT COORDINATES **
3010   REM  ** OF RECTANGLE **
3020   REM  ** COORDINATES ENTERED FROM KEYBOARD **
3030   REM  ** DRAWS A RECTANGLE USING OPPOSITE CORNERS **
3040   REM  ** AS INPUT COORDINATE VALUES **
3050   INPUT "ENTER FIRST CORNER (X1,Y1)";X1,Y1
3060   INPUT "ENTER THIRD CORNER (X3,Y3)";X3,Y3
3080 X2 = X1:Y2 = Y3:X4 = X3:Y4 = Y1
3110   GOSUB 3200
3130   INPUT A$
3190   RETURN
3200   REM  ** SUBROUTINE TO DRAW RECTANGLE **
3220   HPLOT X1,Y1
3230   HPLOT  TO X2,Y2
3240   HPLOT  TO X3,Y3
3250   HPLOT  TO X4,Y4
3260   HPLOT  TO X1,Y1
3390   RETURN
```

Example 5-2, Pages 108–109

```
10   REM ** DRAWING PROGRAM **
20   HGR : HOME : VTAB (21)
30   HCOLOR= 7
40   GOSUB 3800
50   TEXT
60   END
3200   REM  ** SUBROUTINE TO DRAW RECTANGLE **
3210   REM  ** OR PARALLELOGRAM **
3220   HPLOT X1,Y1
3230   HPLOT  TO X2,Y2
3240   HPLOT  TO X3,Y3
3250   HPLOT  TO X4,Y4
3260   HPLOT  TO X1,Y1
3390   RETURN
3800   REM  ** SUBROUTINE TO INPUT COORDINATES **
3810   REM  ** OF PARALLELOGRAM **
3820   REM  ** COORDINATES ENTERED FROM KEYBOARD **
3850   INPUT "ENTER FIRST CORNER (X1,Y1) ";X1,Y1
3860   INPUT "ENTER SECOND CORNER (X2,Y2) ";X2,Y2
3870   INPUT "ENTER THIRD CORNER (X3,Y3) ";X3,Y3
3880   X4 = X3 - (X2 - X1):Y4 = Y3 - (Y2 - Y1)
3910   GOSUB 3200
3930   INPUT A$
3990   RETURN
```

Example 5-3, Page 113

```
10   REM ** DRAWING PROGRAM **
20   HGR : HOME : VTAB (21)
30   HCOLOR= 7
35   FACTR = 1.25
40   GOSUB 4000
50   TEXT
60   END
4000   REM  ** SUBROUTINE TO INPUT COORDINATES **
4010   REM  ** OF POLYGON **
4020   REM  ** COORDINATES ENTERED FROM KEYBOARD **
4040   INPUT "ENTER NUMBER OF SIDES ";N
4050   INPUT "ENTER CENTER (XC,YC) ";XC,YC
4060   INPUT "ENTER STARTING POINT (X1,Y1) ";X1,Y1
4080   RADIUS =SQR (((X1 - XC) / FACTR) ! 2 + (Y1 - YC) ! 2)
4110   GOSUB 4200
4130   INPUT A$
4190   RETURN
4200   REM  ** SUBROUTINE TO DRAW POLYGON **
4210   REM  ** CALCULATE STARTING ANGLE **
4230   GOSUB 5100
4260   HPLOT X1,Y1
4270   DTHETA = 6.2832 / N
4280   FOR K = 1 TO N
4290   X =  COS (START + K * DTHETA) * RADIUS * FACTR + XC
4300   Y =  SIN (START + K * DTHETA) * RADIUS + YC
4320   HPLOT  TO X,Y
4340   NEXT K
4390   RETURN
5100   REM  ** SUBROUTINE TO CALCULATE START ANGLE **
5110   START = 4.7124
5120   IF X1 - XC <  > 0 THEN 5160
5130   IF Y1 > YC THEN START = 1.5708
5150   GOTO 5190
5160   START =  ATN ((Y1 - YC) / ((X1 - XC) / FACTR))
5170   IF X1 - XC < 0 THEN START = START + 3.1416
5190   RETURN
```

Chapter 6

Example 6-1, Page 124

```
10    REM ** DRAWING PROGRAM **
20    HGR : HOME : VTAB (21)
30    HCOLOR= 7
35 FACTR = 1.25
40    GOSUB 4000
50    TEXT
60    END
4000   REM  ** SUBROUTINE TO INPUT COORDINATES OF **
4010   REM  ** CENTER AND STARTING POINT OF CIRCLE **
4020   REM  ** COORDINATES ENTERED FROM KEYBOARD **
4050   INPUT "ENTER CENTER (XC,YC) ";XC,YC
4060   INPUT "ENTER STARTING POINT (X1,Y1) ";X1,Y1
4080 RADIUS =SQR (((X1 - XC) / FACTR) ! 2 + (Y1 - YC) ! 2)
4090 XX = X1:YY = Y1: GOSUB 5100
4100 START = ANGL
4120 ENPT = START + 6.2832
4140 N =  INT (12 + .4 * RADIUS)
4150   GOSUB 4200
4160   INPUT A$
4190   RETURN
4200   REM  ** SUBROUTINE TO DRAW POLYGON OR CIRCLE **
4210   REM
4240 X1 =  COS (START) * RADIUS * FACTR + XC
4250 Y1 =  SIN (START) * RADIUS + YC
4260   HPLOT X1,Y1
4270 DTHETA = (ENPT - START) / N
4280   FOR K = 1 TO N
4290 X =  COS (START + K * DTHETA) * RADIUS * FACTR + XC
4300 Y =  SIN (START + K * DTHETA) * RADIUS + YC
4320   HPLOT  TO X,Y
4340   NEXT K
4390   RETURN
5100   REM  ** SUBROUTINE TO CALCULATE START ANGLE **
5110 ANGL = 4.7124
5120   IF XX - XC <  > 0 THEN 5160
5130   IF YY > YC THEN ANGL = 1.5708
5150   GOTO 5190
5160 ANGL =  ATN ((YY - YC) / ((XX - XC) / FACTR))
5170   IF XX - XC < 0 THEN ANGL = ANGL + 3.1416
5190   RETURN
```

Example 6-2, Pages 127–128

```
10    REM ** DRAWING PROGRAM **
20    HGR : HOME : VTAB (21)
30    HCOLOR= 7
35 FACTR = 1.25
40    GOSUB 4000
50    TEXT
60    END
4000   REM  ** SUBROUTINE TO INPUT COORDINATES OF **
4010   REM  ** CENTER AND STARTING POINT OF CIRCLE **
4020   REM  ** COORDINATES ENTERED FROM KEYBOARD **
4050   INPUT "ENTER CENTER (XC,YC) ";XC,YC
4060   INPUT "ENTER STARTING POINT (X1,Y1) ";X1,Y1
4070   INPUT "ENTER ENDING POINT (X2,Y2) ";X2,Y2
4080 RADIUS =SQR (((X1 - XC) / FACTR) ! 2 + (Y1 - YC) ! 2)
4090 XX = X1:YY = Y1: GOSUB 5100
4100 START = ANGL
4110 XX = X2:YY = Y2: GOSUB 5100
4120   ENPT = ANGL:IF ENPT-START <= 0 THEN ENPT=ENPT+6.2832
4140 N = INT (20 + .4 * RADIUS * (ENPT-START)/6.2832)
```

```
4150   GOSUB 4200
4160   INPUT A$
4190   RETURN
4200   REM  ** SUBROUTINE TO DRAW POLYGON OR CIRCLE **
4210   REM
4240 X1 =  COS (START) * RADIUS * FACTR + XC
4250 Y1 =  SIN (START) * RADIUS + YC
4260   HPLOT X1,Y1
4270 DTHETA = (ENPT - START) / N
4280   FOR K = 1 TO N
4290 X =  COS (START + K * DTHETA) * RADIUS * FACTR + XC
4300 Y =  SIN (START + K * DTHETA) * RADIUS + YC
4320   HPLOT  TO X,Y
4340   NEXT K
4390   RETURN
5100   REM ** SUBROUTINE TO CALCULATE START ANGLE **
5110 ANGL = 4.7124
5120   IF XX - XC <  > 0 THEN 5160
5130   IF YY > YC THEN ANGL = 1.5708
5150   GOTO 5190
5160 ANGL =  ATN ((YY - YC) / ((XX - XC) / FACTR))
5170   IF XX - XC < 0 THEN ANGL = ANGL + 3.1416
5190   RETURN
```

Example 6-3, Pages 135–136

```
10   REM ** DRAWING PROGRAM **
20   HGR : HOME : VTAB (21)
30   HCOLOR= 7
35 FACTR = 1.25
40   GOSUB 4000
50   TEXT
60   END
4000   REM  ** SUBROUTINE TO INPUT COORDINATES OF **
4010   REM  ** CENTER AND STARTING POINT OF CIRCLE **
4020   REM  ** COORDINATES ENTERED FROM KEYBOARD **
4050   INPUT "ENTER STARTING POINT (X1,Y1) ";X1,Y1
4060   INPUT "ENTER NEXT POINT (X2,Y2) ";X2,Y2
4070   INPUT "ENTER ENDING POINT (X3,Y3) ";X3,Y3
4072 X1=X1/FACTR:X2=X2/FACTR:X3=X3/FACTR:GOSUB 6000
4073 X1=X1*FACTR:X2=X2*FACTR:X3=X3*FACTR:XC=XC*FACTR
4074   IF ARCTYP <  > 4 THEN 4080
4075   PRINT CHR$ (7): GOTO 4050
4080 RADIUS =SQR ((((X1 - XC) / FACTR) ! 2 + (Y1 - YC) ! 2)
4090 XX = X1:YY = Y1: GOSUB 5100
4100 START = ANGL
4110 XX = X3:YY = Y3: GOSUB 5100
4120   ENPT=ANGL:IF ENPT-START<= 0 THEN ENPT=ENPT+6.2832
4140 N=INT (20 + .4*RADIUS*(ENPT-START)/6.2832)
4150   GOSUB 4200
4160   INPUT A$
4190   RETURN
4200   REM  ** SUBROUTINE TO DRAW POLYGON OR CIRCLE **
4210   REM
4240 X1 =  COS (START) * RADIUS * FACTR + XC
4250 Y1 =  SIN (START) * RADIUS + YC
4260   HPLOT X1,Y1
4270 DTHETA = (ENPT - START) / N
4280   FOR K = 1 TO N
4290 X =  COS (START + K * DTHETA) * RADIUS * FACTR + XC
4300 Y =  SIN (START + K * DTHETA) * RADIUS + YC
4320   HPLOT  TO X,Y
4340   NEXT K
4350   HPLOT  TO X3,Y3
4390   RETURN
5100   REM  ** SUBROUTINE TO CALCULATE START ANGLE **
```

```
5110  ANGL = 4.7124
5120   IF XX - XC <  > 0 THEN 5160
5130   IF YY > YC THEN ANGL = 1.5708
5150   GOTO 5190
5160  ANGL =  ATN ((YY - YC) / ((XX - XC) / FACTR))
5170   IF XX - XC < 0 THEN ANGL = ANGL + 3.1416
5190   RETURN
6000   REM  ** SUBROUTINE TO CALCULATE CENTER **
6010   REM  ** OF 3-POINT ARC **
6020   GOSUB 6400
6025  M1 = 0:M2 = 0
6030   ON ARCTYP GOTO 6040,6110,6160,6390
6040   IF X2-X1 <> 0 THEN M1 = -(1/((Y2-Y1)/(X2-X1)))
6050   IF X3-X2 <> 0 THEN M2 = -(1/((Y3-Y2)/(X3-X2)))
6060  B1 = (Y1 + Y2) / 2 - M1 * ((X1 + X2) / 2)
6070  B2 = (Y2 + Y3) / 2 - M2 * ((X2 + X3) / 2)
6080  XC = (B2 - B1) / (M1 - M2)
6090  YC = M1 * XC + B1
6100   GOTO 6390
6110   IF X3-X2 <> 0 THEN M2 = -(1/((Y3-Y2)/(X3-X2)))
6120  B2 = (Y2 + Y3) / 2 - M2 * ((X2 + X3) / 2)
6130  XC = (X1 + X2) / 2
6135  YC = M2 * XC + B2
6150   GOTO 6390
6160   IF X2-X1 <> 0 THEN M1 = -(1/((Y2-Y1)/(X2-X1)))
6170  B1 = (Y1 + Y2) / 2 - M1 * ((X1 + X2) / 2)
6180  XC = (X2 + X3) / 2
6190  YC = M1 * XC + B1
6390   RETURN
6400   REM  ** SUBROUTINE TO DETERMINE WHETHER **
6405   REM  ** POINTS CAN DEFINE AN ARC **
6410  ARCTYP = 1
6420   REM  ** CHECK FOR THREE DIFFERENT POINTS **
6430   IF NOT ((Y3-Y2 = 0 AND X3-X2 = 0) OR (Y2-Y1 = 0 AND
            X2-X1 = 0) OR (Y3-Y1 = 0 AND
            X3-X1 = 0)) THEN 6460
6440  ARCTYP = 4: GOTO 6540
6450   REM  ** NEXT CHECK FOR TWO VERTICAL LINES **
6460   IF  NOT (Y3 - Y2 = 0 AND Y2 - Y1 = 0) THEN 6490
6470  ARCTYP = 4: GOTO 6540
6480   REM  ** CHECK FOR ONE VERTICAL LINE **
6490   IF Y2 - Y1 = 0 THEN ARCTYP = 2
6500   IF Y3 - Y2 = 0 THEN ARCTYP = 3
6510   IF ARCTYP = 2 OR ARCTYP = 3 THEN 6540
6520   REM  ** CHECK FOR PARALLEL LINES **
6525   IF X3 - X2 = 0 AND X2 - X1 = 0 THEN 6535
6528   IF X3 - X2 = 0 OR X2 - X1 = 0 THEN 6540
6530   IF (Y3-Y2)/(X3-X2) <> ((Y2-Y1)/(X2-X1)) THEN 6540
6535  ARCTYP = 4
6540   RETURN
```

Example 6-4, Pages 138–139

```
10   REM ** DRAWING PROGRAM **
20   HGR : HOME : VTAB (21)
30   HCOLOR= 7
35   FACTR = 1.25
40   GOSUB 4000
50   TEXT
60   END
4000   REM  ** SUBROUTINE TO INPUT COORDINATES OF **
4010   REM  ** CENTER AND STARTING POINT OF CIRCLE **
4020   REM  ** COORDINATES ENTERED FROM KEYBOARD **
4050   INPUT "ENTER CENTER (XC,YC) ";XC,YC
4060   INPUT "ENTER STARTING POINT (X1,Y1) ";X1,Y1
```

```
4080 RADIUS =SQR (((X1-XC)/FACTR) ! 2 + (Y1-YC) ! 2)
4090 XX = X1:YY = Y1: GOSUB 5100
4100 START = ANGL
4120 ENPT = START + 6.2832
4140 N =  INT (12 + .4 * RADIUS)
4150  GOSUB 4200
4160  INPUT A$
4190  RETURN
4200  REM  ** SUBROUTINE TO DRAW POLYGON OR CIRCLE **
4210  REM
4240 X1 =  COS (START) * RADIUS * FACTR + XC
4250 Y1 =  SIN (START) * RADIUS + YC
4260  HPLOT X1,Y1
4265 XN = (X1 - XC) / FACTR + XC:YN % Y1
4270 DTHETA = (ENPT - START) / N
4272 CODTH =  COS (DTHETA)
4274 SIDTH =  SIN (DTHETA)
4280  FOR K = 1 TO N
4290 X = XC + (XN - XC) * CODTH - (YN - YC) * SIDTH
4300 Y = YC + (XN - XC) * SIDTH + (YN - YC) * CODTH
4310 XD = (X - XC) * FACTR + XC:YD = Y
4320  HPLOT  TO XD,YD
4330 XN = X:YN = Y
4340  NEXT K
4390  RETURN
5100  REM  ** SUBROUTINE TO CALCULATE START ANGLE **
5110 ANGL = 4.7124
5120  IF XX - XC < > 0 THEN 5160
5130  IF YY > YC THEN ANGL = 1.5708
5150  GOTO 5190
5160 ANGL =  ATN ((YY - YC) / ((XX - XC) / FACTR))
5170  IF XX - XC < 0 THEN ANGL = ANGL + 3.1416
5190  RETURN
```

Example 6-5, Page 141

```
10   REM ** DRAWING PROGRAM **
15   HOME : HGR
20   HCOLOR= 7
30   GOSUB 11000
40   VTAB (22): PRINT "PRESS ANY KEY TO CONTINUE";
50   GET A$
60   HOME : TEXT
70   END
11000  REM  ** SINEWAVE DRAWING SUBROUTINE **
11010  REM  ** ACCESSED FROM A MAIN PROGRAM **
11020  REM  ** SYSTEM ALREADY IN GRAPHICS MODE **
11030  HPLOT 20,40: HPLOT  TO 20,120
11040  HPLOT 20,80: HPLOT  TO 275,80
11050  HPLOT 20,80
11060  FOR X = 0 TO 12.5664 STEP .2617
11070  Y =  SIN (X)
11080  YD = - 40 * Y + 80
11090  XD = 20 * X + 20
11100  HPLOT  TO XD,YD
11110  NEXT X
11130  RETURN
```

Chapter 7 _____

Example 7-1, Page 159

```
1200   REM ** SUBROUTINE TO ENTER DATA FOR PIE CHART **
1205   REM ** ARRAYS DIMENSIONED IN MAIN ROUTINE **
1210   PRINT : PRINT "ENTER DATA FOR PIE CHART":PRINT:
           ENTRIES = 0:TTAL = 0
1220   FOR K = 1 TO 25
1230    INPUT  "ENTER VALUE FOR ELEMENT (0 IF FINISHED) >";
           VLUE(K)
1240    IF VLUE(K) = 0 THEN 1290
1250    INPUT "ENTER NAME OF ELEMENT > ";NAM$(K)
1260   TTAL = TTAL + VLUE(K):ENTRIES = ENTRIES + 1
1270    NEXT K
1280    REM
1290    RETURN
```

Example 7-2, Page 160

```
1300   REM ** SUBROUTINE TO ENTER CHART NAMES **
1302   REM ** FOR PIE CHART **
1304   REM ** ARRAY DIMENISIONED IN MAIN ROUTINE **
1310   INPUT "ENTER DESIRED CHART NAME (TOP OF CHART) >";
           CHART$(1)
1320    PRINT
1330    INPUT "ENTER DESIRED CHART NAME (BOTTOM OF CHART) >";
           CHART$(2)
1340    RETURN
```

Example 7-3, Page 163

```
100   REM   ** SUBROUTINE TO SUBDIVIDE PIE **
110   REM   ** USES DATA FROM DATA ENTRY ROUTINE **
115 XC = 139:YC = HEIGHT
120   HPLOT XC,YC: HPLOT   TO XC + SIZE * FACTR,YC
130   PIESM = 0
140   FOR K = 1 TO ENTRIES
150   ANGL(K) = ((PIESM + VLUE(K)) / TTAL) * 6.2832
160   X =   COS (ANGL(K)) * SIZE * FACTR + XC
170   Y =   SIN (ANGL(K)) * SIZE + YC
180   HPLOT 139,HEIGHT: HPLOT   TO X,Y
185 PIESUM = PIESUM + VLUE(K)
190   NEXT K
200   RETURN
```

Example 7-4, Page 164

```
210   REM ** SUBROUTINE TO LABEL SECTIONS OF PIE **
212   REM ** CALLS A CHARACTER PLOTTING ROUTINE TO **
214   REM ** CREATE LABEL NAMES **
215 PIESUM = 0
220   FOR K = 1 TO ENTRIES
225 RADIUS = SIZE
230 ANGL(K) = ((PIESM + VLUE(K) / 2) / TTAL) * 6.2832
240   XS =   COS (ANGL(K)) * .75 * RADIUS * FACTR + XC
250   X =   COS (ANGL(K)) * 1.1 * RADIUS * FACTR + XC
260   YS =   SIN (ANGL(K)) * .75 * RADIUS + YC
270   Y =   SIN (ANGL(K)) * 1.1 * RADIUS + YC
280   HPLOT XS,YS: HPLOT   TO X,Y
282   REM   ** PRINT LABEL NAME
283   GOSUB 5500
284   GOSUB 900
285 PIESUM = PIESUM + VLUE(K)
290   NEXT K
300   RETURN
```

```
5500  REM ** SUBROUTINE TO PRINT LABELS FOR **
5502  REM ** PIE SECTIONS **
5504  REM ** USES CHARACTERS FROM A SHAPE TABLE **
5506  REM ** (NOT SHOWN) TO CREATE LABELS **
5510  REM ** WITH XDRAW **
5520  XLOC = X + 10
5530  YLOC = Y + 4
5535  GOSUB 5620
5540  FOR J = 1 TO  LEN (NAM$(K))
5545  TO =  ASC ( MID$ (NAM$(K),J,1)) - 32
5546  IF TO < 1 OR TO > 63 THEN 5555
5550  XDRAW TO AT XLOC + J * 7 - 7,YLOC
5555  NEXT J
5560  RETURN
```

Example 7-5, Page 165

```
5600  REM ** SUBROUTINE TO CHANGE LOCATION **
5610  REM ** OF STARTING POINT OF LABEL **
5620  IF ANGL(K) < 1.58 OR ANGL(K) >4.7 THEN GOTO 5640
5630  XLOC = XLOC - 7 * ( LEN (NAM$(K)) + 3)
5640  RETURN
```

Example 7-6, Page 166

```
310  REM ** SUBROUTINE TO PRINT PIE CHART TITLES **
320  REM ** XDRAWS CHARACTERS FROM SHAPE TABLE **
330  XSPOT =  INT (139 - 3.5 *  LEN (CHART$(1)))
335  FOR K = 1 TO  LEN (CHART$(1))
336  TO =  ASC ( MID$ (CHART$(1),K,1)) - 32
337  IF TO < 1 OR TO > 63 THEN 345
340  XDRAW TO AT XSPOT + K * 7 - 7,16
345  NEXT K
360  XSPOT =  INT (139 - 3.5 *  LEN (CHART$(2)))
365  FOR K = 1 TO  LEN (CHART$(2))
366  TO =  ASC ( MID$ (CHART$(2),K,1)) - 32
367  IF TO < 1 OR TO > 63 THEN 375
370  XDRAW TO AT XSPOT + K * 7 - 7,180
375  NEXT K
390  RETURN
```

Example 7-7, Page 167

```
400  REM ** SUBROUTINE TO DRAW AXES FOR LINE CHART **
410  REM
420  XRGIN = 75:YRGIN = 191 - 70
430  HPLOT XRGIN,YRGIN
440  HPLOT  TO 279,YRGIN
450  HPLOT XRGIN,YRGIN
460  HPLOT  TO XRGIN,0
470  RETURN
```

Example 7-8, Page 169

```
500  REM ** SUBROUTINE TO LABEL THE ORDINATE **
505  REM ** XDRAWS CHARACTERS FROM SHAPE TABLE **
510  SCALE= 1
520  CNTR =  INT ((YRGIN - 0) / 2)
530  BGIN = CNTR -  INT (4 *  LEN (LABL$)) + 4
535  FOR K = 1 TO  LEN (LABL$)
540  TO =  ASC ( MID$ (LABL$,K,1)) - 32
550  XDRAW TO AT 15,BGIN + 8 * K
560  NEXT K
565  SCALE= 280 / 192: GET A$
566  GOTO 600
570  RETURN
```

Example 7-9, Page 169

```
600   REM *** SUBROUTINE TO CALCULATE X INTERVAL ***
610  XNT =  INT (270 - XRGIN) / 13
615   GOTO 630
620   RETURN
```

Example 7-10, Page 170

```
630   REM ** SUBROUTINE TO PLACE TICK MARKS ON ABSCISSA **
650   FOR K = 1 TO 12
655  NX = XRGIN + K * XNT
660   HPLOT NX,YRGIN + 4
670   HPLOT  TO NX,YRGIN - 4
680   NEXT K
685   GOTO 800
690   RETURN
```

Example 7-11, Page 170

```
700   REM ** SUBROUTINE TO CONVERT DATA "Y" VALUES **
710   REM ** TO SCREEN COORDINATE "Y" VALUES **
720  YSCREN = YRGIN + (10 - YRGIN) / 192 * YDTA
730   RETURN
```

Example 7-12, Page 172

```
800   REM ** SUBROUTINE TO PLOT POINTS ON CHART **
810   FOR K = 1 TO ENTRIES
820  XDTA = ELNAME(K): GOSUB 750: REM  XSCALE ROUTINE
830  YDTA = VLUE(K): GOSUB 700: REM    YSCALE ROUTINE
840   HPLOT XSCREN,YSCREN
850   GOSUB 900
860   NEXT K
870   RETURN
900   REM ** SUBROUTINE TO DRAW A CROSS AT BEAM POS **
902   REM ** BEAM POSITION (X0,Y0) SPECIFIED BY **
904   REM ** CALLING ROUTINE **
910   X0 = XSCREN:Y0 = YSCREN
920   HPLOT X0 - 2,Y0: HPLOT  TO X0 + 2,Y0
930   HPLOT X0,Y0 - 2: HPLOT  TO X0,Y0 + 2
940   REM
950   RETURN
```

Example 7-13, Page 177

```
3000   REM   ** SUBROUTINE TO DELETE A DATA PAIR **
3010   FOR K = I + 1 TO ENTRIES
3020  NAM$(K - 1) = NAM$(K)
3030  VLUE(K - 1) = VLUE(K)
3040   NEXT K
3050  ENTRIES = ENTRIES - 1
3060   RETURN
```

Example 7-14, Page 177

```
3200   REM   ** SUBROUTINE TO INSERT A DATA PAIR **
3210   FOR K = ENTRIES TO I STEP  - 1
3220  NAM$(K + 1) = NAM$(K)
3230  VLUE(K + 1) = VLUE(K)
3240   NEXT K
3242  NAM$(I) = NUNAM$
3244  VLUE(I) = NUVLUE
3250  ENTRIES = ENTRIES + 1
3260   RETURN
```

Example 7-15, Page 178

```
3400  REM   ** SUBROUTINE TO REPLACE A TITLE LINE **
3410  REM   **        WITH A NEW ONE           **
3420  INPUT "ENTER NUMBER OF TITLE LINE TO REPLACE";N
3430  INPUT "ENTER NEW TITLE LINE";T$(N)
3440  RETURN
```

Chapter 11

Example 11-1, Page 256

```
7000  REM ** THIS CODE POKES A SHAPE TABLE INTO **
7002  REM ** MEMORY TO CREATE A GRAPHICS CURSOR.**
7004  REM ** THE CURSOR CAN THEN BE DISPLAYED   **
7006  REM ** USING "XDRAW 1 AT X,Y" **
7010  FOR K=7676 TO 7697
7020  READ RN
7030  POKE K,RN
7040  NEXT K
7045  REM ** TELL SYSTEM WHERE SHAPE TABLE IS LOCATED **
7050  POKE 232,252:POKE 233,29
7060  DATA 1,0,4,0,63,63,191,146,73,73,36,36,36,36
7070  DATA 76,73,146,18,63,63,7,0
7080  RETURN
```

Example 11-2, Page 259

```
7200  REM ** GRAPHICS CURSOR CONTROL ROUTINE **
7205  REM ** ASSUMES HGR2:HCOLOR=7:SCALE=1 ARE ALL **
7210  REM ** SET BY CALLING ROUTINE **
7220  REM ** PROVIDES ALTERNATE KEYS FOR APPLES WITHOUT **
7225  REM ** UP-ARROW AND DOWN-ARROW KEYS **
7230  GOSUB 7420
7240  GET A$:A% =  ASC (A$)
7242  REM ** TAB KEY (CTRL-I) TOGGLES SPEED CHANGE **
7245  IF A% = 9 THEN  GOSUB 7500: GOTO 7240
7248  REM ** ESC KEY ERASES CURSOR AND EXITS (RETURNS) **
7250  IF A% = 27 THEN  GOSUB 7420: RETURN
7255  IF A% > 32 AND A% <  > 59 THEN  GOTO 7240
7260  GOSUB 7420:REM ** ERASES CURSOR **
7262  REM ** SPACE BAR RETURNS TO CALLING ROUTINE **
7265  IF A% = 32 THEN  RETURN
7267  REM ** RIGHT-ARROW (OR CTRL-U) MOVES CURSOR RIGHT **
7270  IF A% = 21 AND XG% <= 279 - DX THEN XG% = XG% + DX
7275  REM ** LEFT-ARROW (OR CTRL-H) MOVES CURSOR LEFT **
7280  IF A% = 8 AND XG% >  = DX THEN XG% = XG% - DX
7284  REM ** DOWN-ARROW (OR CTRL-J) OR SEMICOLON (ASCII 59) **
7286  REM ** MOVES CURSOR DOWN **
7290  IF (A% = 10 OR A% = 59) AND YG% <= 183 - DY THEN
      YG% = YG% + DY
7294  REM ** UP-ARROW (OR CTRL-K) OR RETURN KEY (ASCII 13) **
7296  REM ** MOVES CURSOR UP **
7300  IF (A% = 11 OR A% = 13) AND YG% >= DY THEN
      YG% = YG% - DY
7310  GOTO 7230
7420  XDRAW 1 AT XG%,YG%: RETURN
7500  IF FLAG < 2 THEN FLAG = FLAG + 1:DX = 5 * FLAG:
      DY = 4 * FLAG: RETURN
7510 FLAG = 0:DX = 1:DY = 1: RETURN
7520  REM
```

Example 11-3, Page 274

```
12000   REM ** SCREEN DUMP SUBROUTINE **
12002   REM ** PRINTS A SMALL PICTURE ON **
12004   REM ** A NEC PC-8023A-C PRINTER **
12006   REM ** A LARGER PICTURE WOULD REQUIRE **
12008   REM ** MAPPING TO A NEW SET OF VALUES **
12010 SE = 16384 + 7168 + 896 + 80
12020   PRINT : PRINT
12065   PRINT  CHR$ (4);"PR#1"
12070   PRINT  CHR$ (27);"T";"14";
12100   REM
12110   REM  ** DUMP SCREEN TO PRINTER **
12130   FOR J = 0 TO 39
12140   PRINT  CHR$ (27); CHR$ (83);"0192";
12150   FOR K = 0 TO 2
12155 SF = SE - 40 * K
12160   FOR L = 0 TO 7
12165   FOR  M = SF + J - 128 * L TO SF + J - 128 * L - 7168
            STEP - 1024
12170 D =  PEEK (M)
12173   IF D = 13 THEN D = 12
12174   IF D = 9 THEN D = 8
12180   PRINT  CHR$ (D);
12190   NEXT M
12200   NEXT L
12210   NEXT K
12220   PRINT
12230   NEXT J
12240   PRINT  CHR$ (12)
12250   PRINT  CHR$ (4);"PR#0"
12260   REM  ** BOTTOM OF LOOP **
12280   RETURN
```

Chapter 12

Example 12-1, Page 290

```
21000   REM  ** THIS SUBROUTINE READS AND STORES DATA **
21012   REM  ** FOR USE IN THE THREE DIMENSIONAL **
21014   REM  ** DISPLAY ROUTINES **
21016 NDTA = 0
21018   FOR J = 1 TO 50
21020   READ X(J),Y(J),Z(J),P(J)
21021   IF X(J) = 999 GOTO 21026
21022 NDTA = NDTA + 1
21024   NEXT J
21026   RETURN
```

Example 12-2, Page 290

```
22100   DATA  9
22102   DATA  0,0,0
22104   DATA  0,2,0
22106   DATA  4,2,0
22108   DATA  4,0,0
22110   DATA  4,0,3
22112   DATA  0,0,3
22114   DATA  0,2,3
22116   DATA  1,2,3
22118   DATA  4,2,1
```

Example 12-3, Page 292

```
22148   DATA   7
22150   DATA   5
22152   DATA   1,2,3,4,1,0
22154   DATA   5
22156   DATA   1,4,5,6,1,0
22158   DATA   5
22160   DATA   1,6,7,2,2,0
22162   DATA   5
22164   DATA   3,9,5,4,3,0
22166   DATA   5
22168   DATA   5,8,7,6,5,0
22170   DATA   6
22172   DATA   2,7,8,9,3,2
22174   DATA   4
22176   DATA   5,9,8,5,0,0
```

Example 12-4, Page 293

```
22000   REM ** THIS SUBROUTINE READS IN THE INFORMATION **
22002   REM ** FOR THE VERTICES TO BE USED WITH THE FACE **
22004   REM ** METHOD. VERT-VERTEX COORD.,NUMVERT-NO. **
22008   DIM VERT(20,3)
22010   READ NUMVERT
22012   FOR K = 1 TO NUMVERT
22014   READ VERT(K,1),VERT(K,2),VERT(K,3)
22016   NEXT K
22018   RETURN
22050   REM ** THIS SUBROUTINE READS IN THE INFORMATION **
22052   REM ** FOR THE FACES TO BE USED WITH THE FACE **
22054   REM ** METHOD. NMFACE-FACE NUMBER,FCVERT-NO. **
22056   REM ** VERTICES/FACE, VN-VERTEX NUMBER **
22058   DIM FCVERT(10),VN(20,10)
22060   READ NMFACE
22062   FOR M = 1 TO NMFACE
22064   READ FCVERT(M)
22066   READ VN(M,1),VN(M,2),VN(M,3),VN(M,4),
            VN(M,5),VN(M,6)
22068   NEXT M
22070   RETURN
```

Example 12-5, Page 297

```
23100   REM ** THIS IS THE FRONT VIEW SUBROUTINE **
23102   REM ** IT REQUIRES THE READ/STORE SUBROUTINE **
23104   REM ** FOR THE DATA AND NUMBER OF COORDINATE **
23106   REM ** POINTS **
23108   SF = 30:X1TRAN = 20:Y1TRAN = 180
23110   FOR J = 1 TO NDTA
23112   XPLT = X(J) * 1.25 * SF + X1TRAN
23114   YPLT =  - Y(J) * SF + Y1TRAN
23116   IF (P(J) = 3) THEN  HPLOT XPLT,YPLT: GOTO 23120
23117   IF J = 1 THEN   HPLOT XPLT,YPLT: GOTO 23120
23118   HPLOT   TO XPLT,YPLT
23120   NEXT J
23122   RETURN
```

Example 12-6, Page 298

```
24000   REM ** THE ORTHOGRAPHIC PLOTTING ROUTINES USING **
24002   REM ** THE FACE METHOD **
24100   REM ** THE FRONT VIEW **
24104 X1TRAN = 20
24106 Y1TRAN = 180
24108   FOR K = 1 TO NMFACE
24110 LMAX = FCVERT(K)
24112   FOR L = 1 TO LMAX
24114 V = VN(K,L)
24116 XPLT = SF * VERT(V,1) + X1TRAN
24118 YPLT = - SF / 1.25 * VERT(V,2) + Y1TRAN
24120   IF (L = 3) THEN  HPLOT XPLT,YPLT
24122   HPLOT   TO XPLT,YPLT
24124   NEXT L
24126   NEXT K
24128   RETURN
```

Example 12-7, Page 301

```
25150   REM ** THIS IS THE OBLIQUE SUBROUTINE **
25152   REM ** IT REQUIRES THE READ/STORE SUBROUTINE **
25154   REM ** AND THE VALUES FOR THE SCALE FACTOR, **
25156   REM ** SF AND ZSF, AND THE Z AXIS ANGLE. **
25157   ZSF = 0.5:ALPHA = 3.1416 / 6:X1TRAN = 150:
        Y1TRAN = 100
25158 CA =   COS (ALPHA)
25160   SA =   SIN (ALPHA)
25162   FOR J = 1 TO NDTA
25164 XPLT = (X(J) - Z(J) * ZSF * CA) * SF + X1TRAN
25166 YPLT = - (Y(J) - Z(J) * ZSF * SA) * SF + Y1TRAN
25168   IF P(J) = 3 THEN  HPLOT XPLT,YPLT: GOTO 25170
25169 HPLOT   TO XPLT,YPLT
25170   NEXT J
25178   RETURN
```

Chapter 15

Example 15-1, Page 369

```
1   REM ** STARTUP ROUTINE FOR MENU-DRIVEN DRAWING **
2   REM ** PROGRAM. MENUS AND OTHER MESSAGES COULD **
3   REM ** BE IN A DISK FILE AND READ AS NEEDED. **
10   DIM PNTS%(100,2),LINES%(100,4),RCTNGLS%(20,8),
        CIRCLES%(50,7)
11   DIM TXTSTR%(110,3),P%(2),L%(4),R%(10),C%(7),
        T%(3),MESS$(10)
12   MESS$(1) = "PT=1 LN=2 RCT=3 POL=4 CIR=5 ARC=6
        NXT=7 END=8"
14   MESS$(2) = "PLT=1 GRD=2 TX=3 RD=4 SAV=5 RET=6
        NEX=7 END=8"
15   MESS$(3) = "CHOOSE   (E)XIT   (S)TART NEW DWG
        (A)BORT CMMD"
16 MESS$(4) = "LINES - ENTER START, THEN END"
20   HCOLOR= 7: ROT= 0: SCALE= 1.5:DX = 1:DY = 1
30 XT% = 149:YT% = 79
45   GOSUB 29000
70   HGR2 : GOSUB 100
80   TEXT
90   END
```

Example 15-2, Page 371

```
29000   REM   ** INSTRUCTIONS SUBROUTINE **
29005   REM   ** READS SEQUENTIAL TEXT FILE (NOT SHOWN) **
29010   HOME: TEXT: PRINT "DO YOU   WANT   INSTRUCTIONS
           Y/N": GET A$
29020   N =  ASC (A$): IF N > = 97 THEN N = N - 32
29025   IF A$ = "Y" THEN  HOME : GOTO 29050
29030   IF A$ = "N" THEN  HOME : GOTO 29140
29035   GOTO 29020
29040   REM   ** READ FROM INSTRUCTION FILE **
29050   D$ =  CHR$ (4): PRINT D$;"OPEN INSTR.TXT"
29055   HOME
29060   PRINT D$;"READ INSTR.TXT"
29070   FOR K = 1 TO 1000
29090   INPUT V$
29100   IF V$ = "PAGE" THEN  GOSUB 29160: GOTO 29120
29105   IF V$ = "END" THEN  GOSUB 29160: GOTO 29140
29110   PRINT V$
29120   NEXT
29130   GOSUB 29160
29135   GOTO 29010
29140   PRINT D$;"CLOSE INSTR.TXT"
29150   HOME : RETURN
29160   REM   ** PAGING ROUTINE **
29170   FOR L5 = 1 TO 10000: NEXT:REM * CREATES PAUSE *
29180   HOME : RETURN
```

Example 15-3, Page 373

```
100   REM   **** MENU SUBROUTINE ********
110   HOME
120   MN = 1: GOSUB 950
140   GET A$:A% =  ASC (A$) - 48
145   IF A% < 1 OR A% > 8 THEN  GOTO 140
150   GOSUB 950
160   ON A% GOTO 250,300,350,400,450,500,180,900
180   MN = 2: GOSUB 950
190   GET A$:A% =  ASC (A$) - 48
200   IF A% < 1 OR A% > 8 THEN  GOTO 190
205   IF A% < 1 OR A% > 8 THEN  GOTO 190
210   GOSUB 950
220   ON A% GOTO 600,700,750,550,800,850,120,900
250   GOTO 120
300   GOSUB 2000:REM LINE INPUT ROUTINE
310   GOTO 120
350   GOSUB 3000:REM RECTANGLE INPUT ROUTINE
360   GOTO 120
400   GOSUB 4600:REM POLYGON INPUT ROUTINE
410   GOTO 120
450   GOSUB 4000:REM CIRCLE INPUT ROUTINE
460   GOTO 120
500   GOSUB 4800:REM ARC INPUT ROUTINE
510   GOTO 120
550   GOSUB 6000:REM REDISPLAY ROUTINE
560   GOTO 120
600   GOSUB 12000:REM PRINT-PLOT ROUTINE
610   GOTO 120
700   GOSUB 10800:REM DOT GRID ROUTINE
710   GOTO 120
750   GOSUB 8000:REM TEXT INPUT ROUTINE
760   GOTO 120
800   GOSUB 10200:REM DISK STORAGE ROUTINE
810   GOTO 120
850   GOSUB 10400:REM DISK RETRIEVAL ROUTINE
860   GOTO 120
900   RETURN:REM RETURNS TO MAIN MODULE TO END PROGRAM
```

```
950    REM ***** DISPLAY MESSAGE SUBROUTINE ****
951    REM ** DRAWS LETTERS FROM SHAPE TABLE (NOT SHOWN) **
955    FOR K = 1 TO  LEN (MESS$(MN))
960    XT = 6 * K - 5:TT =  ASC ( MID$ (MESS$(MN),K,1)) - 32
965    IF TT > 0 THEN  XDRAW TT AT XT,191
970    NEXT K
980    RETURN
```

Example 15-4, Page 377

```
2000   REM   ** INPUT ROUTINE FOR LINES **
2005   REM   ** NEXT LINE DISPLAYS PROMPT **
2010   MN = 4: GOSUB 950
2020   IK$ = "":ADDDL = 1:NTFD = 0:SOLDSH = 1:LPEN = 7
2030   REM ** CALL CURSOR ROUTINE (SEE UNDER CHAP 7) **
2032   GOSUB 7200
2033   IF A% = 27 THEN  GOTO 2090
2040   L%(1) = XG%:L%(2) = YG%
2042   HCOLOR= LPEN: HPLOT L%(1),L%(2)
2045   GOSUB 7200
2046   IF A% = 27 THEN  GOTO 2090
2047   L%(3) = XG%:L%(4) = YG%
2050   IF ADDDL = 1 THEN  GOSUB 2400
2060   IF ADDDL = 0 THEN  GOSUB 2600
2070   IF NTFD = 0 THEN  GOSUB 2200
2075   NTFD = 0: GOTO 2032
2080   REM
2090   GOSUB 950: RETURN
```

Example 15-5, Page 377

```
2200   REM   ** LINE DRAWING SUBROUTINE **
2210   HCOLOR= 7 * ADDDL
2215   GOSUB 11000: GOTO 2260
2220   HPLOT L%(1),L%(2): HPLOT  TO L%(3),L%(4)
2225   L%(0) = 0
2230   IF L%(0) = 0 THEN  GOSUB 11000: GOTO 2260
2260   RETURN
```

Example 15-6, Page 377

```
2400   REM   *** LINE DATA STORAGE SUBROUTINE ***
2405   IF LINES%(0,1) = 100 THEN PRINT CHR$(7);:
         GOTO 2460
2410   LINES%(0,1) = LINES%(0,1) + 1
2415   L%(0) = SOLDSH
2420   FOR J = 0 TO 4
2430   LINES%(LINES%(0,1),J) = L%(J)
2440   NEXT J
2450   REM
2460   RETURN
```

Example 15-7, Pages 377–378

```
2600   REM   ** RETRIEVE LINE FOR DELETE **
2610   REM
2620   IF LINES%(0,1) = 0 THEN 2690
2630   FOR I = 1 TO LINES%(0,1)
2640   IF ABS(LINES%(I,1) - L%(1)) <6 AND ABS(LINES%(I,2) -
         L%(2)) <3 AND  ABS (LINES%(I,3) - L%(3)) <6 AND
         ABS (LINES%(I,4) - L%(4)) <3 THEN ROW = I:
         NTFD  = 0:GOTO 2700
2650   IF ABS(LINES%(I,1) - L%(3)) <6 AND ABS(LINES%(I,2) -
         L%(4)) <3 AND  ABS (LINES%(I,3) - L%(1)) <6 AND
         ABS  (LINES%(I,4) - L%(2)) < 3 THEN ROW = I:
         NTFD = 0:GOTO 2700
2680   NEXT I
```

```
2690 NTFD = 1: PRINT  CHR$ (7);: GOTO 2750
2700  FOR J = 0 TO 4:L%(J) = LINES%(ROW,J): NEXT J
2710  FOR J = 0 TO 4:LINES%(ROW,J) = LINES%(LINES%(0,1),J):
       NEXT J
2720 LINES%(0,1) = LINES%(0,1) - 1
2730  REM
2750  RETURN
```

Example 15-8, Page 378

```
11000  REM  ** DASH LINE SUBROUTINE **
11030 R = SQR (((L%(3) - L%(1)) / 1.25) !  2 + (L%(4)  -
        L%(2)) ! 2)
11040 SNTHA = (L%(4) - L%(2)) / R
11050 CSTHA = (L%(3) - L%(1)) / 1.25 / R
11070 X9 = L%(1):Y9 = L%(2)
11080  FOR K = 4 TO R STEP 4
11090 X = X9 + 2.5 * CSTHA:Y = Y9 + 2 * SNTHA
11100  HPLOT X9,Y9: HPLOT  TO X,Y
11110 X9 = X + 2.5 * CSTHA:Y9 = Y + 2 * SNTHA
11130  NEXT K
11140  HPLOT  TO L%(3),L%(4)
11150  RETURN
```

Coded Routines for Tektronix Series 4050

This appendix contains coded routines for Tektronix series 4050 microcomputers. Code is presented for each of the routines covered in Chapters 4, 5, and 6. These are the basic graphics routines that are used throughout the book to create drawings, charts, and graphs. The techniques used in these routines to print text on the screen for data entry can be applied to labeling the charts of Chapter 7 or presenting the menus of Chapter 15. The 4050s have a built in graphics cursor, a system screen dump for hard copy, and a built-in window and viewport capability, so the routines we created in Chapter 10 and 11 for the IBM are not required. The code in Chapters 8 and 9 is very similar to the corresponding Tektronix code and is not repeated here. Students having difficulty writing code for decision making (IF–THEN) are referred to the code in the example for three-point arcs as a guide.

The code segments are organized by chapter, and each segment is keyed to the page of text where corresponding IBM-PC code appears. The segments are self-contained runable routines but are not intended to be complete programs.

The Tektronix BASIC code has been written to be as similar to the corresponding IBM-PC BASIC code as possible. Some differences are unavoidable. For example, the graphics statements are different in Tektronix BASIC. Second, the Tektronix screen resolution is much higher, and the window and viewport are user programmable. Third, the Tektronix does not have selective erase capability (the entire screen must be erased). The fourth, and perhaps most obvious, difference is in the language features available: Tektronix BASIC allows a numeric variable name to have only one letter plus one digit; a character variable name may have only one letter (no digit); and only one statement is allowed per line. Finally, the only form of IF statement supported is IF–GOTO. These features are similar to those found in most minimal BASICs.

You should read the material in the indicated chapters including the flow charts and the example routines before studying the routines shown here.

Chapter 4

Example 4-1, Page 84

```
10 REM ** DRAWING PROGRAM **
20 INIT
30 PAGE
40 GOSUB 1000
50 END
1000 REM ** SUBROUTINE TO INPUT COORDINATES **
1010 REM ** OF SIX POINTS **
1020 REM ** COORDINATES ENTERED FROM KEYBOARD **
1030 REM ** NO VISIBLE ACTION ON SCREEN **
1040 FOR K=1 TO 6
1045 MOVE 1,90-6*K
1050 PRINT "ENTER COORDINATES OF POINT (X,Y) "
1060 INPUT X,Y
1110 GOSUB 1200
1120 NEXT K
1130 REM ** DUMMY READ STATEMENT TO CREATE PAUSE **
1140 INPUT D$
1150 PAGE
1190 RETURN
1200 REM ** SUBROUTINE TO MOVE BEAM TO POINTS **
1230 MOVE X,Y
1390 RETURN
```

Example 4-2, Page 87

```
10 REM ** DRAWING PROGRAM **
20 INIT
30 PAGE
40 GOSUB 1000
50 END
1000 REM ** SUBROUTINE TO INPUT COORDINATES **
1010 REM ** OF SIX POINTS **
1020 REM ** COORDINATES ENTERED FROM KEYBOARD **
1030 REM ** POINTS PLOTTED ON SCREEN **
1040 FOR K=1 TO 6
1045 MOVE 1,90-6*K
1050 PRINT "ENTER COORDINATES OF POINT (X,Y) "
1060 INPUT X,Y
1110 GOSUB 1200
1120 NEXT K
1130 REM ** DUMMY READ STATEMENT TO CREATE PAUSE **
1140 INPUT D$
1150 PAGE
1190 RETURN
1200 REM ** SUBROUTINE TO PLOT POINTS **
1230 MOVE X,Y
1240 DRAW X,Y
1390 RETURN
```

Example 4-3, Page 90

```
10 REM ** DRAWING PROGRAM **
20 INIT
30 PAGE
40 GOSUB 2000
50 END
2000 REM ** SUBROUTINE TO INPUT COORDINATES **
2010 REM ** OF SIX POINTS **
2020 REM ** COORDINATES ENTERED FROM KEYBOARD **
2025 REM ** LINES DRAWN ON SCREEN **
2030 MOVE 1,90
2031 PRINT "ENTER COORDINATES OF FIRST POINT (X,Y) "
```

```
2032 INPUT X1,Y1
2040 FOR K=1 TO 5
2045 MOVE 1,90-6*K
2050 PRINT "ENTER COORDINATES OF NEXT POINT (X,Y) "
2060 INPUT X2,Y2
2110 GOSUB 2200
2111 X1=X2
2112 Y1=Y2
2120 NEXT K
2130 REM ** DUMMY READ STATEMENT TO CREATE PAUSE **
2140 INPUT D$
2150 PAGE
2190 RETURN
2200 REM ** SUBROUTINE TO DRAW LINE BETWEEN POINTS **
2230 MOVE X1,Y1
2240 DRAW X2,Y2
2390 RETURN
```

Example 4-4, Page 92

```
10 REM ** DRAWING PROGRAM **
20 INIT
25 DIM X(6),Y(6)
30 PAGE
40 GOSUB 2000
50 END
2000 REM ** SUBROUTINE TO INPUT COORDINATES **
2010 REM ** OF SIX POINTS **
2020 REM ** COORDINATES ENTERED FROM KEYBOARD **
2025 K=1
2030 MOVE 1,90
2031 PRINT "ENTER COORDINATES OF FIRST POINT (X,Y) "
2032 INPUT X(K),Y(K)
2040 FOR K=2 TO 6
2050 PRINT "ENTER COORDINATES OF NEXT POINT (X,Y) "
2060 INPUT X(K),Y(K).
2070 NEXT K
2080 MOVE X(1),Y(1)
2090 FOR K=2 TO 6
2100 DRAW X(K),Y(K)
2120 NEXT K
2130 REM ** DUMMY READ STATEMENT TO CREATE PAUSE **
2140 INPUT D$
2150 PAGE
2190 RETURN
```

Example 4-5, Page 96

```
10 REM ** DRAWING PROGRAM **
20 INIT
25 DIM X(6),Y(6)
30 PAGE
40 GOSUB 1000
50 END
1000 REM ** SUBROUTINE TO INPUT COORDINATES **
1010 REM ** OF SIX POINTS **
1020 REM ** COORDINATES ENTERED FROM KEYBOARD **
1025 K=1
1030 MOVE 1,90
1031 PRINT "ENTER COORDINATES OF FIRST POINT (X,Y) "
1032 INPUT X(K),Y(K)
1040 FOR K=2 TO 6
1050 PRINT "ENTER DISTANCE TO NEXT POINT (DX,DY) "
1060 INPUT X(K),Y(K)
1070 NEXT K
1080 MOVE X(1),Y(1)
1085 RDRAW 0,0
```

```
1090 FOR K=2 TO 6
1100 RMOVE X(K),Y(K)
1110 RDRAW 0,0
1120 NEXT K
1130 REM ** DUMMY READ STATEMENT TO CREATE PAUSE **
1140 INPUT D$
1150 PAGE
1190 RETURN
```

Chapter 5 _____

Example 5-1, Page 105

```
10 REM ** DRAWING PROGRAM **
20 INIT
30 PAGE
40 GOSUB 3000
60 END
3000 REM ** SUBROUTINE TO ENTER COORDINATES **
3010 REM ** OF RECTANGLE **
3020 REM ** COORDINATES ENTERED FROM KEYBOARD **
3030 REM ** DRAWS A RECTANGLE USING OPPOSITE CORNERS **
3040 REM ** AS INPUT VALUES **
3050 PRINT "ENTER COORDINATES OF FIRST CORNER (X1,Y1) "
3060 INPUT X1,Y1
3070 PRINT "ENTER COORDINATES OF THIRD CORNER (X3,Y3) "
3080 INPUT X3,Y3
3090 X2=X1
3100 Y2=Y3
3110 X4=X3
3120 Y4=Y1
3130 GOSUB 3200
3140 REM ** DUMMY READ STATEMENT TO CREATE PAUSE **
3150 INPUT D$
3160 PAGE
3190 RETURN
3200 REM ** SUBROUTINE TO DRAW RECTANGLE **
3220 MOVE X1,Y1
3230 DRAW X2,Y2
3240 DRAW X3,Y3
3250 DRAW X4,Y4
3260 DRAW X1,Y1
3390 RETURN
```

Example 5-2, Pages 108−109

```
10 REM ** DRAWING PROGRAM **
20 INIT
30 PAGE
40 GOSUB 3800
60 END
3200 REM ** SUBROUTINE TO DRAW RECTANGLE **
3210 REM ** OR PARALLELOGRAM **
3220 MOVE X1,Y1
3230 DRAW X2,Y2
3240 DRAW X3,Y3
3250 DRAW X4,Y4
3260 DRAW X1,Y1
3390 RETURN
3800 REM ** SUBROUTINE TO ENTER COORDINATES **
3810 REM ** OF PARALLELOGRAM **
3820 REM ** COORDINATES ENTERED FROM KEYBOARD **
3850 PRINT "ENTER COORDINATES OF FIRST CORNER (X1,Y1) "
3860 INPUT X1,Y1
```

```
3870 PRINT "ENTER COORDINATES OF SECOND CORNER (X2,Y2) "
3880 INPUT X2,Y2
3890 PRINT "ENTER COORDINATES OF THIRD CORNER (X3,Y3) "
3900 INPUT X3,Y3
3910 X4=X3-(X2-X1)
3920 Y4=Y3-(Y2-Y1)
3930 GOSUB 3200
3940 REM ** DUMMY READ STATEMENT TO CREATE PAUSE **
3950 INPUT D$
3960 PAGE
3990 RETURN
```

Example 5-3, Page 113

```
10 REM ** DRAWING PROGRAM **
20 INIT
30 PAGE
40 GOSUB 4000
60 END
4000 REM ** SUBROUTINE TO ENTER COORDINATES **
4010 REM ** OF POLYGON **
4020 REM ** COORDINATES ENTERED FROM KEYBOARD **
4030 PRINT "ENTER NUMBER OF SIDES "
4040 INPUT N
4050 PRINT "ENTER CENTER (XC,YC) "
4060 INPUT X0,Y0
4070 PRINT "ENTER STARTING POINT (X1,Y1) "
4080 INPUT X1,Y1
4090 R1=SQR((X1-X0)^2+(Y1-Y0)^2)
4110 GOSUB 4200
4140 REM ** DUMMY READ STATEMENT TO CREATE PAUSE **
4150 INPUT D$
4160 PAGE
4190 RETURN
4200 REM ** SUBROUTINE TO DRAW POLYGON **
4210 REM ** CALCULATE STARTING ANGLE **
4230 GOSUB 5100
4260 MOVE X1,Y1
4270 D1=6.2832/N
4280 FOR K=1 TO N
4290 X=COS(S1+K*D1)*R1+X0
4300 Y=SIN(S1+K*D1)*R1+Y0
4320 DRAW X,Y
4340 NEXT K
4390 RETURN
5100 REM ** SUBROUTINE TO CALCULATE START ANGLE **
5110 IF X1-X0<>0 THEN 5160
5120 S1=4.7124
5130 IF Y1<=Y0 THEN 5190
5140 S1=1.5708
5150 GOTO 5190
5160 S1=ATN((Y1-Y0)/(X1-X0))
5170 IF X1-X0=>0 THEN 5190
5180 S1=3.1416
5190 RETURN
```

Chapter 6

Example 6-1, Page 124

```
10 REM ** DRAWING PROGRAM **
20 INIT
30 PAGE
40 GOSUB 4000
60 END
4000 REM ** SUBROUTINE TO ENTER COORDINATES OF **
4010 REM ** CENTER AND STARTING POINT OF CIRCLE **
4020 REM ** COORDINATES ENTERED FROM KEYBOARD **
4050 PRINT "ENTER CENTER (XC,YC) "
4060 INPUT X0,Y0
4070 PRINT "ENTER STARTING POINT (X1,Y1) "
4080 INPUT X1,Y1
4090 R1=SQR((X1-X0)^2+(Y1-Y0)^2)
4100 X9=X1
4105 Y9=Y1
4110 GOSUB 5100
4120 S1=A1
4122 E1=S1+6.2832
4125 N=INT(30+0.4*R1)
4130 GOSUB 4200
4140 REM ** DUMMY READ STATEMENT TO CREATE PAUSE **
4150 INPUT D$
4160 PAGE
4190 RETURN
4200 REM ** SUBROUTINE TO DRAW POLYGON OR CIRCLE **
4260 MOVE X1,Y1
4270 D1=6.2832/N
4280 FOR K=1 TO N
4290 X=COS(S1+K*D1)*R1+X0
4300 Y=SIN(S1+K*D1)*R1+Y0
4320 DRAW X,Y
4340 NEXT K
4390 RETURN
5100 REM ** SUBROUTINE TO CALCULATE START ANGLE **
5110 IF X9-X0<>0 THEN 5160
5120 A1=4.7124
5130 IF Y9<=Y0 THEN 5190
5140 A1=1.5708
5150 GOTO 5190
5160 A1=ATN((Y9-Y0)/(X9-X0))
5170 IF X9-X0=>0 THEN 5190
5180 A1=A1+3.1416
5190 RETURN
```

Example 6-2, Pages 127−128

```
10 REM ** DRAWING PROGRAM **
20 INIT
30 PAGE
40 GOSUB 4000
60 END
4000 REM ** SUBROUTINE TO ENTER COORDINATES OF **
4010 REM ** CENTER AND STARTING POINT OF ARC **
4020 REM ** COORDINATES ENTERED FROM KEYBOARD **
4030 PRINT "ENTER CENTER (XC,YC) "
4040 INPUT X0,Y0
4050 PRINT "ENTER STARTING POINT (X1,Y1) "
4060 INPUT X1,Y1
4070 PRINT "ENTER ENDING POINT (X2,Y2) "
4080 INPUT X2,Y2
4090 R1=SQR((X1-X0)^2+(Y1-Y0)^2)
4100 X9=X1
```

```
4105 Y9=Y1
4110 GOSUB 5100
4115 S1=A1
4120 X9=X2
4122 Y9=Y2
4124 GOSUB 5100
4126 E1=A1
4127 IF E1-S1>0 THEN 4129
4128 E1=E1+6.2832
4129 N=INT(30+0.4*R1*(E1-S1)/6.2832)
4130 GOSUB 4200
4140 REM ** DUMMY READ STATEMENT TO CREATE PAUSE **
4150 INPUT D$
4160 PAGE
4190 RETURN
4200 REM ** SUBROUTINE TO DRAW POLYGON OR CIRCLE **
4260 MOVE X1,Y1
4270 D1=(E1-S1)/N
4280 FOR K=1 TO N
4290 X=COS(S1+K*D1)*R1+X0
4300 Y=SIN(S1+K*D1)*R1+Y0
4320 DRAW X,Y
4340 NEXT K
4390 RETURN
5100 REM ** SUBROUTINE TO CALCULATE START ANGLE **
5110 IF X9-X0<>0 THEN 5160
5120 A1=4.7124
5130 IF Y9<=Y0 THEN 5190
5140 A1=1.5708
5150 GOTO 5190
5160 A1=ATN((Y9-Y0)/(X9-X0))
5170 IF X9-X0=>0 THEN 5190
5180 A1=A1+3.1416
5190 RETURN
```

Example 6-3, Pages 135−136

```
10 REM ** DRAWING PROGRAM **
20 INIT
30 PAGE
40 GOSUB 4000
60 END
4000 REM ** SUBROUTINE TO ENTER COORDINATES OF **
4010 REM ** THREE POINTS ON ARC **
4020 REM ** COORDINATES ENTERED FROM KEYBOARD **
4050 PRINT "ENTER STARTING POINT (X1,Y1) "
4060 INPUT X1,Y1
4065 PRINT "ENTER NEXT POINT (X2,Y2) "
4066 INPUT X2,Y2
4070 PRINT "ENTER ENDING POINT (X3,Y3) "
4075 INPUT X3,Y3
4076 GOSUB 6000
4077 IF A2<>A4 THEN 4090
4078 PRINT "CANNOT DRAW ARC THROUGH THESE POINTS "
4079 GOTO 4050
4090 R1=SQR((X1-X0)^2+(Y1-Y0)^2)
4100 X9=X1
4105 Y9=Y1
4110 GOSUB 5100
4115 S1=A1
4120 X9=X3
4122 Y9=Y3
4124 GOSUB 5100
4126 E1=A1
4127 IF E1-S1>0 THEN 4129
4128 E1=E1+6.2832
```

```
4129 N=INT(30+0.4*R1*(E1-S1)/6.2832)
4130 GOSUB 4200
4140 REM ** DUMMY READ STATEMENT TO CREATE PAUSE **
4150 INPUT D$
4160 PAGE
4190 RETURN
4200 REM ** SUBROUTINE TO DRAW POLYGON OR CIRCLE **
4260 MOVE X1,Y1
4270 D1=(E1-S1)/N
4280 FOR K=1 TO N
4290 X=COS(S1+K*D1)*R1+X0
4300 Y=SIN(S1+K*D1)*R1+Y0
4320 DRAW X,Y
4340 NEXT K
4390 RETURN
5100 REM ** SUBROUTINE TO CALCULATE START ANGLE **
5110 IF X9-X0<>0 THEN 5160
5120 A1=4.7124
5130 IF Y9<=Y0 THEN 5190
5140 A1=1.5708
5150 GOTO 5190
5160 A1=ATN((Y9-Y0)/(X9-X0))
5170 IF X9-X0=>0 THEN 5190
5180 A1=A1+3.1416
5190 RETURN
6000 REM ** SUBROUTINE TO CALCULATE CENTER **
6010 REM ** OF THREE POINT ARC **
6020 GOSUB 6400
6025 M1=0
6026 M2=0
6030 GO TO A2 OF 6040,6110,6160,6390
6040 IF X2-X1=0 THEN 6050
6045 M1=-(1/((Y2-Y1)/(X2-X1)))
6050 IF X3-X2=0 THEN 6060
6055 M2=-(1/((Y3-Y2)/(X3-X2)))
6060 B1=(Y1+Y2)/2-M1*((X1+X2)/2)
6070 B2=(Y2+Y3)/2-M2*((X2+X3)/2)
6080 X0=(B2-B1)/(M1-M2)
6090 Y0=M1*X0+B1
6100 GOTO 6390
6110 IF X3-X2=0 THEN 6120
6115 M2=-(1/((Y3-Y2)/(X3-X2)))
6120 B2=(Y2+Y3)/2-M2*((X2+X3)/2)
6130 X0=(X1+X2)/2
6135 Y0=M2*X0+B1
6150 GOTO 6390
6160 IF X2-X1=0 THEN 6170
6165 M1=-(1/((Y2-Y1)/(X2-X1)))
6170 B1=(Y1+Y2)/2-M1*((X1+X2)/2)
6180 X0=(X2+X3)/2
6190 Y0=M1*X0+B1
6390 RETURN
6400 REM ** SUBROUTINE TO DETERMINE WHETHER **
6405 REM ** POINTS CAN DEFINE AN ARC **
6410 A2=1
6420 REM ** CHECK FOR THREE DIFFERENT POINTS **
6425 IF (Y3-Y2=0 AND X3-X2=0) OR (Y2-Y1=0 AND X2-X1=0) THEN 6535
6430 IF Y3-Y1=0 AND X3-X1=0 THEN 6535
6440 GOTO 6490
6450 REM ** NEXT, CHECK FOR TWO VERTICAL LINES **
6460 IF Y3-Y2=0 AND Y2-Y1=0 THEN 6535
6480 REM ** CHECK FOR ONE VERTICAL LINE **
6490 IY Y2-Y1<>0 THEN 6500
6495 A2=2
6500 IF Y3-Y2<>0 THEN 6510
6505 A2=3
6510 IF A2=2 OR A2=3 THEN 6540
6520 REM ** CHECK FOR PARALLEL LINES **
```

```
6525 IF X3-X2=0 AND X2-X1=0 THEN 6535
6528 IF X3-X2=0 OR X2-X1=0 THEN 6540
6530 IF (Y3-Y2)/(X3-X2)<>(Y2-Y1)/(X2-X1) THEN 6540
6535 A2=4
6540 RETURN
```

Example 6-4, Pages 138−139

```
10 REM ** DRAWING PROGRAM **
20 INIT
30 PAGE
40 GOSUB 4000
60 END
4000 REM ** SUBROUTINE TO ENTER COORDINATES OF **
4010 REM ** CENTER AND STARTING POINT OF CIRCLE **
4020 REM ** COORDINATES ENTERED FROM KEYBOARD **
4050 PRINT "ENTER CENTER (XC,YC) "
4060 INPUT X0,Y0
4070 PRINT "ENTER STARTING POINT (X1,Y1) "
4080 INPUT X1,Y1
4090 R1=SQR((X1-X0)^2+(Y1-Y0)^2)
4100 X9=X1
4105 Y9=Y1
4110 GOSUB 5100
4120 S1=A1
4122 E1=S1+6.2832
4125 N=INT(30+0.4*R1)
4130 GOSUB 4200
4140 REM ** DUMMY READ STATEMENT TO CREATE PAUSE **
4150 INPUT D$
4160 PAGE
4190 RETURN
4200 REM ** SUBROUTINE TO DRAW POLYGON OR CIRCLE **
4240 X1=COS(S1)*R1+X0
4250 Y1=SIN(S1)*R1+Y0
4260 MOVE X1,Y1
4265 X9=X1
4266 Y9=Y1
4270 D1=(E1-S1)/N
4272 C5=COS(D1)
4274 S5=SIN(D1)
4280 FOR K=1 TO N
4290 X=X0+(X9-X0)*C5-(Y9-Y0)*S5
4300 Y=Y0+(X9-X0)*S5+(Y9-Y0)*C5
4320 DRAW X,Y
4330 X9=X
4335 Y9=Y
4340 NEXT K
4390 RETURN
5100 REM ** SUBROUTINE TO CALCULATE START ANGLE **
5110 IF X9-X0<>0 THEN 5160
5120 A1=4.7124
5130 IF Y9<=Y0 THEN 5190
5140 A1=1.5708
5150 GOTO 5190
5160 A1=ATN((Y9-Y0)/(X9-X0))
5170 IF X9-X0=>0 THEN 5190
5180 A1=A1+3.1416
5190 RETURN
```

Example 6-5, Page 141

```
10 REM ** SINEWAVE PROGRAM **
20 INIT
30 PAGE
40 GOSUB 11000
60 END
11000 REM ** SINEWAVE DRAWING ROUTINE **
11010 REM ** ACCESSED FROM A MAIN PROGRAM **
11030 MOVE 10,75
11035 DRAW 10,25
11040 MOVE 10,50
11045 DRAW 125,50
11050 MOVE 10,50
11060 FOR X=0 TO 12.5664 STEP 0.2617
11070 Y=SIN(X)
11080 Y8=25*Y+50
11090 X8=9*X+10
11100 DRAW X8,Y8
11110 NEXT X
11140 REM ** DUMMY READ STATEMENT TO CREATE PAUSE **
11150 INPUT D$
11160 PAGE
11190 RETURN
```

APPENDIX

Flowcharting and Documentation

Introduction

Sources

This appendix is divided into two parts. The first part explains graphical flow-chart symbols and presents an example flow chart. The second part deals with program documentation. There are many sources for the items listed here, but there are four that are especially important. The first source is our experience with students in the classroom; the second is the programming guidelines used by Precision Visuals, Inc.; the third is the "Guidelines for Writing Transportable Code," by Tom Walliser, a graduate student in the Ohio State University Department of Mechanical Engineering; and the last is the American National Standards Institute (ANSI) standards, which were used specifically for the flowcharting symbols.

Practical Aspects

Two items must be kept in mind when talking about flowcharting and documentation. The first is that, when the program to be created is large, the amount of planning and scheduling prior to writing code is much greater than when preparing to write a one- or two-page program. However, the approach should be the same: "Top down" and "modular" are the governing characteristics. The second item to be kept in mind is that the documentation process must be reasonable, so that programming personnel can get the job done.

Flowcharting

Flowcharting is a process that should be completed before any coding is started. Flow charts come in a variety of styles, and the style shown here is a system using graphical symbols. Some programmers like to draw the tree diagram, shown in Chapter 15, prior to the preparation of the flowcharts because such diagrams provide an overall structure that the programmer can follow while creating flow charts for the modules. It is wise for any programmer to consider and to try each type of flow chart before adopting or abandoning one type. Most of the graphical symbols shown here have been adopted, or are in the process of being adopted, as part of the ANSI program flowcharting standard. However, some symbols that we have found to be useful have been included even though they are not part of the standard.

Two levels of flow charts may be employed by the programmer. The first is one in which the programmer uses the standard symbols to show the overall flow with few details included. In this case, each flow-chart block may represent several operations. The second, and later, level shows the program in enough detail that the programmer can use the chart to write code. In both cases the following symbols are used.

START/END Each block of code needs to have a recognizable starting and ending point. The symbol shown in Figure C-1 is used only for starting and ending subroutine modules.

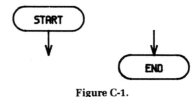

Figure C-1.

INPUT/OUTPUT The standard input and output symbol is the parallelogram, shown in Figure C-2. Other standard symbols include the punched-card input symbol, shown in Figure C-3 and the trapezoid used at OSU for keyboard input, shown in Figure C-4. Specific output symbols include the "torn" page, shown in Figure C-5 and the "CRT tube," shown in Figure C-6.

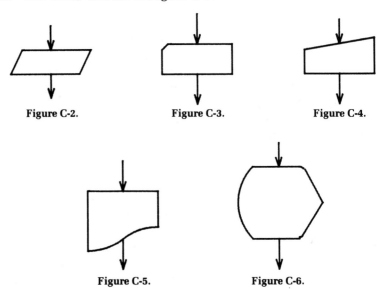

Figure C-2.   **Figure C-3.**   **Figure C-4.**

Figure C-5.   **Figure C-6.**

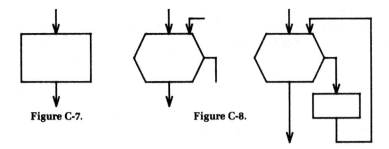

Figure C-7. **Figure C-8.**

ASSIGNMENT STATEMENTS OR CALCULATIONS The rectangle, shown in Figure C-7, is used for assignment statements.

LOOPS The squashed hexagon symbol, shown in Figure C-8, is used for DO loops. Other loops can be drawn using a combination of decision symbols.

DECISIONS The IF-GOTO statement is represented by the diamond, shown in Figure C-9. This symbol indicates that the program flow is down the page unless the condition is met. Figure C-10 shows the symbol for the IF-THEN-ELSE construct and Figure C-11 shows the symbol for a multiple-decision statement, such as a computed GOTO or ON-GOTO.

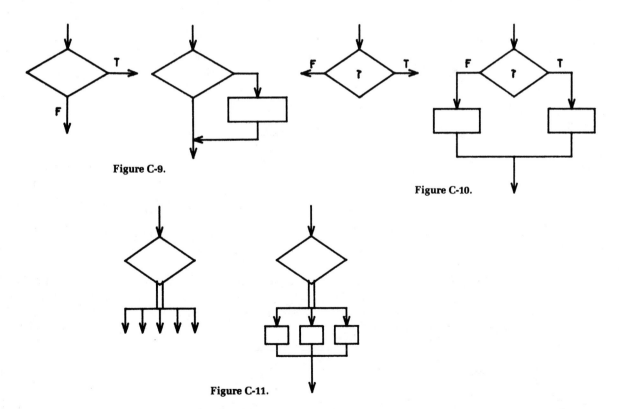

Figure C-9.

Figure C-10.

Figure C-11.

SUBROUTINES OR FUNCTIONS Program modules such as subroutines, functions, or procedures are represented by a rectangle with double side bars, as shown in Figure C-12. The name of the module and the arguments that must be passed to that module are shown inside the box.

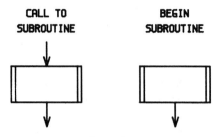

Figure C-12.

CONNECTORS On-page and off-page connectors are required for flow charts. On-page connectors provide a mechanism for drawing the flow chart without having lines crossing lines. The off-page connectors are required when the flow chart is larger than a single page. The two symbols are shown in Figures C-13 and C-14.

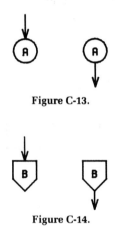

Figure C-13.

Figure C-14.

FLOWLINES These are lines with arrowheads to show the direction of program flow.

The following flow chart was created prior to writing the subroutine for reading instructions from a file and writing them to the CRT screen. This program module, SUBROUTINE INSTR, is found in Chapter 15.

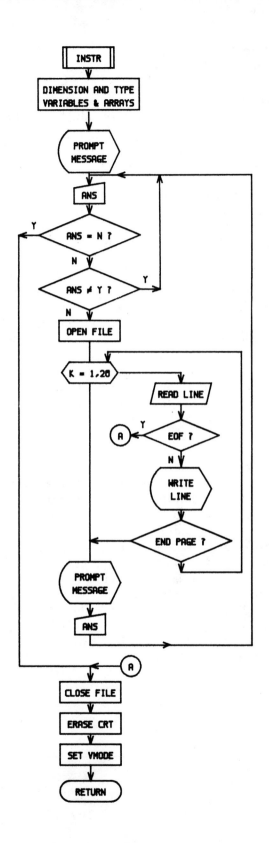

Documentation

Documentation, including headers and intraline comments, is necessary for a program to be planned, created, used, and maintained. Many professional programmers advocate that the documentation be written following the creation and verification of the flow chart and prior to writing the actual code.

Header Documentation

The *header documentation* is required for each main program and for each subprogram or procedure. The header contains the purpose, the list of variables (and their type: integer, real, or character), the list of subroutines required for the program or subprogram to operate properly (this includes the system libraries of functions and subroutines), the input/output devices that are required, and the list of programs or subroutines that call the particular subroutine.

The main program lists all variables that are used in the program, preferably in alphabetical order, and all subroutines and libraries that are needed for the program to function. The subroutines that are called directly by the main program should be in a separate list from the complete list of subroutines and libraries.

The programmer's name and the date on which the program was created should be placed on a line immediately following the program title. If there are any revisions, the revisor's name should be added beneath the original programmer's name along with the date of revision.

Intraline Documentation

Intraline documentation aids the program maintenance personnel in following any steps within the program that are not made clear by the statement of purpose in the header. Such documentation information can be written prior to writing any code so that the persons writing the code can "fill in the blanks."

As with any large design process, a program is created through a series of iterations and it is conceivable that the programmers will have to include or omit items as the program is being written and checked. In addition, students are generally learning their systems while they are learning to program and thus will use more iterative steps in creating a good program than will experienced programmers working on familiar systems.

Example Subroutine

```
C*****************************************************************
C                                                               *
C       SUBROUTINE INSTRUCTIONS                                 *
C                                                               *
C                                                               *
C       WRITTEN BY: WM. ZAGGLE          DATE: 2/25/84           *
C       REVISED BY: K. KRUMM            DATE: 4/26/84           *
C                                                               *
C       PURPOSE:                                                *
C          THIS SUBROUTINE ALLOWS THE USER TO CHOOSE TO         *
C          READ THE PROGRAM INSTRUCTIONS OR NOT TO READ THEM.   *
C          IF THE USER CHOOSES TO READ THE INSTRUCTIONS THE     *
C          INSTRUCTIONS FILE IS OPENED AND THE INSTRUCTIONS     *
C          ARE READ IN AND WRITTEN TO THE SCREEN A LINE AT A    *
C          TIME. A MAXIMUM OF 20 LINES OF INSTRUCTIONS PER      *
C          PAGE IS ALLOWED. THE PROGRAMMER MAY MAKE THE PAGES   *
C          SHORTER BY PUTTING A '>' IN COLUMN ONE OF ANY        *
C          LINE. EACH TIME THE '>' IS ENCOUNTERED THE PROGRAM   *
C          STOPS AND WAITS FOR THE USER TO TYPE A CHARACTER     *
C          FOLLOWED BY A CARRIAGE RETURN <CR>.                  *
C                                                               *
C       I/O SPECIFICATIONS                                      *
C          INPUT - THIS PROGRAM READS INFORMATION FROM THE      *
C             KEYBOARD AND FROM A DATA FILE                     *
C          OUTPUT - ALL OUTPUT IS TO THE CRT SCREEN             *
C                                                               *
C       THIS SUBROUTINE:                                        *
C          IS CALLED BY - MAIN                                  *
C          CALLS TO - PROGRAMMER WRITTEN SUBROUTINES - NONE     *
C                     PLOT10 SUBROUTINES - ERASE, ANMODE,       *
C                     VMODE                                     *
C                                                               *
C       VARIABLES                                               *
C          TEXT (CH*1) - A CHARACTER ARRAY TO TRANSFER LINES    *
C                        OF CHARACTERS FROM THE FILE TO THE     *
C                        CRT SCREEN                             *
C          ANS (CH*1)  - A SINGLE CHARACTER VARIABLE USED TO    *
C                        HOLD RESPONSES TO PROMPTS              *
C                                                               *
C*****************************************************************
C
C
C
       SUBROUTINE INSTR
       CHARACTER*1 TEXT(71),ANS
       CALL ANMODE
   10  WRITE (6,620) 'DO YOU WANT INSTRUCTIONS ?'
  620  FORMAT ('1',A30)
       READ (5,630) ANS
  630  FORMAT (A1)
       IF (ANS .EQ. 'N' .OR. ANS .EQ. 'n') GOTO 999
       IF (ANS .NE. 'Y' .AND. ANS .NE. 'y') GOTO 10
C
C  **  OPEN DATA FILE AND PUT TERMINAL IN ALPHA MODE
C
       OPEN(UNIT=1,NAME='INSTRCTNS.DAT',TYPE='OLD',READONLY)

       CALL ANMODE
C
C  **   BEGIN READ-WRITE LOOP   **
C
    5  DO 70 K = 1,20
         READ (1,640,END=999) TEXT
         WRITE (6,650) TEXT
```

```
C
C   **    TEXT FOR END-OF-PAGE (>) INDICATOR     **
C
          IF (TEXT(1) .EQ. '>') GOTO 15
   70     CONTINUE
  640  FORMAT(71A1)
  650  FORMAT(' ',71A1)
C
C   **    PAUSE FOR OPERATOR READ, THEM ERASE AND OUTPUT NEXT
C   **    PAGE
C
   15  READ (5,631) ANS
  631  FORMAT (A1)
       CALL ERASE
       WRITE (5,635)
  635  FORMAT ('1')
       GOTO 5
  999  CONTINUE
C
C   **    CLOSE THE INSTRUCTIONS FILE,  ERASE   THE   SCREEN,
C   **    RETURN TO GRAPHICS MODE
C
       CLOSE (UNIT=1)
       CALL ERASE
       CALL VMODE
       RETURN
       END
```

Bibliography

Albrecht, R. L.; Finkel, L.; and Brown, J.R. *BASIC.* (2nd ed.). New York: John Wiley & Sons, 1978.

Artwick, B. A. *Applied Concepts in Microcomputer Graphics.* Englewood Cliffs, N.J.: Prentice-Hall, 1984.

Beakley, G. C.; and Chilton, E. G. *Introduction to Engineering Design Graphics.* New York: Macmillan, 1973.

Chasen, S. H. *Geometric Principles and Procedures for Computer Graphics Applications.* Englewood Cliffs, N.J.: Prentice-Hall, 1978.

Cress, P.; Dirksen, P.; and Graham, J. W. *FORTRAN IV with WATFOR and WATFIV.* Englewood Cliffs, N.J.: Prentice-Hall, 1970.

DeVoney, C.; and Summe, R. *IBM's Personal Computer.* Indianapolis: Que Corporation, 1982.

Earle, J. H. *Engineering Design Graphics.* Reading, Mass.: Addison-Wesley, 1983.

Eckhouse, R. H., Jr. *Minicomputer Systems.* Englewood Cliffs, N.J.: Prentice-Hall, 1975.

Etter, D. M. *Structured FORTRAN for Engineers and Scientists.* Menlo Park, Calif.: Benjamin/Cummings, 1983.

Foley, J. D.; and Van Dam, A. *Fundamentals of Interactive Computer Graphics.* Reading, Mass.: Addison-Wesley, 1982.

French, T. E.; Vierck, C. J.; and Foster, R. J. *Graphic Science and Design.* New York: McGraw-Hill, 1984.

Giloi, W. K. *Interactive Computer Graphics.* Englewood Cliffs, N.J.: Prentice-Hall, 1978.

Goetsch, D. L. *Introduction to Computer-Aided Drafting.* Englewood Cliffs, N.J.: Prentice-Hall, 1983.

Harrington, S. *Computer Graphics, A Programming Approach.* New York: McGraw-Hill, 1983.

Hartman, R. A.; et al. *Computer Graphics.* College Station, Texas: Creative Publishing, 1983.

Hume, J. N. P.; and Holt, R. C. *Better BASIC for the Apple.* Reston, Va.: Reston Publishing, 1983.

Hume, J. N. P.; and Holt, R. C. *Better BASIC for the IBM-PC.* Reston, Va.: Reston Publishing, 1984.

Hume, J. N. P.; and Holt, R. C. *UCSD Pascal: A Beginner's Guide to Programming Microcomputers.* Reston, Va.: Reston Publishing, 1982.

Ledgard, H. F.; and Chmura, L. J. *FORTRAN with Style.* Rochelle Park, N.J.: Hayden, 1978.

Ledgard, H. F.; Nagin, P.; and Hueras, J. F. *Pascal with Style.* Rochelle Park, N.J.: Hayden, 1978.

Lewis, T. G. *Pascal Programming for the Apple.* Reston, Va.: Reston Publishing, 1981.

Lewis, T. G. *Pascal Programming for the IBM-PC.* Reading, Mass.: Addison-Wesley, 1983.

Luzadder, W. J. *Fundamentals of Engineering Drawing.* Englewood Cliffs, N.J.: Prentice-Hall, 1981.

Machover, C.; and Blauth, R. E. *The CAD/CAM Handbook.* Bedford, Mass.: Computervision Corporation, 1980.

Meissner, L. P.; and Organick, E. I. *FORTRAN 77.* Reading, Mass.: Addison-Wesley, 1980.

Moore, J. B.; and Makela, L. J. *Structured FORTRAN with WATFIV.* Reston, Va.: Reston Publishing, 1981.

Myers, R. E. *Microcomputer Graphics.* Reading, Mass.: Addison-Wesley, 1982.

Nagin, P.; and Ledgard, H. F. *BASIC with Style.* Rochelle Park, N.J.: Hayden, 1978.

Newman, W. M.; and Sproull, R. P. *Principles of Interactive Computer Graphics.* New York: McGraw-Hill, 1979.

Ryan, D. L. *Computer-Aided Graphics and Design.* New York: Marcel Dekker, 1979.

Seiter, C.; and Weiss, R. *Pascal for BASIC Programmers.* Reading, Mass.: Addison-Wesley, 1983.

Steidel, R. F., Jr.; and Henderson, J. M. *The Graphic Languages of Engineering.* New York: John Wiley & Sons, 1983.

Waite, M. *Computer Graphics Primer.* Indianapolis: Howard W. Sams & Co., 1979.

Index

A

alphanumeric terminals, 27
American National Standards
    Institute (ANSI), 44
animation, 10, 11, 211
ANSI (American National
    Standards Institute), 44
applications software, 45–47
arcs, 125–137, 196
arrays, 185–189, 192, 194–202
    dimensioning, 56–58, 186–189
    packed, 58
    storage, 197–198
    working, 194–197
arrow keys, 222, 249, 259
art, computer applications in,
    10–11
as-built drawings, 6
ASCII characters, 184, 253, 254,
    272, 273
assembler languages, 44–45
AT END DO statements, 70
audio input/output, 11, 41
auto-execute files, 350
axonometric projections, 282,
    305, 306–311, 318–319

B

bar charts, 146–148, 150, 153,
    173–175
BASIC, 13–14, 342, 356, 359
    arcs, 127–128, 135–136
    arrays, 58
    branching, 63, 65
    character variables, 52
    circles, 124, 138–139
    clipping, 238–241
    color, 320
    cursor control, 253, 255–262,
        265–266
    curves, 141
    data-entry techniques, 159
    data retrieval, 204, 206
    data transfer, 198, 199, 200–201
    detail deletion, 216, 219–220,
        224, 226, 227
    digitizing tablets, 263–266

editing techniques, 177, 178
erasing, 226, 227
error handling, 344
files, 60, 271, 272
graphics mode, 82
initialization, 369–370
integer variables, 50
joysticks, 260–262
light pens, 266–267
line chart, 167, 169, 170, 172
lines, 88, 90, 92, 226, 227,
    376–378
logical operations, 66, 67
logical variables, 52–53
loops, 61
menus, 371, 373–374
modularity, 71
parallelograms, 108
pie charts, 159, 163, 164, 165
plotters, 276–277
plotting, 85, 87, 96
point selection, 83, 84
pointers, 119
polygons, 113
program description, 73
real variables, 51
rectangles, 105
relative coordinates, 93, 96
sample graphics program, 369,
    371, 373–374, 377–378
screen dump, 274
search routine, 224
subroutines, 55
three-dimensional objects, 290,
    292, 293, 297, 298, 301
Battelle Laboratories, 324
bits, 23
boolean variables, 52–53
branching, 62–66, 70
built-in functions, 53
business, computer applications
    in, 7–10
bytes, 23, 24, 183–184

C

cabinet drawings, 300
cameras, 35

cancellation capability, 335
CASE statements, 64–65
cathode ray tubes. See CRTs
cavalier drawings, 300
character variables, 51–52
charts, 6–9, 145–181, 243
    bar, 146–148, 150, 153, 173–175
    line, 146, 147, 148, 149, 150,
        153, 157, 167–173, 176–177
    map, 148
    pie, 146, 147, 148, 150, 151,
        152–153, 156–157, 160–166
    surface, 146, 150
Chasen, 14
CIRCLE statements, 237
circles, 122–125, 137–139, 196
clipping, 15, 237–243
closeness factor, 224–225
Cohen-Sutherland clipping
    algorithm, 242–243
color, 11, 12, 213, 319–320
    with dot matrix printers, 34
    with ink jets, 35
    with pen plotters, 31, 275
    with raster terminals, 30–31
    with thermal copiers, 34
    See also color insert
command language, 42–43
command structure, 353
commands, 333
COMMON statements, 54–55,
    288, 372
communication, 328–331
communications diagrams,
    358–359, 364, 365–366
compiled languages, 44
computers, 19, 22–25
connected-vertex method,
    284–285, 321
constants, 50
constructs, 70
CRTs, 26–31, 76, 77, 334, 336, 346
crystallography, 6–7
cursors, 37, 221–222, 249,
    253–262, 265–266, 353
    creating, 255–257
    displaying, 257

software bugs, 337
sonic digitizers, 38
Spencer, 278
Sproull, 14
stacks, 192–193
status messages, 354–355
stepped approach, 71–72
storage, 49–50, 55–58, 155–156, 179, 182–209
  screen, 28
  updating, 213–220
  See also disks; tape storage
storage arrays, 197–198
storage devices, 25–26. *See also* disks
storage terminals, 28
  detail deletion from, 211–212
STRIG statements, 261–262
string variables, 51–52
subroutines, 17, 45, 54–55, 70–71
  writing, 359–360
surface charts, 146, 150
surfaces, 286–287

T

tape storage, 25, 58, 156, 179
task appropriateness, 355–356
task names, 365
terminals, 20, 21, 26–31
  alphanumeric, 27
  graphics, 27–28
  raster, 29–31
  storage, 28, 211–212
  vector refresh, 29
thermal plotters, 34
three-dimensional drawings, 15–16, 278–304

thumbwheels, 38–39, 249
titles, chart, 151, 152, 155, 160, 165–166, 177–178
top-down approach, 16, 337
track balls, 334
transferring data, 198–202
translation, 244
trees, 192, 193–194
trimetric projections, 282, 311
turnkey programs, 349–378
TURTLEGRAPHICS, 82, 83, 85, 88, 93, 94–95

U

University of Rochester, 324
user-defined functions, 53–54
user interface, 327–347
users, 363–364
utilities, 47

V

values, storage of, 49–50
Van Dam, 14
variable list, 74
variables, 50–53
vector refresh terminals, 29
vectors, 315–318
Vierck, 278
viewport range, 243
VIEWPORT statements, 235–236, 237, 244, 246

W

WEND statements, 61, 62
WHILE DO loops, 61, 62, 70

WHILE EXECUTE statements, 70
WINDOW statements, 237, 244, 246
windows, 235–236, 237–243
wire-frame modeling, 283–285, 287–293
WITH statements, 70
words, 23, 183
working arrays, 194–197
workstations, 334, 336–337, 345–347
WRITE statements, 187, 268, 270

X

X axis, 79–80, 100–101, 280–281, 282, 283, 287, 294, 298–300, 315–316
  in charts, 150, 151
  rotation about, 309–310, 311
XDRAW statements, 255, 257

Y

Y axis, 79–80, 100–101, 280–281, 282, 283, 287, 298–300, 315–316
  in charts, 150, 151–152
  rotation about, 307–309, 311

Z

Z axis, 280–281, 282, 283, 287, 294, 298–300, 315–316
  rotation about, 309